The Best Team
Money
Could Buy

The Best Team Money Could Buy

THE TURMOIL AND TRIUMPH
OF THE 1977
NEW YORK YANKEES

STEVE JACOBSON

Atheneum   New York   1978

Dedicated to Larry Brooks, Murray Chass, Joe Donnelly, Henry Hecht, Moss Klein, and Phil Pepe, who survived a season with the Yankees and made them the most thoroughly covered running story in sports.

Most of all, dedicated to my wife, Anita, and the kids, Mathew and Neila. They put up with me after all those days with the Yankees.

Contents

The Best Team
Money
Could Buy

Like No Other Season

Believe it or not, 1977 is right there in the books. It happened. You could look it up.

The New York Yankees won the Eastern Division championship of the American League, the American League playoff, and beat the Dodgers in the World Series. It was just what the great Yankees did in the dynasty years.

But no Yankee season ever played like 1977. There was nothing in history to prepare the baseball world for what went on inside those sanctified pinstripes.

And to hear some of them tell it, that season really didn't happen. "The controversy was created by the press," said Chris Chambliss, the first baseman who batted in 90 runs and never looked at what was swirling around him in the clubhouse. What conflict? What chain of events? What jealousy? What animosity? What deceptions? Are you going to believe me or your lying eyes?

It happened. And the 1977 Yankees will be remembered for it. All season players on other teams rushed to read about and laugh at the soap opera in the Bronx.

Keep in mind that 1977 was the dawn of a harsh new era for baseball. It was the first year of competition for players who were free to leave their old teams and auction themselves to the highest bidder. There had been isolated instances in the two preceding years, but after a century of players being bound to teams endlessly, baseball suddenly found there were no familiar guidelines. There was no precedent to prepare for the pitfalls of assembling a team the Yankee way.

Within those new rules—with a wealthy owner craving recognition—the Yankees were able to outbid the world for the most costly pitcher and the most costly slugger. While the old Yankees were hated by the rest of the world for their eternal superiority, the new Yankees were hated because they had been assembled not by the traditional trading and de-

1

velopment but by the checkbook. They represented everything middle America—and California, too—hated, feared,
and coveted in New York. And the world never does get
tired of resenting Goliath and rooting for a David.

In the midst of this upheaval we had three highly volatile
men contributing to the upheaval like Shakespeare's witches:
"Double, double toil and trouble. Fire burn and cauldron
bubble." They made it bubble.

George Steinbrenner was the managing partner among the
nineteen listed owners, the only one with any voice. His is a
loud voice.

Billy Martin was the manager. He had won the pennant
with the Yankees the season before. He had won two pennants and finished a rousing second at three previous stops
only to be fired before the next season was complete.

Both are self-made, but what good is it to be a self-made
man if nobody knows about it? So it was vital to both Steinbrenner and Martin to keep the world aware of who and
what they were.

And there was Reggie Jackson, the slugger who chose the
Yankees' from among offers that would have made Midas'
head spin. He is a magnificent athlete, blessed with a rare
personal magnetism and marked by the brooding pride and
sensitivity of an opera star.

It was a season of the anonymous quote. Players felt they
had to say things, but were afraid of the consequences. So
they became known as "a prominent Yankee" or "a teammate who asked not to be identified." Or they sat in twos in
front of their rows of lockers, leaned close to each other, and
murmured their suspicions.

The old Yankees won with consummate ease, grace, and
dignity. These Yankees won with dirt on their faces.

"They won it. They're world champs," Billy Martin said
with champagne running out of his hair, stinging his eyes.
"You analyze how they got there. If you can.

"Good luck."

That is, if you want to believe a word of it.

ASK NOT FOR WHOM THE WIND BLOWS

Folk singer Bob Dylan gave a generation of radicals a
catchword by singing, "You don't have to be a weatherman

to know which way the wind is blowing." For a whole season with the Yankees, nobody could be sure which way the wind was blowing. Wait ten days or ten minutes and it shifted.

The month of August became a season in microcosm. The worst of times became the best of times. And underneath the best of times was the simple truth that nothing at all had changed except on the scoreboard.

The contrast was most extreme in two scenes that occurred three weeks, a continent and a world apart. The atmosphere went from tears and open rancor, when it looked as if they would never pull themselves together, to the confidence that they were going to win and nobody could stop them except themselves.

Years from now, it will be the tears that are remembered as representative of the season, tears when a trip to the West Coast threatened to be the epitaph for the season.

The Yankees had lost another punishing game to the expansion-weak Seattle Mariners and Billy Martin sat slumped on the small round stool in his office in the Kingdome. His eyes were red and very full. And he looked very small.

It wasn't just the 5–3 loss, it was the whole grinding six months and the anticipation of two more. Martin played a lot of scenes in a boiling career that he began as an undersized, undertalented second baseman spurring the Yankees to championships in the early 1950s, but few of those scenes could be called poignant. Now, even for people who were repelled by his frequent disregard of truth, for his frequent rudeness, for the obvious obstacles he put in the way of the press, Martin became a sympathetic character. He was a pathetic little man who appeared about to lose the thing he held most dear.

Martin's trademark as a Yankee player was that he overcame his size. He occasionally took offense when his talents were described as marginal, but he never missed a chance to describe how he had fought his way into the big leagues and how Casey Stengel, whose memory Martin reveres, had loved Martin's spunk.

As a manager, Martin is belligerent, but—on his own terms—a cheerful sort. He can tell a funny story before a game, and a half hour after a loss can even kid himself. But by August 5 there was no humor to relieve the moment as he sat and absently ran a finger around the rim of an empty beer can.

The embroidered message on his shirt, left over from spring training, was ironic. It said: "Yankee Greats Golf Tournament." Maybe Martin hadn't been great, but he had been a Yankee. When he was traded from that team in 1956, he wept. In his seven seasons as a Yankee they won seven pennants. Now he was in a situation that was more difficult to overcome than a mere shortage of talent.

Martin cherishes his job. It was Stengel's job, and Stengel is Martin's link to Yankee glory. Stengel, with his fractured syntax and lumpy legs was Martin's patron, a surrogate father.

He has been close to losing the job at least twice. Now it seemed to be hanging by a hair. Despite the reality of the standings, the Yankees continue to be caught up in petty issues that would be laughable in a sane community. But then, who calls this a sane community?

Jackson still permits himself to be involved in reruns of the question of whether he hates being here so much that he will refuse to return next year.

And Thurman Munson is wearing an eight-day growth of beard. Whiskers, for goodness' sakes. That's a deliberate violation of Steinbrenner's rules, whatever they are worth. There has been a phone call to Martin from the home office in response to what's been in print.

"Petty bullshit," Martin snapped at the reporters in his little office. "Worried about beards, like babies." Weeks later he conceded that if he were running a newspaper and his man on the Yankees overlooked the issue, Martin would fire him.

Martin calls himself "the people's manager." He sees himself as a symbol of every workingman who feels put upon by his boss. Martin is caught in the undercurrents, some of them clearly his own fault.

Munson's beard is not Martin's doing. It is one more demonstration of the animosity Munson and several other players feel for Steinbrenner. But before this game Munson went to Martin and said, "I'm going to wear a beard. I hope it doesn't get you into trouble."

Munson refuses to explain the beard. He denies that he is trying to force Steinbrenner to trade him but Munson has said he certainly wouldn't mind being traded to Cleveland.

As captain and acknowledged leader, Munson has certain responsibilities and obligations. Steinbrenner could see this defiance as the ultimate indication that Martin can't handle people. "You mean another excuse to fire him?" Munson said. "That's been hanging over Billy's head all year, hasn't it?"

Of course it has. But what the Yankees don't need now is still another issue interfering with baseball. Like the continuing Jackson situation. Tonight Jackson hit his 300th home run; only thirty-seven men have ever hit as many as 300. After the game congratulations came from only Catfish Hunter and Mike Torrez. Jackson feels every slight, like the princess and the pea.

Tempers are thin; two weeks since his last near-firing, Martin's sense of security is thin. All defiance is gone from his tone. "What ever happens to me doesn't count," he says. "Winning this year is the most important thing."

He sounded like some Union general plucked from Martin's Civil War history collection; it was preservation of the Union that counted, not any man's career or his life.

The next night the Mariners beat the Yankees again and while the players were eating their post-game salad and beef sandwiches in the clubhouse—ball players can manage to eat free food even in the gravest of circumstances—Lou Piniella's voice cracked the silence.

"Let everyone speak up now after getting beat by a horseshit ball club like that," Piniella snapped. Nobody looked up. "All that shit in the papers," Pinella said. "I want to go here, I want to go there. Everybody should speak up when you get your ass beat by a horseshit ball club."

The eating resumed with only the sound of the murmuring between players with their heads close together. The Murderers' Row Yankees were now reduced to "murmurers' row."

Scarcely three weeks later, the Yankees post-game snack was a banquet in celebration of themselves. In the middle of the Yankee Stadium clubhouse, players sat in various stages of undress, cheek to cheek with Martin, snapping and sucking at the dozen peppered crabs the manager had flown in from Baltimore. They were to reward his team for coming from the depths to take command of the race.

It was the kind of thing Martin does to remind his players he is on their side. The Yankees chattered and laughed together after being for so long the crabs who—win or lose—skulked off to sanctuary, off-limits to their inquisitors.

It appeared to be something close to the best of all possible worlds as Jackson leaned against a pillar, his round face lighted with the glow that had charmed the multitudes while the tempestuous Oakland A's dominated baseball. "Almost," Jackson said, "but not quite."

Call them crocodile smiles. There was as much joy in Jackson's smile as remorse in the tears of a crocodile eating lunch.

What Jackson felt was relief and vindication. He could no longer be blamed for the failure of the Yankees—they were winning. He was living up to his billing after a season of melodrama. He was succeeding in the role Martin had tried to keep from him. Jackson was proving he was the ball player that he felt the manager could never recognize.

But it wasn't fun and it wasn't joy.

As he spoke, Jackson had bits of pepper on his hands. A trickle of blood ran down his thumb, cut by the shells of Martin's celebration crabs. It was the kind of scene college literature teachers find revealing in Hemingway's "The Killers"—the clock on the wall showing the wrong time to indicate that things aren't as they seem.

"The same problems are always going to be there," Martin said in a burst of candor. "They're there now. They'll be there at the end of the season and next spring, too. They'll still be here next fall. But they realized they still have to do a job."

The conflicts continued in the clubhouse. Martin still needed to be right. Munson still felt betrayed by Steinbrenner. Graig Nettles still felt exploited by the owner. Martin resented Jackson. Jackson choked on Martin's name. Munson resented Jackson. Jackson felt a chill from Nettles. And on and on.

But on the field they had indeed pulled themselves together when there hadn't been the slightest suggestion they would do anything but live out the self-destruct prophecies.

Jackson, batting cleanup for the seventeenth consecutive game, singled home the winning run in the eighth inning as they beat the Twins, 6–4. It was the Yankees' sixteenth game won in their last eighteen; it gave them a two-game lead and it hardly mattered that the Red Sox had also won. If the Yankees won, nothing else mattered in the race.

They were playing what Jackson called "connoisseur's baseball." He indicated that some of his favored newsmen were included among his connoisseurs.

Scarcely three weeks had passed since that West Coast trip that had appeared to be the ultimate disaster, and Steinbrenner reminded them that if they didn't win they would be known forever as "the team that choked."

At that point—perhaps despite themselves—they pulled themselves together. It's a never-ending wonder how superior athletes can play two thirds of a season—a hundred games and more—just dragging along, and then abruptly play so much better than anybody else.

"Things came together on the club," Jackson said. "We said, we got fifty-three games to go; the hell with the bullshit, the talk about cars, handshakes, beards, contracts, and wanting to get traded. Let's play baseball to get the heat off. So we don't have to go home at night, turn on the TV, and see what happened in the soap opera on 161st Street."

In one breath Jackson summarized the season—the jealousy over the Rolls-Royce gift, Munson's beard, Jackson's refusal to shake his teammates' hands. And he underlined the creeping feelings of embarrassment that eventually turned their attention to their business.

Attention to business included Martin's concession to bat Jackson fourth. That's just what Jackson always wanted. Fourth is the cleanup slot; it's the pedestal of prestige for a slugger. Batting Jackson sixth in exhibition games was Martin's original affront. In all but a handful of games through the season, Martin would not trust cleanup to Jackson.

Batting fourth since the day after that dreadful trip, Jackson proved his point. In seventeen searing games he batted .310, drove in 29 runs. He had amassed more game-winning runs batted-in than any Yankee.

Jackson said he felt good about proving himself. At the same time he underlined the tenuous balance of the club. "I won't go into an extreme analysis," Jackson said. "If anything can stop this club from winning, I don't want to be a part of it. I want to stay as far away from that as possible."

Jackson and Munson gradually came together in a grudging respect for each other's talent. But the issues that separated them and threatened the team remained vulnerable to one wrong word.

As he spoke, it occurred to Jackson that he was saying his piece while standing in front of Munson's locker, half the length of the room distant from his own. Munson, who always felt Jackson talked too much, looked in and winked.

Early Warning

"This has been the worst spring training in my whole history in baseball," Billy Martin said. Undoubtedly that's true.

Spring training, as Martin understands it from his Yankee beginnings, is a time for fun in the sun. Work hard for a couple of hours to get in shape. Play the exhibition games hard enough not to form bad habits, and don't worry about winning all the games. Get through the day's work and play a round of golf with Mickey Mantle and Whitey Ford. Have a couple of drinks at night and get to the ball park in time to supervise the workout. Enjoy the camaraderie of the clubhouse.

But this isn't that kind of spring. It's Martin's second for George Steinbrenner, the onetime college assistant freshman football coach who still has basic football mentality. His concept is of a once-a-week game. Steinbrenner believes in things like undefeated seasons and spending everything to win each game. The fact that last season Martin led the Yankees to their first pennant since 1964 doesn't lessen Steinbrenner's demands. Martin doesn't have any ten-game lead yet. Steinbrenner feels a manager who won last year has to work that much harder.

And this is the year of the free agent. The Yankees added Reggie Jackson and Don Gullett for sums that would have dazzled any players two or three years ago—or even last season. Some players signed contracts and helped the Yankees win, only to find that outsiders had been brought in at higher salaries. Players whose contracts expired while helping the Yankees win held out because they felt they weren't being rewarded like those who had never helped the Yankees before.

It was a new situation for Martin. He was used to fighting with the front office—even enjoyed it because it demonstrated his strength—but he had nothing to counteract the festering resentment among the players.

8

"Baseball better find a cure because it's getting to be a cancer," he said. "The free agent gets it all. Another guy they want to pay nothing because he's too old. Another guy they don't want to give nothing because they don't like him."

The first indications that conflict among the newly-moneyed Yankees wasn't just media speculation came on the first day the regulars assembled. Mickey Rivers came out tardy and pouting. He had instructions to learn to drag bunt and to work more bases on balls. Last season he bunted only to third base and drew only thirteen walks. But there was a good case for him for the Most Valuable Player award that Munson won. When Rivers got on base, the Yankee offense was devastating. They want him on base as often as possible.

Rivers wants to be on base his way. He resents being singled out for his shortcomings. He signed his contract for $90,000, and now he's saying that for all his contributions, and in light of Jackson's contract, he was shortchanged and wouldn't mind being traded. He might even like it.

Maybe the signs were clear when Jackson was introduced to the world after signing his five-year, $2,930,000-contract and announced: "I didn't come to New York to become a star; I brought my star with me." True enough, Jackson had been a star with Oakland and had helped them to three consecutive World Series triumphs, but the Yankees had won the pennant last season without Jackson. There's nothing that alienates new teammates like the suggestion that they weren't nothin' until you got there.

Or maybe we all should have known that it was going to be a year like no other year on January 19, when Thurman Munson, the Most Valuable Player, said he was being screwed. At a dinner in Hamilton, Ontario, Munson said he had been "lied to and deceived" by Steinbrenner.

It seems that Munson had been convinced to sign his 1976 four-year contract and not to become a free agent by certain promises. Munson was promised that if the Yankees signed any free agent, his own contract would be upgraded to keep him the highest-salaried Yankee other than Catfish Hunter. Precisely what that meant was subject to interpretation.

When the Yankees traded for Ken Holtzman and then signed him to a five-year contract, Munson's $120,000 contract was upgraded and he received a bonus. Then when the Yankees signed Jackson, Munson demanded that he be upgraded again. On January 6 Munson's contract was extended two more years at a new price. That procedure was never announced. Jackson's package is confirmed at $2,930,000 for five years with a sixth year at his option. The components were learned to include annual salary of $200,000, annual deferred payments of $132,000, and a cash signing bonus of $400,000. The balance has been a carefully protected secret, as are the details of an interest-free loan believed to be for $1 million.

Baseball salaries have always been carefully hidden by owners who didn't want players comparing. In this case, Jackson also wanted his figures held private; he even insisted on an agreement that the contract would become void if the details became public. Steinbrenner had his own reasons for not making Jackson's contract a point of boasting, and for not revealing that he had given Jackson the gift of a $93,000 Rolls-Royce for the courtesy of talking to him.

Eleven days after signing his new contract, Munson hollered that he had not been given the true figures by Steinbrenner. A day after that both sides said a compromise agreement was reached, and both sides said the point of contention had been a misunderstanding.

"We got together face to face and reached a happy medium," Munson said. "Settling meant a lot to me; you can't play for somebody you mistrust. He asked me if there were any hard feelings that I couldn't get over, and did I want to be traded some place? And I said, 'Hey George, I want to play in New York.' "

As things developed, there were hard feelings that never were overcome. Munson never got over his mistrust of Steinbrenner.

* * *

Martin and Steinbrenner? Well, you may remember that Steinbrenner wanted Martin's spice over the advice of baseball-wise old Gabe Paul at the time the Yankees were getting ready to dump calm and honest Bill Virdon in the middle of the 1975 season.

Steinbrenner must have his finger in the middle of everything on the Yankees. He phones Martin and expects Martin to be available to him or to return calls.

Billy Martin does not answer to anybody. He does not spend much of his off-field time in his hotel room. He does not like all those phone calls. After one particularly galling loss last season, Steinbrenner called Martin's office and Martin let the phone ring. Steinbrenner refused to take no answer and eventually Martin pulled the phone out of the wall. So Steinbrenner phoned the trainer's office to tell him to have Martin call. Martin told the trainer, "Just tell George you gave me the message."

Martin repeats often that he and Steinbrenner are really not always at odds. "He's a frustrated friend," Martin said with his little smile. "I think if I was in trouble, he'd help me. The problem is George wants to win so bad, he doesn't realize we do, too. The yelling and screaming and football shit doesn't solve a thing."

Once when the Yankees were playing on the West Coast, Gabe Paul phoned Martin at eight thirty in the morning after a night game. Martin didn't take kindly to being awakened at such an early hour, even if it was a business hour in New York. So Martin responded by phoning Paul at 2:30 A.M. after a night game.

From the first indications that Steinbrenner was thinking of hiring Martin, dismissed after a startling second-place finish at Texas, it was clear the Yankees were on some kind of collision course. Each has his rigid way of going about things. "Actually we are a lot alike," Martin says, "except that he's rich and I'm poor." The poor man fires the rich man.

Steinbrenner has his bits of advice on how to run the team, whom to pitch on four days' rest, and which player to bat in which slot in the batting order. He insists it's the manager who makes the decisions, but it's difficult to see the situation as anything other than my-wish-is-your-command. Martin hates it.

Martin can't resist slipping in little jabs, ridiculing Steinbrenner's rules on short hair and his penchant for applying the concepts of football. On his side, Steinbrenner has laid an endless path of comment to newsmen—off the record, of course—on Martin's indiscretions that some day may be held against him.

Unlike football, baseball is played in the open. Any dummy can have an opinion. The daily statistics make it clear who is hitting and who isn't pitching. When the question becomes "Why?" then the thinking gets around to the manager.

If the question is asked often enough by the owner, the

manager has a crisis. Martin is a crisis manager. If no crisis develops normally, he'll raise the heat to the boiling point himself. That's how he manages his team and his life.

He thrives on pressure and traces that back to growing up on the streets of Berkeley, California, where he had to be willing to take two punches to get in one. But the pressure this year became such that Martin lost weight. He went to restaurants and merely picked at his meal. Often he thought about telling Steinbrenner he could keep the job—beginning in spring training—but those pinstripes run deep. He wanted that job so badly, he couldn't walk away from it.

Besides, if he quit, he wouldn't get paid for the two remaining years on his contract. Now many men walk away from $160,000. And Martin isn't so sure that he hasn't run out of opportunities. There aren't many owners left like Steinbrenner, who would take a chance on living with Martin.

And all the while Steinbrenner and Martin engage in their ego battles, mistrust swells on the team. Each has earned a reputation for being less than candid. From the first day to the last day nobody knew whom to believe.

And Come Out Fighting

It's the day the regulars come out to play. MVP Thurman Munson is here, Graig Nettles, the home-run champion, and all the guys who won the pennant and had such good fellowship last season. Now we are adding Reggie Jackson. Nobody knows quite how he will fit in. How does he take the clubhouse needling? How does he needle?

Just how big is his ego? "There isn't enough mustard in the world to cover that hot dog," former Oakland teammate Darold Knowles once said. The line made Knowles immortal—for as long as Jackson plays, anyhow. It will also sting Jackson as long as he plays.

Certainly, the press has foreseen the potential for friction between Jackson and his new teammates, especially with Munson, who has just begun to feel he is getting the recognition he deserves.

Jackson has the kind of personality that will divert the spotlight from Munson. And what of Jackson's comments that he was treated coldly as a television commentator by his new teammates?

Now the press is waiting to interview Jackson. Wait, where is Mickey Rivers? The center fielder is late. He doesn't arrive until the brief workout is almost ended. Rivers is a product of the Miami ghetto. His speech is often difficult, his thought processes hard to follow. When he arrives he says he'd like to be traded.

Among all the Yankees, Rivers is probably the most sensitive. Unlike the rest, he doesn't show it. He turns inward, becomes depressed, detached from the game. Now he feels threatened by the front office.

13

Rivers is angry. "I'll only work on the things I'm good at," he said. "Don't do no good to work on the things I'm not good at."

So the Yankees have begun the season.

* * *

The days of standing pat with a winner are not the ways of George Steinbrenner and Gabe Paul. Paul ran impoverished clubs mainly on thrift most of his career, but he has Steinbrenner's bankroll and drive for the top now. Paul didn't have to wait for a farm system to produce a winner for the Yankees. Among last season's pennant winners only Munson and Roy White were home-grown. The Yankee farms that once fed the baseball world have been a dustbowl for nearly fifteen years. They haven't produced a regular infielder for the big team since Horace Clarke—long gone and unlamented—in 1965.

What they have is a chief operating officer who isn't afraid to make players angry by trading their best friends. He made much of last year's team by trading popular Fritz Peterson and Steve Kline, and two others, for Chambliss and Dick Tidrow.

What Steinbrenner doesn't know about baseball Paul does. Chambliss hit the ninth-inning home run that won the final game of the playoff with Kansas City. Tidrow was the winning pitcher.

Paul is sixty-seven. He's been in baseball fifty-one years, beginning as batboy at Rochester in the Cardinal's farm system. He's been a bullpen catcher, a ticket seller, public relations man, and traveling secretary. He succeeded James Reston, the political columnist, as traveling secretary at Cincinnati. Paul assembled the talent with which the Reds won a 1961 pennant and was responsible for the signing of Tony Perez and Pete Rose, who made up so much of the Reds who dominated the National League in the early 1970s. Paul left the Reds before that first pennant and touched down at Houston and Cleveland before coming to New York.

When he joined Steinbrenner's group of Clevelanders who bought the Yankees from CBS, it was assumed that Paul came along to finish out his career in semiretirement. Paul came to do anything but retire.

He is a marvelously energetic man. His hair is silver, his nose prominent and red, and his complexion a normal shade of pink. He has a bag packed with a shirt, a razor, and a toothbrush at all times, ready to go off to make a deal. Phone him at any hour of the day or night and you can expect the line to be tied up with a call to some other club. Unlike many executives, Paul always returns newspaper calls. He won't reveal anything, but he is always courteous.

In the process of not revealing anything about a potential deal, Paul is revealing about himself. About his interest in somebody else's failure or somebody else's interest in a Yankee discard, Paul has a saying: "One man's shit is another man's ice cream." He is saying, let me make up my own mind.

He made the determination to trade George Medich, the pitcher who was en route to becoming a doctor and gave such a nice image, to the Pirates for pitcher Dock Ellis, with his reputation as a troublemaker and minor-league second baseman Willie Randolph. It was Paul who traded the superstar glitter and disappointment of Bobby Bonds for Rivers and pitcher Ed Figueroa.

Around the league, the Yankee haters who slept content since 1965 can rail and cry that the Yankees bought that 1976 pennant, but only Catfish Hunter came for cash alone.

This year that claim is even louder. The Yankees have taken on Don Gullett for $1,990,000 over six seasons, Jackson at $2,930,000 over five seasons. They spent $150,000 to buy Jimmy Wynn to be the right-handed designated hitter and took on veteran Paul Blair for center field insurance. They have Ken Holtzman at $450,000 for three years.

Last year they won in an upset. This year they were favored to win from the first day of training camp. They may have bought a lot of talent with money, but the rules of baseball are the same for everyone.

And they are still shopping for more. All winter they conceded that they weren't secure at shortstop and openly coveted Bucky Dent of the White Sox. Dent is a star and unsigned. The White Sox are hard pressed. If they can't sign Dent, they run the risk of losing him at the end of the season for no compensation. If they trade him, at least they can salvage something. It's the sort of situation the Yankees love.

The history of the Yankees is the highlight of baseball and the ideal of professional sports. From 1921 to 1964 they won twenty-nine American League pennants and nineteen World Series. In the twelve seasons Casey Stengel managed, they won ten pennants and seven Series. They won five consecutive World Series, 1949–53, four consecutive World Series, 1936–39, five consecutive pennants, 1960–64. And then nothing for a dozen seasons.

They were the team of Babe Ruth and Lou Gehrig, Joe DiMaggio and Mickey Mantle. And then nobody.

From November 1964, when CBS bought the Yankees, until January 1973, when Steinbrenner came to town, the Yankees finished as high as second once. They finished sixth, tenth, and ninth. They lost more often than they won. Triple-tiered Yankee Stadium with its monuments to greatness, The House That Ruth Built, became a haunted house. In 1972 they drew fewer than a million fans for the first time since the World War II year of 1945.

The Mets, playing on the Long Island side of the East River, rose from their ridiculous beginnings near the end of the Yankee dynasty to capture the interest and affection of New York. They sold more season tickets than the once lordly Yankees. Even the corporate powers with headquarters and tax writeoffs in New York abandoned the Yankees. Television ratings were twice as high for the Mets.

But for a lot of people over thirty-five, old enough to have grown up when the Yankees won by fulfilling Manifest Destiny, that name was still magic. George Steinbrenner III was old enough. He had made his fortune in shipbuilding and even had a costly fling at owning the Cleveland Pipers in the short-lived American Basketball League of the early 1960s. But he was still an obscure rich man. He didn't have the ego gratification of being known as the owner of a great team.

What Steinbrenner wanted was to be the owner of the 1927 Yankees. The idea of a good Yankee game back then, according to Colonel Jacob Ruppert, who owned the team from 1915 until 1939, was for the Yankees to score seven runs in the first inning and then slowly pull away.

They were lordly, imperious, rude, confident, bullying, and great. They were also boring in their greatness. Rooting for the Yankees, it was said, was like rooting for General Motors. Of course the Yankees were going to win. For all intents and purposes, they clinched pennants in July and August. Mantle was a magnificent player and Whitey Ford a wonderful pitcher, but their constant success robbed the suspense from the only continuing entertainment form with genuine suspense. If a father missed a chance to take his son to see the Yankees win today—don't worry; they'd have a chance to see them win tomorrow.

And if there was no suspense there was no warmth, either. George Weiss, known as "Lonesome George," the architect of the last phase of the great years, rarely returned phone calls. He had contempt for newspapermen, saying "You can buy them with a steak." What other way does a team have of projecting an image than through the daily press?

The greatest Yankees radiated the least warmth. The great DiMaggio was as distant off the field as he was chillingly graceful on it. Mantle was a gallant player as he suffered in pain, but to him a questioning reporter was to be regarded with great suspicion. Mantle was capable of great ribald humor among his teammates and even on occasion to the press. But let the reporter ask one question too many or one question in an undesired direction and Mantle would spin around on his stool, leaving the reporter to stare at the reddening back of Mantle's neck.

Suspicion of the press was institutionalized. It was passed on from one strong silent type to the next, from Vic Raschi to Whitey Ford, whose natural good humor shone through this indoctrination. The wife of trainer Gus Mauch warned wives of players against revealing anything to wives of the press.

Jim Bouton and Phil Linz confounded their elders in the early 1960s by their openness. They dared to smile after a losing game, the worst of sins.

Billy Martin did not miss the lessons nor ignore the tradition. By nature he is an outgoing man, full of funny stories of his stormy career. He loves a good time and loves to tell about getting into trouble, but he tells those stories only on his own terms. He got into trouble at Minnesota and Detroit by being a drinking buddy of some of his players and not others.

After losing games last season he often would seclude himself in the trainer's room. Yankee tradition has made this out of bounds to give the trainer space to do his work. In practice it is used as a sanctuary for players to hide from the press and for management to hide injuries. Often the only Yankee players seen in the open clubhouse after a game are those who had nothing to do with the game.

Martin likes to tell his stories and to convey his personality through the press because it creates a favorable image with the fans for the time management thinks about firing him. At the same time Martin likes both to create the impression among his players that he will protect them against the outrages of the front office, which can't understand how tough it is to be a player, and to establish the concept of the press as the common enemy. The players always like to have someone protect them from the press, which has the audacity to point out that somebody is in a slump.

By protecting his players, Martin forms ties to protect himself at those times when a player feels he's been told something other than the truth.

In the midst of this mistrust of the press are the players who feel they don't get enough favorable ink. If a player is a cordial fellow, reporters—who are interested in the people who play the game as well as in runs, hits, and errors—will find reason to write about his personality. An honest reporter has no reason to make an issue of his relations with a player unless they are pertinent to the story. When a player is unpleasant to the press, he is usually ignored as much as possible. Players don't understand that attractive personalities sell tickets and are worth money, too.

Three classic examples on these Yankees are Munson, Graig Nettles, and Ken Holtzman.

For seven years Munson felt he wasn't appreciated enough. It bugs him no end that Carlton Fisk of the Red Sox is sometimes considered the best catcher in the league—or even his equal. Munson felt the same even when he was rated higher than Fisk. Perhaps Munson's jealous because he looks short and squat while Fisk has the classic looks of the New England Minuteman. Fisk is a good interview, full of keen insights and even a laugh. Most important, he is available. Munson is often grouchy and a forbidding subject. So despite the fact that he is an outstanding player, he gets a minimum of press.

Holtzman's dour disposition is legend around the league. Oakland owner Charles Finley calls him "the most miserable man in baseball." Any kind of testimony from Finley is suspect. But on the Orioles, with whom Holtzman played half of last season, none other than gentle Brooks Robinson says: "Kenny's a barrel of laughs, isn't he?"

Around the Yankees Holtzman is pleasant company for a small group of teammates, most notably Mickey Rivers. Immediately Holtzman becomes guarded with the press. He laments that he was told being in New York would mean considerable outside money, but it hasn't come. Obviously, he hasn't had much New York promotion, for either performance or personality.

Nettles is the most overlooked home-run hitter in years. Ask who led the American League in home runs in 1976 and you'll get a lot of long pauses. Nettles led the league, that's who. For leading the league in homers, the only loot Nettles received was a set of golf clubs from the Louisville Slugger people, whose bat he swings. "I guess it's my nature to be quiet," Nettles said.

Nettles doesn't get publicity because he's another reluctant interview. He is a king-sized pain in the ass to the official scorer, a chore still handled by newsmen covering the team. He is one of those people who seclude themselves in the trainer's room while newspaper deadlines tick away. His answers to questions are rarely revealing, despite the fact that he should understand the business better than most players; he has a cousin working the copy desk at a San Diego paper.

Nettles is also a terrific third baseman, but it seems nobody knows his name. That's all right with Nettles, he says, but he feels the owner of the team hasn't paid attention to him, either.

If the fans and the press overlook him, that's one thing. But if the owner overlooks him, that's another. Nettles feels he isn't being paid in line with the new order of things, the result of the free-agent market. Whatever big stick he swings, Nettles is speaking softly, but it's a sign of those complaints some owners predicted. There is resentment brewing in Nettles for the money Jackson got.

Of course, Nettles signed a three-year contract last July when he could have continued the season unsigned and become a free agent. Munson got an increase based on what Jackson got, but Nettles got nothing.

"When I signed my contract I was one of the highest-paid players on the club," Nettles said. "Now I'm one of the lowest. I guess I'm partly to blame because I don't believe in blowing my own horn. But I wish the front office would recognize what I've done. It seems the guys who make the money are the flamboyant, controversial guys. At least on this club." He means Jackson.

Jackson does a job on selling Reggie Jackson. "More power to him," Nettles said. "My argument is that I shouldn't suffer because I don't call attention to myself. If guys signed with the Yankee organization, I don't see why guys here who made the Yankees an attractive package shouldn't be taken care of."

That's a fundamental contention in the clubhouse. A number of players who were on last year's pennant winners feel that the new people were taken care of and the loyal ones were ignored. Rivers obviously feels that. An outsider-vs.-insider separation is forming.

The obvious outsider is Jackson. He comes to work alone, he leaves alone. He is separate from the banter that goes on in the clubhouse. "The only people I've found who I can relate to are the writers," he says.

He's acutely aware that everybody is watching him. He works harder than anybody, running extra laps, doing extra exercise. His elbow already hurts from the throwing. Quietly, he says Martin's camp isn't nearly as much work as the one Dick Williams used to run with the As. Alvin Dark sold Jackson on his kind of religion when Dark was the Oakland manager, but Williams is still Jackson's paragon as a manager.

Jackson says he never got to the ball park when Williams hadn't been there for hours. Martin often gets to the ball park after the players are supposed to be dressed and ready for action. Martin likes to sleep late.

Friday, March 11

Pompano Beach

Exhibition games begin today. After ten days of workouts, the pain of early conditioning has passed, leaving the boredom of calisthenics and batting practice all in the home park. The games are welcome. That will last about three weeks and then only the men still struggling to win a place on the team will want them to continue. For the players going to Syracuse or being released, there can never be enough exhibition games. By the end of the month the regulars will be impatient to start the season.

Billy Martin, or any of the reporters, can sit down now and fill in the lineup at eight of the nine positions. Only the batting order and the shortstop are in question, besides the pitching staff.

On paper the pitching looks like the best in the world, but beneath the glitter are some questions. Ken Holtzman was so mediocre at the end of last season that Martin didn't pitch him in the playoffs or the World Series. Hunter struggled to win as often as he lost and now admits that he lied to conceal arm trouble. Dock Ellis had his best year since 1972. Don Gullett's last two seasons were restricted by injuries, and that appears to be the mark of his career. Those are the starters.

In the bullpen Sparky Lyle was the best in the league for the first two-thirds of last season. He had a couple of bad outings and the front office soured on him. He's unsigned and giving ultimatums that he won't pitch in a game until he gets a contract good enough to sign. He says he will leave camp next week if no progress is made toward his demands, $475,-000 for three years.

Steinbrenner has no patience with ultimatums and is looking to make a deal. He'd like to have Ron Guidry as his short man in the bullpen on the basis of a sensational half season in triple A. It's dangerous business entrusting the main job in the bullpen to someone who's pitched a total of thirty-one innings in the big leagues.

The issue raised most often during the winter was over shortstop. Fred Stanley did a nice job after taking the full-time job last season. He got outs on balls that should be outs, the first requisite of the job. But the shortstop for the first exhibition game is Mickey Klutts, MVP in the International League.

Gabe Paul is predictably close mouthed about a prospective trade or expressing any need, except with regard to Stanley and shortstop. Paul lists that position as his main concern. He had dinner with White Sox boss Bill Veeck at Tampa last night to talk about Bucky Dent, who says he will play out his option. Paul doesn't think Stanley is good enough. Stanley feels that's because he isn't flashy. The skill of playing good position and of having sure hands are subtle. He tied with Dent for the best fielding percentage of shortstop, and after four seasons in the big leagues Stanley feels he has finally learned a position. He is hurt.

"You have your best year, the team wins when it hasn't won in twelve years, and all of a sudden you're not good enough at shortstop," Stanley said. "Same old shit."

One time-honored baseball explanation is that Stanley hasn't signed and the club is trying to intimidate him. He was paid less than $30,000 last year and is looking for the security of three years for something like $180,000. "They get on people who have no alternative," said Munson, who is growing cynical. "Fred is a good shortstop. People talk about loyalty to an organization; where's the organization's loyalty to him?"

Billy Martin says he is in Stanley's corner. He says he doesn't see the great range in Klutts the scouts have raved about. Klutts: what a name for shortstop!

*   *   *

Toby Harrah, whom the Yankees have sought for two years to play shortstop, hit two homers as the Rangers beat the Yankees in the first exhibition game. Jackson batted sixth; he didn't like the implication.

Saturday, March 12

Fort Lauderdale

The official reason for mystery and intrigue opened in the second game. Klutts made a tag to complete a double play and came out of the game. The official announcement called it "a jammed sprain" in his left hand but later in the day several players said they had learned it was a damned break.

Hiding injuries enjoys a special place in Yankee tradition. It was only last spring that Munson's broken index finger was described as "bruised" for a week while the Yankees were trying to find a backup. Besides the normal inclination to be devious, they don't want the price on Dent to go up because the Yankees' need is known. Martin concedes that much, but the whole world will know about it by the morning anyhow. Ball players don't keep secrets.

That the press learned of the injury in the first place is another story. It's standard procedure for the press to be in the clubhouse during exhibition games because most of the players leave before the end of the game. This time Klutts was observed in the table in the trainer's room with an ice pack on his hand. Then the door was shut. When Klutts dressed hastily and was taken for X-rays, questions were raised.

Before Martin had a report from the hospital he had a new rule for the press: The media would no longer be permitted in the clubhouse during a game, when such things as injuries might be observed.

The interesting development in the game was a grand-slam home run by Jimmy Wynn, who has to demonstrate that he can still hit after two bad years with the Braves.

Sunday, March 13

Miami

The official word on Klutts is still "jammed sprain," but Brooks Robinson of the Orioles said, "Their guys told me it was broken." Martin appears chagrinned that the ruse was so transparent. He kidded about it. "Almost identical to the Munson thing," he said with a lopsided smile. He said there would be a better diagnosis in two days. "That's it; these things take forty-eight hours." Note: The interleague trading period ends at midnight of the fifteenth.

Monday, March 14

Fort Lauderdale

The most eloquent thing Catfish Hunter said was wordless. He just shook his head. The head shake said, When a man has pitched 3,083 innings, is coming off a season of pain, and his arm still does not feel right after a winter's rest—even before the age of thirty-one—there's nothing dismal anybody can suggest that he has not already considered himself.

He pitched three innings, allowed five hits and some well-hit outs. His fastball was clocked by the Rangers' radar gun at 70-odd mph, as compared to 85 by Texas pitcher David Clyde, or to Hunter's own standard 87. As Martin put it, "Catfish didn't throw hard at all."

Martin said it didn't worry him at this early stage of the

spring, but Hunter conceded he was worried. "In a way I am
scared," Hunter said. "I want to go and earn my money; I
don't want to sit and have it come to me. I couldn't stand
that."

Hunter could stand learning he would never pitch again,
but he couldn't stand the thought of being mediocre after
years of greatness. After five seasons as a 20-game winner, he
was 17–15 on a Yankee team thirty-five games over .500.
The rotation was extended to give him four days of rest between starts. It still seemed that there was never enough time
between starts.

It was a curious scene as Hunter described himself in the
awkward ritual Martin has set up for the press. The game
was still in progress when Hunter had showered and completed the ice bath for his arm. The reporters were seques-
tered in the manager's office, out of sight and hearing of any
secret proceedings. Hunter sat down behind Martin's desk,
surrounded by notebooks, tape recorders, and grave faces. He
placed Martin's bifocals near the tip of his nose like a comic
professor.

It's Hunter's nature, like Davy Crockett's, to try to grin the
bear to death. "I don't think the arm's worn out," he said. "It
needs a new screw, that's all."

* * *

The Yankees got Marty Perez from San Francisco as a
backup infielder in exchange for rookie outfielder Terry
Whitfield.

Tuesday, March 15

Fort Lauderdale

Dock Ellis, master of inflamed rhetoric, is practicing inflamed rhetoric. He won seventeen games for the Yankees after a miserable season with Pittsburgh. He thinks he is being
treated badly in salary negotiations.

Ellis had a reputation as a troublemaker with the Pirates—things like wearing his hair in curlers on the field and
talking back to the manager. With the Yankees he's been a
perfect gentleman. He was even recognized as a valuable

voice in the clubhouse last year, needling moody Mickey
Rivers just when he needed it. Now Ellis is threatening to
make trouble if his contract problems aren't solved. "When I
become the oppressed, that's when I become very hostile," he
said.

Ellis made $80,000 last year and is asking for three years at
a lot more. The Yankees have Hunter at $250,000, Gullett at
$166,000, Holtzman of $165,000, and Figueroa at $120,000.
They say Ellis is asking for too much, and he's saying he
won't negotiate anymore once the club breaks camp.

* * *

Ron Blomberg, remember him? "The Boomer" hit a towering two-run homer against the Twins. It was Blomberg's first
hit since April 4, 1976, his first home run since July 8, 1975.
He has to prove all over again he can play. He had two at
bats last season. He's lost a season and a half with a shoulder
injury that Yankee doctors first diagnosed as a strain and
which required surgery almost a year later.

Now he's an outsider in the roster battle. Martin likes Oscar Gamble; he doesn't care for Blomberg.

Wednesday, March 16

Fort Lauderdale

An exhibition game becomes more when the Yankees play
the Red Sox. Each is trying to establish itself in the mind of
the other as the team to beat in the Eastern Division. And
they don't like each other from the last picture. When Carl
Yastrzemski hit the first of his two homers in the fifth inning
and George Scott followed with another, Ed Figueroa sailed
his next pitch a menacing foot inside and a foot over the
head of Boston catcher Carlton Fisk. Fisk started toward the
mound and both benches emptied.

Fisk has been in two fights with the Yankees in past years.
Nothing came of this one but an accidental shove; there
could have been a free-for-all like the one in which Boston
pitcher Bill Lee had his shoulder wrecked last season.

Each team was demonstrating it wouldn't be intimidated.

"They hit two home runs," Figueroa said. "I don't like to take too many crap. Two home runs, I not going to throw another pitch over the middle again. I have to show those people over there I am pitching."

There is also the personal animosity between Munson and Fisk that may be the root of little things like this. "We're not the best of friends, nor are we the worst of enemies," Fisk said. What does that mean? "It means I don't like him worth a damn."

Before the game Steinbrenner, the old college freshman assistant football coach, posted a clipping that had Boston manager Don Zimmer saying he was tired of hearing how good the Yankees were. Steinbrenner is moved by traditional football things like bulletin-board motivation.

If not for the history of Lee's arm injury, the evening would have come off as comic opera. Certainly, Lee lends his own touch. He was watching on the sidelines in street clothes while events were unfolding—street clothes for him, that is: a flowing white shirt with a Nehru collar and Indian sandals. "I was afraid they might step on my feet," he said.

Lee still has trouble with the shoulder he hurt wrestling with Graig Nettles last May, but he says he has more trouble accepting what he calls the Yankees' "win-at-any-cost mentality."

"Last year I was assaulted by George Steinbrenner's Nazis, his Brown Shirts," Lee said. "He brainwashes those kids over there, and they're led by Billy Martin—Hermann Goering II. They've got Steinbrenner, a convicted felon running the club. What else do you expect?"

Oh, the Sox hit five homers and won the game, 7–4. In ten innings.

Thursday, March 17

Vero Beach

Martin yanked Rivers from the Dodgers game after he didn't run out a ground ball as first batter of the game. Who knows what goes on in Rivers' head? He grumbles about not being appreciated.

He objects to practice as early as 10 A.M. He had to report

to the ball park at Fort Lauderdale at 8:30, ride two and a half hours on the bus, was the first batter of the game, waited idly another two and a half hours while the game was being played. The ride back was another two and a half hours.

Rivers said he thought Martin wanted to give Larry Murray some work in center field. "Billy didn't say anything to me," Rivers said. No, Martin agreed, "but three players and one of my coaches did." Martin avoids face-to-face confrontations when he can.

Some of the players think Rivers was punished for an accumulation of things like arriving late for workouts and leaving early. Jackson wonders if Martin got through to Rivers at all. "Is it possible that the man can be punished and not even know it?" Jackson asked. "I wish I had that going for me."

Rivers is pleasant enough. He shows no malice or guile. He is hard to understand. "He doesn't mean anything bad," Martin said. "He gets on the wrong foot and you got to get him on the right one again."

* * *

Stanley got his three-year contract. The deal for Dent appears dead. Steinbrenner is still trying to get the Yankees to Cuba for exhibitions, but the commissioner wants to send an all-star team. Steinbrenner would love the designation as the first American team there since 1960.

Friday, March 18

Fort Lauderdale

In the apparently comfortable clubhouse needling there's a core of bitterness. Lyle, Chambliss, Gamble, Ellis, newcomer Marty Perez, Gene Locklear, and Roy White are all unsigned. White won't comment on his status, but Chambliss will. "It's unfair what they're doing to Roy," he said. White is the senior man here. He's been a Yankee of great dignity since 1966. He hit .286 on a championship team and led the league in runs scored, for which he was originally offered no raise on his $90,000 salary.

Graig Nettles still hasn't appeared in a game. He had a

deep wart removed from his left hand and it is healing slowly.

Jackson is coming to a painful conclusion. Making his way from the clubhouse to the parking lot, he turned and grimaced. "I don't know if I'm going to fit in, man," he said. It was a cry of pain.

Sunday, March 20

Fort Lauderdale

More trouble with Rivers. Apparently Martin's action at Vero Beach didn't get him back on the right foot. Rivers feels picked on. Today he dawdled after a hit and, on the next batter, made a casual attempt and failed to catch a fly ball. Martin is aware that his handling of the situation is being watched closely from the clubhouse and the front office.

With other teams as manager or player, Martin made a show of strength of one kind or another. But Martin fears losing Rivers' motivation entirely. "He might quit on you," Martin said. He doesn't think a fine would be effective, but what can he do?

Martin, smiling faintly, laid out a scenario for tomorrow. "This is exactly what I'm going to do," he said. "I'll tell him, 'How would you like it if you were the manager and I didn't run balls out? Would you like it if I showed up the manager? Would you like to punch me? I'm surprised some of your teammates haven't beat the daylights out of you already.' "

At his apartment several hours later, Rivers' explanations were cryptic. He didn't like being one of the few regulars who had to make that trip to Vero after playing seven innings the night before. He objected to having to stay at the game Saturday night even though he wasn't used.

"If I do my work, I want to go home and relax like everybody else," Rivers said. "Why do I got to keep on my toes all the time? They think I should run 3.3 seconds down the line, catch everything, hit everything."

While Rivers talked, his wife moved silently about the room. She's a stunning woman, with a marvelous figure and the warmth of ebony.

Monday, March 21

Fort Lauderdale

The fine hand of George Steinbrenner is now evident. He invited Reggie Jackson to breakfast, then invited Thurman Munson to the same breakfast. Munson and Jackson haven't been at sword point yet, but Jackson has winced at the things Munson says in jest. They haven't broken bread together before, but Steinbrenner has ways. It can only ease the tension for Munson and Jackson to be more comfortable around each other.

Just before gametime Steinbrenner made his way to the corner of the clubhouse where Rivers and most of the other black players congregate. Steinbrenner put his arm around Rivers' shoulders and kidded him. The message was clear: The manager makes the first move; the next belongs to the owner. "It's Billy's problem to handle," Steinbrenner said. "If he doesn't handle it, then I will get involved."

Martin and Steinbrenner say they understand the nature of Rivers' problems and will try to help. Fining him would only make it worse. Rivers is not the kind of man who can leave his troubles behind when he goes on the field. When too much money is being spent at home, there's just so much a ball club will do with salary advances. If Rivers were a less important ball player, he wouldn't get as much help as he's had.

"He's a good kid," Steinbrenner said. "He smiles and I can't help but like him. But if this continues, he leaves us with no alternative but to look for a deal."

Martin says he understands that every player has a time to pout; he even had some himself. He tells about the time Casey Stengel benched him, and Martin was so angry he took his glove to the farthest end of the bench and sulked.

"Casey kept watching me out of the corner of his eye and along about the eighth inning, he pinch-hits for the second baseman," Martin recalled. "And here comes Casey down to the end of the bench to put me in the game. But I wouldn't give him the satisfaction of looking up at him.

"Finally, the Old Man comes over to me and says, 'Awww, is widdew Biwwy mad at me?'

"I started to laugh and I picked up my glove and went out to second base."

* * *

The rhetoric over contracts has escalated. There are angry words and ultimatums from Lyle and Ellis. "If that's their final offer, then I want to get out of here," Lyle said. He's looking for $500,000 for three years and the Yankees are offering about $350,000. The bid-and-asked are about the same with Ellis.

Steinbrenner makes the point that Lyle will be thirty-three in July, Ellis is thirty-two, and Roy White is thirty-three. "That's nobody's fault, but it is a fact of life," Steinbrenner said. Who wants to give big-money three-year contracts that run past the Plimsoll line of age thirty-five? Long-term contracts are new to players and owners. Somewhere along the line both sides have to learn about them.

* * *

The atmosphere of contention is contagious. After an outstanding career marked by silence, Elston Howard is speaking in anger. Bobby Cox is the first-base coach now. That leaves no place for Howard, who says he did not sign to be a bullpen catcher. He's offended that nobody told him he wasn't going to be at first base after nine seasons in the job. "As long as I've been with this club, I think that was the least they could have done," he said. "That would have been a little class."

Howard is a legacy, not Martin's choice. For that matter, none of the coaches are really Martin's selections. The one he really wanted was Art Fowler, his pitching coach at the other three stops. But Fowler called Gabe Paul "a son of a bitch" when Fowler was pitching for Cincinnati. Paul doesn't forget easily.

Thursday, March 24

Orlando

Martin is becoming concerned about the pitching. Lyle repeats that he won't pitch in a game until he's signed. Ken Holtzman took another battering from the Twins today, which boosted his earned run average to 5.25. Ron Guidry has a pulled muscle in his side and hasn't pitched in a week. He wasn't getting anybody out before that. "Tell me if there's anybody you can get out and I'll let you pitch to him," Martin told Guidry. That makes the question of Lyle bigger than ever.

Friday, March 25

Clearwater

Lyle and White both accepted contracts of about $450,000 for three years. It looks as if Ellis is not going to be satisfied and will have to play out his option, which could make for an ugly summer. It doesn't look as if the Yankees are interested in signing Perez, either. He turned down $200,000 for two years from the Giants and is here at the Yankees' 20-percent cut of his $65,000 1976 salary. He's here for the Yankees' convenience and all it means for him is grief.

Saturday, March 26

St. Petersburg

Now we have the ugly scene to go with the ugly words. The Mets beat the Yankees 6–0 and Steinbrenner is furious. The loss was televised back to New York—where the Yankees have passed the Mets in season-ticket sales for the first time in nine years—and Steinbrenner, with Gabe Paul in tow, roared into the clubhouse demanding to talk to Martin. George doesn't take exhibition games with traditional baseball indifference.

"I want to talk to you," Steinbrenner stormed. "Now!" The whole ball club heard it.

Steinbrenner has already had impatient words with Martin because the manager doesn't like to ride the team bus to games. He prefers to drive behind the bus with his coaches; he says he can talk about things better with the privacy. Steinbrenner prefers togetherness, and also prefers winning. He and Paul have been considering a switch to Yogi Berra. He was considered a mistake here and later with the Mets, but he won a pennant at each place.

"I ought to get rid of you," Steinbrenner yelled at Martin.

"Why don't you fire me right now?" Martin shouted back.

That's when Martin's hand struck the bath of ice and water the pitchers use, splattering Steinbrenner and Paul. It was right out of a Donald Duck tantrum cartoon—or maybe Dagwood and Mr. Dithers.

They've had their comic scenes before, like last September when the Orioles completed a sweep of four games at the Stadium, cutting the Yankee lead to seven and a half games. Martin hid in the trainer's room for a long time, then consented to answer questions in his office. The phone rang and rang and rang, perhaps twenty-five times, and Martin didn't even look at it. Nobody had to guess who was calling. Eventually the phone stopped ringing, but after the clubhouse was cleared, Steinbrenner made his entrance into Martin's office. Martin was ready.

"When I'm seven and a half games behind, you can come in here and rant and rave," Martin said. "But when I'm seven and a half in front get the fuck out of here."

Martin was dealing from strength. He doesn't have that kind of insulation now. It would be awkward as hell to fire a manager at this point, but then Steinbrenner does impulsive things. He is an impulsive man.

Once, when he owned a team in the American Basketball League (not to be confused with the later ABA), Steinbrenner seated himself in the top row of the stands at the start of the game to keep himself from becoming involved. Gradually he moved closer. He wound up drawing a technical foul seated on the bench.

The first spring Steinbrenner owned the Yankees (actually,

a now shrinking group of silent partners largely from Cleveland bought the team) the Yankees were off to a good start until they played in front of Steinbrenner in Cleveland. When they took off their caps for the national anthem, George M. Steinbrenner III was close enough to determine that he didn't like their hair cuts. He wrote a note to Ralph Houk, then manager, to read at a clubhouse meeting.

The players didn't think that it was so harsh; an owner is entitled to some rules of appearance even if it isn't the style of the day. What did disturb the players was that Steinbrenner named them as "1, 17, and 28."

One time Steinbrenner was sitting next to the dugout while the Yankees were playing in Texas when shortstop Gene Michael put his hand into his glove and withdrew it in horror. The practical jokers used to put crawly things or clots of chewed tobacco in Phil Rizzuto's glove to see him jump, but that didn't make the Yankees a bad team. Michael frantically shook his glove and out fell half of an uncooked hot dog. Michael sighed and tossed it off the field. End of practical joke.

Except that Steinbrenner sent for whatever it was that Michael tossed away. When the game ended in a Yankee victory, rare enough at that time, Steinbrenner vaulted the railing and followed the team to the clubhouse. When Houk expected a compliment on the victory, Steinbrenner held up the hot dog, all crusted with gravel.

"This!" Steinbrenner said. "I want you to find out who is responsible for this and discipline him."

"You won't believe this, but . . ." Houk said at the time.

All of that was before revelations of Steinbrenner's Watergate involvement. Ball players are much more concerned with petty issues that involve themselves than with the greater moral issue of making illegal campaign contributions to Nixon and directing his employees to lie to the FBI about them.

Steinbrenner pleaded guilty to felony charges and was fined $15,000. The commissioner of baseball then suspended Steinbrenner from active participation in the running of the Yankees for two years, a sentence later reduced to what amounted to suspension of one playing season.

That suspension proved to be so superficial that Steinbrenner played a critical behind-the-scenes role in the house revolt that nearly deposed Bowie Kuhn as commissioner. The

Yankees' vote was changed at a late hour, and the following season Steinbrenner was reinstated as visible head of the Yankees.

To the players, in their self-interest, it all amounts to a judge's warning to beware. As one player put it in the midst of the tumultuous season: "Billy has lied to me, I know that. George has been convicted of lying. So how do you know who to believe around here?"

For people who work for Steinbrenner, there are more significant aspects to the man than merely an illegal attempt to curry favor in the government.

"George is the essence of the Jekyll and Hyde mentality," Campbell W. Elliott, who worked for Steinbrenner for three years as president of American Ship Building Co. and is still a close friend, has said. To people outside his business interests, "George is the most charming guy in the whole world, a real Mr. Nice," Elliott continued. "But to people who work for him, George's attitude is that they're damned lucky to have a job—and if they don't like the way he treats them, they can just get the hell out."

And that's precisely what a number of Steinbrenner's Yankee employees have done. Lee MacPhail became president of the American League. Clyde Kluttz, the head scout who won Catfish Hunter for the Yankees, moved on to Baltimore. Pat Gillick had Elliott Wahle, Nos. one and two in player development, moved on to expansion Toronto, Tal Smith to Houston. Two public relations men, Bob Fishel— nearly 20 years with the Yankees—and Marty Appell, left. And more. Steinbrenner says he is proud that people in his organization are so much in demand. But when so many people uproot themselves, the suggestion is more that it became too unpleasant for them to stay.

One time in his first years of running the Yankees, Steinbrenner reacted strongly to a newspaper story critical of the Yankees. It is said that Steinbrenner's voice on the telephone to Paul could be heard over half the South Bronx ordering the publicity staff to get a "good story" into the papers.

The man has ultimate confidence in his own ability to handle the job of any employee better than the employee. He is impatient with disagreement and intolerant of anything other than immediate results. Low-level employees are constantly in fear of their jobs.

Steinbrenner pays attention to microscopic details. He is

very strong on adequate policing of the grandstand, which is necessary. He is equally strong on less important details. He has his thing about what kind of music will be played in his ball park. It will be of some conservative nature, with its roots in an earlier generation. When an electrician used a rock recording to test the sound system in an empty Yankee Stadium, Steinbrenner came roaring abuse at the powerless electrician.

Apparently Steinbrenner's harsh treatment is not reserved for little people. His disregard for the wishes of his stockholders has made a number of them sell their stock to him. There was no fun in ownership even of a championship team.

Billy Martin still feels strongly about being a Yankee, even if it isn't the same organization he played with. He's taken more abuse to hold this job, he says, than he would take for any other job in baseball.

Sunday, March 27

Tampa

Jackson made no throw home on a single to right field as the winning run scored for the Reds, and players on both sides asked why. Jackson's elbow is still sore and he was due for a cortisone shot after the game. He was told not to throw hard, but Martin didn't tell the Yankee players. Jackson was needlessly embarrassed.

Tuesday, March 29

Dunedin

Now Steinbrenner has the fight he says he's been spoiling for. Graig Nettles has jumped the team over dissatisfaction with his contract. When the team took the bus from its hotel in Tampa to play in Dunedin, Nettles was on his way back to Fort Lauderdale.

Steinbrenner sees himself as the leader of the Young

Turks, filling the power vacuum left by the aging Dodger owner Walter O'Malley, long the strongman among the owners. Steinbrenner says he is ready to make an example of Nettles for failing to honor his contract. Athletes in other sports have signed long-term contracts and then tried to force new contracts when they had a good year. Steinbrenner said he will sue to prevent that's happening here.

He told Nettles' agent, LaRue Harcourt, "I hate to see Graig in the middle of a monumental case, but somebody has to tell the athlete he has to live up to his contract. We're going to take a stand."

Steinbrenner thinks Nettles is one of the most selfish athletes he's ever met. Nettles chose to participate in the television competitions of Superstars and Superteams because of the fees and put off having that wart taken care of until it forced him to miss so much playing time here.

Nettles, who was moving toward playing out his option and becoming a free agent last July, signed a three-year contract for approximately $390,000—plus an option year. With that security, Nettles then led the league in home runs. Now he sees how much he could have made. He insists he is not looking to renegotiate, but that's splitting hairs. He will be thirty-three by the time this season ends. The contract will carry him through next season. He says he wants an extension of two years on the contract. And he wants it reworded so that the tax bite will not be so great on deferred payments. He says the rewording won't cost the Yankees a thing and will save him some money.

To the contrary, according to the current player agreement, any rewording would make it a new contract and the Yankees would lose the option year. Steinbrenner is not willing to give that up. He's says he's not willing to risk $140,000 a year on a player who will be thirty-five or thirty-six, either. He won't give in. Nettles must. "If Graig admits publicly that he made a mistake, there will be no fine," Steinbrenner said.

Steinbrenner can see a victory in this for his side. Nettles will surrender quickly enough. But what will be the residue of unpleasantness? Martin is concerned about that.

So are several players. "If this club starts losing a lot early, the whole thing could blow up," said Jimmy Wynn, a perceptive fellow. Things are sensitive already.

A strong division has been formed between the good ol'

boys who won last year and the newcomers. Newcomers got money and they got the jobs that belonged to last year's pals. "It seems the only way to make any money from the Yankees is to play for another team," Nettles said.

Wynn didn't get all that much money, but he did get Lou Piniella's job, which violates everybody's sense of security. If a team wins a pennant and players still lose their jobs, when is there ever any security? Maybe there never is any security—ever—when a team constantly tries to improve itself, but the resentment is mounting.

Jackson, of course, is the chief irritant and he hasn't had anything to do with it. He's worked very hard, knowing he was always being watched, and he's been quiet. "It's just that I'm the problem," he said. "I cause problems just being here."

That's oversimplification. The explosion could come among the players or it could come from the top. If Jackson and Gullett have something to do with early success, then they will quickly become part of the group. If the opposite happens, it could be awful on this team.

It could be most awful at the top. "Martin, he's like a little rat," a player said. "You don't know when he's going to feel threatened and strike out at somebody or a whole bunch of people."

Players are already afraid of being identified with what they say. "There is craziness, from the top down—owner, manager, and players," another player said. "They think they can be like Oakland, but it's not the same. The players could unite in Oakland around hating Finley. There's too many different people to hate here."

Thursday, March 31

Fort Lauderdale

Nettles is back in camp with his mimeographed apology. How do you type an apology with your fingers crossed?

To Steinbrenner it's a major victory. He is saying to players and other owners alike: Send them a message. Now he can see himself as the big shaker and mover among the new ruling faction. "Turks, Young Turks, Old Turks, whatever you want to call them," Steinbrenner said.

Chris Chambliss, twenty-eight, was signed to a five-year contract worth close to a million dollars, which is Steinbrenner's evidence that he is willing to pay for services performed and anticipated. Getting Nettles back without making any concessions is more far-reaching. "Pretty God damn important," Steinbrenner said.

He has held Nettles to his contract, and Steinbrenner said he had three phone calls from other owners complimenting him. He wouldn't give their names. "We set a precedent," Steinbrenner said proudly. "From now on guys are not going to be too quick to pull something. If the development had gone the other way, it could have been very difficult for baseball."

*   *   *

Ron Blomberg has his left leg in a cast as a result of a collision with a fence two days ago. The official line says he has bruises and swelling. After four weeks, the line still says Mickey Klutts has a jammed sprain. Klutts says the bone in the back of his hand was broken in two places and the middle finger was dislocated. So much for the truth.

Friday, April 1

Miami

Thank goodness for Sparky Lyle. When this camp needed a laugh more than anything in the world just a week before the season opens, there was Lyle.

And if there was Lyle, there had to be a foil. Gene Monahan, the trainer, is perfect. He's so very serious. He's a young man, but being the trainer of the Yankees costs a man some youth. Monahan dresses all in white and smiles broadly at the right time, but he's very careful to do things the company way lest he get caught in the middle. He reacts very gravely.

Like tonight in the middle of the game against the Orioles in Miami. Between innings of his highly encouraging six-inning workout, Hunter hollered into the trainer's room that Jimmy Wynn had been hit "upside the head." Monahan dispatched assistant Herman Schneider before Hunter stopped him. "April fool," Hunter said. "That's all right, Catfish," Monahan said. "I'm never going to trust you again."

Ten minutes later Hunter leaned on the door to the trainer's room and said loudly, "God damn, Reggie, what are you hopping around like that for? Does it hurt that bad?" Again Monahan came at a run and found Hunter wasn't talking to anyone. "Damn, I'll never believe you again," Monahan promised.

That was the warmup for Lyle, who took over after Hunter's best six innings of the spring. Lyle made his first two preliminary tosses from the mound and then doubled over clutching his left elbow. He walked around the mound as if suddenly the season had ended right there.

Monahan had been primed, of course. As he was going into the clubhouse to ice Hunter's arm, dour-looking Dick Tidrow had halted him and told him to watch Lyle because his arm had felt stiff in the bullpen. When Monahan saw Lyle, his arm drawn and quivering, the trainer ran for the mound. Lyle told him, "Gene, I popped something in my elbow." He slurred his words. And Monahan turned whiter than his uniform.

"I'm thinking, Jesus, my gosh, this is a hell of a time for this to happen," Monahan said. He grabbed the elbow and asked if Lyle could straighten it. Lyle said, "Not too much." And Monahan started to walk Lyle off the mound.

Then Lyle said, "April fool. Ha, ha, ha, ha."

"And there I was standing there," Monahan said, his face flushing at the combination of relief and embarrassment.

His retaliation while the whole team roared with laughter was to pick up the rosin bag behind the mound and fling it as far as he could toward second base.

Later Monahan thought it was all wonderful. He'd spent the spring worried about Willie Randolph's knee, Hunter's shoulder, Don Gullett's neck and shoulder, and all the little things nobody foresees. And then there was a laugh because everything was looking bright in the medical department. "It's wonderful how Sparky loosened up the whole club," Monahan said. "We're flying home now and everything's all right."

Well, maybe not everything. The best of jokes doesn't change the nature of the relationships here. "What we should have done," Hunter said, "is about ten of us go to George all together and said we all wanted to renegotiate our contracts. Then we should have yelled out, 'April fool.' Steinbrenner probably would have shot us all."

Saturday, April 2

Chapel Hill, North Carolina

The Yankees beat the University of North Carolina, 8–1. Jackson hit a two-run homer and Steinbrenner got to show off his proudest possession at the school where his daughter will be in her freshman year by World Series time.

Sunday, April 3

Fort Lauderdale

It's time for a declaration of independence by Martin. The spring has gone along about as expected. There hasn't been a big blowup, just little ones all along the line. The atmosphere is heavy in the clubhouse.

Steinbrenner thinks it's been a lousy spring. He thinks they haven't worked hard enough, Martin included. He thinks they're not going to be ready to open the season. He thinks they haven't won enough here.

Martin thinks it's been a lousy spring because Steinbrenner has asked for all that. "This emphasis on winning in spring training has been horseshit. . . . This is the time you've got to relax; when the hell else are you going to? You can't during the summer."

Certainly not this summer with this team.

Martin and anybody else who looks can see the kind of team this is. It's full of explosive talent and explosive personalities. Martin knows about explosive situations; that's what he's had wherever he's been. Even caused some of it himself.

"They could win without me," Martin said, "but it would be hard."

Martin is caught in an absurd paradox. He wants always to

be his own man with responsibilities to no one and accountable to no one. Yet he wants to be the manager of the
Yankees. He says it's the only manager's job he ever really
wanted. He has Casey Stengel's job.

There was a wake at Stengel's house in Glendale the night
after he was buried in 1975. Martin, then the Texas manager,
was there, and there was a lot of drinking. Martin wound up
the night sleeping in Stengel's bed, as if he might be blessed
with the Old Man's genius.

The Stengel for whom Martin played didn't have to answer
to anyone. He was Casey Stengel. But he was also clever
enough to know when his owner and his general manager had
authority. And above all things, Stengel never put himself in
open conflict with management. Martin doesn't know how to
stay out of it.

The Jackson situation is the classic case in point. Martin
makes his role in Jackson's presence perfectly clear: "I didn't
buy him, George did."

About himself, Martin says: "I won last year, remember."
Then he laughs and points to the club directory taped to the
wall above his desk. "He won," he says mockingly. "We won."
Then he counted out the nineteen owners listed.

About his accountability he said: "I'm not going to explain
to George everything I do."

That appears to be just what Steinbrenner wants.

"My secret of managing is getting into players' hearts,"
Martin said. "I can get something extra from them. I can't
get petty and do certain things George sometimes wants or
I'll lose them. Something happens and he sits in the stands
and says, 'Find that son of a bitch, Martin.' I wait until the
next day. If it can't wait until the next day, it's not worth it."

Steinbrenner was in the stands on opening day last year
when Munson lined up without his cap for the national anthem. And Steinbrenner phoned the dugout to order Munson
reprimanded. "I told him I didn't like phone calls during the
game," Martin said. "I didn't get any more all season."

He now says he regards that scene after the Mets game in
St. Petersburg as a victory for himself. "It was a good thing
the players saw I wouldn't take shit from anybody," he said.

Of course, when the manager and the owner have words
often enough and strong enough, the owner can always have
the last two, "You're fired."

Martin is in the first year of a three-year contract. This

year, he indicates, his salary is about $75,000 plus expenses for car and apartment, which brings it to about $100,000. But there are certain clauses in the contract that are rules of conduct; if Martin breaks those rules then he is considered to have broken the contract and couldn't collect the balance of the money. He fully expects to be fired before the run of his contract.

"With him here," Martin said, "he might do it just for the publicity. I want to stay the Yankee manager as long as I can. This is as far as I can go. I don't think I'll ever come back as a manager again. I'll go fishing."

There are strong suspicions that if Martin is fired here, he might not get another managing job. It takes a man like Steinbrenner to take a shot with a man like Martin over the advice of Gabe Paul. Martin has come to conflict with the front office at other spots over players he wanted or didn't want. He came to blows with an aged farm director and an out-of-shape traveling secretary as well as with players.

Martin says he won at Detroit because he was able to break up the cliques in the clubhouse and keep the players from going over his head to the general manager. Eventually, he says, the players found their way back to the front office and Martin was fired.

"The manager has got to live and die on his own convictions," he said. "They hire you to manage, that's what it means."

Sometimes it seems that it means more to Martin to be right than to win, and it is most important of all to be Billy. He wears that label on his back the way he wears the number 1 on his uniform.

"Have you ever had to stand in line for food? I did," he says. "I slept in the same bed as my grandmother until I was fifteen."

Not only was he a poor kid when he was growing up on the wrong side of San Pablo Street in Berkeley in the depths of the Depression, but he was small. "Nobody ever believed I'd be a baseball player, I was so small. I made up my mind."

By his definition, he made it to eleven seasons in the big leagues by being aggressive. He'd like it to be acknowledged that he had better tools as a player than he's given credit for. But if there were a choice, he'd prefer to be thought of as willing to scrap for everything he got.

"I joined the YMCA, and some other guys thought I was

too uppity. I had to fight two guys when I got back home. I beat up enough of them and they left me alone. I was small, but I could hit hard. I would take two or three punches to get one in."

In 1953 he was in a celebrated brawl at second base with St. Louis Browns catcher Clint Courtney. Martin gets laughs now telling the story, and about how shortstop Phil Rizzuto stepped on Courtney's eyeglasses. In 1960 Martin went to the mound after being hit by a pitch and broke the jaw of pitcher Jim Brewer. It later cost $10,000 in a civil suit.

The acceptable term for that kind of behavior in an athlete is "a competitor." That's what Martin was, no question. He sees himself as the perpetual underdog. To him the whole world has always been "they" and "they" were always out to get him.

It still bothers him that when the 1950s New York papers discussed the World Series matchups between Martin and Jackie Robinson of the Dodgers, it was dismissed as no contest. Martin points to his record and argues that in the World Series he was superior. He rose to the challenge. "I wanted to do better than Jackie," Martin recalls. "He was a hell of a competitor. If we'd been on the same club, we'd have been close."

Near the end of Martin's career, playing for Cleveland, he had several bones broken in his face when he was hit by a pitcher. For a time after that, he had difficulty making himself stand at the plate. "My heart was in the batter's box but my tail wasn't," he said. He attacked that problem by putting on a heavy jacket in batting practice and making himself be hit by the pitches.

What he doesn't care for is his reputation as an abusive person, a man who baited umpires and battled with players on both sides. He doesn't care to be reminded that he played for seven teams in his last five seasons. The cruelest blow was the first trade, when he was traded from the Yankees in 1957. It was the aftermath of a brawl during the celebration of Martin's birthday at the Copacabana nightclub in New York. Martin, Mantle, Ford, Hank Bauer, and the other Yankees present were cleared in court, but Martin was fined $1,000 by the Yankees for his part and George Weiss banished him to Kansas City because he feared the influence Martin had on Mantle.

Martin had always been Stengel's pet. He was so hurt by

the trade that he did not speak to Stengel for several years afterward.

Martin is also remembered for the knockout he scored over Dave Boswell, his own pitcher, while Martin was managing the Twins in 1969. "When he came off the wall, I hit him again and he was out before he hit the ground," Martin said at the time. He also explains that Boswell was in the process of beating up burly outfielder Bob Allison.

Now Martin says: "If you can't play for me, you can't play for anybody.

"I push myself as hard as I push my players. When I come into the clubhouse, I'm sort of like—don't ask me why— something just reaches in and takes hold of me.

"I can't take a loss easy. To me it's pride. When we lost the World Series to the Dodgers in 1955, I had to go in a back room because tears were coming out of my eyes. I didn't want anybody to see. I had a good Series, but we lost. That's pride."

Martin takes great pride in what he sees as his relationship to his players. With these Yankees, that aspect of the manager is worth special consideration. "If he could handle Steinbrenner for a year, he can handle anything," says one veteran player. There are those who think Martin's greatest value will come as a buffer—or a barrier—between the owner and the players.

Steinbrenner thinks that's been one of the faults in Martin's managerial style at the other stops, that he turns players against management, that he is too much the players' manager, keeping those good old friends on the team and retarding the development of young talent.

Martin has made some concessions on that score, or rather he was forced to make some. He was opposed to the trade of utility infielder Sandy Alomar. He wanted Elrod Hendricks kept as a third catcher rather than assigned to Syracuse.

Certainly he and Steinbrenner will have their arguments. It's remarkable that we're this close to opening day and Martin still has his job. "There'll be ones better than we've had; we're always going to argue," Martin said.

Steinbrenner finds a positive side to that, too. His point is that he and Martin had those harshest words at 10:30 at night and were able to breakfast together at eight the next morning.

Steinbrenner calls the whole process "constructive volatilism." We'll see just how constructive.

Monday, April 4

Fort Lauderdale

There is no such thing as a small issue on this team. Anything big enough to be an issue is an issue. Martin announced his opening day batting order and it's an issue.

So it's not a big deal: Munson bats third, Chambliss bats fourth, and Jackson bats fifth. But that's a big deal; Jackson has batted fourth for years.

"I'm worried about getting a chance to play and they're worried about where they bat," said Lou Piniella, the man without a position. "That's the egos involved."

The egos involved are, of course, Martin and Jackson. "Everybody is happy right now except one person; that's Reggie," said Jimmy Wynn. "It doesn't seem that his head and his heart are in the right place." Jackson's head and heart are in the fourth spot; that's called "cleanup." Cleanup has a certain heft that appeals to Jackson.

Wynn calls the affliction "mosquito bites." Mosquito bites itch. And sometimes they become infected.

When Ron Blomberg got the grim word this morning that his knee required surgery, he accepted Jackson's good wishes and vowed that he'd be batting behind Jackson in two months. "Then you're going to be awfully far down in the lineup," Jackson said. There was an itch to be scratched right there.

Some players are getting impatient with Jackson. "He's worried about not driving in a hundred runs," Wynn said. "With this club, there's going to be a lot of guys on base in front of him wherever he bats."

In the exhibition game today, right-handed Wynn batted fifth against the Mets' left-handed Jerry Koosman, and lefty Jackson batted sixth. It's Martin's lineup. He won the pennant with Munson batting third and driving in 105 runs, and Chambliss cleanup and driving in 96 runs. When Munson objected to batting second here, that experiment was dropped after one day. Martin doesn't move his men; the newcomer has to move. It's the same thinking as in the combat infantry platoon: The replacements are the ones picked for the dangerous patrols.

"I've never moved around like this, from second to sixth," Jackson said. "I've never had to think about where I was going to bat when I came to the ball park. Maybe I'm going to have to get used to it." It was said with dismay.

Martin's rationale is that Chambliss makes better contact than Jackson—80 strikeouts compared to 108. That's more influential, he says, than Jackson's 28 homers to Chambliss' 17. Jackson wouldn't argue the point for the record, but when his displeasure became known to Martin, Martin called Jackson into the office before the game. "The guy has had his way all along," Martin said later. "He's not used to playing the way other people want him to. But it's no big deal."

Any time the $3,000,000 man and the manager have a potential for conflict, it is a big deal. Any time Martin has a point to prove, it's a big deal. While the Mets' colossus Dave Kingman was hitting two towering home runs and Steinbrenner was getting red in the face willing Jackson to answer them, Chambliss twice drove in runs with singles. His single in the sixth inning drove in the run that gave the Yankees a 4–3 win.

"How about that number four hitter?" Martin crowed. "He'll come through all through the year, you'll see. Watch how consistent he is. He's a tough out."

Chambliss is a tough out. He's also a member of the team. Jackson hasn't achieved that status yet. He's still Steinbrenner's man, and any time Martin gets a chance to demonstrate his strength over Steinbrenner's, Martin grabs it. Jackson is Martin's way to get at Steinbrenner. "We're not playing egos," Martin challenged. "We're playing pennant, what's best for the ball club."

* * *

Poor Blomberg has his own kind of lament: "I made the club. I did good. I was going to play. I was going to be there opening day. The fans were going to see I was still there. I'd been out a year. I was going to run out there with the team.

"I bit the dust."

What was originally diagnosed as a bruise was revealed yesterday as a torn knee cartilage. Now he won't be able to play until late in July at the earliest, and there's another season gone. He's twenty-eight. He was supposed to be the Jewish slugger made for Yankee Stadium and the Bronx, and now what does he have left? Bad luck.

"Buzzard's bad luck," Jackson sympathized. "Can't kill nothin' and nothin' won't die."

Blomberg was never completely accepted by his teammates, either. He is the big friendly dog who tried to be too friendly and drove the others away. He never learned how to behave around them any more than he learned to play a position. By default, Blomberg's place on the roster goes to Elrod Hendricks, and any time Hendricks makes the team it's good news. "I still feel sorry for Bloomie," Hendricks said.

"I don't know," Blomberg said. "I don't know. I just don't know."

Tuesday, April 5

Fort Lauderdale

With one last phone call and one last dip into his deep pockets, Steinbrenner got Bucky Dent to play shortstop. That fills the vacancy in George III's crown. Now he can gaze upon his Yankees and at every position he can see a man who has been an all-star. It's just what he always wanted. It's the kind of team the Reds had when they swept the Yankees in four straight games in the World Series and embarrassed Steinbrenner.

All it took to complete the long-pending deal was more money for the White Sox, who didn't have the money to sign Dent in the first place. Dent has accepted the Yankee terms. A shortstop at $400,000 for three years is worth more to an owner who can smell the pennant than to an owner who can smell sixth place and the nearby stockyards.

And what about poor Chicken Stanley? That's as much an illustration of the game as the cast on Blomberg's knee. The front office never believed in Stanley.

Martin says he believed. "I hate to see Chicken moved out," Martin said. "I'm in Chicken's corner. I made him my shortstop; he did a hell of a job for me."

The Yankees gave up unsigned Oscar Gamble for Dent. It was as Steinbrenner threatened when he told Gamble he had twenty-four hours to sign or he'd be traded. Now there are still Dock Ellis and Marty Perez unsigned. And Rivers has those continuing personal distractions. The Yankees are talking with Oakland about Mike Torrez, who pitches, and Bill North, who plays center field and steals bases.

Wednesday, April 6

New York

The cocktail party is over. It's been all talk and no action. Tomorrow is opening day, the games begin to count and the animosity becomes a factor to be measured. Can it be separated from the job on the field? Is it all merely newspaper talk, as Gabe Paul says? Or does it wreck the team? Do they run away and hide from the league? Or do they run away and sulk?

"It's a hell of a club," says Dock Ellis. He says he's decided to put away the hard feelings over his contract and try to be as cheerful as he was last season. It's the easiest way for him to live. But he has a feel for the shadows and the murmuring voices in the lockers. "Something is going to happen," Ellis said. "You can see it. You can feel it. Hopefully, it won't happen. But I don't see how to get around it."

Ellis isn't alone in what he sees. Wynn is worried, too. They are two highly perceptive men. Wynn after twelve seasons in the National League went onto the field before the workout to examine the monuments to Yankee history in center field. "If the guys' minds are right, they can run away from the league," Wynn said. "If these guys' minds are not right then there's trouble. Anything can happen with a club like this. You don't know from day to day who's going to jump the ball club."

If they play well at the start and they find they are comfortable with themselves, then they should play that much better. If they start poorly and start picking at themselves, they can scuttle the whole operation by May. If Catfish Hunter doesn't have to worry about his own survival, he can exert a lot more influence than just his pitching. His country-boy wit disguises a lot of insight. He has the respect of the ins and the outs. He can talk to Munson and to Jackson, and he has the confidence of the black players.

Hunter can help by kidding with the right guys when the right other guys can see him. He calls Rivers "Wonderboy," as in "I wonder if you're going to show up at the ball park?" It's an unaccustomed role for Hunter, but he acknowledges that he may have breakfast often with people on opposing sides of issues.

Hunter and Jackson were teammates for seven seasons on the A's, who won in spite of their tempest. Jackson predicts that Hunter will turn out to be his greatest ally.

There are still players who say the whole issue of conflict on the team is a media creation. Wynn is not one of them. They say there isn't a player around who wouldn't try to drive his worst enemy home from second base. But it's still a game played by people, and the psychology of it has so much to do with performance. If the heads aren't right, how can the performances be?

Wynn remembers how the 1975 Dodgers were torn apart when some players felt that too-good-to-be-true Steve Garvey was more interested in promoting his own image than in winning. "It destroyed a good ball club," Wynn said. After winning the National League pennant in 1974, the Dodgers finished twenty games behind Cincinnati. "It is possible," Wynn said.

Things have been quiet lately, but on this team "lately" is limited to maybe the day before yesterday, the way "oldies-but-goodies" on rock radio mean records made six months ago. Jackson and Munson have been compatible and the team has played well for more than a week. "I don't think the turmoil is over with yet," Hunter said. "There will be some problems, but there is so much talent here it's hard to let any one guy get in the way."

Of course, all of that is between the players. George Steinbrenner III is still the owner. He still advocates a "constructively volatile" club. That much is out of the players' control.

"Let him stay up in his box, count the money, push buttons, and stay the hell out of the clubhouse," Ellis said.

Steinbrenner is certainly not going to like reading that an unsigned player is telling him where he can go and where he can't.

Maybe none of this makes any difference. Maybe it really
is all talk. There hasn't been anything like this team as precedent. "Thurman and I can still have a fistfight a week," Jackson said, "and I'd still hit thirty home runs and he'll bat
.300."

That's Jackson's bravado speaking. By admiring Munson's
talents, Jackson makes it known that he has no hard feelings
toward Munson and, at the same time, calls attention to his
own talents. Jackson needs to be recognized as much as he
needs to succeed. Jackson says he knows what he can do,
that there's no way he won't get 30 home runs and drive in
100 runs. One breath later he concedes that those figures are
the minimum that will be acceptable and that the pressure to
achieve them may be choking. George Steinbrenner didn't get
Jackson at that price to be merely very good.

Jackson won't be thirty-one years old until May 18, and he
has already made his mark and his fortune. He accepted a
five-year $2,930,000 contract (plus an interest-free loan
presumed to be another million) that may be worth as much
as $5–6,000,000 after twenty years. He had already accumu-
lated wealth he estimates at $9,000,000 from land trading in
Arizona. He was the Most Valuable Player in the American
League in 1973, led the league in runs batted in once and in
home runs twice. He has batted cleanup on three World
Series winners.

He says he has nothing to prove by playing baseball anymore. He says it with pain, with his round face crinkled into
a grimace. He is asking why he has to put himself through
what he is feeling at this point with this team.

With Jackson's history and his contract, as Casey Stengel
used to say, "The only thing you got to worry about is your
health." But Jackson is afraid he accepted the wrong fortune.
To say he is scared out of his wits would be only a slight ex-
aggeration.

He had his sweet time in Oakland despite the periodic grief
Charlie Finley handed out, before being traded to Baltimore,
where he chose to put himself on the market. Maybe Jackson
could have had that sweet time again with the Angels or the
Padres or the Phillies or the Dodgers. But he is afraid he cannot have it with the Yankees, not in New York.

The life Jackson sees for himself was more visible out on
the fishing pier in Fort Lauderdale one afternoon before a
night game. Jackson wore just snug-fitting shorts and thong

slippers and pointed a long-lens camera at everything he saw. He crept up to sea birds as they perched on the railing and he sought interesting faces among the elderly men and women who fished. The warmth with which they indulged the young man delighted Jackson.

People responded to Jackson's inquiries before they knew who he was, and when a man who had grown up in the Bronx identified Jackson, the tone on the pier changed hardly at all. It was hometown comfort even if Jackson had smirked earlier when the white gas station attendant addressed the black driver as "Mr." Jackson.

There was no rush for autographs, no pulling at his hands. When a woman from Pittsburgh asked for an autograph: "Please, Reverend Jackson," Reggie pointed out that he was the ball player Jackson, not the civil rights leader Jesse Jackson. But he signed anyhow and smiled away the woman's embarrassment.

The New Yorker on the pier pointed out the half dozen torpedo-shaped barracuda lurking in the water, discussed marine biology, and told of stealing radishes from the Bronx farms that became the site of Yankee Stadium. When the man said he'd be out at the park to watch him, Jackson replied, "Sit in right field, I'll say hello to you." He meant it.

It was an idyllic moment. He was a nice-sized fish in a comfortable-sized pond. He had just enough attention and no demands, no scream piercing his comfortable shell. He had delighted in the attention of the New York press when he was visited in Oakland and in the thrice-yearly visits to Yankee Stadium, but now the constant scrutiny from greater numbers of notebooks, cameras, and microphones and the demands on his time are more than he ever imagined. At the price he's getting, it's fair to say he should be able to put up with a lot, but no fat bankbook can make a man impervious to all that. On the pier he was afraid he was living a moment in time he has lost forever.

He's apprehensive about his relations with his teammates, and of being consumed by the city. He is fearful of the sociology of a whole section of the country. And his fears are all of his own choosing.

From the end of last season, when he became a free agent, until early December when he accepted the Yankees, Jackson had the freedom to pick and choose. Now he feels he was overwhelmed, that he didn't have time to make the right choice and didn't know how to go about picking the right spot. "It was the most mentally strenuous thing I've ever done," he said.

When Steinbrenner applied pressure, flying to Jackson's side twice in a day and giving him a $63,000 Rolls-Royce just for the courtesy of listening, Jackson caved in. In December, when he was introduced to the Big Apple, Jackson said he had been won over by Steinbrenner's style of operating, courting Jackson as if he were "hustling a girl at a bar." Now Jackson said, "I wanted to get it over with."

From a baseball standpoint, a left-handed hitter like Jackson should have picked a team where the power was right-handed, not lefty like Chambliss and Nettles. But the man does not live by home runs alone. "I haven't found anybody I can relate to yet," he said.

Jackson is a very perceptive man. By his count, he has an IQ of 160. His commentary is often one-sided and self-serving, but he has an awareness of the needs of others and an understanding of what's going on around him that few ball players can match or care to match. He can never have the protection of ignorance.

The Yankees are major-league ball players because they have physical skills. "Eighty percent of ball players are one way and Reggie is part of the other twenty percent," former Oakland teammate Bill North once said. "He's intelligent; the rest of them are dumb asses."

He has the skill to manipulate the press like few other athletes—the knack of saying the commonplace in terms that leap into a newspaper story. When he was discussing the brilliance of pitcher Tom Seaver before facing him in the 1973 World Series, Jackson said: "He's so great that blind people come to the ball park to hear him pitch." When he was sidelined from the 1972 Series by a torn hamstring, he wept openly and was proud of it. That's not in the Yankee tradition.

With Oakland, where he played his first eight seasons, he had long-established relationships. He had grown up with many of his teammates. They understood and accepted his emotional need to talk in a business where the ideal is the strong, silent type.

Jackson is divorced. He drew much support from his relationship with outfielder Joe Rudi and laments their separation. "When you have that relationship on a team, it gives you a feeling of being home," he said. "It takes a lot of pressure off you, gives you a feeling of security, of sharing. Sharing—that's what man's all about."

Jackson paused in his musing to admire his own words. "That's a good quote, isn't it?" he asked.

Of course it is. Merely inquiring reveals the man. He is fundamentally insecure, and psychologists say even one ally can be enormously beneficial. That's why the army prefers two-man foxholes. Jackson hasn't found anybody to share his.

He hasn't made an enemy yet, but is acutely aware of that potential. He has worked hard on the field and has been quiet in the clubhouse. "Laid back" is what he calls it. When his original number 20 shirt was mislaid, he considered wearing number 42 because it was the number Jackie Robinson wore and Jackson is also acutely aware of his blackness. But he decided that would be too obvious, so he chose Henry Aaron's number 44.

"I have no problem getting along with anybody," he said. "It's just that I'm the problem. I cause problems just being here."

It's well known that Gabe Paul wanted to make an offer Bobby Grich couldn't refuse. Paul wanted Grich to play shortstop. Martin wanted Rudi, the right-handed counterbalance. Steinbrenner wanted Jackson's charisma. And Steinbrenner had Munson's blessing. Munson advised that Grich could never return the investment with his play, while Jackson could give them speed and an arm they needed in the outfield, and he could bring fans.

Immediately, as agreed in advance, Munson got more money, although not as much as he said was in the agreement. How much resentment is yet to come is only a guess. "How come, after eight years, everybody expects me all of a sudden to become a jerk about Jackson?" Munson protests.

Hardly anybody expects conflict to be deliberate, but the clubhouse needle is a way of life. Jackson is sensitive. Munson's needle is generally blunt. In the heat of the season he is likely to blunder into saying the wrong things. He has already come close. But Jackson has adopted his best self-control. He says he will not permit himself to be drawn into a fight some teammates think possible.

He has developed a way of drawing into a protective shell when fans blurt something awkward or challenging. "They ask, 'What are you going to do with all that money, Jackson?'

They don't mean to say the wrong thing. But they want to say something and it's the only thing they can think of. I understand that.

"If I want to punch a sixty-year-old in the mouth, I can't do that. If he says, 'You're a no-good son of a bitch,' I hear it slowed down: 'You're . . . a . . . no . . . good . . . son . . . of . . . a . . . bitch' "

He is disappointed that he hasn't been drawn into the clubhouse razzing, but feels it improper for him to tease them first. How can he needle them about money or talent when he feels he has so much more of both?

The area where he feels he must step most carefully is leadership. Munson is the man they look up to here, whether he has the verbal qualities or not. Jackson's ideal is Frank Robinson, for whom he once played winter ball. Robinson led with deed and with word. Jackson feels he is a leader but will wait to assert himself.

Usually the role seeks the man. Like the day in Fort Lauderdale when Mickey Rivers had his pre-game lecture about hustling from the manager. On the field Jackson complimented Rivers on one dash to first base, and when Martin indicated that Rivers had played enough for the day, Jackson advised Rivers to stay in the game. Then it was Jackson who waved off Rivers' replacement. "There are a lot of things I do to keep the heat off," Jackson said afterward. He told them to Rivers: for instance, to play an extra inning, run back to your position when you've chased a ball into the alley. "They mean nothing, but they impress some people," Jackson said. "It's all eyewash and I've mastered it."

Those people who are impressed by false hustle often find black players lacking in it. "It's a natural thing for black people to move slowly," former St. Louis pitcher Bob Gibson once said. "What was the point in hurrying to be a slave?"

If Jackson has helped Rivers through his next episode—or merely through this one—he has made a contribution.

He made a contribution to the 1976 Orioles after reporting a month late after being traded by Oakland. Jackson was holding out for more money but was suffering intense personal shock as well. Still he came close to driving an underpowered team up the Yankees' back. Any expectation of internal strife wrecking the Yankees, says Baltimore pitcher Jim Palmer, "is purely wishful thinking."

But even if life on the Yankees goes smoothly, Jackson is

frightened by the city. Of course, coming to New York has put money in his pocket. Geoffrey Beene is considering a clothing line bearing Jackson's name. Ben Kahn wants to put Jackson in furs. And remember when Jackson said if he played in New York, "they'd name a candy bar after me"? Well, Standard Brands is close to announcing a tentatively named "Hey Reggie" bar with caramel, chocolate, and nuts. Its potential for Jackson can be one of the best deals ever for an athlete.

But it's still New York, and even though Jackson grew up in the Philadelphia suburb of Wyncote, he has been California for a long time. He has a home in Berkeley. He has a collection of old cars he likes to tinker with. He has a Porsche with license plates "MVP-73" and a 1939 Chevrolet with a more recent Cadillac engine, bearing the equally anonymous plates "REG-9." But he likes to withdraw into familiar company. "I remain a stranger for a long time," he said. "I was a stranger in Baltimore all season."

He turned down an offer from Montreal that was nearly $4,500,000 because Montreal was "foreign." New York is foreign, too. As bright as Jackson is, he agrees that he is not especially curious. "I don't like to travel," he said. "I don't want to go see Europe; I don't want to go to the Orient or Latin America. I like California. Maybe some day I can have a house in Hawaii where it's quiet and I can walk the beach alone.

"I don't know if I'm going to fit in New York. People already have me fit in a glamorous mold like Joe Namath. I have glamour; I don't have the life-style. Do they expect me to replace him? How much private life will I have? If any. I'm not a city guy."

He is not a chaser of women the way many ball players are. It's not his thing to seek to be seen with the great beauties of our time. He says the only woman he ever lived with he was married to.

He is aware of the public reaction to any man making his kind of money, but he argues that he's earned it, and it didn't come all at once. In 1966 he made $500 a month and $800 a month the next year. He made $140,000 one year at Oakland and was cut to $112,000 the next. He says he has an accountant watching his money and if he spends "$7,000 or $8,000 in a month," he gets a warning.

"I don't want to spend that much," he said. "If I piss my

56 *Steve Jacobson*

money away, I make sure I spend it on somebody." He drank
one beer at the Banana Boat Lounge the other night and
bought $20 worth of drinks for the bar. He likes the feeling.

When he went to Arizona State, he had no car. "I couldn't
dream of owning a car then," he said. In high school he had
a '55 Chevy, "which is why I own one now." He bought his
father, a retired tailor in Philadelphia, a car for $9,800. "I
tell him, 'Dad, if you want something, get it.' How much
longer is he going to live? Why shouldn't he have anything he
wants?"

The real estate money he worked for, too. "I worked every
day for eight years, jacket and tie every day," he said. "Guys
lying around all winter won't find that."

Jackson could find the solitude he says he craves and a
place to tinker with his cars if he sought a place to live outside the city, but business arrangements will put him in Manhattan. It's his choice.

He's apprehensive about the East in general. "The East
Coast is not philosophically or socially as liberal as the West
Coast," he said. "I don't think the East is used to the black
man standing up and saying what he thinks. Out of the ordinary."

Jackson is afraid that his keeping company with an attractive blond woman he says he may some day marry will not
be accepted in New York. He remembers growing up in
Philadelphia as a Dodger fan because his father used to take
him to see the Dodgers, the team with the black stars.

He feels the Mets were not interested in competing for him
for the same reason they didn't draft him after his sophomore
year at Arizona State. "The Mets are a lily-white organization," he said. He said he was passed over when the Mets had
first choice in the amateur draft because, he was told, as long
as he was serious about his girl friend, of Mexican descent,
the Mets couldn't be serious about him. Oakland drafted him
and he married her. He feels the baseball establishment
resents giving big money to black players, especially to black
players who speak out.

Some players, however, feel Jackson is one who ultimately
survives. A former teammate recalls Jackson, when drinking,
saying he wished he were white. And when does one believe
Jackson most? "When he's drunk," a former Oakland teammate said. "I won't take the crap of some of the racial slurs
he used to pretend he didn't hear."

Now there is a pressure he's never had before. He insists he knows what he can do and will do it. Then he concedes "just a ray of doubt." If he concedes "a ray," how much uncertainty really is there? "Last May," recalls Paul Blair, who was with Jackson on the Orioles, "when he was telling people he was good, he was telling himself at the same time."

When he didn't have a hit in his first seven times up in exhibition games here, he felt the pressure. Then he got a single and a searing line-drive double and felt the relief. "That double, that's what separates me from the rest of the guys," he said. "How many others can hit it that hard? Everybody knows I'll hit. But I felt the relief: 'Whew! They still want to see it now.' "

But what if he gets off to a bad start? "It will eat me up. It ate me up in Baltimore." And what if he has a bad year? He scoffed. "I can play," he said. "You know I'm going to hit."

He shrugged. "Maybe I'm wrong. Maybe I can have a rotten year."

How is a rotten year measured? He has hit as high as .293, hit as many as 47 home runs, batted in as many as 118 runs. He can steal a base at a critical time. He can make a spectacular play or a mistake in the outfield. He has a magnificent, but undisciplined, arm in an outfield with no other arms. Take off his number, put him with any six players running thirty yards, and he instantly would appear as the superior athlete.

"If I do well, people will say, 'He's supposed to do that.' If I come short of it, if we don't win, it will be my fault," he said. "They'll say, 'Steinbrenner fouled up. Jackson's no good. He hurt the club. He created dissension.' "

That much is obvious. The Yankees are expected to win. Anything less than winning the World Series will be falling short. Jackson's performance will be measured against a standard he never saw in Oakland or Baltimore. New York is bigger, knows more baseball, is more sophisticated than anything Jackson has experienced. "Everybody thinks I'm going to electrify New York," he said. "So I hit thirty-five home runs. How do I turn that city on?"

Will the city overwhelm him? "How much will I have to deal with every day?" he asked. "I'm not allowed to have a headache, be tired, not allowed to have time to be with myself. That's the way it's going to be. There are a lot of things you'll accept for a couple of million dollars."

Jackson's contract is for five years with an option—his option—for a sixth year. There is a spoken agreement that says he can direct the Yankees to trade him. After two years the heaviest part of the contract will have been paid. The salary of $200,000 a year plus $132,000 deferred is not staggering in today's market. "If I can't relate to the people off the field, then I'm not going to stay there," he said. "I'm not sure I want to play five more years, anyhow."

There is much more going on in Jackson's mind than the simplicity of taking a round bat and making it hit a round ball—squarely. There's a danger that Jackson's apprehensions will become self-fulfilling, that he will court his own unhappiness by fearing it. "It's demanding as hell to be Reggie Jackson," Bill North of the A's says.

Jackson sees himself as Jonathan Livingston Seagull. On the fishing pier he crept up on gulls on the railing, trying to capture them with his camera, wings poised at the first moment of flight. "Birds have a sense of freedom I admire," Jackson said. "They're loners. I'm a loner. Look at me. Watch me."

If he feels trapped, penned in by the pinstripes, he can't say it's a world he never made.

* * *

Tomorrow we start finding out.

The Plot Thickens

New York

The season opened with the Reverend William Kalaidjian praying over the speaker system, which took his plea to the crowd of 43,785. "We pray this year," the Reverend Kalaidjian intoned, "that from your great heaven we receive the world championship."

It wasn't enough that the Yankees bought those ball players; now they needed God. Who ever heard a chaplain at a ball park pray for victory before? Not in public, anyhow.

I don't think Reggie Jackson prays for personal success; he thinks too much of God for that, but a prayer for love would be something else. He got love in the eighth inning of his first game for the home fans, his first game as a Yankee, his first game as a New Yorker.

Love came to Jackson in great waves as the fans filled Yankee Stadium with a huffing, puffing "Reg-gie, Reg-gie, Reg-gie," as if they wanted to love him as much as he wanted their love. "You hear that sound, 'Reggie, Reggie, Reggie,' and it turns on your adrenalin," Jackson said. "It makes you feel liked. It makes you feel loved." It's not a bad name for a candy bar, either.

He'd hardly done anything yet for the fans and he'd won his first victory in anticipation. He got two singles, made one hands-first slide and one feet-first slide, and he had that sound to feel down to his gut. He's not the kind of man who can ignore that sound.

He flied out with two on in the first inning. In the fourth

he singled and scored on a nifty suicide squeeze bunt by
Willie Randolph, sliding home outside the line, a half-step beyond the catcher's lunge. In the sixth he singled and scored
on a wild pitch. And in the eighth inning he went to the plate
with none on, the game apparently all but in the clubhouse,
and the crowd wanted more: a third-act show-stopper. "They
were saying, 'Come on, man, finish off our day, hit one out!"
he said. "I'd have loved to hit one. It wasn't because I wasn't
trying."

The contrast with Baltimore was extreme. He recalled
people kicking in the door of his car in the parking lot. He
remembered going three for three against lethal Frank
Tanana and being booed when he struck out the last time. He
remembered hitting home runs in six games in a row and
when he struck out against Nolan Ryan's smoke, he was
booed.

Today when he drove a ball foul long enough to be a
home run and then grounded out, the sound he heard was
cheering. "It was nice," he said. "I want to see what they're
like when I hit one. That crowd can make me play over my
head."

Jackson seemed somewhat bewildered by it all. Most of the
crowds he played for in Oakland could have been fitted into
one section of the Stadium. And that cheering, was it something that was due him? Or was this really a special occasion?
But he had his audience, and no actor plays at his best to an
empty house.

"Thank you," Jackson said from the clubhouse, and he
took his bow there.

* * *

Responses to special moments come in different shapes
for different people. Jimmy Wynn, in his first at bat as a
Yankee, hit a startling home run over the most distant fence,
across territory known as Death Valley for the long drives it
has killed. In the Astrodome in Houston, where Wynn—all of
five ten and 165 pounds—was known as the Toy Cannon,
there is a black cannon painted on one of the seatbacks in
honor of Wynn's 500-foot shot. This one carried a mere 450
feet into the Yankee bullpen, which was reached twice last
season. "Toy Cannon, my ass," said Catfish Hunter.

Wynn's feeling was intellectual rather than visceral. He's
thirty-five, coming from the tail-end Braves to a pennant-race

favorite. The last time he did that, he went as a star from Houston to the 1974 Dodgers. "I felt excited with the Dodgers," he said. "Today I felt nervous." With the Yankees he is the designated hitter who came in a closeout sale. He hit a home run on opening day for the 1974 Dodgers, too. The roles are different.

Hunter pitched a sweet seven innings before retiring with a swelling lump on his left instep where he was struck by a hard grounder. Because he pitched so well, he dismissed the bruise even though X-rays were scheduled as a precaution. "This was as good as I ever pitched on opening day," he said.

Chicken Stanley had his ovation from the fans, who sympathize, when he went to shortstop for the ninth inning. "It was the biggest ovation I ever had," he said.

And Jackson had his moment to kid about the fight that broke out in the stands as he came to bat for the first time. A fight in the first inning on opening day is a record. "See what I breed," he said. When he was asked about his communications with Munson during the game, Jackson said, "He punched me in the mouth after I got my two hits, so I didn't get any more."

Friday, April 8

New York

Hunter's bruise is a little worse than he thought yesterday. He'll probably miss his next turn.

Ron Blomberg's knee was operated on.

Dock Ellis continues unsigned and outspoken, but he's been moved up in the pitching rotation. He's been named to pitch Monday, which would make him the No. 4 pitcher, and Ken Holtzman, who was thought to be No. 4, drops back to the irregularity of the fifth spot. But that may be short-lived since they're trying hard to trade Ellis. "I just don't want unsigned players on this ball club," Steinbrenner said.

Ellis has been offered about $360,000, about $100,000 less than he thinks he should get. Steinbrenner says Ellis is "a fine pitcher, who, unfortunately, has talked too much." Ellis did say quite bluntly Steinbrenner ought to stay up in his office and out of the clubhouse. The present rumor is that a deal is working that would send Ellis and Mickey Rivers—pitcher and center fielder—to Oakland for Mike Torrez and Bill North—pitcher and center fielder. Gabe Paul denied everything. "We're as far apart as New York from California," he said.

Saturday, April 9

New York

So they won't have an undefeated season. That happens only in football.

The Yankees aren't a perfect team, either. The Brewers beat them, 3–2, and they ran on Thurman Munson every chance they got. They think they saw something in the way the Reds ran on Munson in the World Series. The Brewers inquired whether Munson had a sore arm. "The ball was like floating, it had no zip," Don Money said.

"My arm is fine," Munson said.

Jimmy Wynn, the Toy Cannon again, hit a 410-foot drive that one-hopped over the wall in left center for a ground-rule double. And Reggie Jackson misjudged a fly ball in the wind, which opened the door for all three Milwaukee runs.

Sunday, April 10

New York

By Billy Martin's reckoning, the Yankees have played three games and have an even split. One game they won, one game they lost, and one game the umpires stole from them. Martin can manage his team and he can manage against the other team, but how can he be expected to beat the umpiring team? That's what he explained to Steinbrenner when he phoned from his home in Tampa into Martin's steaming office.

Officially, the Brewers beat the Yankees, 2–1, but not in Martin's heart. "We got a pretty good screwing," Martin told the owner. "The umpire is flat full of shit."

Than Martin got up and did a pantomime, wearing only his mustache in a kind of colorful Marcel Marceau routine, of the two plays he decided were the Yankees' undoing. It was a run-of-the-mill tempest for Martin; he likes to blame umpires. It would have been funny, except that Martin was so serious. But how much dignity can any man maintain when he's doing a jumping-jack in the nude?

Martin was ignoring the fact that Sixto Lezano, the Brewers' $45,000 right fielder, hit home runs the first two times he ever faced Don Gullett, the Yankees' $180,000 left-hander. One of Martin's complaints was that the Brewers' first baseman touched a drive by Graig Nettles in fair territory and not foul as the umpires ruled.

The big complaint was over the last of the ninth, when Jackson was picked off after leading off with an infield single. Martin insisted that the pitcher, Doug McClure, had balked. He said McClure's illegal move was identified right there in his scouting report and waved a document to prove it. "Here it is, right here," Martin said.

Jackson didn't dispute the call; he accepted the blame. Both decisions were made by Vic Voltaggio, who was working his first series in the big leagues. "It was," Martin decided, "the worst one he ever had."

* * *

Jackson missed a fly-ball double he might have caught. He looks awkward in the outfield for a man who is regarded as a competent fielder.

Monday, April 11

Kansas City

Silly night. Both teams played as hard as if it were the sixth game of last year's playoffs. This time Mark Littell got Chris Chambliss' fly ball to stay in the ball park, and the Royals won in the thirteenth inning, 5–4.

There was a fan in a long black raincoat behind the Yankee dugout at the start of the game. He had lettered the front of the coat "STEIN/BRENNER" and wore big Elton John sunglasses with dollar signs on the lenses. And he tossed around Monopoly money as if it were real. With the potential winning run on first base in the last of the ninth, both sides stood on the top steps of their dugouts to watch a fistfight in the stands between two men in jackets and neckties. In the top of the eleventh a fan lurched across the outfield to the left field corner and, finding no escape, tried to grab the hands extended to him from above the twelve-foot wall. Three times he tried a running jump. Each time he ran, he jumped—*splat*—against the wall and fell to the dirt. Finally he was led staggering away.

Two infield errors gave the Royals two runs in the first inning, and the Yankees sent the minimum twenty-four batters to the plate over the last eight innings. Paul Blair was out stealing in the eleventh and Rivers in the thirteenth. It's the third time Rivers has been caught in four tries. Against Rivers, Kansas City manager Whitey Herzog called a pitchout on the third pitch and got his man. Not on the second pitch because Martin might have expected it. "I thought that he thought that I thought," Herzog chortled.

Martin will make the first change in his lineup. Munson will bat second. Jackson, who homered with none out, will move from sixth to third. "I'll bat anywhere they tell me," Jackson said. He has been to the plate seventeen times, fourteen times with none on. Chambliss hasn't been getting on base. "We will get better," Martin promised. "I don't worry about it one bit. I may be the only one who believes it."

The game was the first Monday night network telecast. which meant that it was carried back to Steinbrenner in Tampa.

"Full pads tomorrow," Martin announced.

Wednesday, April 13

Kansas City

The hotel here is the Sheraton Royal and Royals' owner Ewing Kaufman is part owner. So the Yankees stay here. It's a half mile from the stadium and an $8 cab from downtown, so much of the group kills time at the hotel. It was damp and windy and the tennis courts at the hotel were unplayable, so four reporters on the trip spent more than two hours standing under the marquee chatting with Jackson. It was very pleasant give-and-take and much of it was directed to and from Jackson, who is alert to anything.

We talked about Jackson's youth in Wyncote, Pennsylvania, about sleds and kids' street games, about his 160 IQ, and about the pronunciation of the name of the Royals' rookie left fielder, Joe Zdeb. And after a while Jackson casually took his wallet out of his pocket and rearranged the $100 bills. Everybody knows he's making big money and already has big money. When he does that wallet bit, which he does often, is he showing his wealth to others or to himself?

He had been shopping earlier in the day with Hunter, Lou Piniella, and Don Gullett. Only Piniella, lowest-paid member of the group, had bought anything, a couple of $26 shirts. Jackson said he wouldn't wear a $26 shirt; he's Gucci and Beene and Pierre Cardin. He said he wouldn't even consider $50 shoes the others looked at.

* * *

So the lineup was changed. Mickey Rivers and Bucky Dent batting first and eighth, got five hits, and batted in three runs to win, 5–3. Dent broke the tie with a hit in the eighth when everybody thought Martin was going to hit for him as he had twice in the first four games. "Keep yanking him out and he's going to go down the drain," Martin said. He's aware of those emotions.

Hunter, whose wit is not impaired by his bruised foot, kidded Dent, "You ought to hit fourth." He said it loud enough to reach Jackson, who wants to bat fourth, and Munson, who doesn't want to bat second.

Ron Guidry was the winner in relief, with his best pitching since February. Jackson took himself out of the outfield in the ninth. "I can't throw anybody out," he said. No team can avoid questions about events like that. After it was already known, the trainer conceded that Jackson's sore elbow had been examined by the Royals' doctor in the clubhouse and would be examined again tomorrow in Milwaukee. It bugs Gene Monahan that Jackson talks openly about things the Yankees hide as a matter of course. Monahan is caught in the middle.

Thursday, April 14

Milwaukee

Jackson is disturbed about his sore arm. He's never had one. "The doctor said if it's not better in a month, I should be concerned," he said. "It's already been six weeks." He had a cortisone shot three weeks ago. X-rays showed only what wasn't wrong and produced no medical name for the inflammation, according to Monahan. With this team you have to attribute every injury report to a source.

Martin is furious that Jackson told two reporters he passed in the coffee shop about his visit to the doctor. Martin's protocol says those things come from Martin only. Martin called Jackson out of dinner at the Marc Plaza and they sat together with coach Dick Howser in the hotel bar for two hours until Jackson left. He had one beer.

With Oakland he never had to be afraid to speak his mind.

Friday, April 15

Milwaukee

When Martin is troubled or when there is trouble brewing, he goes out on the field for batting practice and fields grounders at second base. He's playing his old position and he can't be reached by the press when he's behind second base.

Trouble was that the lineup card on the dugout wall said Jackson wasn't playing. Jackson was left to face the questions. "I could play. I don't know why I'm not," he said. Does it piss you off? he was asked. "No comment," he answered. There was no need for a comment.

Jackson was punished for being candid with the press. When Martin finally came off the field, he was pressed for an explanation. "His arm is bothering him; he told all the press it's bothering him," Martin said. A sneer was discernible. If Jackson was going to tell the press he was hurt, then he was going to be treated as if he was hurt. "A couple of days' rest and he can come back strong," Martin said. He turned to Jackson farther down the dugout bench. "Right, Mr. Jackson?"

"Right," Jackson said. And there he sat all night.

He didn't pinch hit in the eighth or ninth inning with two on when a home run would have tied the score either time. So the Brewers beat the Yankees, 7–4, with Fran Healy, a nice fellow who has hit 20 homers in six seasons, making the last outs both times. As much as Martin wants to win, it's more important for him to be Martin.

The doctor said Jackson could play if his elbow didn't hurt, but Martin did not ask him if he could swing. Jackson would have said yes, but he didn't volunteer. It is evidence of the barrier between them.

Jackson sat while lefty Jerry Augustine was holding the Yankees hitless until the fifth inning, and to one hit until they broke through with a flurry of singles in the eighth. Against Augustine last season Jackson had three hits in eight times at bat, two home runs (one of them a grand slam), and five runs batted in. He was one of three against Augustine last week. Steinbrenner often says Martin doesn't pay enough attention to the performance charts; Martin maintains that he manages best by what he has in his head. He indicated that he'd probably use Jackson as DH tomorrow, but it's Martin's war to wage.

We don't have an open struggle yet between Martin and the owner's high-priced star because the high-priced star chooses to back down as he promised in Florida. "I'm trying to think correctly," Jackson said. "I'm goin' along with the program." He's trying to see things through his slowed-down viewer, but underneath he is stunned. He is caught between Martin, whom he distrusts, and Steinbrenner, whom he has no reason not to trust.

The polarity is apparent to Sal Bando, the Milwaukee third baseman who grew up with Jackson at Arizona State and Oakland. "It's sad," Bando said, for Martin "to use it as an excuse to get on Reggie. That's not right."

In the meantime, the Yankees played another lousy game and Martin got all over the clubhouse attendant for permitting the press into the room a few seconds too early.

And Catfish Hunter threw thirty-odd pitches on the sidelines before sitting down because his sore foot was making

him throw unnaturally. He'll miss his second start Monday.
He's supposed to be X-rayed again tomorrow.

Saturday, April 16

Milwaukee

Jackson is a wreck. He felt another insult from Martin in
the ball game and couldn't leave his emotions at the ball
park. Jackson is too sensitive—touchy, too—not to wear his
emotions like an arm band. He encountered two newsmen he
regards as friends just when he thought he was going to have
dinner alone. He sat with them for a long time with his emotions turning over. He feels he's too smart, has too much
money, and has proven too often how much ball player he is
to have to prove himself again to Martin—over Martin's obstacles.

Jackson picked at his food—the Maryland Steak Ranch
isn't what it used to be—wrung his hands, and pondered leaving the team or turning in his contract and begging to be sent
elsewhere. He's terribly depressed.

The offense came in the fifth inning of one more loss, 4–2.
The Yankees had a 2–1 lead and Martin had Rivers try to
steal third base with two out and Jackson at bat. Jackson is
on the Yankees because he drives in runs. With two out,
Rivers can score from second on almost any kind of hit;
third base has no value worth risking the third out. Rivers
was out.

"It's a good play," Martin said. It was a bad play with no
rational defense. "He doesn't think I can play ball," Jackson
said.

In the clubhouse after the game Jackson tried to evade inquiries about this return to the lineup by keeping on the
move or by being cryptic. "I was glad to be in there," he
said. He conceded that he felt "uncomfortable."

He was asked by a Milwaukee reporter if he had anticipated the situation in which he now finds himself. "No," he
said. "And why do you look so puzzled? Do you think someone would anticipate something like that and then go there?"
Certainly, Jackson anticipated problems back in spring train-

ing, but not of this intensity so soon. With that comment, Jackson left for the showers. "Let me go away before you get mad," he said.

It was another losing game and that raises the question of how much the unrest in the clubhouse affects play. "They're thinking of so many petty things, nobody can think properly about the games," said Bando after watching the Yankees and chatting with them for the second day. "They have a lot of people whose egos are important. They have to learn everybody can't be satisfied."

Martin's benching of Jackson was one statement of ego. One day later the manager was applying conciliatory words in patronizing fashion. "He didn't know that I don't allow players to tell the press about injuries," he said.

It seems a petty thing for Martin to pick at and it seems a minor disturbance to have caused such reaction in Jackson. "You may think they are petty things and that you ought to be able to play in spite of them," Bando said. "But the game is played mentally before you go on the field and after you leave the field. It's six months of baseball all the time. If you're going to have your mind distracted, you're going to get the short end."

Jackson isn't the only disturbed voice in the clubhouse. Let us not forget the forgotten man, Ken Holtzman. Until the last of the ninth it looked as if he had put the Yankees on the long end. Pitching on seven months' rest, Holtzman made his first start since the last day of last season and allowed only one run and four singles over eight innings. He took a 3–1 lead into the ninth inning.

Sparky Lyle hung a slider and Cecil Cooper hit a two-run homer that tied the score, and Mickey Rivers played a single into a double, which set up the losing run. All of which turned Holtzman's golden effort to dross. Holtzman was remarkably effective considering his struggle for control and rhythm. He was promised by Steinbrenner over the winter that last fall's slight was past, that he would be in the rotation from the start of the season. He didn't pitch the last ten days of training and it is now two weeks into the season. He feels he must pitch every fourth day for his change of speeds to be effective. The situation is almost as difficult for him as having the press ask him about it.

Asked how this game related to his situation at the end of last season, he grew dark. "I don't want to talk about last year," he snapped. "It's not relevant." But everything a player does is related to what's come before. "If it's not relevant to me and I'm the central figure," he said, "I don't see how it's relevant to anybody else." Then he doesn't see.

"You're trying to make something out of nothing," he said. Holtzman is reportedly a very bright man. Condescending, too. An honest reporter isn't trying to make something out of nothing, but he does try to report something if it exists, even if the central figures say it's nothing.

Martin has instituted new rules regarding the press. The press is no longer permitted in the Yankee clubhouse or dugout in the twenty-five minutes before the game. "They want it," Martin said. Funny how no other team has it and the players' desire has followed Martin from Minnesota to Detroit to Texas to the Yankees. "It can be put to you in such terms that it sounds as if you asked for it," a Yankee player said.

X-rays of Hunter's foot were reported negative, but he still can't pitch Tuesday.

Bando says baseball is a six-month season. Good grief, this one is only two weeks old.

Sunday, April 17

Milwaukee

There was a little lightness in the clubhouse for a change. Reggie Jackson, meet Thurman Munson. Thurman Munson, meet Reggie Jackson. How long the warmth will last is only a wild guess, but Munson did go out of his way to break through the frost around Jackson.

Munson went out to Jackson in the outfield during batting practice and they stood side by side while the baseballs whizzed past. Jackson has not been able to reach out to his teammates and make himself one of them. Those who perceive Munson as the leader have not opened themselves to Jackson.

Munson, normally brusque, has not been hostile. He has done some subtle nice things, like wordlessly brushing his hand across Jackson's shoulder in the coffee shop or in the clubhouse, but he had not made the strong move that the others observe.

Jackson, who was at his deepest depression last night, was prepared to be receptive today. For now, he has decided to put mind over matter and do what seems to be the easiest thing. He is deliberately cheerful.

"I decided," he said, "that there was no sense in walking around with my head up my ass all season."

As a preliminary to the summit meeting there was the regular Sunday morning chapel session in the clubhouse. Jackson also had a private conversation with the minister afterward that he found beneficial even if the minister was not particularly impressive. Some players pay little or no attention to these rituals. Once Gene Michael was asked why he wasn't in the manager's office with the others and he replied, "I'm hypocrite enough as it is."

Jackson, who found his religion under Alvin Dark's counsel in Oakland, says he feels these sessions. This one told him that he wasn't as important as he sometimes feels he is. "He took me out of myself," Jackson said. "I was reminded that when I strike out, a billion people in China don't care."

The first evidence of his frame of mind was that he did something frivolous. Ball players are always doing something frivolous. Some people say that being a ball player is frivolous to begin with, but Jackson has been so heavy. He put a clipped picture of a fat man in Munson's locker with the penned inscription: "To George, Best Wishes, Thurman Munson." Jackson then called Graig Nettles, one of the more distant of the establishment players to see it. He beckoned Catfish Hunter to join in a laughing argument in the trainer's room, and then Sparky Lyle, everybody's pal: "Sparky, come in and defend yourself."

It sounds childish among professional athletes, especially for one who too often reminds everybody that he has a $3,-000,000 contract, but it's a game where emotions often govern performance and Jackson is among the most emotional. The separation he felt from his teammates has been growing and his gloom was spreading to others.

Elrod Hendricks remembers what that meant at Baltimore last year. "Reggie needs to be loved," he said. "More than that, he needs to be shown he's loved even when he fouls up."

Jackson thought he got that reassurance for the first time

from Munson. "He said he hadn't realized I was as sensitive and emotional as I am," Jackson said. "He's going beyond the problems he's had and helped me with mine. He said, 'Hey, man, don't let it bother you. Go after them. We need you.'

"Thurman is a good human being, even if he seems sarcastic sometimes."

Munson is struggling, himself, with a very small batting average and embarrassment in throwing to second base, but he has an unconscious understanding of some things. "We want Reggie to play baseball," Munson said.

He was pleased with the team's immediate response, even if they did lose their third in a row and sixth in eight games. "We played super today," Munson said. "Everybody pulled for everybody else. Sometimes the heads are screwed on right; you just got to tighten them a little bit."

What does all this mean over the course of the season? Maybe nothing at all. But maybe everything in the world. Undoubtedly Jackson will have his depressions from time to time, and he and Martin will probably always have their differences, but the door between Jackson and the team has been opened.

Maybe the day wasn't wasted, but a fine complete game by Dock Ellis was. And Hunter will take his sore foot home to rest on his farm in North Carolina tomorrow. He says he can drive the tractor with that foot propped up and wear soft shoes. Ellis offered him a pair of Pumas. "Can't," Hunter said. "I got a contract with Adidas." He's missed two starts with what is announced as a bone bruise and is likely to miss two more starts after he goes on the disabled list tomorrow. Gil Patterson, who had a good spring, will probably be recalled to replace him.

Monday, April 18

New York

Another loss, 5–1, to the Toronto Blue Jays, who came to life twelve days ago. The Yankees made four hits and four errors. When the press entered the clubhouse it was occupied by only the batboys and a couple of players who had not been in the game. The rest of them were in the lounge with the "Yankee Players Only" sign over the door. Martin was there, too. So the writers moved on to wait in Martin's office; sooner or later he'd be there, or go home in his uniform. They waited forty-five minutes. Then Pat Kelly, the stadium manager, stuck his head into the room. "Mr. Martin will not be in today," Kelly said. "He has no comments." That was comment enough.

Steinbrenner is due in New York tomorrow.

Tuesday, April 19

New York

The smell in the air is like the smell of electric trains that aren't hooked up right.

Munson and Jackson may have moved closer together but Martin and Steinbrenner appear to be farther apart than ever. Martin continues to suggest that the owner is trying to tell him what to do, and Martin continues to display his independence by his treatment of Jackson. The players smell the ozone, too. "One thing Billy has going for him is that he has more players on his side than the owner has," one player said.

Martin alienates a player from time to time, but in buying loyalty from some players Steinbrenner has alienated some, too. Some he has struck deeply. "The more we lose," one player said to Murray Chass of the *New York Times*, "the more often Steinbrenner will fly in. And the more he flies, the better the chance will be of the plane crashing." That's as strong as feelings get without a player taking them into his own hands.

Martin has dropped comments—and sometimes whole statements—about the areas where he feels his authority has been infringed upon. He wanted Sandy Alomar as the backup infielder, but Alomar was traded. He didn't like Mickey Klutts's being forced on him early in the spring and said he objected to Bucky Dent's being obtained late in the spring to replace Fred Stanley, last season's loyal shortstop. He values Dock Ellis for his seventeen victories last season and his influence in the clubhouse; he objects to Steinbrenner's efforts to trade Ellis because of his resistance to signing, and his strong comments. Martin fears that Steinbrenner will trade Mickey Rivers, too. Martin feels he can handle Rivers' occasional lapses.

* * *

The business day in the front office began when Martin dropped in on Steinbrenner "to clear the air."

Then Steinbrenner had reporters from the papers that regularly cover the team summoned to a hasty conference in his office.

Nice office. Big windows that overlook the playing field. Big soft leather chairs in the shape of baseball gloves. Big table with more businesslike chairs. A bar. Drinks were offered. Steinbrenner had a lot to say. He is obviously stung. It's his team. Let him speak:

"I have things to get clear in a factual way. The newspaper has the last word, but somebody has to take you guys to task when you are not factual.

"I don't give a shit what you say about me. I'm a hard guy; I have skin like an alligator. But I'd be lying to you if I said it didn't bother me when I read that one player said he wished I'd go down in a plane crash. It hurts me that someone on the club feels that way. I pity that man. I must have done something to hurt him that much.

"I've had fifty phone calls about that. To think a player feels that about you is a terrible, terrible thing.

"You're never going to change my image. I'm stuck with it. I'm such an ogre in the United States now that even my father asks me why I'm such an ogre . . .

"If anybody says I've been on Billy Martin's back, they're a liar. The last contact I had with him was in spring training. I haven't talked to him but one time since. Before he went to Kansas City he asked for help on a real-estate deal. And we had no conversation there."

From a stack of papers on his desk Steinbrenner produced a scrap on which a telephone number was scribbled, and held it up to be seen. "Billy left this number on my desk where he could be reached. He wanted me to call. I tried to reach him three or four times but failed."

He was making the point that Martin had to leave a number because he was not staying at the hotel with the team.

"The Sandy Alomar trade was not made by me. That was

Gabe Paul's trade. I backed him. You know how well he's traded.

"Nobody is trying to hurt Billy. I didn't lay Bucky Dent on Billy. About five days before the end of spring training he came to me. He said, 'I got to have Bucky Dent. I got to have him and Stanley.' The Bucky Dent deal was dead until he came to me.

"About Dock Ellis. When he spouts off that I came screaming into the locker room after the game in St. Petersburg—I didn't come in screaming. The loss to the Mets had nothing to do with it. It was a matter of procedure I wanted to discuss and I knew Billy wasn't going back on the team bus." The manager not riding the team bus was another point to be made. Steinbrenner feels his manager belongs with the team.

"No Dock Ellis is ever going to tell me to stay out of the locker room. Ever. Maybe he realizes he shouldn't have spouted off. It doesn't bother me. He is not going anywhere.

"All the things Billy says about Dock's value to the team, the question is the money in his contract. I go with my guy in charge, Gabe. I respect Dock; nobody is going to trade Dock in spite . . .

"Mickey isn't going anywhere . . . he was requested as part of a deal. We considered it, but he's too valuable to us.

"Billy will make it or break it on the basis of what the club does. The players are not going to drive that wedge between us. It's not a win-or-else situation; in many ways it is, to the extent that the club performs up to capabilities."

Of course, it was Steinbrenner who assembled the team and he is the judge who determines what capabilities are.

"I'm not going to stick a lineup down his throat. I tell him I'd like to see the lineup: Rivers, White, Jackson, Munson. But I say, 'Nobody is telling you what to do.' Not a word has been said that he has to do something, never has. We make suggestions . . .

"These are tough times for him. He's going through a hell of a time. Nobody is panicking. If you want to place blame, put it on me for putting the team together. If things stay shitty, put the blame on me.

"I have not a single doubt that Billy will get the job done. My biggest worry is whether to run my horse in the Kentucky Derby . . .

"Reggie is going through a hell of a stage of adjustment.

All the weight is on his shoulders. It's natural for there to be some overreaction [to batting sixth] . . . Where he belongs, he'll end up.

"His adjustment is that he's on a team. Oakland won because it had great individual ball players. For this team to win, it has to have leadership from Munson and performance from Jackson."

About the business of lying about injuries, Steinbrenner claimed responsibility for both known instances, because trades were involved. "I did it. I'm not going to do it again.

"If they feel I'm on Billy's ass, they're wrong. I'm going to go down and meet with the players in a few minutes."

Steinbrenner said he would tell them the same sorts of things he told us in the office. He would not exhort them, he had learned some things about the nature of a 162-game season as contrasted with a football season when a championship team can win thirteen of fourteen games.

"Look, I'm not Little Red Riding Hood, and I did not ride into town on a load of pumpkins, either. But I'm learning. I'm learning the hard way in some cases. Sometimes from what you guys write. I've ridden guys to exhort them in the past in both business and sports. There are times to exhort and times not to . . .

"I wish I had a nickel for every time Billy came in with his pipe and sat down to talk to me. I'd be a millionaire."

Oh?

That brought the best laugh of the session.

Then Steinbrenner went down to address the troops. And then they went out and played another rotten game. Munson was charged with two errors and a passed ball. Gil Patterson hit a batter and threw a wild pitch. Guidry threw a wild pitch. And Toronto beat them, 8–3.

Gabe Paul, who said he had been feeling light-headed, was admitted to Lenox Hill Hospital with what was believed to be a slight stroke.

Wednesday, April 20

New York

A five-game losing streak and an address to the troops by an impatient owner calls for something special, a stroke of genius by the manager. Perhaps a change of the lineup and a gimmick of some sort? Most of all it calls for a winning game, which in the Yankees' case means more hitting.

So Billy Martin picked the lineup out of a hat and it produced 14 hits. They beat Toronto, 7–5. Out of a hat? First name out bats first, second name, third name . . . At least that's what the manager said. "Is that what Bill said?" one player asked.

"You really don't believe that magic hat lineup stuff, do you?" said another.

Well, Chris Chambliss batted eighth and Mickey Rivers batted fifth—unusual placements. But Willie Randolph batted leadoff, which he did most of his time in the minors, and Munson batted second. Jackson, Nettles, and Roy White were in the middle of the order. And Bucky Dent was last, as usual. Remarkably logical hat.

Anyhow, the lineup produced three runs in the first inning, which is one way to break a losing streak. Same lineup tomorrow.

And Munson wasn't talking. "Thurman never talks to the press," Martin explained. Except, of course, when he wants to.

Thursday, April 21

New York

Same lineup, same results, same story: magic hat lineup produced 13 hits and beat the Blue Jays, 8–6. Chambliss had two doubles and a three-run homer for the first five-RBI game of his career and may be the best eighth-place hitter in creation. Either that, or that hat is a genius.

Chambliss was asked if he believed the story about the hat that created the batting order. "That's what I heard," he said with his mystical smile. Chambliss may not care where he bats, but Jackson does. Just so things were on the up-and-up, Martin said, he had Jackson do the actual picking. "If the manager says I picked it out of a hat, then I picked it," Jackson said.

The defense didn't come out of any hat; that would be asking too much. Graig Nettles played third base so he could make a sensational stop and a sitting-down throw to begin a double play, and a diving stop in the hole for another. He also managed to hit a home run for his first run batted in of the season.

Same lineup tomorrow. "Why change?" Martin explained. "If anybody has any arguments, he can talk to the hat."

Friday, April 22

Cleveland

Dock Ellis and his lawyer, Tom Reich, have made a written appeal for peace to Gabe Paul. Their letter said that Ellis would back off his belligerent stance and try to do his best for the team. At this point Ellis seems to hold some advantage he didn't have a month ago: Hunter is hurt, Gullett isn't sound, and Figueroa and Holtzman have not pitched well. If the pitching should continue scarce and Ellis should pitch well, then he might have a good shot at the money he's demanding. It's clear now in Reich's eyes that Ellis isn't going to be traded.

Saturday, April 23

Cleveland

Same lineup: Thirteen hits, 9–3 over the Indians, and a break because the second game of the proposed doubleheader was called off. Steinbrenner thought it was a mistake to play even that one on the sodden field in 35-mile-an-hour winds, even if there was a big advance sale. "This is stupid," Steinbrenner said. "They won't learn until somebody gets seriously hurt." Wait until there's a big advance on a lousy day in Yankee Stadium.

Sunday, April 24

Cleveland

One of the funniest scenes of last season was the argument conducted in mock rage between Mickey Rivers and Carlos May over who was more intelligent. "You're so dumb," May said in his show-stopper, "you don't even know how to spell IQ."

The correlation between measurable intelligence and what works on a baseball field is difficult to draw. There are so many ways Rivers can win a game with his speed that he can outrun his mistakes.

The Yankees swept both games from the Indians by big scores, 10–1 and 7–1, so there's little statistical evidence that the run Rivers produced in the seventh inning of the second game made the difference. But the score was 1–1 at the time and so much of the Yankee offense begins when Rivers gets on base, even when he's batting fifth.

He led off the inning with his third bunt single of the afternoon, stole second base, and advanced to third on a ground out. That brought up Roy White and started wheels spinning in Martin's mind. He called for his favorite play, the suicide squeeze. Then he took it off because he was afraid the Indians would anticipate and pitch out. But White recently developed a system of his own with Rivers, by which White could tell Rivers a bunt was coming in such a situation. So White flashed his sign to Rivers and then pushed his bunt toward third base. And Rivers broke late.

Buddy Bell picked up the ball and counted his multiple options: He could concede the run and throw to first for one out; he could throw home and prevent the run and get nobody out; he could fake a throw to first and try to trap Rivers off third, but Rivers is so quick that the shortstop might not be able to get there in time. Or Bell could try to chase Rivers himself, which would have been an exercise in futility unless Rivers fell down. Rivers hesitated, but Bell committed himself to a hurried throw to first base and threw the ball into the dirt past the first baseman. White was given a single and Rivers trotted home with what proved to be the winning run. "It was a good play," Bell said. "I'm not going to say Rivers made a good play because I'm not sure he knew what he was doing."

Just what Rivers is thinking is a continuing puzzle. Some Yankees feel that Rivers was their most valuable player in 1976 but blew his chance by deliberately taking too long to recover from a shoulder injury in September. Not long before that, Rivers was fined for bringing his wife on a road trip although several other Yankees brought wives. They had asked permission and Rivers hadn't, according to Martin. Rivers didn't see the distinction. Martin was also annoyed that one night Rivers said his legs were too sore to play, but he had spent the afternoon walking Baltimore with his wife.

It's obvious Rivers feels he took a trimming in the contract negotiations. "There are a lot of guys who ain't doin' a lot of things and I ain't making their salaries," he says with a peculiar inverted logic. And he doesn't like the idea that Martin will not permit him to steal on his own. "I could lead the major leagues if the man would let me run," Rivers says.

When he runs, he scampers like a racing dog out of the starting box, but when there's no hurry Rivers moves slowly, as if his neck and his back and his feet hurt just too much to bear. "If I didn't know who he was, I'd figure he walked on hot coals for a living," Sparky Lyle once observed. At those times Rivers' nickname of "Old Man Rivers" is just right.

But he can make almost all of them, other than Jackson, laugh. Rivers is five ten and 160 pounds, and he likes to needle Cliff Johnson, six four and 227 pounds. One time Rivers was being fitted for a suit by the tailor who somehow has been granted permission to do business in the Yankee clubhouse. He pleaded with the man, "Please don't make me look like Cliff Johnson."

Rivers has some strange expressions. He calls some of the players in his regular motel-room poker game "gozzle head" or "warple head," and there are no standard English translations. According to Rivers, a gozzle head is someone with a "big funny face, just, ya' know, like a bullfrog face." A warple head, "that's a different shape. A funny-looking creature. Odd-shaped."

Those expressions are uniquely Rivers. Nobody else can handle them. But he has two other expressions that white and black players have adopted as their own. One, used for bringing flights of fantasy back to earth, is: "Well, uh—let's not get ridic-a-lus." The other, sometimes to stall a puzzling questioner or sometimes just an abbreviation of the first is simply, "Well, uh," drawn out to a deep-voiced *uhhh*.

"It's really not what Mickey says, it's how he says it," Paul Blair said. "You sit back and half of what he says doesn't mean a thing. Someone else says it and it's not funny. But when he says it, he's funny."

Some of what Rivers says cannot be understood at all; it comes from too deep in the Miami ghetto to be understood by the whites around him or even by some of the black players. They call him "Hardy," which is short for "Hard Mickey," which has no satisfactory translation into English on the team, either.

Rivers grew up about an hour down Interstate 95 from the Yankees' Fort Lauderdale spring training ball park and a whole world away in point of view. He grew up in the care of his grandmother in the Brownsville ghetto in northwest Miami, and it is said he was even scrawnier than he is now. In his second spring with the Yankees, Rivers visited his grandmother several times and he also stopped by the old Brownsville neighborhood and saw some of the old friends. It was Mickey Rivers, the $100,000 ball player touching old memories, seeing what might have been, and giving thanks that it wasn't.

"Some guys always have things pulling them down," Rivers said in a rare moment of public introspection. "When I go home, I see the guys I used to play ball with and they'll say,

'Hey, buy me some wine.' I'll hand them a couple of dollars. I figure, 'Well, these guys must know what they want to do.' And these guys don't want anybody to help them, anyway."

Not all of the old friends are at liberty to see Rivers. "I used to get into some fights when I was growing up—serious fights," he recalled. "I'd have at least one fight every day. Every neighborhood would be fighting another neighborhood. It was rough. In the parks, a couple of guys used to carry around guns. Those are the guys I used to play baseball with."

He's proud of the guys who made it as he did. "Jeff, he's teaching. Lee, he's driving a bus. Bob's got a good job, he's a technician. Eddie, he's working out at Eastern.

"I understand a couple of the guys I used to play ball with are dead. My friends—well, it they weren't involved in robberies, they'd be involved in dope."

Like so many kids who managed to survive the climate of the ghetto, Rivers had a strong figure in his family. And like a lot of those who survived, Rivers had a grandmother. Rivers' father, John, was a longshoreman on the Miami docks until he was disabled at work ten years ago, the year before Mickey went away to be a ball player. As Rivers recalls it, John Rivers didn't want his eldest son fooling around playing ball, so Mickey moved in with his grandmother, who even encouraged him. Rivers remembers that he was eight at the time, but don't press him for facts. The age is irrelevant, anyhow.

"I'm playing now for my grandmother," Rivers said. "That's the main thing, my grandmother. I promised that I'd make it just for her. Without her pushing me, I just don't know what would have happened to me."

Flora Fambro, now nearly seventy, lives with Mickey's mother and is the guardian of the three children Mickey has fathered. He's been married twice. They get some of the guidance she gave to their father. She used to escort Mickey through the streets to practice. "If she had to ride the bus to practice with me, she'd do that," Mickey said. "If she had to walk with me to the park, she'd do that, too. She didn't make much money—maybe $15 a week cleaning other people's houses. But she'd buy groceries, then use the money left over to buy me a bat or a glove.

"Sometimes she'd give me a dollar to take to school, even when lunches were only a quarter or thirty-five cents. Everybody would see me with the dollar and they'd say, 'Hey, what are you doin' with a dollar in this area?' I had to fight to keep my money. Sometimes a man would come up to me and say, 'You give me a dime a day or I'll hurt you.' "

Mickey Rivers didn't grow very big, but he grew quick. He didn't stay in one spot long. He was an awkward ball player at Northwestern High, but he was good enough for the game to keep him off the streets. "There was nothing on the streets but trouble," he said.

Baseball took him on to Miami–Dade Community College North, where he made the same kind of technical mistakes he still makes. He hit off his front foot and he didn't throw even as well as he does now. And sometimes he didn't show up for practice. Being at a prescribed place at a prescribed time every day just didn't fit in with Rivers' background.

After his freshman season, Rivers was arrested as an accessory in a car theft. Rivers says he was taking his friends fishing and he thought it was their car. With the urging of the college coach, the judge didn't hand Rivers the jail sentence that might have snuffed out his baseball career. "That taught me a lesson," Rivers said. "I learned I had to watch the people I be with."

With the right company on the Yankees, Rivers is usually smiling. He has a special kind of sense of humor. He had his pranks at Dade North, too. There was the time when he and a teammate showered the homecoming queen, a black girl, with eggs. The assumption on campus was that the eggs had been thrown by whites, and there was an uproar on the campus. But the guys on the team knew who was responsible. Not long afterward at a ball game, a teammate told Rivers there were some black guys waiting near the dugout to get him after the game.

At the end of the inning, Rivers grabbed his glove and ran his best dash out toward his position in center field and right on through it. He jumped the fence and disappeared.

Rivers doesn't give the best testimonial for the English department at Dade North, but that seems beside the point. There are a lot of people who come in contact with Rivers who feel he's incredibly dumb, that he really might not know how to spell IQ. But he's half of the oddest partnership you can imagine in the clubhouse game of pluck, a baseball's cousin of bridge. His partner is Ken Holtzman, the aloof white man who displays the manner of a superior intellect.

They go to the racetrack together often. "Of all the guys, getting two together, I can never picture Holtzman and Mickey together," Jimmy Wynn said. "And they're tight buddies—tight, tight buddies."

Well, maybe it's because they're both college men.

Monday, April 25

Baltimore

Reggie Jackson won't say he likes being a hate object, but he has this concept of himself that says he will rise to any occasion. He says he likes being the hunted because only the best are hunted.

He came back to Baltimore tonight, the place he abandoned with a lot of hard feelings after one season in which the fans saw only the seamiest side of the free-agent business. And the fans brought their own hard feelings, and hard objects to throw. Jackson says he minds only the hard objects; the harsh sentiments are his spur. "Sure it was brutal, but it's a psych game so they're playing right into my hands," he said after the game. "The more pressure, the more I respond. It makes me play better."

Just what was his response? All Jackson did was hit the game-winning home run and two doubles as they beat the Orioles and ran the winning streak to six games. He did it in the face of a sign that said "Reggie is a Bozo." He was booed, insulted, and reviled. He was the target of nuts and bolts, rocks, a cup of beer and a plastic water bucket, and he was hanged in effigy.

A lot of fans went to the trouble to let Jackson know they remembered he had refused to play after he was traded to the Orioles last April, until management increased his salary. They remembered how he had helped drive the Orioles almost into the race and then walked away from the team. Surely some of those people merely objected to the money Jackson got from the Yankees; he got his ration of hate last year when he was still in the Orioles' uniform. If there is such a thing as charisma, then there is negative charisma, too. Jackson is not a man to be ignored. To him that would be the greatest insult.

The money part he will have to get used to. The Yankees, and he in particular, are going to hear about that wherever they go. Much of the public is not ready to understand how a ball player can be worth $600,000 a year to anyone. The idea that any big-league player is one of the best 650 men at his business in the whole world, and in Jackson's case one of the very best of those, offends people who accept the salaries of other entertainers. Wayne Newton makes more, points out Phil Pepe of the *Daily News*, and he's not even one of the top 650 singers.

"This could be the best year I ever had," Jackson said. "More is demanded of me because everyone is watching me. I'll have to concentrate all the time. And tonight, that was a tremendous amount of satisfaction." Whether he would have said the same things if he had a bad night, who knows? At some point crowd behavior can be an awful distraction.

There are other, more subtle benefits in nights like this, when a team can throw the abuse back at the fans by winning. When a man climbed on top of the dugout at the end of the game and then jumped onto the field, Graig Nettles tackled him and held him for the cops; Nettles does not love Jackson, but there is something about the unity of the uniform. "One thing about a night like tonight," Jackson said, "it brings the guys together."

*   *   *

Don Gullett slipped on the wet mound, sprained his ankle, and strained muscles in his neck. He missed most of the first part of last season with muscle problems in his neck and came out of the World Series when he sprained the same ankle. He'll miss at least two turns. Catfish Hunter can't come off the disabled list until May 4, and some teammates think he won't be ready to pitch for another two weeks after that.

But the Yankees have scored 50 runs in the last six games, Jackson has 11 hits in his last 25 at bats, and that much hitting can obscure a lot of problems.

Tuesday, April 26

Baltimore

Give this one to the Orioles. They broke the Yankee streak, and all the fans did was make a lot of noise and throw one white rubber ball at Jackson as he was catching a fly. Martin rushed onto the field to demand that the umpires protect his players and later threatened to take a bat to any fan who threatened his players. The worst part of the 6–2 loss was that Ken Holtzman gave up four runs in the first inning, and Nettles had to sit out because he bruised his hand grabbing the intruder last night.

* * *

Elrod Hendricks has been optioned out and pitcher Ed Ricks recalled. Martin wanted to keep Hendricks despite the shortage of pitching.

Wednesday, April 27

Baltimore

It came as no surprise to Dock Ellis when Martin called him into the manager's office to tell him that he, with Marty Perez, had been traded to Oakland for Mike Torrez. Neither Martin nor the Yankees in the clubhouse were pleased with the deal that spotlighted their insecurity one more time. The players remembered a week ago Steinbrenner had said Ellis wasn't going anywhere. "That was a dead giveaway there was going to be a deal," one said.

They also didn't care for the arithmetic of the deal. Ellis has helped them win with a 17–8 record. He was one of them. Torrez has been a twenty-game winner and averaged seventeen wins over the last three seasons, but he didn't do it for them. "Dock fit in super," Thurman Munson said. "It's funny because of all the stories about him with Pittsburgh. To us he had a head that worked."

To baseball people, Torrez is a better pitcher. Gabe Paul had been working on the deal since March; actually for years, he said. They didn't make it in March because Oakland watched the best of the Yankee prospects, Ron Guidry, Mickey Klutts, and Gil Patterson. When Paul returned to work after his short hospitalization (it was called a "cerebral spasm"), the price had come down. And Steinbrenner insists that he said Ellis wouldn't be traded unless the deal would help the Yankees, not just to spite Ellis.

Martin's complaint is that he has now lost three of his best agitators in Ellis, Hendricks, and Gamble, guys who did a subtle job of keeping other players thinking in the right direction. It was also another front office rap at the manager, trading against his wishes.

Three of the noisiest dissenters are Jimmy Wynn, Sparky Lyle, and Dick Tidrow. All three of them came to the Yankees on trades. Tidrow came to the Yankees in 1974 over the storm of player opposition to the deal that brought Chris Chambliss.

Ellis took it all most realistically. He expected to go. He was holding out for $450,000 and the Yankees were offering $350,000, and he was very loud in criticizing Steinbrenner's manner and policies. "I'm going to get my money, so I'm happy," Ellis said. "Finley wouldn't have traded for me if he wasn't going to pay me."

That remains to be seen. In Torrez, Steinbrenner is getting a pitcher who may eventually cost twice as much as Ellis. Torrez thought he should get more than the slight raise to $80,000 Charlie Finley offered in the required first contracts, but Torrez outsmarted Finley by signing it. That way Torrez avoided the 20-percent cut Finley gives all his players he can't sign, and still Torrez is free to go after this season. He is supposed to start for the Yankees in Ellis' turn Friday night.

* * *

Oh, the ball game. That always seems to be an afterthought with this team. The Yankees scored a run in each of the last three innings to win, 4–3, with Chambliss tying the score with a homer in the eighth and Jackson knocking in the winning run with his second sacrifice fly.

Friday, April 29

New York

No word from Torrez. His agent, Gary Walker of Phoenix, the man who guides Reggie Jackson, sent word that Torrez was home in Montreal because his wife was having problems after the birth of their first child. So Martin reached into the bullpen and pulled out a plum.

Ron Guidry, who had started once since the 1973 season at Kingston in the Carolina league, was asked to pitch six innings. He threw the hell out of the ball until Lyle relieved in the ninth. For such a skinny guy, not even 160 pounds, Guidry throws a live fastball and an impressive slider. He also has a sense for a line that's welcome in the dour clubhouse. About his wildness in the first inning, which might have been his last, Guidry said, "I think the ump and I were both trying to find the strike zone." Munson hit a two-run homer and now Guidry goes back to the bullpen.

In Boston, Ellis showed up for the A's and got thoroughly knocked around in five innings by the Red Sox. And he refused to knock the Yankees or Steinbrenner.

Saturday, April 30

New York

It looks as if they really are on a streak. Jackson hit his first home run at home, Figueroa pitched nine innings, and they beat Seattle, 7–2. That's nine out of ten.

But where is Torrez? First, agent Walker said Mike was in Montreal. Then Torrez' brother, John, at Torrez' home in Montreal, said over the phone that Mike wasn't there yet, that he was fishing with Walker. And a few minutes after that Walker's wife said the men were fishing in northern Arizona. So where is he? Not here.

Sunday, May 1

New York

Officially Torrez has seventy-two hours to report to his new team, but traditionally only players going down in the standings take that long. Players going to a team like the Yankees usually report as fast as possible so nobody calls off the deal. Martin says he'd like to call it off. "I'll tell you what I'd do if I was the general manager," Martin said. "I'd nail him with the biggest fine baseball ever saw." He suggested $5,000 a day for starters.

The delay suggested that Torrez was trying to force contract demands of a million over five years to be accepted right now. The Yankees are down to Holtzman and Figueroa as regular starters. "He'll probably try to hold a gun to our heads," Martin said. "He hasn't pitched an inning for me and already I'm pissed at him."

Walker says he expects Torrez to be in New York Monday. If he is, he'll pitch Tuesday.

* * *

Voilà, Mike Torrez has been found. He phoned Yankee vice-president Cedric Tallis and said he'd be here in time to pitch tomorrow night.

Munson homered for the third straight day. Holtzman pitched well enough for six innings and Lyle pitched the last three of the 5–2 win over Seattle. Tomorrow Lyle will be married to Mary Massey, his companion of some time. "For me," Lyle said, "getting married is like coming in with the bases loaded: I've been there before."

Monday, May 2

New York

First, to end the suspense, Torrez showed up and ran in the outfield on the day off.

Now the social note. Lyle and Mary Massey were married at the Marble Collegiate Church as scheduled.

When they stepped out of the church, they discovered that their chauffeured limousine had been replaced by a 1936 fire engine that had played a supporting role on the Milton Berle show in the pioneer days of television. With sirens wailing and bells clanging, the fire engine took bride and groom, ushers and bridesmaids from the church on Fifth Avenue and 29th Street all the way uptown to the reception at McTeague's on East 79th Street.

The fire engine was the idea of a restaurant-owner friend of Sparky and Mary. Lyle was the Fireman of the Year in 1972, so it was suitable. It was also suitable to play a practical joke on Lyle, who has a taste for practical jokes. "It was quite a surprise," Lyle said, "but frankly it's not as bad as I expected." Surely he would have thought of something more outlandish himself.

Among the teammates, coaches, friends, and owner at the wedding was Reggie Jackson, who signed autographs beside his maroon Rolls-Royce. "I usually charge $3,000 for an appearance," Jackson said. It was Jackson's attempt at kidding, but that's just the kind of emphasis on wealth that irritates his teammates.

Tuesday, May 3

New York

Torrez pitched the first five innings of the 8–1 victory over the Angels before a blister formed on his pitching hand, and then cleared up the mystery of his absence.

He had, indeed, gone from the A's in Anaheim to Phoenix to discuss his contract with agent Walker. Torrez insists he intended to fly to New York Friday and pitch that night as planned. But late Thursday night he got a call from Montreal that his wife, Danielle, who had given birth to a son on April 8, lost a great deal of blood so he rushed to her side. The baby was christened Iannique Michael John on Sunday, the mother was released from the hospital Monday. And then Torrez flew to New York.

The business of the fishing trip was the work of the agent's wife. Walker handles Lenny Randle, who is still involved in legal action over punching his manager in spring training, and Don Carrithers, who recently was in an automobile accident. "My wife got tired of the phone calls," Walker said over the phone. "Hell, I don't even know how to fish. My wife just said it."

Torrez said he wanted to be happy wearing the Yankee uniform, his fourth in slightly more than three seasons. "I'm just tired of being traded," he said.

Thurman Munson got two hits, which he said was pleasing to any man with a .189 average, but preferred to keep moving from locker to lounge to sauna to trainer's room to exit rather than discuss it. He said if he talked about it, maybe he'd get back to his bad habits. "Talk to Reggie," he said, "he knows a lot about me." Perhaps that was Munson's sarcasm.

Jackson knows a lot about a lot of things. He says Munson is the best hitter he's ever played with. Perhaps that is a politic comment. "Contrary to the exterior person, Thurman's got a lot of depth and intelligence," Jackson said. "And he's very sensitive. He's my best friend on the team." That sounds politic, too.

Thursday, May 5

New York

The luncheon was at the 21 Club in Manhattan, set off from the teeming street by wrought-iron gates and a phalanx of front-lawn figures holding lanterns and wearing the racing colors of the Whitneys, the Phippses, and other illustrious patrons. The guest of honor was Reggie Jackson, whose prophecy was coming true.

They were naming a candy bar after him.

The idea first flickered on the tongue of Jackson back in July of 1970, when he was just turned twenty-five years old and a modest young man at the brink of stardom. He was the statuesque fellow in the corner locker whom Oakland owner Charlie Finley used to show off to noted guests like an art collector might show off a statue by Rodin. Jackson was on his way to 47 home runs that season and had hit his thirty-seventh just before the All-Star break.

He was twenty-three games ahead of Babe Ruth's pace the year he hit 60. Jackson was asked if he thought he could catch Roger Maris, and if he could catch Babe Ruth. "I'm no Babe Ruth," Jackson replied. "There'll never be another Babe Ruth. The man had a candy bar named after him."

Well, that wasn't exactly right, because the candy bar was introduced in 1920, before Babe Ruth's great fame, and was named for the daughter of President Grover Cleveland. And the Oh Henry bar wasn't named after Henry Aaron, either.

Some years later, when Jackson's stardom was established and the obscurity of playing in Oakland was established, Jackson decided that if he played in New York a candy bar would be named after him. And so the first candy bar named for an athlete has come to pass.

The name was spawned in Yankee Stadium on opening day from the mouths of the people Standard Brands, Inc., intends to fill. The candy bar will be called "Reggie, Reggie, Reggie." "In a form that delivers the kind of mouth feel the public wants," said Robert Cappadocia, president of the Curtis Candy subsidiary, to the assembled. Mouth feel?

Jackson's financial advisers say the deal will be one of the three largest off-field contracts an athlete ever had. "The deal is a good one," Cappadocia said. "And if the bar is successful, it can be a very good one." Consider that nearly $65,000,-000 worth of Baby Ruth is sold every year, and compute—say—three-fourths of one percent of that potential as Jackson's share.

Jackson says that his presence in New York was not required for him to make that deal, but Cappadocia said he got his strongest thoughts about the alliance when Jackson signed with the Yankees in November. There are other facets of his contract involving representation of the larger Standard

Brands' name, which could pay Jackson $300,000 a year for the next ten years.

There are benefits Jackson says he insisted upon that are nice public relations gestures. "Reggie's Regiment" has been established with the distribution of 140 right-field tickets to each home game through police precincts. And for each home run, $500 is to be distributed to charity, $1,000 for a grand slam. "All I have to do," Jackson said, "is go out, play baseball, hit twenty-five or thirty home runs, and Reggie Jackson comes looking like a hero. My job is basically very easy."

The candy bar is expected to be ready for promotion sometime before next season. All Jackson has to do is play baseball.

*   *   *

When is a losing game not a game lost? When Catfish Hunter can come back and pitch nine innings after being idled almost a whole month. Hunter threw 123 pitches in the 5–2 loss to Oakland and pronounced himself fit. He even survived another shot off his instep, this one missing the old bruise by two inches.

Friday, May 6

New York

If there is any real poetic justice in baseball, the Yankees should clinch the pennant on a day like today, with Roy White hitting a three-run home run in a 4–1 victory like this one against Oakland. White has been with the Yankees longer than anyone. He goes back to 1966, the year they finished tenth. Tenth place was last in the league that year and the Yankees hadn't been last since 1912, when they were still called the Highlanders. The very presence of White on those teams in the dark years was taken as evidence of how the mighty had fallen.

It would be all right, too, if White hit a sacrifice fly to get the winning run home from third instead of the home run. It would be more in keeping with what White has done for the

Yankees over the years; a fly ball would say simply that Roy White got the job done.

Over the years, White's ability has been questioned often. When Bill Virdon took over in 1974, he wanted to move White out of left field and out of the lineup. White won the position back, the Yankees made a healthy run at the division championship, and Virdon conceded that he had made a mistake in judgment. "He's a professional; I don't say that about a lot of people," Virdon said when he had seen more of White.

For his age, thirty-three, White has a much younger man's body. He has his name on two karate schools near his home in New Jersey and his own karate-trained body is so supple that he can reach out and gently tap a friend on the top of the head with his toe. By his own description, he is "skinny but strong."

The longevity of his career with the Yankees is a contradiction, but then the last fifteen years of his life are a paradox too. His body is too small and flat-chested for the deep, rich voice that comes from it. His body is too small for him to be as dangerous a hitter as he is. His career started too slowly for him to be recognized among the best players in the league.

In 1970, when the dynasty had disintegrated into a string of lasts and next-to-lasts, White was the cleanup hitter. And Oakland broadcaster Harry Caray marveled that the Yankees had a cleanup hitter who choked up on the bat. White was five feet ten and barely 165 pounds. "I guess I had to be the lightest man in the big leagues batting fourth," he reflected. He batted in 94 runs that year and scored 109 runs, and there was a measure of sadness for students of the game that the fact that he couldn't throw worth a damn kept White from real stardom. It made him sad too.

If his arm isn't strong, he understands that and has educated himself to hit the cutoff and to charge balls to shorten his throw. Rivers, who doesn't throw well either, hasn't learned that. And when a game might be saved by a strong throw by the left fielder, White cries a lot. But he is playing his twelfth season in that uniform. (By the end of the season, the only Yankees to have played in more games were all in the Hall of Fame. He was among the top ten Yankees in at bats, hits, and doubles; in the top twenty in runs, home runs, and runs batted in.)

At thirty-three White is among the most insightful of athletes, perhaps the most sophisticated of the Yankees. He is an elegant man who is willing to accept the probing questions on good days and bad, a reporter's measure of a man. His growth as a player who embarrassed himself in his first efforts at second and third base and in his first tentative trial in left field is no greater than his growth as a man. Before the first entry under his name in the *Baseball Register*, his performance was noted in the precinct houses in Los Angeles.

He tells about the time when he was a junior in high school, the scouts had just begun to watch him closely, and the voice over the loudspeaker in his classroom said: "Roy White, go to the principal's office." There was a badge on a blue suit waiting for him, and then there was the voice in the stationhouse telling him: "It looks like you're in real trouble."

White can be seen with a hard-cover book in the clubhouse where the prevalent taste runs to stacks of split-beaver girlie magazines. He goes to the Broadway theater. He passes up the free food in the clubhouse and on the planes so he can enjoy the best restaurants around the league. He feels for the plight of the brother—white or black—who doesn't have it made. Despite his $125,000 salary and a home in suburban Wayne, New Jersey, where he lives with his wife, daughter, and son, he doesn't hide from the recollection that he once helped beat up a man he didn't even hate.

Sometimes when the Yankees are in California, White sees old friends from the Watts ghetto, and they tell him of the fortunes of one of his peers. "He was my best friend back then," White related. "The other guys tell me he's back in."

"Back in" means the stripes run across the grain of Yankee pinstripes and the numbers on his back run to six digits. "Back then I could never have conceived of what my lifestyle has become," White said. "Being able to get a new car when I felt like it, a nice home, clothes when I want them, vacation when I want to. The best part of it is that I'm able to give it to my children. I hope they will appreciate it."

Growing up for him meant a white father and a black mother who divorced when White was nine. He grew up with his mother, who worked as a waitress to augment what welfare provided, and there was seldom enough of anything. Sometimes when there was a need for more clothes, White would take them from a department store.

There were more menacing events. "One time a car followed five of us," White said. "We were sixteen or seventeen and they were in their twenties. They had chains and bottles. They got out and started walking behind us and we started running. I ran into a park to get away and slipped in the wet grass. As I was going down, I remember thinking: 'This is it. They're going to beat the hell out of me.'

"But they must have been high on something. They didn't see me turn in. It was pretty close."

White feels that he was "too level-headed to get into drugs or heavier crime." He suspected that there were interesting things in books, and he was doing interesting things on the ball field at Centennial High School, where he played second base and Reggie Smith played shortstop. But pressure from the peer group was very strong.

"Not going along with the crowd was very difficult," he said. "There was a sense of power to be with a group of guys ganging up on another guy. A father can make you listen to him; I didn't have any male direction in my family. I would take advantage of my mother to go off when she told me not to.

"My best friend's both parents had committed suicide. One shot the other and then turned the gun on himself. And he saw the whole thing. I'm sure that had a lot to do with his life. He used to stay with foster parents. They were good to him. He had more money and clothes than the rest of us, but he was the worst."

The concept of money and clothes—or the lack of money and clothes—was very strong then. "My brother, my sister, and I would have one pair of shoes to wear for a year. It was always kind of embarrassing when the only pair of shoes I had came apart. Maybe I'd have two shirts and two pairs of pants and I'd always be changing combinations to make them look different.

"That's probably why you see so many black players paying so much attention to their clothes. They never had enough to wear growing up."

He remembers the feelings he had when he and the gang did things he knew he really didn't want to do. "When we'd gang up on somebody, I felt bad afterwards," he said. "It wasn't in my heart to do that to anybody, especially a guy who didn't have a chance."

He remembers most clearly breaking into the school cafeteria and being seen by a man who knew their names and began yelling at them. "So we beat him up," White said.

"What were we going to find there? Nothing of any value. Maybe some change, some bottles of pop, some ice cream. We took ice cream. Just think, we had so much to lose for a bar of ice cream."

That was all when White was in the ninth grade. When he was a high-school junior the police were tracking whatever it was that police track, and they came across White's tracks. In the principal's office they told him they had some of his friends. "Being dumb, I said I was on all four of the break-ins," White said. The others had confessed to one, and so White was singled out for prosecution.

"I knew there was a chance of me going to the reformatory," he said. "It's a scary thing. You can change your whole life in the ninth grade. One of the other guys has been in and out of jail since. He was my best friend then."

What did a best friend mean then? "He tried to get me to take drugs then," White said. "The big thing was pills, and a little bit of marijuana. I had a couple of friends who were tough. At a party, if they were thinking of jumping some guy, they'd leave me alone."

By the time White went before the judge, he had already turned his life. The judge was impressed by White's school record, and sentence was suspended. A year of probation and White made good his escape to another life. In recent years he has even established a relationship with his father, who goes to games when the Yankees are in Anaheim.

"It's not father-and-son, but it's friendly," White said. Marcus White is an artist and a collage of his hangs in Roy White's home. "I've been in his home," Roy said. "I don't resent him. I know mixed marriage must have been hell in the 1940s. I always considered myself black, but being in the middle like that made it difficult to hate white people when white is part of you."

What he is most proud of as a ball player is that he is still here after twelve years. He has made the most of the time. "The big leagues gave me a chance to explore," he said. "I had other guys take me out and say, 'Have a glass of wine.' I never had a glass of wine with a meal in my life. It was in Washington—Tom Tresh, Phil Linz, Jim Bouton, Al Downing, and I—and we had a bottle of Lancer's. Then I tried cold duck. I acquired a taste for other wines.

"I went to a Broadway play and found I enjoyed it. I tried musicals later. I thought before I went, 'Hell, I wouldn't like that.' But I did and started going often."

Often in the pregame lull, when White has already done his twenty minutes of meditation, he can be seen sitting and reading in front of his locker. "I've read a lot in the last couple of years," he said. "The kind of books I never thought of reading. James Baldwin. Claude Brown. Iceberg Slim.

"Basically, I like the story of a guy who has nothing, is in the dirt, and was able to make something out of his life."

Saturday, May 7

New York

With the players crowded in front of the television in the lounge to watch their master's horse in the Kentucky Derby, the realization came across that the Yankees have been in good spirits for some time. There's a kind of peace about them. Maybe it's because they've won thirteen out of fifteen—or maybe they've been winning because they're getting along better. That's a chicken-and-egg discussion. "The guys are happier now, everything's going our way," Rivers said. "But some days it's going to be bad, too."

Rivers hit a home run, White hit another three-run homer, Nettles homered, Don Gullett pitched a complete game, and they beat the A's, 11–2. Then they ridiculed Steinbrenner's horse, Steve's Friend, for finishing fifth in the Derby. "I'd come closer than that," Rivers said. "Well, he ran a pretty good race down the stretch, but I'd stand a good chance against a couple of them horses."

That claim provided an interesting flurry of discussion among the players who had forgotten or never knew that sprinters had run against race horses before, usually trotting horses pulling a sulky. In short distances, a human can beat a horse.

But Rivers' feeling about the way he runs is bigger than that. It's bigger even than a home run. "A home run in a game like today's don't mean that much," he said. "Stealing bases, that's what counts." He still feels cheated that Martin doesn't let him run on his own.

Martin spent most of his postgame discussion profaning the official scorer's ruling of an error on George Zeber's first time at bat in his first major-league game.

At Churchill Downs, Steinbrenner had his winner with Sweet Little Lady's eleven-length romp in the Debutante Stakes. And at least one in Steinbrenner's party at the track took his advice. "Say, George," Charles Finley said, "I had $200 on that horse." Steinbrenner had thrown in two tickets to the Kentucky Derby in the trade that brought Mike Torrez to the Yankees for Dock Ellis.

Sunday, May 8

New York

The definitive illustration of the workings of Thurman Munson's mind came in the sixth inning when he popped up with the bases loaded and flung his batting helmet.

The Yankees already had a lead of 8–2 on the way toward the 10–5 victory over the A's. Munson already had three singles, beginning with the hit that set off the five-run first inning against old friend Ellis. He had hit in his sixteenth consecutive game, longest streak in his career. With the home run he hit in the eighth inning, Munson's average has climbed to .337 and his .424 pace during the streak neatly parallels the team's streak. And what did Munson have to say about it? "Yeah," he said, "and before that I was hitting one-something."

When he goes four for five, he thinks he should have been five for five, even when the team wins by a big score. "Believe it or not, up until today I didn't feel like I hit well," he said.

He said that after his customary long period of seclusion in the lounge and trainer's room. He is as sound a player in all respects as there is on a very good team. The one visible flaw in his game is his throwing. Teammates can kid him about it—carefully. One day in spring training Munson had his youngest son in the clubhouse, and Fred Stanley was amused by the remarkable resemblance the boy showed to his father. "Thurman," Stanley said, "when he throws his toys, do they go like this?" And Stanley drew with his hand the banana arc

many of Munson's throws take on route to second base or beyond.

Munson's throws often look worse because Martin doesn't
permit the shortstop or second baseman to cover the base
until the batter can no longer hit the pitch. That prevents
some hit-and-run ground balls from going through the infield.
but also makes it difficult to save some of Munson's throws.

So Munson is generally sensitive about his throwing. He
would like the recognition other players give him to come
also from the fans. But he is uncomfortable dealing with the
press, the players' link with the fans. He would like to be appreciated without having to talk about himself. Whether he
resents the way the press gravitates to Jackson is fully understood only by Munson.

"Reggie likes to get attention," Munson said. "The guys
around the league would tell me, 'You watch, you go four-
for-four or hit a home run to win a game, and the writers
will be around Reggie's locker.' He likes that. I'm the exact
opposite. I can't hold that against him."

Munson is not holding anything against Jackson, at least
not anything that can be noticed from the outside. What was
expected to be an inevitable collision course is now a comfortable path. Munson speaks more to Jackson than any other
player does, and the conversation with Jackson three weeks
ago in Milwaukee has put Jackson in a tolerable frame of
mind. "I've had a lot of conversations with Reggie," Munson
said. "I've tried to help him adjust to the club. Reggie is the
kind of guy who would like to have some say on the club and
rightfully so.

"When you hit a certain peak, everybody is going to shoot
at you. I can understand his feelings and his problems. I like
Reggie; he likes to play. He has problems because he talks a
lot. But he likes to play, and long as you play baseball, you're
going to get along with me. One thing I have tried to relate
to Reggie is, don't worry about what other guys think of you.
Just go out and play. The hell with what anybody thinks."

Of course, Jackson must care what everybody thinks of
him, but it was a strong statement for peace on the ball club.
The only shot fired in the clubhouse was by Graig Nettles.
The Yankees made 16 hits and Nettles tried to recall the
outs. The only out he could remember was Munson's pop-up,
the one that caused the helmet to be thrown.

Nettles shrugged. "Somebody," he said to Munson, "has to make the outs."

Wednesday, May 11

Seattle

The Yankees had their first look at the Kingdome, the American League's first indoor ball park. It's impressive. The last time the Yankees played here was in 1969 when the expansion Seattle Pilots played in Sicks Stadium. The Kingdome is right downtown. Sicks Stadium was inconveniently located on the outskirts; it had been and still was a minor-league park. The Pilots became the Milwaukee Brewers the next spring.

After a day off, the Yankees flew in here all rested. They had also won fourteen of sixteen. The Mariners, losers of twelve of sixteen—expansion team that they are again—didn't get home from Toronto until 1 P.M.—just about time to come back to work. But they beat the Yankees, 5–2, and Martin jumped on his reason. Obviously, things had been too quiet with all that winning business. If Martin couldn't find an issue with the umpires or his players or with the other team, he found his front office a target: The front office was keeping the third-string catcher at Syracuse.

With one out and runners on first and third in the seventh inning, the only left-handed pinch hitter Martin had was switch-hitting George Zeber. So Martin felt compelled to go with right-handed Jimmy Wynn against the right-handed reliever. Wynn struck out.

"I want Elrod Hendricks," Martin said. "I need three catchers plus a left-handed pinch hitter. I've been asking for Elrod for a week and a half. But George and Gabe think I'm kidding. Why are we going with twenty-four players? Are we that fucking great? It cost us tonight's game, as far as I'm concerned."

Thursday, May 12

Seattle

Munson agrees. Not that the absence of a man hitting .105 at Syracuse cost a game, but that the Yankees need a third catcher. It's only the middle of May and Munson's legs are tired. "I'd like to know how a major-league team can go through a season without three catchers," he said. Well, it has been done before. "If you think I'm going to catch a hundred and fifty-five games, you're crazy," he said.

Catching is a special position. It is very hard work and catchers take more than their share of bumps and bruises. That's why so few catchers have ever won a batting championship. Munson is a good hitter and being on base takes even more out of his legs. And not everybody can fill in at his position.

We can't use that as an excuse for losing to the Mariners again, 8–6. The Yankees did make five errors—three ground ball errors in a row—and gave away six unearned runs. Munson left the game in the seventh inning after hitting into an embarrassing double play. He thought there were two outs and didn't run hard.

But he did make his point, calmly and rationally. He rarely makes his complaints public, but wants them understood. He has missed only six innings as catcher. He caught only 121 games last year and did the rest of his hitting as DH, occasional outfielder, and pinch hitter. That enabled him to stay strong enough to win the MVP award. Now his knees are sore and tired.

He was thinking about the long game he had played and the prospect of the flight to Anaheim to be followed tomorrow night by a game with the Angels, who have all those runners to challenge his throwing. "Well, what the hell," Munson said. "It would have been nice just to DH. I coulda been fresh tomorrow."

But the other catcher is Fran Healy, who isn't nearly the hitter Munson is. If Munson is the DH, Martin can't pinch-hit for Healy because Munson would then have to catch and the pitcher would go into the batting order.

Martin says he is thinking more long-range. "I need Thurman for the whole year," he said. "I talked to Gabe two times today about another catcher. I'm worried about Thurman. If he gets down emotionally, I lose my best hitter."

Munson is disturbed about other things too, obviously about the Steinbrenner touch. "We had so much fun last year," he said, "and I want us to have fun like that this year. But there's too much pressure, too many things created. Someone says this guy [that would be Carlos May] is a few pounds too heavy. Someone's hair is too long."

Friday, May 13

Anaheim

Try to think of the last time a manager was fined by his employer. You'll think a long time. But then put Billy Martin and George Steinbrenner together for any length of time, and you'll see things nobody has seen before.

Martin was fined $2,500 by the club today for his comments on the absence of the third catcher. Who ever heard of such a thing?

Purportedly, Martin was fined for missing a scheduled meeting with Gabe Paul before the team left New York Tuesday. That would be in keeping with Martin's contract. But there are other clauses in Martin's contract that are just coming into view and defining the owner-manager relationship more clearly. One of the clauses stipulates that Martin is not to criticize the front office publicly.

Since the beginning of spring training, Martin has been letting the press know that Steinbrenner's intereference with the way Billy the Kid was running the club would jeopardize its chances. Whatever the reason, Steinbrenner kept his distance, but Martin doesn't know how to keep his mouth shut and Steinbrenner's clauses scratch. He could fire Martin and contend that it was Martin who broke the contract, and then Martin would be due nothing on the remaining two years of his contract. There is some thought that if Martin blows his job, he might not manage again. Steinbrenner has mentioned that to Martin.

The New York *Post* carried Martin's relatively noninflammatory remarks back to Steinbrenner's eyes under the head-line "Martin Blasts Steinbrenner." That's the *Post*.

But Martin did agree to the Tuesday meeting about the roster vacancy and then didn't show. That's Martin. Now he says, "I talked to Gabe for an hour and a half the night be-fore. I let him know my needs. Going to a meeting with him is having repeated to you what he already said."

When he was informed that Paul had indeed filled the va-cancy with outfielder Dell Alston, Martin expressed his dis-agreement, but quietly. Alston, who was around in spring training, was hitting .388 at Syracuse, while Hendricks was hitting .105. "If the success of this club depends on a player hitting .105 at Syracuse, then we're all in trouble," Paul said.

Even after Ed Figueroa shut out the Angels, 3–0, Martin was presenting his best beleaguered image to clarify his silence on the fine. "I'm like a submarine being attacked by depth charges," he said. "Complete silence, and I'm cruising on batteries."

The whole business has become a soap opera.

Saturday, May 14

Anaheim

Don Gullett beat the dreaded Nolan Ryan, 4–1, but Mun-son proved Martin's point. Munson took a foul tip on the base of his right hand and may not be able to play tomorrow night. The trainer said Munson had broken blood vessels. Nothing very serious, but if Munson can't catch, only Fran Healy can.

Nettles provided three of the four runs with two home runs.

And Hunter's arm is sore again. He'll miss his turn Tues-day.

Sunday, May 15

Anaheim

It turned out that Munson's foot, hit by his own foul ball, was more painful than his hand. He took himself out after batting in the sixth inning and says he won't be able to play tomorrow. He had been up during the night to get painkillers from the trainer but said he wasn't surprised that he was in the lineup for the thirty-first consecutive game. "Because they want me to play," he explained. "Don't I always play? But I'm not going to kill myself. If they think I'm going to catch a hundred and sixty games, they better run somebody else in."

He said he played because the Yankees' record against left-handers was three won and eight lost, and would have come out if either team got a big lead. It obviously wasn't the Yankees who got the lead, as lefty Frank Tanana beat them, 8–2. And Munson still has never had a hit off Tanana in 34 at bats, even if Munson has hit some balls well.

Paul is sitting tight on the catching situation. "If Healy gets injured, we'll take appropriate steps," he said. "Hendricks is within three or four hours. But Healy isn't injured." If Munson is out, then the backup catcher is Chicken Stanley, who once caught seven innings at Syracuse in 1973. "We can't have everything," Paul said. "If Billy had come and had our meeting, there wouldn't have been any problem. A deal might have been worked out then."

* * *

Paul Blair took over center field in the sixth inning after Mickey Rivers bobbled one ball for an error and looked less than enthusiastic chasing down some other hits. Martin said there was no connection. "He just doesn't hit Tanana too good," Munson said. So who does? And was that something Martin didn't know before the game?

And Dick Tidrow, the essence of the noncomplainer, had a closed-door session with Martin after game. "He just wants to pitch more," Martin said.

It seems that no day goes by without some disturbance.

Monday, May 16

Oakland

Billy Martin's forty-ninth birthday. He spent the afternoon with his mother at the house where he was born in Berkeley. "I think this is the first time in thirty years I've been home on my birthday," he said. She served him home-made ravioli, which he said he ate with relish.

What he did not enjoy was playing catch-up baseball. The Yankees gave away another game with defense. They made four more errors, bringing their total to fifteen on the six games of the trip. Frank Healy, Reggie Jackson, and Chris Chambliss each made an error in the first inning, and Ken Holtzman was started and finished with only one out. He was charged with five runs in what wound up an 8–4 loss.

Holtzman has lost three of his last four starts and says he has no feeling for his rhythm and control. "I seem to be all right if I can get to the third inning, but there was no way he could wait that long," he said.

The middle of the batting order—Jackson, Chambliss, and Carlos May—hit a collective one for twelve. After hitting a home run in his first at bat on the trip, Jackson has had one more hit in 25 at bats. He struck out awkwardly on two bad pitches tonight. He continues to say that there's no way he won't hit, but then he never had this kind of pressure before. "The only thing this does to me is see how much a man you are," he said.

And the Yankees are now in third place.

Tuesday, May 17

Oakland

Jackson is seething at Martin, at the press, at anything he can find. First, Martin benched Jackson against Vida Blue because Blue is left-handed and because Jackson is in that slump. That's hard enough for Jackson to take. He feels he's proved to anybody who'll look that he can hit—and will hit if he's permitted to find himself. Then the game went into the fifteenth inning and when a pinch-hitter was called for, Jackson found himself still on the bench. Dell Alston, one day up from Syracuse, was sent to the plate.

"Yeah," Jackson said when asked about the lineup, "I'm a mediocre ball player and I'm overpaid. That's what the press says, isn't it?"

Honestly, no, that's not what the press says. There have been some critical pieces in New York, most of them saying that what Jackson did in Oakland and the pressure he played under in Oakland hardly count in the face of New York demands. The reporters who have been on the Yankees regularly since spring training have noted Jackson's fielding problems but have been largely understanding of Jackson's situation in the city, on the ball club, and aware of Jackson's playing record. Some of the out-of-town press has been more caustic, but then they regard Jackson and the Yankees as the enemy. The problem is that Jackson isn't able to see an 80/20 split as being in his favor.

What was in the Yankees' favor was a terrific combined pitching effort by Ron Guidry and Sparky Lyle in beating the A's, 5–2, in fifteen innings and ruining a marvelous pitching job by Vida Blue. Guidry lost his shutout in the last of the ninth when Manny Sanguillen and Dick Allen homered to tie the score. Lyle allowed no runs over the last 6 ⅔ innings.

And Alston began the winning rally. He has the inscribed baseball in his locker to prove it: "1st Major League Hit, Double vs. Oakland to Start Three-Run Rally to Win Game 5–2 in 15 Inn. 5–17–77." It is a thing a man can cherish forever.

"If I go down tomorrow, I can say I got a hit in the big leagues and scored a run," Alston said.

For everybody else, the atmosphere in the clubhouse is very heavy. It seems that Martin encourages the sulking.

* * *

Steinbrenner, Paul, and Whitey Ford are off on a two-day tour of Cuba to observe the baseball program and meet Fidel Castro. Steinbrenner would love to have his team be the first American baseball team to play in Cuba since 1960.

Thursday, May 19

New York

Other clubs like to pitch left-handers against the Yankees. Orioles manager Earl Weaver started Mike Flanagan tonight and even though the Yankees beat him, 9–1, Weaver plans to start lefties in three of the remaining four games this series. The logic of it is that the Yankees are 3–10 against lefties and 16–4 against righties.

One easy explanation is that Jimmy Wynn, the right-handed DH, is 1 for his last 31 after starting off with 9 for 25. A less comfortable explanation is offered by one of the players, who sees a difference in Martin's approach to the game this season compared to last year, when they got off to such a great start. "We sit and wait for a home-run ball instead of the way we won last year, the hit-and-run, the stealing bases, getting two or three runs—and then it'd be nice if someone hit a home run."

They won tonight on Figueroa's fifth straight complete game—nobody in the league is pitching better—on a homer, triple, and single by Munson, and four hits and four runs scored by Willie Randolph. "Hits don't thrill me that much," Randolph said. "What thrills me is crossing home plate."

Catfish Hunter is annoyed because Martin won't tell him when he is going to pitch. "I'm supposed to pitch Sunday," Hunter said, "but now I don't know. I told him I could pitch Tuesday and he told me to wait. So I waited."

Martin said he'd have Hunter throw batting practice tonight and then decide whether he would pitch one of the Sunday games. So Hunter threw and said he was pleased. And Martin insisted, "I will announce my starting pitchers for Sunday on Saturday, not before."

Martin is especially testy. Word is out that the new issue of *Sport* magazine has an article about Jackson in which he comments about Munson's insecurity and his leadership qualities—or rather what Jackson sees as a lack of leadership qualities.

Martin's response was a rip at Jackson. "Leadership is done by example, not by mouth," Martin said.

The feeling in the clubhouse is ominous.

Friday, May 20

New York

Martin needs his third catcher again, but is holding his tongue as best he can. Munson had four hits, including two doubles, then made a tag on Lee May at the plate in the seventh inning and needed four stitches to close the gash on his right thumb. The Orioles won, 6–5, with Fran Healy, Munson's replacement, making the third out of the eighth inning with the tying run at the plate. Martin could have pointed to a number of strategic turning points, but chose the most tactless one again. Instead of pointing out that Alston's pinch double started the near-miss rally, Martin preferred to point out that he could not have Jimmy Wynn hit for Healy because there was no third catcher.

But Martin wasn't going to go further; he had made his point. "I'm not going to talk about that," was his disclaimer. "The last time I said anything about that, it cost me money. No, I don't want a third catcher."

By saying no when everybody knew he meant yes, Martin had accused the front office again. He was saying in his own way, How can I be expected to win with what those people give me? And if it wasn't the front office to blame, then Martin would have found something else—anything but himself and the players he put on field.

Martin won last year. He has the best personnel in the league and is in the best position he's seen in his life, but he always has to push somebody to the wall. He has to have a crisis. "There is a way to simplify most situations and a way to make them more complicated," Brooks Robinson of the Orioles said. "Martin seems to be able to make things more complicated every time."

Psychiatrists in the press box call it Martin's death wish.

Saturday, May 21

New York

This time Martin shut the door of his office and posted a scrap of paper on it like "Beware of Dog." His notice read: "No interviews."

Martin had reason to be angry. His team let a 2–0 lead get away and lost to the Orioles, 4–3, in twelve innings on a two-out single off Sparky Lyle. Munson was out with his sore hand and Jackson was out because Martin wanted it that way. And then Mickey Rivers didn't run out a grounder in the seventh inning and was immediately replaced by Paul Blair.

Apparently Martin shut his office door and posted his notice from the outside because he wasn't inside the office. Shortly afterward he was spotted in the players' lounge at the far end of the clubhouse. That room is off limits to the press. Dick Young of the *Daily News* has small patience with the barriers established by managers in New York. Young is constantly at war with the powers of television and is on guard against inroads on freedom of the press. He is also the reporter with the best contacts in baseball and the support of the largest newspaper in the country. He is sometimes cranky. He is silver-haired, usually well dressed, and always ready to take someone on. Martin is always suspicious of the press. Young attempted to question Martin through the door of the lounge, and Martin responded by shouting, cursing, waving his arms, and pushing past Young toward the trainer's room, the other off-limits room. In the process he spilled some coffee on Young's lapel.

Rivers, who has been at odds with Martin from time to time, also made himself unavailable.

The whole scene was something out of the Marx Brothers. Baltimore manager Earl Weaver, who has exchanged barbs with Martin for years, tried to kid the situation. On one level, he can enjoy Martin's discomfort. "Bill's got nothing to say, eh?" Weaver said in welcoming the New York reporters. "Jeez, I'm happy to talk."

On the next deeper level, Weaver doesn't kid Martin.

There are twenty-six managers' jobs in the big leagues. Weaver's job is precious to him, and he understands that Martin's is precious to Martin. But Weaver is broad enough to see how Martin is his own undoing, as illustrated by the sign Martin has on the wall of his office: "Company Rules— Rule 1: The boss is always right. Rule 2: If the boss is wrong, see Rule 1."

The conflict is that Martin sees those rules as the manager's authority over his players. But Steinbrenner once had a pair of Yankee blue baseball hats made with naval officers' braid on the bill, and they illustrate the situation better. Martin wears number 1 on his uniform, but Steinbrenner put that single figure on his own cap where the Yankee monogram goes. For Martin he had "1½." Martin may be the boss on the field, but he still works for Steinbrenner. Martin often forgets that; Steinbrenner does not.

Weaver says he never forgets in his dealing with the Orioles' front office he is their employee. "Billy understands baseball, but he doesn't understand life," Weaver said. "You got to do what the owner says. That's not baseball, that's life. That's always Billy's undoing.

"I think the Yankees get along with each other. The only problem I see on that club is Billy and Steinbrenner. Billy told the owner in Texas, 'You sell pipes and I'll run the ball club.' Well, you don't tell the owner and the general manager what to do. You make suggestions."

Certainly, the manager should not deliberately make the owner look bad in public. A man who has accumulated great wealth in industry generally does not invest in a baseball team in order to make more money. He may get lucky, but he could probably make more dollars in more conventional business. He goes into baseball for the glory—call it ego gratification or whatever. Steinbrenner had owned the Yankees only a year when he observed that he had already gained more notice than in all his years in business, and that was before Watergate.

"They want to hear people say how smart they are for the moves the team makes," Weaver said. "They want to be in the papers. Above all, they want to be loved in their city."

They don't want conflict on the team to make them look foolish for having assembled that team. Steinbrenner has already been embarrassed by the fan reaction to his new ticket prices and has been forced to back down on some of them. He does not need ridicule from his manager.

Steinbrenner brought a box of expensive cigars back from Cuba for Martin. Steinbrenner appears to have an affection for Martin, but there is some question of how much affection Steinbrenner can have for anything or anyone who embarrasses him.

* * *

Martin does finally have Elrod Hendricks. Sort of, anyhow. Hendricks is not on the roster, but he is in the clubhouse. "He's not on the roster, but in a holding pattern," public relations man Mickey Morabito explained. Morabito, a first-string publicity man for the first time has a hard job with this combination.

Hendricks doesn't know anything more himself. "All I know is I'm here and if they tell me to go back tomorrow, I'll turn around and go back," he said. If he goes on the active list, then somebody has to be taken off.

* * *

The whole question of the relationship between athlete and press has never been resolved. It never will be except for a few very special athletes. Bill Bradley of the Knickerbockers, a Rhodes scholar and a campaigner for a senatorial nomination in New Jersey, described it as a "waltz" in his book *Life on the Run.* The waltz has two dancing partners who need each other. The working newsman needs the athlete for the commentary, analysis, and emotion that lend a feeling of the human beings who play the game and separate the story from the numbers of the box score. The athlete needs the newsman for the attention and acclaim most athletes need as much as they need food and beer. And he needs the newsman for the publicity that will put money in his pocket, through salary or outside activities.

Phil Linz, an undistinguished Yankee utility infielder with a marvelous sense of humor, is the classic example. He gathered much favorable publicity because he was one of the few cordial people in the hostile clubhouse of the late dynasty years. He usually had a funny line or at least a welcome smile in the most grim situations. Before he was out of baseball he opened a boy-meets-girl bar named Mr. Laughs on Manhattan's East Side happy hunting grounds. He said he made three times as much from the bar as he did playing ball, and owed it all to the publicity he received.

Most athletes regard the press as an enemy, or at least an opponent. A reporter who writes that a player dropped a fly ball and it cost the game or that a player struck out three times is regarded as "a ripper." Somehow most players expect their successes to be broadcast to the world and their failures hidden. "These guys want you to kiss their ass," Al Downing once said while he was a Yankee pitcher, meaning the reporters who went to his locker even when he lost. "That's not the point, Al," Jim Bouton pointed out. "If you want them when you win, you have to expect them when you lose."

Managers—and Martin is among them—regard the reporter who reports conflict on the team as having caused it. Actually, any reporter who wrote half of what he knows that goes on off field could wreck a team. There is no end to the examples of the reporter taking the elevator up from the lobby, meeting player and a girl getting into the car on the second floor. Most newspaper men regard that kind of thing as the player's business and try not to be guardians of the team's morality.

Understanding the personalities on the Yankees this season imposes another kind of obligation on the press. This season writers are in the position of possibly making some problems worse by quoting players directly. Exaggerating aspects of what were delicate but dormant situations could cause them to flare. The writer has to understand that, too.

Many managers try to sell themselves to their players by making the press the common enemy. Martin does it a little more skillfully than most of them, but not always.

When he was managing Texas, Martin once reacted to reports of a fight between two of his players by attacking the report. "Nothing but a sports writer could have caused it," Martin said.

For years with the Yankees Ralph Houk made himself enormously popular with his players by exploiting that concept. He would choose the right psychological moment for his attack—and he is a master of the psychology of the team. There would be a question after a tough defeat or in a losing streak and the substance of the question would have little to do with his outburst. The identity of the questioner would have everything to do with it.

The man would have to be regarded as an outsider by the

players. He would be someone Houk thought had few sympa-
thizers on the team—a new man on the assignment, a man
from a paper that covered the team irregularly, or a man
Houk thought the players disliked. Martin prefers unknowns
and the little-known out-of-town writers as his straw men.

Houk would scream and order the questioner out of the
clubhouse at the risk of his life. The players would always
hear the stream of abuse. Rarely was there real physical contact with the reporter. But Houk once pulled a button off the
coat of Trenton reporter Jay Dunn. Once Houk held Maury
Allen of the *Post* against a wall for writing that Houk put on
a tough show for the public but was the opposite to his players. "A marshmallow," Allan called him.

Once after a galling Yankee defeat in Baltimore, Joe
Trimble of the *Daily News* climbed onto the team bus and
muttered: "I guess you have to carry knives to beat these
guys." It was said in total admiration for the Orioles, not as a
put-down of the Yankees, who were just becoming competitive again. But Trimble had been critical of the Yankees in
print and Houk seized the moment to combat a defeatist attitude among the players.

Houk filled the bus with vile abuse for Trimble—his courage, honesty, journalistic talent, and the clothes he wore.
When he was finished, the players applauded.

Within a day or so, Houk would find the opportunity to
apologize—but, as usual, in private: in a hotel elevator or in
the empty clubhouse when the players were all on the field.

When Herman Franks managed the Giants, he responded
to probing questions with: "What the hell kind of a question
is that?" Often, in his tobacco-juice-stained underwear, he
would abuse the reporter in the Latin-flavored clubhouse with
a stream of insults in Spanish that obviously the fool reporter
couldn't understand.

A couple of years ago Cleveland manager Ken Aspro-
monte shut the door of his coaches' room while inside a reporter was held and struck. The reporter and his paper settled
for an apology. When Eddie Stanky's 1967 White Sox lost
their grip on first place by losing a doubleheader in Kansas
City in the last week of the season, Stanky ridiculed a young
reporter from Topeka who dared to ask if the losses would
cause a change in the announced pitching.

Standing in the middle of his team in the clubhouse,
Stanky—now a college coach, who guides young people—de-

manded: "Young man, how old are you? How long have you been covering baseball?"

The next year Stanky ridiculed the reporters covering the White Sox by running in the outfield after games until many of their deadlines had passed. Ted Williams shut the press out of his clubhouse for ten minutes after every game. With a ten-minute start, almost any player can be dressed and gone before embarrassing questions are asked. Unless he has something to say, Martin isolates himself on the field before the game. After it, Martin likes to keep on the move or take up residence in the trainer's room or the lounge until deadlines press hard. His players follow his example.

Maybe fifteen of the twenty-five Yankees welcome the interference with the press and most of the others easily go along with it. Individually many of them are cordial, but even those join in the cold front. So if a player is willing to stand out in the light, he is marked as an outcast, as Jim Bouton was with those old Yankees. Either that or he is so good or so beloved that the others don't object.

On a few teams—like the Baltimore Orioles with Frank and Brooks Robinson, or the old Brooklyn Dodgers with Pee Wee Reese—the example of openness set by the stars was such that the whole clubhouse followed suit. Those Orioles and those Dodgers never feared there'd be a question they couldn't handle.

Thurman Munson resents his own lack of acclaim and the attention given Carlton Fisk, yet a couple of seasons ago Munson spit on a reporter who tried to kid him about a passed ball. Former Yankee Bill Sudakis threatened to hit the sixty-year-old Trimble, who, as official scorer, charged an error on what Sudakis felt should have been a hit.

Official scoring is another point of contention. Baseball has paid newmen for years to handle the responsibility of making the decisions and filling out the official box score. Presently, the scorer is paid $50 a game, a whole lot less than it would cost the league offices to put their own man on the job. In recent years, however, a number of newspapers have judged that a conflict of interest. They believe that a man who is covering the news shouldn't be making the news. They also feel that the animosity inherent in the scoring duties can interfere with properly covering the team. Some players are impossible to work with after a scoring decision has gone against them. Nettles is among them.

Basically, the press is there to be used. Wouldn't any film producer love to have each of five metropolitan newspapers give him 800 words plus pictures every day? That's what the ball clubs get. They also get a forum for their point of view.

Martin has used the press to give his side of the argument with his bosses. For those purposes he can be charming. On the other side, he warns players about what they say to the press. In his one year managing the Twins, Martin put a $5,-000 gag order on pitcher Jim Kaat. Two years earlier Kaat wrote an open letter to the newspapers protesting the dismissal of pitching coach Johnny Sain and the replacement of manager Sam Mele with Cal Ermer rather than Sain. Martin wasn't going to let that kind of loyalty (or disloyalty) go on while he was manager. But before Martin finished winning the division title with the Twins in his first shot at big-league managing, he was sniping at the farm director and assistant farm director and punching the traveling secretary. And getting dismissed before the first snowfall in Minneapolis.

When the first hints of the *Sport* magazine piece were heard, Martin attacked the press. "People write what sells papers," he said. "The press has been on my back all year, and I don't think they'll get off my back even if we get a fifty-game lead. It's newspaper articles that cause problems."

Jackson, who basked in the New York attention when he played with Oakland and only one reporter traveled with his team, is stung by the scrutiny of New York. Often he is unable to distinguish the source of his irritation. When the gossip section of the *Post* ran his home address, Jackson was rightfully angry. A ball player has enough invasion of privacy not to have his residence advertised in the public print. But Jackson took his anger out on Henry Hecht, who merely covers the Yankees for that paper and had been understanding of Jackson's struggles. What Jackson wasn't willing to accept was the fact that the *Post* paid $25 for tidbits like that. It could have been the doorman or a delivery boy who sold the address.

"I'm not talking to the guy from that paper anymore," Jackson said.

"The sports department can't take the blame for that one," Hecht said.

"Well, it's the same damn paper, isn't it?" Jackson said. "You ought to quit."

Later that night, not having found another job, Hecht approached Jackson and was cursed out. Jackson proceeded to snub the rest of the press by talking in Spanish.

Some time later Jackson accepted Hecht's explanation, but not before having written one more chapter in the Yankee soap opera at someone else's expense.

Feud for Thought

New York

Fran Healy caught both games against the Orioles and Munson was the DH. Since Elrod Hendricks is not on the active list, he is not allowed in uniform and has no place to be. Martin knows Hendricks is an old favorite of Weaver's, so he had Hendricks phone the Oriole manager during the first game and confide that he was in uniform in the Yankee bullpen. Weaver ran out of his dugout and protested that it wasn't permitted. And Martin told Weaver it was all a put-on. Later in the first game, which the Orioles won, 5–1, Weaver sent the batboy with a note to Martin saying: "It's OK to use Hendricks now."

After the second game, won by the Yankees, 8–2, Weaver accepted the split with a reference to Martin's no-interviews sign yesterday. Weaver had a sheet of white cardboard on his office door announcing: "Press–Media welcomed at all times."

Catfish Hunter pitched into the sixth inning and said he felt better even if he lost. Ron Guidry, the spot starter, won the second game, allowing four hits until he was relieved with one out in the ninth. It was his third start, his third win, and the third time he has lasted one out into the ninth inning. He threw 128 pitches, almost all of them hard, and expressed the confusion of sometimes starting and sometimes relieving. "My arm doesn't know if it's supposed to rest three days or four days, or throw every day," he said.

Jackson played the second game, got two hits, and advised reporters: "Save your breath, fellows."

118

Monday, May 23

New York

The magazine article is out. Munson has the pages of it folded into his back pocket and the contents committed to memory. The rest of the team has followed Munson's chill. Jackson has his own personal way of reacting.

All those things take precedence over even a 4–3 loss to the hated Red Sox. The Yankees don't have to have another team to hate.

Jackson tied the game at 2–2 in the seventh inning with a mammoth shot into the bleachers in right-center field. It was a dramatic moment, to say the least. But the Yankees did not exactly pour out of the dugout to welcome him. They did gather at the end of the dugout nearest home plate, where Martin stood. And Jimmy Wynn was on the top step to greet Jackson.

After circling the bases, Jackson veered to his left and went directly to the vacated first-base end of the dugout. He deliberately snubbed his teammates, in front of 30,000 fans and the largest crowd of reporters this season. That's the worst crime in the game and it was undoubtedly premeditated. Even if it wasn't, the Yankees thought it was. "That's not spontaneous; you have to have that in mind," Chicken Stanley said.

To make matters worse, having tied the score with his home run, Jackson then overran a bloop single into two bases in the eighth inning, permitting the winning run to reach second base. The worse the conflict gets, the worse his fielding gets.

There seems to be a link. His feeling about Martin has interfered with his concentration. Anybody can pay attention for the brief moments at the plate, especially if he has confidence in his ability to hit. But defense means bearing down on every pitch and anticipating what might happen. And Jackson is not as confident an outfielder as everybody thought. He isn't ready in right field.

Now what's going to happen? Life had been placid and Jackson and Munson had been moving closer together. The magazine piece, even if it was written from things said back in spring training, has broken the spell. That stunt of running to the wrong end of the dugout has to make it worse, no matter what Jackson's explanation.

He didn't even offer much of an explanation. He was poking around the food table in the clubhouse when he was asked for his side of the story. "I had a bad hand," he said, hardly caring if anybody believed him. Nobody did.

"He's a fucking liar," Munson said. "How's that quote?"

At first Munson offered his standard "I'm just happy to be here," disclaimer he uses for all awkward circumstances. Then there was no longer any point in pretending. Whatever he had going with Jackson is shot. The most punishing remarks Jackson made in *Sport* were about the leadership role he saw for himself in what was Munson's territory.

"I'm the straw that stirs the drink. It all comes back to me. Maybe I should say me and Munson but really he doesn't enter into it . . . Munson thinks he can be the straw that stirs the drink but he can only stir it bad."

Jackson, who openly concedes that he needs to be shown he is appreciated, also said that Munson suffered from his own insecurity and was jealous of Jackson. Munson's insecurity was apparent around the Yankees for years, but for the outsider to say that about the insider is a bad risk. Given the basic mentality of the clubhouse, for Jackson to say Munson is jealous is the more explosive because there is an element of truth to it.

"I wish that George would buy me a Rolls-Royce," Munson said. As Munson sees it, the only thing Jackson has that Munson doesn't is that Rolls-Royce gift and a few million dollars.

Munson allowed that perhaps the quotes were not entirely accurate. "But for a man to think Thurman Munson is jealous of anybody else in the world, he has to be ignorant or an imbecile," Munson said. "I've got the cutest kids and a lovely wife and everything I need. I could go home tomorrow, and I don't need material things to make me jealous of someone."

Munson also feels hurt that he was the one who tried to ease Jackson's integration with the team and this is what he gets for it. "I've never done anything except make him feel at home here," he said. "I've probably talked to him more than anybody else."

The thought that Jackson said those things before he got to

know Munson and might feel otherwise now had nothing to do with anything. Munson was so stirred that he stood in the clubhouse and answered all the Reggie questions, calmly and patiently. "You know," he said, "I've had some people hint to me lately . . . they're trying to sway me about keeping my mouth shut. They don't want me to open up." Then he launched into an expression of how much he wanted to play and how much the others wanted to play. He named a string of players with desire, without including Jackson. "Don't let me start," Munson concluded.

He walked out of the clubhouse with the magazine sticking out of the pocket of his jeans, folded open to the Jackson story. "I'm gonna go home and read it again," Munson said.

Around the clubhouse, there was no voice lifted in defense of what Jackson did in the dugout. "It was embarrassing," said Paul Blair, who feels he understands Jackson at least a little.

Martin now has an overt act to support his original feelings about Jackson. "Mabye Reggie was mad at me 'cause I didn't play him a couple of games against left-handers," Martin said. "You ask him. I'm sure he'll have some answers for you. Also ask him about the ball that got away from him in the right-field corner to start the eighth. He probably forgets about those things."

Jackson said he had no comment now, nor would he later. "I'm not gonna talk no more, write whatever you want; you've been doing that all year," he said. "I'm not talking."

It seems that he said enough in March.

* * *

Before the game, Bill Lee of the Red Sox lent his own special rational insanity to the event. He then pitched seven innings to gain credit for the win. Lee has his personal feelings about Martin and Steinbrenner, growing out of the fight in which his pitching shoulder was injured a year ago. He has strong feelings about the universe, and he spills them out stream-of-consciousness style:

"Baseball will become extinct. It's just a game. It'll be extinct before it's a holy war. The weather is going to change before then and we'll go into a glacier age. The earth will go on and we as a species will become extinct. The designated hitter, AstroTurf, and concrete stadiums instead of the quaintness of a Fenway Park or a Wrigley Field. The system's view of baseball. We're moving toward Rollerball."

He said all that. And more. The "Rollerball" concept came from the movie of the same name, as influenced by the incident in which Graig Nettles threw him to the ground on his shoulder. Lee is disturbed by trends of violence in society and in sports, and he sees the Yankees as the advocate of violence. It was the thinking he applied in spring training when he called the Yankees in pinstripes "Steinbrenner's Brown Shirts" and called Martin "Hermann Goering."

"The players are brainwashed by him. His win-at-all-costs type of attitude has to have limits. When you limit it, that makes you civilized, and it's the reason we will survive—as long as we don't go blindly on, as Billy Martin would have you. There's a part of him that functions perfectly and a part of him that's not screwed on."

Lee went out to pitch with a golden artichoke decal on his arm, right where his six-year-old son put it while Lee was sleeping. He wore a T-shirt inscribed "Friendship First, Competition Second."

Martin has reacted to Lee's expressed views before. Once, Lee recalled, they went at it from bench to bench when Martin was on the brink of being fired by Texas. "I had him swinging from the chandeliers," Lee recalled. "He thought I was crazy and he tried mimicking me. Next day he was gone. If I'm insane, then it's a response to an insane world."

There may be some sense in what Lee says. And right now, Martin may be at the brink again with the Yankees. Whatever the turmoil on the team, Steinbrenner charges Martin with controlling it.

Tuesday, May 24

New York

Steinbrenner called Martin up to the owner's office to discuss the condition of the team. Then Martin called Jackson into the manager's office to discuss his behavior. And, as if Martin didn't have enough to concern him, he made time to respond to Lee.

The Yankees won the game, 6–5, a classic kind of Yankee-Red Sox game that drew the fans into its tension. Graig Nettles and Carlos May hit home runs on consecutive pitches in the seventh. Mickey Rivers scored the winning run on a single by Munson, sprinting all the way from second base, past the plate, and into the dugout to the comfortable cushion of Herman Schneider, the ample assistant trainer.

But Jackson and Munson aren't discussing their problem, and the tension in the clubhouse is thick. Martin said he was satisfied by his discussion with Jackson about the handshake snub. "It's resolved. It went fine," Martin said, obviously nothing more than window dressing. Jackson still hates being here and may be nearing some kind of nervous breakdown. Refusing the congratulations may be the early warning.

Martin said Jackson's explanation was "that he had no reason for it, that it just happened." But the players still see it as premeditated. They have heard no apology.

It's nothing new for teammates to dislike each other. In the celebrated togetherness of the Miracle Mets, Ron Swoboda and Jerry Grote had contempt for each other. Martin recalled hostilities on earlier great Yankee teams. "But no one said anything [publicly] about it," he said. "I didn't like Johnny Mize and some of the other guys Stengel brought in."

The point was that what the players had against each other was not a problem because nobody on the outside knew about it. That's Martin's solution: Don't tell anybody about the problem and it will go away. He recalled the World Series game in which Carl Erskine of the Dodgers struck out 14 Yankees. "Mize was second-guessing us all game," Martin said. "He was getting on everyone for swinging at bad pitches, curveballs in the dirt. So what happens? He gets sent up in the ninth and swings at not one ball in the dirt, but two, and strikes out. I said, 'Gee, John, what did that ball do—take a bad hop?'"

Martin was the hero of his story of how real Yankees handle their differences. He was living up to his Yankee self-image and Jackson does not. Martin would not have spilled his dislike for Mize to any magazine writer. Martin has not read this story. "I'm not going to read it," he said. "I heard about it."

Munson said he does not expect an apology. "I don't know what Reggie's going to do," he said. What Munson is going to do is ignore Jackson. And Munson's resentment will fester.

His comment last night was, "Imbecile!" His feelings must have been stronger.

Jackson said he was unaware of Munson's feelings. "I don't read the papers," he said. "I'm sensitive and emotional. If I read the papers, I get upset. So now I get up in the morning and turn on the cable channel on television and see the standings. I'd like to read the papers, but I don't." Sometimes it seems that Jackson tries to live up to his sensitivity to the point that he courts unhappiness. There's no question he is unhappy.

In professional sports, the requirement is to cope, and the money is good. The slights Jackson feels, which are real enough, hurt him too much. They rob him of his talent. Maybe if Martin could talk to him without making it a challenge, Jackson could pull himself and the team out of its mood. But then, if Martin could approach Jackson that way, they never would have gotten to this situation. And if Jackson could minimize instead of maximize—as with that slowed-down perception he said he could employ back in Fort Lauderdale—he could pull himself up. Instead, Jackson chose to shoot back at the press after the game. When he was asked questions, he answered again in Spanish.

Then he turned to Carlos May and said, in English: "My face hurts. I haven't smiled this much in a month and a half."

He can't last the season looking to put everybody down, can he?

* * *

Martin has room to put down one more enemy, Bill Lee. "The next time he pitches against us, I'm gonna be all over him and I can jockey pretty good," Martin said. "He'll wish he never made those comments . . . Ask anyone who's ever played for me and they'll tell you that I'm a player's manager.

"He's way off base. If he played for me, I wouldn't handle him with a strong hand. I'd handle him with a straitjacket like the rest of the nuts."

Wednesday, May 25

New York

Call it a split doubleheader—on the field and on the Yankee stage, which is more suspenseful.

The first act was played early in the day between Paul and Steinbrenner. Billy Martin didn't get fired, but it was close.

Steinbrenner said, "I didn't have strong feelings either way, but Gabe felt strongly and that was enough for me." It had to be the weakest vote of confidence an owner ever gave his manager.

Martin and Steinbrenner had a pregame meeting for the second night in a row and they talked about, among other things, the reports that Gabe Paul had talked Steinbrenner out of firing the manager. Other ball clubs may keep things secret in the front office, but not this one. Rumors are not to be dismissed as merely rumors. Paul has been a baseball man for fifty years, going back to days as a batboy at Rochester. He understands the grinding of a 162-game season. Steinbrenner wants things done, as he shouted in the clubhouse in St. Petersburg, "right now." Maybe Martin's manner does inflame already troubled situations, but taking over this pack would be too much to ask from any new manager.

Steinbrenner said that Martin "had not done right" in criticizing club policies, but said that the issue had been smoothed by a discussion of the rules Steinbrenner insisted upon before he would agree to Martin's new contract last year. Better say, smoothed for now. "It's important for Billy to know I'm on his side," Steinbrenner said in explaining his meeting. "I wouldn't say Gabe salvaged his job."

Paul refused to discuss his role in the decision. "Just say," he said, "that as of right now Billy's job is secure."

In the other part of the clubhouse doubleheader, Jackson asked to hold a meeting so he could apologize to the players, and especially to Munson, for the magazine quotes and for the snub. Martin refused.

Steinbrenner said he thought Jackson showed "a lot of class and a lot of humility" in asking for the meeting. Certainly it would have been a hell of a lot easier for Jackson to say his piece in a mass session than to have to bend to Munson, man-to-man. Perhaps it would have closed the wound for the time being.

"I didn't want to have a meeting," Martin said. "I explained my reasons to him, that everybody understands what he's going through and his emotions, and everyone respects him. I told him if you want to say anything on a man-to-man basis, do it, but you don't have to have a meeting to do it."

Martin would like a personal admission of guilt by Jackson. Martin is not flexible enough to understand Jackson's concept of face. By Martin's code, that's what Jackson should have done, and maybe Jackson should have done it, but the responsibility of the manager is to do what has to be done to get the job done. As Texas owner Brad Corbett once said, reflecting on Martin's term as manager of the Rangers: "He's the easiest guy in the world to work for as long as you just do it his way."

Munson is stewing over the printed word. He was the MVP last season; he did have a hell of a year, he did have a magnificent World Series even if the Reds swept the Yankees in four games. And he finally got the recognition he longed for. Now his leadership has been maligned and that stings, even if those things were said nearly four months ago. "I don't care if he said it four years ago," Munson said.

Martin later said that Jackson went around to each player to make his peace. It never happened. The issue is right where it was, ticking away.

Friday, May 27

New York

So Jackson has taken a different way of showing his contrition. He hit a home run and the Yankees beat the White Sox, 8–6, with 15 hits, but Jackson chose to claim the blame for a ball he didn't catch. "I should have caught the ball," he said.

Actually, Jackson was pleading *mea culpa* although Richie Zisk's drive into right center was a legitimate double, splitting the difference between Mickey Rivers in center field and Jackson in right. It did start off the two-run Chicago first inning, and Jackson did get the tip of his webbing on the ball.

Jackson appeared to give his best effort and it would have been a fine catch. "But I should have had it," he said. "Right off the edge of the glove."

Jackson's homer began a five-run Yankee second inning and he singled in another run later, but the significance of the evening is that Jackson tried to come out of his self-imposed exile. He knew his claim of guilt would get around the clubhouse. He had flattering things to say about Munson, and that, too, would get around the clubhouse.

"He's been a man about the whole thing," Jackson said.

It isn't clear what Jackson intends to do about the distance between the two of them in the clubhouse. "But that's my business, really," Jackson said. He doesn't know what to do, really.

* * *

Catfish Hunter left the game before he could get a batter out in the Chicago second. It was the earliest Hunter had been taken out of a game since 1970, but he said he felt better.

He hasn't won since opening day and has been rapped for 11 runs in his last three starts, covering all of 8⅔ innings. But Martin said he would leave Hunter in the rotation "because I think he's coming around."

Sunday, May 29

New York

A little more subtle diplomacy by Jackson, a rebuff by Munson, and a little more diplomacy by Jackson.

Jackson struck out three times while the Yankees were beating the White Sox, 5–2, and Martin replaced him with Paul Blair in right field in the seventh inning. Jackson could have seen that as another put-down. After the game he went to the brink of saying it, then stopped himself. "Last year, I swung the bat worse, but I knew I would hit," he said. "This year I'm swinging the bat bad and nobody thinks I'm going to hit. I'm trying to take it like a man. If it means sitting on the bench, I'll sit on the bench and cheer. But it doesn't do much good to play a few innings, strike out a couple of times, and have someone pick me up. I'd rather . . ." He paused.

"I'm not doing anything to help the club, so you might as well sit me down," he said. "The approach I take is they want to get someone in there to help the ball club, and I haven't helped the ball club. I don't take it as a slight to me."

The facts are that Jackson has been to bat 144 times, has 36 hits, and has struck out 38 times. He said he did not take it as a knock, either, that tonight Munson didn't accept his handshake.

Chris Chambliss homered with Munson on base in the sixth inning. Jackson was coming out of the dugout to take his place on deck as the two crossed the plate. Jackson held out his hand to Chambliss, who slapped it, and kept the hand out for Munson, dawdling a few steps behind. Munson continued past Jackson without accepting the hand. That tied the handshake score at one for Munson and one for Jackson.

"I don't think he saw it," Jackson said.

Munson ignored the question.

It just happens that they begin a difficult road trip tomorrow, five stops and eleven games in eleven days. It begins with two games in Boston and goes on and on: two games and a long plane flight, two games and another long flight. Packing and unpacking, short rest and possibly short tempers. If the gloom in the clubhouse carries onto the field, it could be a very costly trip.

Monday, May 30

Boston

In the midst of the carnival that a Yankee–Red Sox game is at wonderful little old Fenway Park, there was a crack in the ice between Jackson and Munson. Not a real thaw, but a crack. And it was Munson who made the move; give him credit. He shook hands. It was also a marvelous game for the Yankees to win, 5–4. Give Munson credit for that, too.

Jackson hit a home run to tie the score at 1–1 in the top of the second inning. When he got back to the dugout for the routine of congratulations, Munson was waiting with the group to shake Jackson's hand. It was only last week that

Jackson went to a neutral corner of the dugout after hitting a home run. It was only Sunday that Munson spurned Jackson's hand.

"It's not good having all this stuff in the paper every day," Munson said. "If I have to shake his hand to stop this stuff, then I'll do it. I don't have to like it, but I'll do it for the good of the team."

Jackson singled after Lou Piniella's triple in the fourth, putting the Yankees in front, 3–2, and again Jackson and Munson shook hands in the dugout.

In the last of the ninth, the old ball park bubbled with anticipation as Butch Hobson came around third and raced Mickey Rivers' throw to the plate with the winning run. Munson crouched and braced for the impact. Hobson was a quarterback and safety for the 1972 Alabama team in the Orange Bowl. Munson was a linebacker at the Lehman High in Canton, Ohio. "I had eighty letters to play college football," Munson said. And Mike Torrez ran from the mound to back up the play, saying to himself, "Oh, please, nobody cut off the throw."

Rivers, who was challenged and failed to make a strong throw to the plate on Boston's third run, got his throw off quickly, straight, and on a good bounce to Munson. The catcher had the ball ahead of Hobson, crouched, and left no avenue for Hobson to reach the plate. Two out. Torrez hung on to get the third out with the tying run on second base.

And this time, Jackson, who had given way for Blair in right field, sought Munson as he came away from the plate. "There hasn't been much of that lately, has there?" Jackson said. He seemed relieved that the first steps of coming together had been taken.

What does it all mean, Kremlin watchers? What's in a handshake, anyhow? Eventually it may prove to mean nothing. But then it may mean a lot in soothing the antagonism that goes beyond the two principals. "Regarding winning and losing, I'd say it means about fifty per cent," said Jimmy Wynn.

It's like a panel out of Pogo, the philosopher, who said, "We have met the enemy and he is us."

The others are watching with their own feelings about the Munson-Jackson affair and the quoted insults that set off the only rift that Munson acknowledges. "Reggie made all the rest of us like pawns," Blair said, and he considers himself Jackson's ally.

Jackson says that magazine writer Robert Ward violated off-the-record confidences with the story. "But he did say those things, didn't he?" Munson said with consummate logic.

How does Jackson come to bare his deepest feelings to a writer he has never seen before? How can he trust a stranger he may never see again to keep remarks like that off the record? Jackson listened to the criticism in the privacy of the empty dugout and acknowledged that he was foolish. It is precisely that naiveté that makes Jackson rewarding company much of the time. But it gets him into trouble. He did not claim he never said those things. And Munson is not forgiving. "When somebody takes a shot at you, you remember it," he said. "It can never be good between us. But any animosity I feel toward Reggie won't affect the way I play baseball."

So far, it has not. Munson is remarkable for his ability to blank out what goes on around him. "It bothers him less than it bothers me," Jackson said. It bothers Jackson a great deal. His mind wanders back to his feelings about Martin. "The man doesn't think I can play," Jackson said. He is afraid to make a mistake and that causes him to make mistakes, like the error tonight that led to Boston's third run.

He now also concedes that he made a mistake in letting his feelings toward Martin push him to avoiding the dugout handshakes. "I lost my Christianity," he said.

"Others can't cope with the turmoil like Thurman," Wynn said. "He is a baseball man. What goes on around him makes Rivers' problem deeper. Mickey told me if he had Reggie's contract, he would be doing more to help the club win games. Mickey can play when he wants to; sometimes he doesn't want to."

Wynn doesn't take the stance that the conflict is a media creation. "It's nothing you have to stir up," he said. "It's there. It's wide open."

Gabe Paul still insists that it doesn't affect play on the field, but then none of the players remembers playing on a team like this. Blair, who played on the great Oriole teams that were oh-so-smooth, thinks it just makes matters more difficult. "We could win by fifteen or twenty games if we were smooth," he said. "Everybody would prefer it. I'd love to be on a club like that, like Baltimore. It made it so much easier to win that way, all pulling together. But you don't have to have that to win; there's so much talent here."

One of the problems Blair sees is that too much is being expected of Jackson because of his enormous contract. Worst of all appears to be what Jackson has laid out for himself. When Jackson got to the Orioles last year and Earl Weaver wrote him into the lineup in center field, Jackson immediately advised Weaver: "Hey, I'm not as good a fielder as you think I am." Jackson wouldn't think of making an admission like that here, and he could never be sure Martin wouldn't take it as evidence of cowardice.

"Reggie is a good player with exceptional power," Blair said. "Don't take him for more than that. All this plays on Reggie's mind. It's a distraction for him."

If Martin could accept that kind of emotion, perhaps he could ease the whole situation. But it's not Martin's nature to reach out like that.

"He could hold a team meeting and demand that everybody play baseball," Wynn said, "but he's so lackadaisical. Anything people do in the playing field, they never hear about it. Guys—not just Reggie—don't run balls out, on the field or on the bases." Wynn is still an unreconstructed National Leaguer. The game is a little more intense in that league.

It's apparent that Jackson has to make the strong overture toward Munson, but Jackson is so consumed by his own feelings toward Martin that he can't see straight. "I'm trying to prove to the man that I can play," Jackson said. "This is the hardest thing I've ever had to do. I just wish they would leave me alone and let me play ball."

But they won a game and in the Red Sox' own ball park. It was a good beginning for a trip that could prove some things. "We proved something tonight," Blair said. "We won a close game, and we ain't a family." He giggled off toward the bus.

Jackson, on his way out the door in an improved frame of mind, said he would make a move toward Munson, some time on this trip. "I'll go to Thurman's room and ask him to go to dinner," he said. "I'll do that."

* * *

The game had a special flavor of Fenway Park, where the young people seem to dig baseball more than any other place in either league, and are the hippest. You can smell the excitement and the pot in the stands before the game begins. The fans remember how Bill Lee referred to the Yankees as "neo-Nazis." As Martin walked across the field before the game they must have recalled that the league president had warned Lee about the temper of his remarks. So the fans picked up for Lee, chanting, *"Sieg heil . . ."*

"What really tees me off," Martin said, "is he doesn't even know I'm Italian." Billy, just whose side was Italy on, anyhow?

Tuesday, May 31

Boston

The division race that's supposed to be a tale of two cities, Boston and New York, included Cleveland and Patterson.

Gil Patterson, the loser, was very impressive for a rookie, striking out eight in 5⅔ innings. Reggie Cleveland, with a mediocre history, turned out better. But he was the second to admit the Yankees let him off the hook. Martin was the first. The Yankees had runners on second and third with none out in the sixth inning, when the Boston lead was 3–1. Cleveland had to face Jackson, Roy White, and Graig Nettles, all batting lefty. "I'd say the odds were a thousand to one," Cleveland said. "I got lucky."

Patterson was not so lucky and, Martin said, not as smart. Martin, a second-guesser, pointed out that Patterson got hurt when he threw his change-up, which was what the manager had run to the mound to warn against. Carl Yastrzemski of the Red Sox agreed that Patterson did them a favor when he threw anything but his fastball.

"Of all the young pitchers I've seen in the last seventeen years, I'd have to rank this one in the top five," Yastrzemski said. Yastrzemski had two doubles in three at bats against Patterson. It was reminiscent of the comments Whitey Ford made in 1961 after striking out the rookie Yastrzemski three times in their first meeting. "He's going to be a good one, you can tell by the way he stands in there," Ford said. Yastrzemski has gone on to win two batting championships.

What Patterson has to learn is how good his fastball really

is. He's twenty-one and he got hitters out at Syracuse and in Venezuela with his change, which in the big leagues is just a lousy fastball. It took Tom Seaver eight years to develop a change good enough to use in a tight spot. "I don't think I'm smart enough for these guys," Patterson said. He was delighted to hear what Yastrzemski had to say.

Jackson was not delighted about anything. He grounded out with two on in the first inning, with two on in the third, two on in the sixth, and popped out with one on in the eighth. That gave him an inglorious total of seven runners stranded during the game. When he failed with the two runners in scoring position in the sixth, he threw his head back in pain.

"I left seven men on base and I'm not even swinging bad," Jackson said afterward. "No excuses. I look good in the lobby and it ends there."

Now a flight into the night to Minneapolis.

Wednesday, June 1

Minneapolis

The last hitter you want to face with a one-run lead, bases full, and two out in the last of the ninth is Rod Carew. So that was just what Sparky Lyle did—and it was the last batter he faced.

Lyle walked twenty-four-year-old Roy Smalley, batting .225, giving Carew his chance. Psychologists have a theory about that: A man concentrates so hard on what he does not want to do that it's precisely the thing he does do. "I did exactly the opposite of what I wanted to do," Lyle said. And Carew, taking the chicken-soup cure for a sinus infection that has cut him to .364, singled to center for the tying and winning runs.

That wrecked another near-miss at a complete game by Ron Guidry, who took a 3–1 lead into the ninth inning. The lead could have been bigger, but Jackson, struggling painfully now, twice went out with two men on base. He has stranded eleven in the last two games.

Thursday, June 2

Minneapolis

Jackson goes around as if he were about to burst into tears or proclaim right now that he wants out of New York. He is terribly depressed. "I don't like playing baseball," he said. "I don't even like myself. This has made me an unpleasant person. All I do is go back to my hotel room. I don't want to see friends. I don't want them to be with me like this. This has made me not a nice person to be around."

The more he thinks about being depressed, the more depressed he becomes. He feels he has few friends and few allies on the team. And he may be right.

One voice he hears belongs to Lou Piniella, who has enough troubles trying to keep himself afloat without trying to save Jackson. But Piniella is one of the special guys.

Piniella was one of last year's regulars who lost his job in the Yankees' spending spree. He lost right field to Jackson and he lost the right-handed DH job to Jimmy Wynn. Now it appears Wynn has lost the job back to Piniella, who was considering going home to Tampa and sponsoring a softball team with himself in the lineup batting fourth.

"When you're thirty-four and not playing, you feel like you're lying down in your own coffin," Piniella said. Sitting out the remainder of his career or not, Piniella managed to keep smiling and to keep his hand out to Jackson. The smile keeps Piniella prepared for the chances he does get to play. He hit a two-run homer, drove in another with a sacrifice fly, and singled and scored again as they beat the Twins, 10–3. But what he can do for Jackson in his misery may be more important.

Piniella gives pep talks, even if Jackson doesn't like his shirts. "I'll do it," Piniella said. "Reggie doesn't understand that everybody here is for him. There's nobody on the club, including Thurman, who doesn't wish him well."

Jackson doesn't see that yet. He feels all eyes are watching him and he feels Martin is looking for every little flaw. He felt it in Martin's pregame pep talk in which the manager said that too many people were concerned with what Jackson did. That effectively reminded everybody that Jackson had his string of stranded runners.

Piniella, in his way, acknowledges that is not the way to get the most out of Jackson. "Reggie needs to be wanted on a club and he needs to know he's wanted," Piniella said. "That's what he's like. If he needs to be pampered, then I'll pamper him a little."

Billy, knowing only how to be Billy, does not take that function on himself. Piniella, being Piniella, can even offer personal criticism to Jackson. "He came in here with too many trumpets blaring," he said. "I told him he doesn't have to blow his own horn to be recognized for the kind of ball player he is."

In his one turn at bat with runners on tonight, Jackson singled a run home. He even made two better-than-ordinary catches. "I feel Lou is an ally," said Jackson, in need of any ally even after two hits.

Piniella can even shush George Steinbrenner at times. "I like the owner a hell of a lot," he said, identifying himself with the minority of players. "I can talk to him because we're both bullshitters."

It is not clear just who can get through to Mickey Rivers. He stole a base, which brings his discontent to mind. He's been thrown out seven times and there are thoughts among some of the players that Rivers purposely gets himself caught because Martin does not permit him to steal on his own.

"A green light? Now you're talking," Rivers said. "Run when it's not a good time and get caught and it takes everything out of you. Last year he let me go on my own for a while. There's too many veterans on this club for that; you got to have fun your own way."

Now a night flight to Chicago.

Friday, June 3

Chicago

Bill Veeck—as in "wreck"—on his second time around as owner of the White Sox has his own grasp of the economics of the game. His is not the same as Steinbrenner's. Veeck invested $182,000 in three free agents and he's on top of the

Western Division and filling his ball park. But he does have
an admiration for Steinbrenner. "His signing Jackson was the
only logical move in the whole draft," Veeck said. "He's the
only one who puts people in the stands."

Veeck recounted his bidding for pitcher Wayne Garland,
who eventually signed with Cleveland for $2.3 million over
ten years. Veeck said he offered $350,000 for five years for
the pitcher who had won twenty games for the first time.
"The agent said to me, 'That was a token offer, of course,'"
Veeck said. "I said, 'No, that's it.'

" 'You left off a zero.'

" 'No. That's what I think he's worth.' "

Veeck loved beating the Yankees when they were the bul-
lies of the league and George Weiss, Dan Topping, and Del
Webb were so haughty. He loved beating the Yankees tonight
just as much. "I don't think David ever gets tired of beating
Goliath," Veeck said. "George Weiss is gone and Topping
and Webb are gone and I'm fond of Gabe Paul, but George
Steinbrenner is there."

*   *   *

If he didn't have so many of his own problems, Catfish
Hunter might be able to ease the clubhouse tensions. He tries.
Before the game he planted a simulated gorilla cage in Carlos
May's locker, taped a picture of King Kong on it, and hung
May's uniform inside the cage. Then Hunter sat to one side
and waited for May to come in from batting practice.

May, who is not called Kong Junior for nothing, reacted
with mock rage. When the laughter had subsided, Hunter and
May posed together inside the cage for a photo. "On this
club, nothing is sacred," Sparky Lyle said. "Now I should
send a thousand copies of that photo to Catfish's hometown
in North Carolina." Whatever Hunter's problems, his relationship with the black players is not one of them. The idea
that nothing is sacred may be true, but unfortunately the personalities are not that resilient. When Hunter played for Oakland, the A's took the needle more easily. "Here, well, we
really haven't gotten to know everyone that well yet," Hunter
said. It is June.

At Oakland, the A's had one collective hate object in Charlie Finley to divert the hostility from the players. "We might
have a Charlie here, too," Hunter said, rolling his eyes. That
would be Steinbrenner.

* * *

The White Sox won, 9–5, but Martin wasn't around to see the end of it. He was thrown out in the fourth inning with the score already 8–1. By the end of the game, Martin was ready to make light of the event. He thought lasting until June 3 before being thrown out was a remarkable accomplishment for him, and probably was his record. An automatic fine by the league goes with an ejection and Martin has been fined by Steinbrenner already. "I may be the first manager to finish the season in the red," Martin said.

The umpires indicated deeper implications in Martin's behavior. Martin said it was a bad thing for the same combinations of umpires and teams to meet often and recalled that he had trouble with plate umpire Terry Cooney in Boston, too. "He brought up the Boston game," Martin said. "You're not supposed to carry over a grudge from the last game."

"We're trained not to," said crew chief George Maloney, a forty-nine-year-old who wears jeans, in opposition to official taste. Cooney and Maloney said it was Martin who brought up the Boston game. "Something must be on Billy's mind to think that came from the night in Boston," Maloney said.

Perhaps Martin's thoughts grew from the Chicago newspaper column that examined the Yankee problems, sight unseen, and called Martin "a mouse trying to grow up to be a rat." But Martin said that hadn't bothered him. Perhaps it was concern about the pitching staff. Martin thinks about that often. Don Gullett is to start tomorrow after long absence, and Catfish Hunter on Monday. They have contributed a combined four victories and five losses. If both are fit, Martin must choose his fifth starter from between Ron Guidry and Gil Patterson, who have held the fort effectively. It will not be Ken Holtzman. "He was in the rotation and couldn't do the job," Martin said.

Holtzman snapped a response to a question that included the word "ineffectiveness." He did relieve, with an earned run average of 5.82. To that he added 2⅓ innings with five hits and three earned runs. He is struggling to regain his rhythm without the benefit of a four-day rotation to which he had become accustomed. "You know the circumstances of how I pitch, when I pitch," he said. "How was I ineffective? What happened on the first batter I faced?"

With the infield drawn in, second baseman Willie Ran-

dolph made a bad throw to the plate. Unfortunate. After that
came a triple, a single, and another single. Ineffective.

The Yankees were left to their bus ride through traffic-
choked streets amid a gnashing of gears and some sharp
baiting of the driver and only his patience and sense of
humor turned to friendly teasing. "Bussie," Jackson said,
"you're the only guy I've seen all season going worse than I
am."

"The company got $40 for the charter," Lou Piniella said.
"It cost $38 in gas, $50 in rubber, and $107 for a burned-out
clutch. I think I better sell my Gray Lines stock."

"How," the driver responded, "would you like to be making $5.60 an hour?"

Saturday, June 4

Chicago

Yankees who have friends among the press from other
stops around the league find it comfortable to lay the blame
for the heaviness about the team on the New York press.
"They exaggerate everything," Holtzman told Rick Talley of
the Chicago *Tribune*. "It's so competitive that everybody's
looking for a different angle. Hell, you can't even find a true
account of the actual game anymore."

What Holtzman would like would be a strict accounting of
how the runs were scored. That would be a whole lot easier
for the New York press, too, but this team doesn't permit the
luxury of that kind of coverage. And the league is laughing at
the Yankees. "I can't wait to get the papers every day and
read what's going on with the Yankees," said White Sox manager Bob Lemon, the Yankee's pitching coach last season.
"It's like *Mary Hartman, Mary Hartman*."

The long, probing talk Jackson had with White Sox coach
Larry Doby before the game was relevant to Jackson's most
impressive performance in some time. Doby, the first black
player in the American League and a long-time friend of
Jackson's, told him to examine himself for the resolution of
his problems. Jackson responded with two of his best shots in
weeks, a lucky break, and some very eager base running. He
has hit one ball hard in a game recently, but not two. Mostly

he has been feeling for the ball at bat and at times his running has seemed almost desultory. But not tonight. "Nothing I can say can help anything," Jackson said with a shrug.

The Yankees won the game, 8–6, just barely, Richie Zisk's searing line drive smacking into Roy White's glove for the final out with two White Sox on base. A few feet to either side and a double would have tied the score. A fraction of an inch under the ball, Zisk would have had his second home run of the night and the Sox would have won the game. "If they hit the ball hard at someone and it's an out, fuck it," said Sparky Lyle. He had relieved Dick Tidrow, who had relieved Don Gullett, who was making his first start since May 20. Gullett pitched six innings and looked almost well again.

Sunday, June 5

Chicago

It's a good thing people shake hands right-handed because Lyle could not have raised his left to congratulate George Zeber. Zeber deserved the gesture. At twenty-six, after ten years as a minor-leaguer, he hit his first major-league home run. After pitching for the fifth time in six days, Lyle deserves a day off.

On the very last play of the game, with a runner on and the winning run waiting for a chance at the plate, Lyle fielded an easy grounder—paused—and bounced his throw to first. Chris Chambliss saved it and the 8–6 decision. "It was as hard and as far as I could throw," Lyle said. "If there had been another batter, I don't know if I could have pitched to him."

With the starters floundering, Lyle and Tidrow have saved the pitching staff. They have thirteen saves in fifteen chances and a combined earned run average of 1.48 in 109 innings. Tidrow has pitched only three days in a row; he can pitch tomorrow night. Lyle has to have the day off after his eleventh save.

The barrage of homers by Jackson, Munson, Nettles, Carlos May, Bucky Dent, and Zeber made it six for the Yankees for the first time since 1974. That team production and the last five years spent at Syracuse and West Haven obscured the event for Zeber. At this stage of his life, maiden home runs don't hold much more than a brief flutter of excitement and the acknowledgment that tomorrow at Texas he will sit while Willie Randolph plays second base.

Zeber accepted congratulations and turned his attention to the too small television screen where the last seconds of the NBA championship flickered away. He has no more illusions, no more delicious stardom fantasies. "I imagine I had them when I first started out, but not anymore," Zeber said. "I don't even remember what they were, it's been so long." Now he would be delighted to get in four years as Randolph's backup and qualify for the pension plan. Zeber is a switch-hitter with a little sting; he makes the double play somewhat better than Fred Stanley. That's qualification enough for the job.

The decision between Guidry and Patterson as fifth starter was made for Martin when Patterson came up with his sore shoulder in the second inning. He'll go back to Syracuse, and Ken Clay will be recalled.

And Jackson has had seven hits in fourteen at bats, including an impressive shot upstairs in center field. After a stretch last week when he looked hopeless in the outfield, he looks less timid out there. "For about a week I lost my confidence," he said. "I had no audacity. Then I said, the hell with it for a while."

He has been hitting the ball through the middle, a fundamental way of breaking a slump and one way to hit a home run to center field. "My fundamental is having my mind at ease," Jackson said. "I wish the only thing I had to worry about was playing ball."

Even on a good day, Jackson lapses into his feelings of insecurity and awkwardness among these players. He identified himself on the TV screen with George McGinnis, star of the Philadelphia 76ers having a dreadful time in the play-offs.

On the TV, McGinnis missed a shot. "Don't worry," Jackson said. "If you lose, you'll get it all winter like I got it all season. Do you think McGinnis won't get some heat?"

McGinnis missed the last shot. "I know how he feels," Jackson said.

Munson slipped a gentle needle into Jackson, the first casual encounter since the fateful magazine hit the stands. Jackson searched for a comeback; he turned the aluminum foil pan of unidentifiable meat and gravy on the clubhouse table. He plunged in his hand. "Take some of this for tomorrow," Jackson said. He had a second thought, however, and rubbed the meat on the uniform leg of Lou Piniella, who had not played. Piniella winced. "Lou," Jackson said, "it looks like you were in the meat of the lineup." Bystanders winced.

The bus was carrying them to the airport when Rivers stood up in the middle of the group-encounter session in the rear. In his deep voice he mocked Jackson. "Reggie-fuckin'-Manuel-Jackson," Rivers crowed, twisting the middle name of Martinez, but not intentionally. "His first name is white, his middle name is Spanish, his last name is black. You don't know what the fuck you are." Score one for Rivers.

Then on to the flight to Dallas in hope of finding a restaurant open late on Sunday night.

Monday, June 6

Arlington

It's the mark of Catfish Hunter that when life is most bleak he looks for humor even at his own expense. When things look brighter he'll examine the dark side.

The darkest side for Hunter wouldn't be the end of his career, which has been suggested lately. He's had his full measure of success and all the money he'll ever need. But when the end comes, he wants it swift and certain. Anything but the mediocrity of last season and the lingering uncertainty of this one.

"I think about last season all the time," Hunter said after turning in the kind of gem the Yankees needed and had no right to expect. "I'd like for someday to say, 'Your arm, some bones are in the wrong place. That's it.' When I quit, I want it fast like that. Hang around for a while? Uh-uh."

Hunter pitched a complete game, beating the Rangers, 9–2. He threw only 107 pitches, in choking heat. It was a touch of the Hunter of Oakland. "Probably the best news we've had all year," Billy Martin told Gabe Paul when he phoned into the clubhouse.

"It was a very important game," Hunter said. "It was for

me. I was happier on the last pitch than I've been for a long time."

Hunter was the first of the free agents, liberated after the 1974 season when Charlie Finley failed to meet the payments on Hunter's contract. Hunter won twenty-three games in his first season with the Yankees and managed to wring a 17–15 record out of his arm last season while successfully hiding the pain. There is no escaping the questions now when he hasn't pitched in so long. For a long time he couldn't even run; all he could do was pace up and down.

Jackson watched Hunter and knew what was going on in his mind. They were Oakland teammates while Hunter was winning eighty-eight games over four seasons, and Jackson has a sense of the other man when he chooses to. "He was wondering if he was done," Jackson said. "He was wondering if his arm could come back, wondering if he was worth the money the owner paid him, wondering when the press was going to get on him."

No, that last thought came directly from Jackson's own subconscious. Hunter has always had the best of press. Jackson withdrew the thought.

Hunter has also always had the unqualified respect of his teammates. "I've been telling you all along," Munson said, "if one guy can come back, it's Cat."

Kind thoughts were nice, but not enough. "I was going bananas, that's what I was doing," Hunter said. "I was doing crazy things, running around the clubhouse. I felt like the guys who sit on the bench—like Chicken Stanley. That's why utility players go flaky. They got to."

It's probably harder for a man like Hunter to accept sitting. Utility players generally know their role. George Zeber does, and Stanley will learn. "When you've been a great pitcher, you know the owner is looking for you," Jackson said. "It's all the difference in the world."

From the beginning of the game, the Yankees measured Hunter's fastball against their recollections. The word for a fastball used to be "speed." Now "velocity" is the in word. "Einstein used it for relativity in space," said Munson, a former junior at Kent State. Hunter had good velocity.

Suddenly there's an obvious lightening of the mood. Jackson hit two home runs, driving in four. He has nine hits in 19 at bats. The Yankees have 40 runs in their last five games and have won three in a row for the first time in a month.

There's even increasing evidence of a slight warming trend between Jackson and Munson. "Winning causes everything to be healed," Munson said.

Or is it the other way around?

Tuesday, June 7

Arlington

On the other hand, there is no warming trend to be detected around Ken Holtzman. To the contrary. He has pitched forty-five innings, fewer than any pitcher on the staff except Hunter, and there is no indication that Holtzman will get another chance soon.

In Chicago, at the Associated Press sports editors convention Charlie Finley confided that the presence of Holtzman and Jackson would cost the Yankees the pennant.

"Jackson is a disruptive influence. Holtzman is the most miserable man I have met in baseball," the A's owner said. "He was with the Cubs and he hated it there. We had him in Oakland and he hated it. He hated it in Baltimore and he hates it in New York . . . He hates himself. We won in spite of Jackson and Holtzman, not because of them."

There's no question that Holtzman is unhappy here, but he does get along with the players. And there is some background involved. At Chicago, Leo Durocher used to call Holtzman "the Jew." When Holtzman didn't win, Durocher questioned his courage. Holtzman won nineteen, twenty-one, and nineteen games for Oakland, where Vida Blue said the owner treated "everybody like niggers." Finley's attitude toward Jews is known widely enough in baseball. It has been suggested by one Yankee that religion is Holtzman's problem with Martin, but there is no apparent evidence, and Holtzman will not make the accusation. Besides, Gabe Paul is Jewish.

But Martin did hold Holtzman out of the play-offs and the World Series last fall, and Holtzman says he was promised over the winter by George Steinbrenner that he would be in the rotation from opening day.

Holtzman enjoys the pluck games with Rivers as his partner, and he enjoys trying to drop his outfield practice fungo drives just inside the wall, and—he is careful to add—he enjoys his sizable check on the first and the fifteenth. He identifies himself as a mercenary.

"But that doesn't mean I'm subhuman," he said in a rare display of heat. "I like to get some enjoyment out of the game." He sounded like Shylock saying "Prick us, do we not bleed?"

Holtzman covers the wounds with carefully precise answers: "No comment" and "Correct."

The issue of the moment is that Paul and Texas owner Brad Corbett, who needs pitching, confirm that they are trying to make a deal for Holtzman. One of the obstacles is that when Holtzman signed with the Yankees last season for what amounted to a million dollars guaranteed over five years, he got the right to approve any trade. He wanted to be in one place for those five years and, if he were traded, he would accept only Chicago or Milwaukee, which are near his home in Lincolnshire, Illinois. Paul said he has been working on the deal for some time and that Holtzman has not vetoed it. Yankee players say that Holtzman told Paul a week ago that he would not accept Texas.

Holtzman pays frequent office visits to Steinbrenner and Paul. "They give me the same old run-around," Holtzman said.

Paul says he wants Holtzman as "insurance." What kind of insurance he can be if he doesn't pitch is anybody's guess. "I could probably get used to pitching every fifth day, if they would do it all the time," Holtzman said. "It's the regularity."

The word from Milwaukee this afternoon was that lefty Bill Travers was put on the disabled list, which might mean increased interest in Holtzman. "No comment," Holtzman said. He said there was no reason to ask him about a trade because it's not in his hands. He turned away further questions with an equally rare flash of humor. "Parry and thrust," he said. He was once engaged to the daughter of the University of Illinois fencing coach.

One suggestion around is that Holtzman will hold out for his cities until the last hour of the June 15 trade deadline and then expand his limits somewhat. Idleness can be lethal to pitchers even with long-term contracts.

*   *   *

The Rangers broke the three-game Yankee streak, 7–3, and

Munson did not play because of an infection in the cut he received on his hand at Baltimore two weeks ago.

Another midnight flight, this time to Milwaukee.

Wednesday, June 8

Milwaukee

The bus made its way from the Pfister Hotel through city streets out toward County Stadium with the customary loud banter in the back of the bus. It is ribald back there. One of the standard put-downs is for burly Carlos May to lower his trousers and command, "Kiss my black ass," and there are roars of laughter. Jackson appears to cringe.

A truck passed the Yankee bus on the left side and Jackson pointed out the driver. "There goes Rivers in five years," Jackson said. "Driving a truck."

"Yeah," Rivers replied. "But I'll be happy driving a truck."

"Listen to me," Jackson said, "arguing with a guy who can't read and write."

"Better stop fuckin' readin' an' writin'," Rivers said, "and start fuckin' hittin'."

Everybody roared except Jackson. That made the back-of-the-bus scoreboard 2–0 for Rivers.

* * *

Munson's hand was so sore and swollen this morning that he was sent back to New York and admitted to Lenox Hill Hospital with what was identified as a staph infection. That meant that Elrod Hendricks was put on the roster, which was just what Martin always wanted. Fran Healy caught his second game in a row, which is not really what he wanted.

Healy, thirty, has adjusted thoroughly to being Munson's understudy, because Munson is so good. Even in his absence, Munson exerts influence on the backup catcher's life. When things are quiet at home, sometimes Healy will find himself unconsciously emitting the hoarse bark of a walrus. It's the sound Healy hears from Munson so often in the clubhouse or the hotel. "He's excellent at it," Healy said.

The way Healy tells it, he'll be sleeping and his wife will say, "Get up, Fran," and his first response will be to go warm

up a pitcher. "But don't use that," Healy added. That's what
he always says: "But don't quote me," about things like the
weather. He is one of the most observant on the team, but
avoids controversy. He has a degree in history and hopes to
manage some day. Staying out of controversy always helps.

While Bucky Dent hit two home runs in the 9–2 victory
over the Brewers, Healy hit two doubles and caught nine innings, which is no more common an occurrence. Now Healy
is likely to catch every day for a week. The last time he did
that was for Kansas City in 1975—or maybe it was 1974.
Healy likes being a Yankee, and he says he knows he can
play because he once was a regular. "The trick is to keep
yourself convinced you can still do it," he said.

A dynasty ago, the Yankees had a backup catcher named
John Blanchard behind Yogi Berra and Elston Howard. One
season Blanchard even hit 21 home runs part-time. Then in
1965 he was traded, and he wept. People who consoled him
told him it was his big chance to play every day. Blanchard
sobbed, "But I can't play." It turned out he really couldn't.

Dent's two homers tied his one-season high of five. In four
seasons he had hit ten homers and now he has four in four
days, same as Jackson. "It is fun when you hit home runs, especially with men on base," Dent said as if he had just made
a remarkable discovery. Paul Blair said his big swing in the
ninth ining had been patterned after Dent's. "I was trying to
go deep with the big boys like Dent," Blair said. "Well, uhh,"
Dent said, "let's not get ridic-a-lus."

Thursday, June 9

Milwaukee/New York

It was a pretty good trip, after all. Now that it's over, anyhow. They survived what could have been a damaging trip.
They even prospered. They played eleven days in a row, five
cities—and getting there was at least half the work. They
won seven and lost four. They left home a game and a half
out of first place and returned tonight a game in front.

They beat the Brewers, 10–1, tonight for the sixth victory
in the last eight games just when the fatigue could have taken
its toll. Martin found help on the bench. Credit him.

After a difficult trip there's a great temptation to feel that nobody knows the trouble you've been through. People watching on television think a trip like that is a romp through good restaurants and good hotels. They can't perceive the fatigue, the drag of five airplane flights—flights that three times took four hours or more—five bus trips to the airport and five bus trips to the hotel in the middle of the night, packing and unpacking five times, trying to get laundry out and back in time to repack, irregular sleeping, airplane meals or worse at odd hours, and the blast of two days in temperature near 100 degrees in Texas. Finally, of course, the flight home was an hour and fifteen minutes late and luggage followed forty-five minutes later.

"The worst trip I've been on," Roy White said. "By the fifth inning Monday night in Texas I was really dead. The thirty-four-ounce bat felt like thirty-four pounds. My legs felt heavy. The baseball felt like a shotput."

It was a time for slight bruises to become sore muscles. Football is a contact game, but it is played once a week and the trips are little more than overnights. Baseball's sheer mileage wears the players down. People who don't know the game ridicule baseball players for the injuries that put them out of action. "This isn't some sport," says former football coach Norm Van Brocklin of his machismo game, "where you play eight thousand games and run out to second base and call time because you've got a hangnail."

Football, for the most part, is a strength game. Baseball is a precision game. An interior lineman can play with his leg taped and nobody would know it. A running back can play with his hands virtually in casts, but you can't throw a baseball with a cast on your hand. And those "eight-thousand" games are a drain by themselves.

"Physical and mental fatigue," trainer Gene Monahan said. "Guys sleep late and eat light before a game and can't find a good meal after a game. Or they eat their heavy meal too close to the game and feel sluggish. I know we've been rubbing sore legs for the last three days."

They played four of the hot teams and came out with some major pluses. In those last eight games, they got 62 runs on 93 hits and made it look as if they have just begun to hit. Reggie Jackson left New York with his outlook thoroughly jumbled, had his ups and downs, and came home apparently comfortable with 14 hits in his last 31 at bats. Don Gullett pitched an optimistic seven innings today and now he and Hunter are in the rotation together for the first time since opening day.

They left New York as if the first sharp needle in the clubhouse could set them off and they returned with no brutality too harsh for the bus rides. Jackson has adapted to that by riding toward the front of the bus, away from the heaviest action. He and Munson may even co-exist from now on. And when Billy Martin lifted Mickey Rivers in the first inning today, it could be interpreted only as preservation of Rivers' tender leg. He did his Ol' Man Rivers walk back to the dugout after grounding out and Paul Blair was immediately dispatched to center field. "No, not that time," Rivers said with a broad grin. Blair even made a marvelous catch of a line drive off the grass.

The one battle the Yankees lost was in Hunter's running war with old Oakland A's friend Sal Bando of the Brewers. After Bando left Wednesday night's game in the fifth inning, he sneaked into the Yankee clubhouse and left Hunter's traveling jeans with a ventilation hole in the seat and the left leg tattered like something out of a pirate movie. "I didn't get him, but I will," Hunter vowed.

Friday, June 10

New York

For a guy who looked so bad as a relief pitcher in spring training, Ron Guidry has been a hell of a starter. He has started six times and lasted into the ninth inning five times. He still doesn't have a complete game, but he did get a 4–1 victory. His success has been the greatest obstacle to Ken Holtzman's getting back into the rotation. "To tell you the truth," Guidry said, "a complete game doesn't mean that much to me because I still think like a reliever. A complete game is—well—a complete game. I supposed I'll get one sometime, somewhere along the line."

Jackson had two doubles and Chambliss got his second steal of home of the season when the pitcher bounced a pitch with the squeeze play on. The other time was a double steal and the pitch bounced away that time, too. "That always helps," Chambliss said.

Munson is back after his session of intravenous antibiotics for the hand infection. The doctor said he shouldn't catch before Monday, and Munson wants to make sure the condition doesn't flare up again.

Saturday, June 11

New York

Hunter and Lyle beat the Twins, 6–5, for the Yankees' fourth straight and Willie Randolph hit a two-run homer. And Lou Piniella was thrown out of the game for disputing a called third strike. He flipped his helmet, which is automatic ejection, and then tossed his bat 20 feet toward the plate umpire. A suspension may follow.

Sunday, June 12

New York

End of winning streak. Paul Thormodsgard held them to five hits, and the Twins won, 6–1. "I guess it has to be the best game I've pitched," the twenty-three-year-old rookie said. "I'd have to say so, since I finished."

Ed Figueroa came out with discomfort in his shoulder, but X-rays indicated it was nothing to be worried about.

Monday, June 13

New York

Kansas City dropped the Yankees out of first place, 8–3, and Boston moved into first. "First place is a nice place to be," Red Sox manager Don Zimmer revealed.

* * *

Ken Holtzman has forty-eight hours of rooting before the trading deadline. His agent, Jerry Kapstein—the super-agent—said on television he didn't think Holtzman would be traded to Texas as rumored.

"He said that?" Holtzman said. He's still hoping for Chicago or Milwaukee.

"You're smiling for the first time in two weeks," Holtzman was told.

"For the first time in six months," he corrected.

Tuesday, June 14

New York

The strangest pitching record around belongs to Don Gullett. He pitched his second successive strong game tonight, beating the Royals, 4–2. He has managed to get through only three of his seven big-league seasons without being injured for an extended period, but when he pitches, he doesn't lose. He has the best percentage among active pitchers (97–46, for .678). He has now won six in a row here.

One of the Yankee runs came on Lou Piniella's legs, a feat that will not be repeated soon. Piniella was on second when George Zeber drove left fielder Joe Zdeb back nearly to the warning track. When Zdeb juggled the ball for a moment, Piniella, among the Yankees' slowest runners, tagged up and took off for third and was safe. So, of course, Piniella must have known something about Zdeb's arm. "I didn't know anything about his arm," Piniella said. "But then, he didn't know anything about my speed." Piniella then scored the Yankees' first run in a close game.

Piniella has been fined $200 by the league and suspended three days—to be served at a later date—for his bat-tossing demonstration Saturday. He will appeal. "What bothers me is the suspension," he said. "The fine is fine."

What is not fine is the state of negotiations between the Yankees and Mike Torrez. There have been no negotiations between the Yankees and Mike since Torrez was traded here April 27. "I want to think there won't be any problems, but how can you be sure?" he said. "I don't know if I'll play out my option."

Wednesday, June 15

New York

The trade deadline came and passed, and Holtzman is still here. What the Yankees got was big Cliff Johnson, who hit ten homers for Houston. He can hit but doesn't catch well enough to play enough.

Thursday, June 16

New York

The strangest accent around belongs to Ron Guidry. It's a southern drawl with a French flavor. Either that or it's a French accent with a southern flavor. It's Cajun, originally known as Acadian for the people who emigrated from French-speaking Canada to the bayous of Louisiana, where Guidry was raised. He speaks French because that's how he speaks to his grandparents.

He also pitched his first complete game, shutting out the Royals, 7–0, on a night the Yankees went back into first place. The symbolism is obvious. What if the Yankees had not discovered the real Guidry in the shambles of spring training? They probably would not be in first place going into Boston to begin a three-game confrontation tomorrow night.

It's a big series. One of the teams will most likely win the division championship. It's only June, but the two meet again next weekend in New York, then not again until September.

Guidry pitched a three-hitter, struck out seven, retired seventeen in a row over one stretch. He pitched nine innings when the figure 8⅓ was becoming a mental block. So he decided to fool himself. When he went into the ninth inning he told himself he was still pitching the eighth. "I feel strong," he said, still playing out his self-deception. "If I had to pitch the ninth or even the tenth inning, I could have done it."

He has been nothing short of remarkable. He leads the staff with 58 strikeouts and has managed to hold things together while Hunter and Gullett were out and Holtzman forgotten. He went to spring training with the team made on the basis of an 0.68 earned run average at Syracuse and then did everything possible to lose his job. "I've never seen such long home runs and home runs to consecutive batters" is his summary.

Martin insists he wasn't making any decision on Guidry in spring training. "He has made the club for me," Martin said. "Some other people weren't too happy about it." Ah, a knock at the front office by the manager again.

After a two-game absence because of a sore leg, Jackson returned and got a hit. Rivers got three hits, including a homer, and stole a base. Next stop Boston.

Friday, June 17

Boston

Nobody wants to think the worst about Catfish Hunter, not even his worst opponents, but the evidence is ominous. Huner couldn't get out of the first inning against the Red Sox. He couldn't even get past the first batter.

Rick Burleson, leading off, hit a fly ball that just managed to reach the screen on top of the left field wall for a home run. Then Fred Lynn hit a long home run. Hunter got two outs and then Carlton Fisk and George Scott hit long home runs, and Hunter was gone. And there was no way to avoid the implications. "He felt great and that was a good thing," said trainer Gene Monahan, who nursed Hunter through last season and the three months of this season since the start of spring training. But if Hunter feels as good as the trainer said he did and this is the best he can throw, then it's the worst of signs.

"I've seen Cat give up homers back-to-back," Jackson said, "but I've never seen them rock at the plate at will against him like that. Never."

That development is more significant than the Red Sox' 9–4 victory, which lifted them past the Yankees into first place. Remember that Hunter had trouble with his shoulder all last season and was not comfortable this spring until he had a cortisone shot, even though doctors have found no specific injury. He was brilliant on opening day on what amounted to five months' rest. He hurt his foot and next pitched well on a month's rest. Three more quick knockouts and another cortisone shot. He had ten days off and pitched well. Whenever he's pitched in turn, he's had nothing.

"His fastball was straight," Fisk said. "Usually it jumps a little. A couple of pitches had something on them, but they were not even close to being strikes."

If Hunter has neither stuff nor his customary control, then what does he have? Only a lifetime record of 204–145 and 3,-122 innings worn off a thirty-one-year-old arm. And a lot of friends and admirers.

"Everybody likes him," said Bill Campbell, the Red Sox' relief pitcher. "He's a hell of a competitor. I've never seen him throw like that, just pushing the ball, like something is bothering him."

We have become used to Hunter taking his turn and saying his arm doesn't hurt. He'll continue to do that until the pain is unbearable. That's what they mean by "competitor." But it makes Hunter hard to believe except when he says he will not take another cortisone shot. The potential side effects are more frightening to Hunter than the end of his career.

Rather than examine that thought, Martin dwelled animatedly on the objects that were thrown from the stands at his outfielders. Rivers played center field wearing his batting helmet. Martin submitted one of the objects to the umpires and had another on display, a heavy cube of metal about an inch across. It looked like a printer's em quad. "They could flat kill you," Martin said. "That's what I'm concerned about."

Baseball players have had objects thrown at them before and Martin carried on about it long enough to suggest a smokescreen to some people. "How come I've had things thrown at me all season and he's never said a thing?" Jackson asked.

Eventually the smoke blew away and Martin was left with the fact that the Red Sox hit two more homers off Dick Tidrow, and the more sensitive issue of Hunter. "Yes, I'm concerned," Martin said finally. He hedged about whether Hunter would continue to start. "I'll announce that tomorrow—or some other day," Martin said.

The big play came in the third inning, after the Yankees had tied the score, had knocked out Bill Lee, and were working on a big inning. One run was in, runners were on first and third. With rookie Bob Stanley facing his first batter Martin ordered a suicide squeeze bunt by Bucky Dent. Dent missed the pitch, Lou Piniella was trapped off third base, the rally was broken, and the Yankees didn't score again. The Yankees were left to ponder the wisdom of the play and to reject the emphasis on the thrown objects as one more excuse on a club that always seems to have an excuse.

"Throwing things didn't mean nothing," Jackson said. "What's that got to do with the game?" He has an appointment to have his eyes examined on the twenty-third, the day of the makeup of the postponed Met-Yankee game. Jackson won't confirm that. He did suggest, "It could be a good day to have an appointment."

Later, in the hotel bar, there was an interesting collection of a dozen Yankees around the same table. It was as comfortably mixed racially as the Yankees have ever been and the level of stardom ranged from Hunter down to George Zeber.

Saturday, June 18

Boston

The struggle between Martin and Jackson is out in the open. No more uneasy truce, no more pretense of peaceful coexistence. All that ended with the most un-Yankee display when Martin yanked Jackson from the field in the middle of the sixth inning. Martin then apparently tried to fight Jackson in the dugout in full view of jammed Fenway Park and a TV audience from sea to shining sea.

Probably Martin didn't really want to fight Jackson. No matter what Martin's fight record is, he must know better than to fight Jackson. But he wanted to look as if he were challenging Jackson, especially when it was clear Jackson wasn't going to fight. And there were plenty of coaches to hold Martin back. But then again, Martin might be brazen enough actually to throw the first punch.

It was an ugly scene. George Steinbrenner was at a funeral in Cleveland so he didn't see it first-hand, but it was on the television news everywhere. And Gabe Paul was on hand to make his report. Steinbrenner has to make some kind of decision.

If he decides Martin and Jackson can't get along and one has to go, it's not likely to be Jackson. Jackson was Steinbrenner's selection over the advice of Paul and Martin, and self-made millionaires don't like to stand up and say they were wrong.

Martin's display is not anybody's image of what a Yankee manager should be. It was Martin being Martin. And if Martin should hold his job, the bitterness that was revealed in the screaming back and forth in the dugout will still be there. It will not be healed easily.

Neither Jackson nor Martin would specify what was said, and a remarkable number of Yankees remembered being in the latrine when the action took place. But what got through the curtain of silence was that Martin ordered Jackson in from right field with the Red Sox well on their way to a 10–4 victory, their second in two games this series. When Jackson reached the dugout, he bounded down the steps, spread his arms and asked what did he do? Martin took his well-known crisis posture, jaw extended and neck stretched, and said: "Nobody who doesn't hustle plays for me."

Jackson, almost passive, calmly said: "Billy, nothing I can ever do would please you. You don't like me. You don't think I can play ball. You never have from the first day."

"I treat every player the same," Martin rasped, then added a string of unidentified expletives, concluding with a challenge.

Jackson said there was no way he was going to fight and added the one thing Martin could not let go by: "an old man."

Martin used to play a scrappy second base. He is forty-nine years old and a lot of what used to be up around his chest is near his belt now. Jackson is thirty-one, twice Martin's size and hard as a rock. Martin made a move at Jackson and Elston Howard, who first clamped his arms around Jackson, shifted to Martin, pinning him against an upright. Martin wriggled free but was intercepted by Yogi Berra and Dick Howser. Jimmy Wynn was the only player who stirred as peacemaker.

When Howser suddenly became aware of the spectacle the Yankees were making of themselves, he ordered batboy Ray Negron to drape a towel over the NBC camera at the end of the dugout. But the camera reporting the scene was the one across the field next to the Boston dugout.

What ignited the fumes that had been building up for three months was a checked-swing pop fly by Jim Rice that fell safe in right field. The Yankees were already behind, 7–4. Martin conceded that the ball was not catchable but insisted that Jackson could have played it more quickly and made something better than a gentle toss to prevent Rice from reaching second base. "The guy walks to second base," Martin said later. "No way . . . The only thing I ask as a manager is hustle. I told them in spring training, if a player shows up the team, I'll show up the player."

Martin then went to the mound to replace Mike Torrez with Sparky Lyle. When Martin returned to the dugout, he sent Paul Blair out to replace Jackson.

"I was dumbfounded," Jackson said much later, back at his room at the Sheraton Boston. On his lap he had an open Bible, which he said he reads often for solace. He was sipping from a glass of white wine Torrez had brought to the room. "You cut me off if I go too far," Jackson said to Torrez. "The man took a position today to show me up on national TV. Everyone could see that."

Jackson's explanation was that he was playing Rice, the strongest right-handed hitter in the league, over to right center. When the ball dropped shallow and near the line, Jackson first thought second baseman Willie Randolph would run it down, and then Jackson proceeded "cautiously." He is playing an uncertain outfield. When he did get to the ball he was reluctant to throw hard because he has had a bad elbow and so is also an uncertain thrower. With Randolph out of line, there was no cut-off man. Because one runner had advanced to third, Graig Nettles couldn't be the backup. A bad throw might mean two runs.

"You ask him what happened," Martin said. "Then ask his teammates. They will tell you something different."

"Maybe I played it too cautiously," Jackson said. "I did not loaf on the ball. If they think I did, I'm sorry it happened that way."

Players who were asked refused to comment for the record, nor would they say whether they thought it was appropriate for the manager to pull Jackson in the middle of an inning. "My name is Wes," Roy White said. "Did you ever hear that expression?" he said to Willie Randolph. "Street talk: I'm not in this mess."

During his early difficulties, there was divided opinion on Jackson. Now it appears that he has few allies. "Only the big guy up there," said Fred Stanley, meaning Steinbrenner.

Add Fran Healy, who ran to Jackson's side from the bullpen, and Torrez. While Paul held the press at bay outside the clubhouse, Jackson changed clothes immediately and left by a side door at Healy's suggestion. He walked back to the hotel. If Jackson were still in the clubhouse when Martin came in after losing the game, there's no telling how bad a scene would have resulted.

Some of the players said they had never seen a player taken out in the middle of an inning as punishment. Gil Hodges did walk all the way out to left field to remove Cleon Jones early in 1969, in what was later seen as the catalytic event of the Mets' miracle season. But history doesn't seem to mean much here at this time.

There had been a period of calm for a week. Jackson and Munson weren't cordial, but they weren't hostile, either. And Jackson was playing well. He had two hits today, which extended his streak to fourteen games, and they had won ten of fifteen.

"People were giving Reggie the benefit of the doubt," one player said, no longer giving that benefit. "He can play, but if you don't want to, what good is it? From what I saw, Reggie was happy-go-lucky all day, as if he didn't give a rap. Whatever happened, happened. He forgets the other half of his job is to hustle and play defense."

Out in Oakland, Bill North, who played center field beside Jackson and has been an open but friendly critic of Jackson's, watched on television and had no doubt that Jackson had given a good effort. "I've seen Reggie loaf and I know it when I see it; that wasn't it," North said.

In Jackson's mind, that play was only the surface issue. "I can't win here," he said. "I'm alone."

Martin maintains that the recent settled appearance has been deceptive. "The last couple of games he's been second-guessing the hell out of me," he said. "The other players have been telling me. He thinks he's getting them on his side."

"That's not true," Jackson said.

What happened before the game may be what actually set Martin off. Martin was discussing his order of the squeeze play with Bucky Dent and turned to Jackson farther down the bench for affirmation. "Reggie, don't you think it was a good play?" Martin asked. Jackson answered, "No." Right then Martin saw himself being shown up by a man he didn't want in the first place.

"I don't know anything about managing, but I'll take the heat for whatever the manager says," Jackson said, looking up from his Bible at the hotel. At one point he dropped to his knees and threw out his arms. "I play right field when they let me. I hit anywhere from third to seventh. I do anything they tell me to do. I'll continue to play well all year. I won't ask to be traded. Thank God I'm a Christian. Christ got my mind right. I won't fight the man. I'll do whatever they tell me."

Abruptly, Jackson dropped his reserve and showed all of his pain in a tirade of profanity. "It makes me cry, the way they treat me on this team," he said. "The Yankee pinstripes are Ruth and Gehrig and DiMaggio and Mantle. I'm a nigger to them and I just don't know how to be subservient. I'm making seven hundred thousand a year and they treat me like dirt. They've never had anyone like me on their team before."

He made an exception for Steinbrenner. "I love that man; he treats me like I'm somebody," Jackson said. "The rest of them treat me like dirt."

What the next step might be, Jackson said he couldn't guess. "I got to go out and play to the best of my ability. If the press keeps messing with me . . ." Then he keenly categorized the reporters covering the team that day. "Jacobson, he's on my side. Pepe, he's on Martin's side. Hecht is just interested in a story. Montgomery [Paul Montgomery of the *Times*, who has covered such things as revolutions in Latin America and the killing of the students before the Mexico City Olympics], he couldn't care less either way."

He tried to be light for a moment, but couldn't hold it. He had revised thoughts about asking to be traded. "I can go," he said, sounding like Kirk Douglas pounding his chest and bleating, "How do you know how I feel inside?" Jackson is ready to decide now that he won't be here next year. "I'd go at half the price," he said. "I got nine million, what do I need two hundred thousand to take this for?"

Martin would accept the departure readily. "We won without him last year," he said. That's precisely the view Jackson has felt from their first meeting.

Paul plans to meet with Martin and Jackson in the morning. Actually, the meeting was set for tonight. Jackson was there but Martin didn't show up.

And before the shit hit the fan, Hunter had been told he had been reassigned to the bullpen.

Sunday, June 19

Boston

The crisis manager has his crisis. He chose to take his stand on his conduct of the Jackson affair, and it may be Billy the Kid's last stand.

If Martin was trying to pull the team together and assert his own strength by taking advantage of the general resentment of Jackson, he may have succeeded among the players. But Steinbrenner is totally opposed. He watched the television replay over and over and didn't see the crime as Martin did. Nor did Steinbrenner view the punishment as appropriate. Most important, Steinbrenner thought Martin was doing a poor job in the first place.

"The team looks out of control," Steinbrenner said. Since he was severely criticized for interfering a month and a half ago, Steinbrenner has largely left the operation of the team to Martin, with Paul as overseer. Steinbrenner said he was leaving this matter in Paul's hands, too, but Steinbrenner will join the club in Detroit tomorrow and he is angry enough to fire Martin on the spot. He was humiliated by Martin's action in full view of 25,000,000 witnesses, by Steinbrenner's count.

The manager and the star maintained their opposite stances even after their reconciliation meeting in Paul's room this morning. "He said he was hustling," Martin said. "I told him, 'Maybe what you think you're doing and what my eyes are telling me are two different things.' "

The players I questioned agreed with Martin: "To me it looked like Reggie was not dogging it." Steinbrenner said, "I think he's been putting out pretty good."

The second part of the affair was the manager's pulling Jackson out of the game immediately after the play. Some of the players think that embarrassment was the only way to reach Jackson while a mere fine would have had no effect.

Again Steinbrenner disagreed. "I could have waited to talk to him in the locker room later. It was a bad scene that good sense would have avoided."

Martin wasn't hired for good sense. Tumult has always

been his element. And when it looked as if the team was finally settling into a calm, he has created crisis. When he had to be physically held away from Jackson in the dugout—even though it may have been only a charade—Steinbrenner was horrified. "No manager should do that," Steinbrenner said. "He tried to get at him three times."

From the beginning Martin made it clear that it wasn't his choice that brought Jackson to the Yankees. From the beginning Jackson felt sorry for his decision to come here and may have sought his own unhappiness. Martin certainly hasn't soothed the situation. Paul is certain to tell Steinbrenner about the tone of the breakfast meeting. "Naturally, it didn't start out well, but I think it ended up very well," Paul said. What happened was that Martin rose up out of his chair, called Jackson "boy," and challenged him right there.

If that's where they were this morning, how compatible can they ever be? How can this team ever be the 1927 Yankees with Babe Ruth in right field, as Steinbrenner dreams? He doesn't think Martin has worked hard enough at preparing the team or himself.

The difficulty in firing Martin, though, remains. Who could Steinbrenner give the job to? Yogi Berra is certainly calm, but Steinbrenner doesn't have much respect for Berra. He doesn't think much of Dick Howser, or Bobby Cox, or Elston Howard. Steinbrenner likes the heavyweight image of Frank Robinson, just fired in Cleveland, but the first black manager brings his own problems that would be insoluble here if Jackson were seen by the other players as the cause of Martin's firing.

Add to that mess the wretched game the Yankees played today, the wretched series they played here, and the observations Ed Figueroa made afterward. They were pounded by the Red Sox, 11–1, coming after losses of 9–4 and 10–4. In three games the Red Sox collected 30 runs and 44 hits, and they hit 16 home runs, a record for a three-game series. Thirteen of them would have been home runs in any national park; the Yankees didn't hit even one Fenway Park home run.

Jackson had no comment today about the whole affair, but he had trouble with the bright sun and overthrew a cutoff. He hit a couple of line drives that were caught and had his hitting streak ended at fourteen games. It's the mode of the team to accuse him of not caring enough, but Figueroa blames everybody for not caring enough. "They don't give a shit," he said.

Normally Figueroa keeps his thoughts to himself. "Go ahead and write it," he said. "I'm not afraid to say it. It's the truth. If they don't like it, fuck it. You see them in the showers playing tricks on each other. If you lose three games in Boston, you should be quiet. Now they're going to Detroit and drink and play cards on the plane. In Detroit they will drink and play cards again."

This devastating collection of Yankees has won seven games more than it has lost. Figueroa, who held the Red Sox to one of their five home runs in his 4½ innings today, has lost three in a row and his back has been bothering him. Dick Tidrow is healthy, but he gave up three homers today and six in two appearances here.

Now, in the emergency, Martin is calling on Ken Holtzman to start tomorrow. They need him and Holtzman warned about that weeks ago: "By the time I can find myself, it may be too late," he repeated. "I tried to tell them that."

Steinbrenner is worried about what happens right now. He is worried about the frame of mind they will take into the Boston series next weekend at Yankee Stadium. "We're at a point now where we could go right out of it, or come back," he said. If they don't come back, Steinbrenner may feel he has no choice but to get rid of Martin, whoever the replacement. Steinbrenner says it will be Paul's decision, but nobody believes that.

Those are the trials and tribulations of Billy Martin. "Nobody's trials and tribulations are any worse than mine," Jackson said.

The irony is that Holtzman and Jackson, who feel so alienated from this team, are in a position to save Martin's job. Through the movement of packing bags and eating ice cream in the clubhouse, their eyes met and they smiled broadly to each other. "Sometimes," Holtzman said, "Reggie and I can understand each other without speaking."

* * *

Late tonight Jackson was on New York television with a taped pregame interview with Jenny Paul, Gabe's daughter. Jackson took another shot at the New York press. "They can't accept the idea of a black man being as smart as they are," he said. Sometimes there is no understanding Reggie.

Present Tense

The tension of the day played like a remake of *High Noon*. From the lobby of the posh Pontchartrain Hotel to rusting Tiger Stadium, from early morning to late tonight, everywhere you looked there was another irony. It ended up with Martin keeping his job at a price he would not have paid for any other.

Jackson has publicly appeared to have backed down. He appealed to Steinbrenner to save Martin's job. He referred to a passage in the scriptures that tells him to be obedient to his superiors. In actuality, it's Martin who has backed down. He has chosen to accept the obvious loss of face. In order to keep the job that means everything to him, Martin has promised to accept everything management demands. In Steinbrenner's suite late in the afternoon, when it appeared that Martin was about to be fired, he begged.

At that point, the decision had already been made not to fire him. Early in the day, Steinbrenner and Paul had determined that Martin would be fired, but then, as Paul often says, "until it's been done, it hasn't been done."

The day began with a story by Milt Richman on the United States International wire that Martin would be fired today and Berra named manager. For Martin, it began with his phone ringing with one newspaper or radio station after another asking him for a comment on the story. So Phil Rizzuto, the broadcaster who played shortstop to Martin's second base and is still the man closest to Martin, insisted that they find sanctuary on the golf course. Meantime, Rizzuto fielded Martin's calls.

When Berra was questioned, he said it was the first he had heard of the news. He said the job hadn't been offered to him, and that he might not take it if it were. He said he didn't think any of the coaches would take it, either. Howser and Cox have never managed and a shot at this job at this point might be the end of their aspirations.

Paul insisted that neither he nor Steinbrenner was the source of Richman's story.

Once Martin and Rizzuto left for the golf course, much of the next act was played in the lobby of the Pontchartrain and the sundries shop off the lobby, where there are racks of books, magazines, and greeting cards that shield hidden discussions.

On the way to brunch, Jackson stopped for a newspaper and confided, "I hope he doesn't get fired. If he does, it will be over me. I don't want to be the reason for any man being fired." That's enlightened self-interest. There's also a strain of compassion in Jackson even for an antagonist. "I am not a vengeful man," Jackson said.

If Martin were fired, the Jackson affair would be only the last stroke. Steinbrenner and Paul have more than enough in their minds to be rid of Martin without the Jackson bit. But Jackson feels himself the center of every issue and he certainly doesn't want the ugliness of being blamed the rest of the season. Besides, if Martin is gone, then Jackson loses the best reason for easing himself out of his Yankee commitment.

Shortly after noon, Steinbrenner arrived from Cleveland and found a telegram from Frank Robinson's agent, applying for the job. Steinbrenner found Jackson and, among the bookracks, Jackson appealed on Martin's behalf.

At that time, Fran Healy, who had spoken at length with Jackson in Boston Sunday, was at lunch with Thurman Munson. Healy wanted to bring about a conciliation between Jackson and Martin, but he was also working to pull Munson and Jackson together, which would also help the Jackson-Martin situation. When Healy returned to the hotel, he found Jackson and they went to Healy's room.

Shortly afterward, word spread through the lobby that if Martin were fired, Jackson would go home. The man whose relationship with Martin had been the biggest source of friction was now working to keep Martin in the job.

The discussions with Jackson led Healy back to Steinbrenner in the hotel lobby. They sat side by side, backs against the wall on a bench under the portrait of the late duke of Pontchartrain, and Steinbrenner began to be moved from his position. "He gave me an insight into what the guys on the team were thinking," Steinbrenner said later.

While that was going on, Martin was returning from his round of golf, which was hardly golf and no escape. "He wasn't even looking at the ball," Rizzuto said. "Every third hole he'd ask me, 'Call up the hotel and see if I'm fired.' " Rizzuto told him not to worry because "one hundred percent" of the calls and letters to the station had been in Martin's favor. "If Steinbrenner and the front office are good businessmen, you won't be fired," Rizzuto told Martin. Martin wouldn't believe that.

In Paul's room, Texas owner Brad Corbett was on the phone. He had already fired Martin once, but Eddie Stanky had walked out on the job after managing the Rangers for one day and Corbett was inquiring about Martin's status with the Yankees before hiring again. Players were forming decisions of their own. Lyle and Wynn decided they were going to leave the club if Martin was fired.

After Healy and Steinbrenner concluded their session, Healy sought out Martin and laid out the situation. Then Martin phoned Steinbrenner and went to the owner's suite. Time was growing late. It was nearly 5:30 and the team bus was due to leave for the ball park at six o'clock.

Martin was shaken. "Am I gone?" Martin asked Steinbrenner.

"Your ass is fired," Steinbrenner said.

Steinbrenner had by then decided to keep Martin. Now the owner was in the position to force Martin to examine his ways, to make concessions, to make Martin grovel. He warned that if Martin lost this job he would not get another.

"If you're going to fire me," Martin said, near tears, "please give me dignity. I promise I'll never say one thing bad about the Yankees. Tell me what I have to do."

"You don't prepare. You don't go to meetings. You missed the meeting before the World Series, for God's sake," Steinbrenner lectured. "From the start of the game until the last out, you have no peers. But you're going to have to take the rest of the shit that goes with it.

"What you did last year was good enough to win, not to

repeat. You have to work ten times as hard to repeat." He exacted promises from Martin, including one that he would be more "flexible" in his handling of Jackson. That undoubtedly was the most painful concession for Martin. But then, Martin says that he has bent to demands here in the past that would have made him quit his three previous jobs before he was fired.

"Down deep, Billy's a hell of a guy," Steinbrenner said. "He's a Yankee through and through. He bleeds Yankee. If anybody had taken this away from him, it would have killed him."

Next, Jackson was called into the session and Steinbrenner virtually forced the two into conversation. Then Martin and Jackson took the short cab ride together to the ball park and appeared in the clubhouse with their arms on each other's shoulders. "We are allies," Jackson announced.

During batting practice Martin sat on the bench with all the questions still swirling about him. He still had the job, but he knew how close he had come to losing it and how little security he could ever have.

"I've taken a lot," Martin said, his voice trembling, his face gray. He did not tell Steinbrenner to keep the job. "Yes, it's the Yankees," Martin said, very softly adding the pledge of allegiance. "I couldn't let the New York fans down. They depend on me to pull the team through. I've got an obligation." There was no Billy the Kid in his voice.

He said he never was mad at Reggie. "A manager can't let personal feelings enter into it." Then he found a parallel in history for his trials. "I wonder how Truman felt when he dropped that bomb?" he said. "Nothing is easy if you lead. Either you're a leader or a follower."

He was choosing his words carefully. "I'm trying to be careful," he said. "I don't want the press hurting this club any more, or hurting management. I'm management, too."

Steinbrenner and Paul arrived shortly before the end of batting practice, the decision having been sealed, and called the team together. With neither the press nor the mass of players informed of the decision, Steinbrenner drew the picture for the team. He touched on the smoke of racial conflict that Jackson had introduced. "God damn it, I don't want any more bullshit about race—black, white, or purple," Steinbrenner said.

"Do you know how close your manager came to being

fired? Everybody in every city is trying to pull us apart. If you guys are pulling against each other, we don't have a chance to win."

Martin emerged from his last words with Steinbrenner with tears in his eyes. Steinbrenner is mindful that Martin has made and broken promises before. "Billy was shook, shook," Steinbrenner said. "It may really have hit home for the first time."

How much Jackson's intercession had to do with saving Martin is locked in Steinbrenner's mind. Jackson feels he had much to do with it. "If we didn't think we could get all the aspects healed, it would have made no difference," Steinbrenner said. But it would not be possible to keep Martin in the job if the owner came out and said that the man the manager had humiliated had indeed saved his job.

It's more likely that the combination of promises of cooperation by Jackson, Martin, and Munson were more influential than any one thing Jackson said.

When the game began, Gabe Paul went up to the press box to announce that the organization had decided not to change managers at this time. Steinbrenner stayed in his seat behind the Yankee dugout, saying that it had been Paul's decision but indicating that Steinbrenner, of course, had made the final decision.

"If the man will grow up, he will be the greatest manager in baseball history," Steinbrenner said. Growing up at the age of forty-nine is very difficult when a man has been Billy Martin all his life. He spends less time at the ball park than any manager around, according to players and coaches.

And now players wonder whether the concessions and Jackson's intercession have left Martin with no balls at all. "I think he still has our respect," Fred Stanley said, "but you know it can't be the same as it was."

* * *

How inextricably Martin and Jackson are linked was demonstrated in the ball game that followed as the anticlimax. Martin wanted so much to win the first game of his new life, and Jackson wanted so much to do well under the scrutiny of the day. And then Jackson missed the fly ball that led to the winning run in a 2–1 defeat.

Jackson's pain was real and obvious. "I couldn't feel

worse," he said later. "That's probably the worst I've ever felt on a ball field. I ought to quit. Give up."

It had been a grueling day. Don Gullett pitched his best game as a Yankee and Mark Fidrych was dazzling for the Tigers. Jackson drove in the first run with a sacrifice fly in the top of the fourth and the Tigers tied it in the bottom of the inning. There was no hint that either team would score again until the Detroit seventh.

A leadoff walk, and Jackson ran in for Mickey Stanley's line drive to right field. Jackson reached up his glove for the ball and at the last moment ducked away. The ball sailed over his right shoulder for two bases and then Aurelio Rodriguez singled home the winning run.

Just minutes before, the Tigers had announced that their lights had been measured as the brightest in the American League. Jackson lost the ball in the lights.

When the half inning was over, Jackson went directly through the dugout into the seclusion of the clubhouse. Martin and Dick Tidrow, who has not been a great supporter of Jackson's, either, followed to console him. "What would you have done?" Tidrow said.

"He felt so bad," Martin said. "We told him not to fault himself."

Maybe for a while there can be some shared feelings. Before long, Jackson changed his clubhouse stance. "If it had to happen to somebody," he said, "I'm glad it happened to me. People expect it of me."

In the Tiger clubhouse Fidrych expressed the resentment against the Yankees felt by many players around the league. He allowed himself a laugh at the discomfort of the man he called "Steinberger."

"You can't go out and buy everything in life," Fidrych said. "If they finish second, that'll prove it. They'll watch the World Series just like us."

*   *   *

The day's manipulations were not over; Healy was still at work. He convinced Munson and Jackson to have a late supper with him. They spent three hours at it. "You'll see," Steinbrenner said. "Thurman and Reggie will be much closer after this."

Tuesday, June 21

The next question is whether the cure was as lethal as the affliction.

One immediate effect of Steinbrenner's maneuvering was the reconciliation—partial, anyhow—of Munson and Jackson. Munson had been resisting taking the big steps. Jackson gives Healy credit for working out the agreement. "I think Thurman has actually wanted it for a long time," Jackson said. "So have I."

They were cordial enough in the clubhouse, even after losing again, for Munson to ask Jackson to "please" get him a soda and for Jackson to comply. "Thanks."

Their thaw can mean a considerable lessening of the tension for the whole club. Meantime, Munson feels he was made the patsy by Steinbrenner. He resents that Steinbrenner virtually directed him to make peace with Jackson in order to save Martin.

Munson's resentment toward Steinbrenner has been building ever since Munson felt Steinbrenner was welching on salary promises last winter. Now he feels that he was given the title of captain and then made to play a role secondary to Jackson. He feels he has been forced into being an intermediary in situations that weren't his responsibility.

Yesterday Steinbrenner told Munson he was shirking his duties as captain. "I thought Jackson was the captain," Munson replied.

"You're the captain," Steinbrenner barked. "When I want Jackson to be my captain, I'll tell him, and you too. You're the captain. Now be the captain."

Munson grumbles at that. "One day they stress one thing and the next day something else: Reggie and I have to get along, then Billy and I," Munson said. "If they just let us go out and let us play, we'll get together. It's been something all year.

"One thing pisses me off: I can't stand to be part of a circus every day. It's like the fucking big top here. I'd rather be on a last-place club, enjoying myself."

This may turn out some day to be a very good baseball team, and Munson likes winning more than the next guy, but there is no hint that it ever will be any fun to be on this team.

Nobody can see an escape from the inflammability here as long as these personalities are together. There are side effects yet to be counted of these fifty-four hours that shook the franchise. Just the thought that Martin had been at the brink disturbed some players. Munson is annoyed at Steinbrenner's emphasis on the three games with the Red Sox this weekend in New York. "Coming in and saying this is the most important series of the year," Munson snorted. "We got enough series all year."

Some players entirely dismissed what Steinbrenner had to say last night. "He's talking about some other sport, not an every-day game," Roy White said.

Now Steinbrenner says he's going to be more active after two months of silence. "We're going down the rat hole if this keeps up," he said. "I'm going to project myself into it and take the blame from this point on." He conceded that he made the decision to keep Martin. But his respect for the way Martin handles the job is as thin as ever.

"How long can you sit back and watch when your manager doesn't return the general manager's calls, doesn't show up for meetings? I had to step in."

Steinbrenner was speaking from his home in Tampa. Wisely, he had told Paul to leave the club and give it a chance to relax after its trauma. But the tension was still evident. The Tigers beat them again 5–2, and Martin was there in the walk-in closet office, but he was Little Billy, and Billy the Kid was nowhere to be seen. There was no carrying on about the umpires, no defiance of the press.

"I'm going to tell Billy to loosen up now," Steinbrenner said. "I'm going to tell him, 'Get your ass moving. Don't go into a shell. That's the one thing I don't want you to do.'"

But that's what has happened to the team as a whole. They were smothered by a pitcher named Jim Crawford and lost their fifth straight. They struck out ten times, five times on called third strikes. Taking strikes is a fundamental indication of hitters' being too careful.

Now the Yankees have slipped 4½ games behind Boston and a lot of us are waiting for the other shoe to drop—kick Martin out of office. "Of course he'll be fired unless we start winning," Jackson said. "We all know it," Jimmy Wynn agreed.

Steinbrenner insists that's not so. He said he had a different concept of the action that so many players feel brought tempestuous Billy to his knees. "If he doesn't do the things we agreed upon, he's finished," Steinbrenner warned. "But if he loses, there's no danger the rest of the year—as long as he does those things."

What are the long-lasting effects of Jackson's role in saving Martin's job? "I don't think he had that much to do with it," Martin said. More would be too difficult for him to concede.

Have Steinbrenner's repeated demands to drive players harder and his proclamation of how close he came to firing Martin in effect left Martin with no clout at all?

"The players know that's not so," Martin said. "I can tell. If my balls were cut off, I would have walked out. I've always said I had to manage my own way. If I don't, my value as a manager isn't any good. Every place I've been, players have given me the complete hundred percent. I get more out of them than a lot of managers ever got. How can you push them more?

"I've played the game as a player on a winner, coached on a winner, managed in the minor leagues, been a scout in the major leagues, and managed winners in the major leagues. I think I have a conception of how to motivate players and their breaking point—when to push them and when to back off. The game is every day; mental pressure is so great; the constant travel, it tends to wear them out mentally."

Steinbrenner is full of the idea of spending everything to win now, of bulletin-board motivation, of the notion of the big series the players object to. He is impressed by the technology of computer printouts like a football coach. He is impressed by the Gene Mauch cerebral approach. Martin worships Casey Stengel, not Univac.

"What did Mauch ever win?" Martin asked. Nothing, actually. "My mind is a computer," Martin said. "I know what guys hit in situations, where others pitch . . . Don't they think I'm going over things all the time when I'm driving to the park and back? I'm thinking all the time when I'm playing golf—what I should say to the players, if it will upset them or make them play better. What's the good of telling a pitcher a guy can't hit a slow curve if the pitcher doesn't have a slow curve?"

Even more than earlier attendance at the ball park, Steinbrenner wants Martin to keep in contact and not to miss appointments. Martin had trouble in Minnesota because he preferred to drink in the lively press bar at the ball park when Calvin Griffith wanted discussions in his office.

Steinbrenner has made that an ultimatum. "You cannot have an organization with no respect for the guy who gives the orders," said the man who gives the orders. "He's not going to push me to the wall without getting thrown over it."

And if the winning and losing isn't turned around, whatever the disclaimers, who can expect Martin to survive for long?

Right now they have played five games in the best home-run ball parks in the league and have not hit one. Tomorrow night lefties Chambliss and Rivers will sit against the left-handed pitcher and Martin will go with an all right-handed lineup, except for Jackson.

Wednesday, June 22

Detroit

Martin was still reeling when he left the clubhouse in the aftermath of a remarkable game won. "Out of my way before I pass out," Martin said with a mock stagger. It was his wife, Gretchen, whose relationship with Martin has been no less stormy than his managerial career, who reached out and touched him on the cheek.

"Aren't they ever easy on you?" she asked.

"No," Martin said, shaking his head.

What ever remained easy or simple for Martin? What condition was ever so serene that he couldn't turn it into a crisis? They took a 7–2 lead, fell behind, 10–7, with Sparky Lyle pitching, then scored five runs in the top of the eighth to go ahead, 12–10. And then Ken Clay had to get the last out for Lyle with the bases loaded. That's what left Martin reeling. But it was the game on the field that had done it and that's a lot simpler than what's been going on. On the good side, the Yankees had scored 12 runs on 13 hits. Nettles had hit his fourteenth home run, Cliff Johnson his first as a Yankee, Munson had three hits and Jackson two.

It broke the five-game losing streak and stirred some life into the Yankees. "We needed a win," Lyle said. "We needed that. We had to win a game before we went back to New York to play Boston this weekend. Lately we've been getting our asses beaten and we just needed this."

The appearance was his 577th in relief—a record for a pitcher who has never started a game.

Thursday, June 23

New York

How irrational are the Yankees? They complicated an exhibition game with the Mets; they couldn't get their stories straight about Reggie Jackson's eye examination. That's how irrational.

"What eye exam?" Jackson said when he arrived at the clubhouse at Shea Stadium. "I didn't have an eye exam."

Perhaps Jackson was up-tight about the implications that his fielding was so bad there must be something wrong with his vision. But the scheduled appointment was known for some time, and Martin mentioned it in explaining the absence of Jackson from the lineup for the Mayor's Trophy Game.

"He did?" Jackson said. "If that's what the man said, I guess I did. I got nothing to say about nothing."

In the process of testing for new lenses, Jackson's eyes were thoroughly examined and the drops used to dilate the pupils left his vision blurred. So he didn't play. "I wish you guys would stop trying to make so much about it." Jackson said. "I just went to have my eyes examined."

The Mets beat the Yankees, 6–4, in the routine of what once was a classic ritual between the two rivals for the affection of the city.

The interesting bit of news is that Martin has decided to take Hunter off the bullpen list and start him in the opening game of the Red Sox series tomorrow night. "Let's face it," Dick Tidrow said. "Billy's looking for anything to give this team a lift. He's using Catfish for emotional reasons." It's a gamble a manager makes only with a pitcher who has a special place in the thinking of his teammates.

If Hunter can struggle through the first couple of innings

and find himself at a time the Yankees are beginning to doubt themselves, he can reverse the trends single-handedly.

Friday, June 24

New York

It was the kind of game baseball fans dream about like the surfer dreams of the perfect wave: the Yankees and the Red Sox opening a big series on a beautiful Friday night before the largest crowd in the new Yankee Stadium and the largest regular season crowd at night in the Bronx since 1961. The Dodgers and the Giants are gone as a rivalry these many years, and the Yankees and the Red Sox are the last of the perennial rivals, with feelings that stir both players and fans.

For the Yankees it was the kind of game that qualifies to be called a victory and not just a win. They won it on a single by Reggie Jackson in the eleventh inning, 6–5. They tied it with two out in the last of the ninth inning on a two-run home run by Roy White, and, if the Yankees do win the championship, that home run is worth remembering as a turning point.

The Red Sox came to town hot as can be. They had won seven in a row and thirteen of fourteen. They had a five-game lead over the Yankees and were pounding out home runs at the staggering pace of 30 in their previous nine games. The Yankees have been threatening to break apart.

A week ago the Red Sox pounded Catfish Hunter for four homers in the first inning. This time the Red Sox hit three homers off him in the first four innings, but he lasted into the ninth. Carl Yastrzemski and Butch Hobson homered to give Boston a 3–1 lead and Paul Blair's first homer as a Yankee tied the score in the second inning.

George Scott homered after a walk to Yastrzemski in the fourth inning and the game ground into the ninth inning with the Red Sox leading, 5–3. The Yankees had knocked out two pitchers but hadn't been able to score again. Lyle replaced Hunter with runners on second and third in the top of the ninth and got Fred Lynn on a foul pop to end the inning.

Then all the Yankees had to do was tie the score against Bill Campbell, who has fifteen saves already. Campbell got

the first two outs. Willie Randolph lined a drive to left center.
Yastrzemski, a skilled outfielder, cut across from left field
and appeared to overtake the ball, but it sailed behind his
frantic grab and Randolph wound up with a triple. White hit
the next pitch for a home run.

It was in that inning that Jackson entered the game as a
pinch hitter. The role infuriated him. He was removed from
the original starting lineup, Billy Martin said, because his
vision was still impaired by the drops. Martin wrote White's
name in Jackson's slot, which eventually made for good
drama, but renewed hostilities between Jackson and the manager.

The route by which Jackson got into the game describes
Martin's conflict with Jackson. Martin sent a coach to ask
Jackson about his vision before the game, and Jackson gave
what was interpreted as a less-than-certain reply that he
wanted to play. Martin inquired of the trainer, who was no
more positive. Martin then made the decision. It shocked
Jackson. Martin never went to ask Jackson personally.

Jackson feels he has earned that courtesy. For years Casey
Stengel went to Mickey Mantle to ask if his injuries would
permit him to play. Dick Williams went directly to Jackson
in Oakland. Martin feels he shouldn't have to go to Jackson.
Martin will not treat Jackson as a Mantle. He doesn't have to
with most of his players. But what's so difficult about asking
Jackson, if it means that much to him? The newer breed of
manager sees communication as the greatest requirement of
the job. Martin either doesn't understand that or refuses to
accept the need. He's often said he wishes managing the team
were as easy as managing the game.

During the second inning Jackson was examined by the
team physician, Dr. Maurice Cowens, and was told he could
play. Gabe Paul then got word to Martin that Jackson was
available.

"I don't want to comment about that," Jackson said later.

Were his eyes okay? "My eyes are okay."

How did he feel before the game? "I forget how I felt. I
forget a lot of things lately . . . I can't say anything. If you
were in my water for a week, you'd understand why."

In any case, Jackson could see well enough when he came
to bat in the eleventh inning. Graig Nettles led off with a
walk from lefty Ramon Hernandez, Boston's fourth pitcher.
Mickey Rivers, another late entry into the game, fouled away

a sacrifice, but Hernandez balked Nettles to second. Rivers was intentionally walked to set up a double play, but Jackson lined the first pitch into right field, scoring Nettles with the winning run. That turned the boos for Jackson to cheers and sent several of the Yankees out to first base to give Jackson the welcome he thrives on.

"It had to be nice for him, considering all the controversy around here," White said, willing to accept the smaller half of the credit for the comeback.

Jackson was less willing to accept his credit. "Yes, I feel good," he said with no enthusiasm.

Was he excited about it? "Yes, I was excited."

Did it make him happy? "Oh, yes, I'm happy. Real happy."

Jackson sees himself as a "gamer," a player who rises to the occasion in big games and big situations. He felt he should be in this game even at less than full strength and was offended by the ease with which he was taken out of the lineup. The decisive hit was his evidence.

"Just lucky, I guess," he said.

Lucky to be a Yankee? "Mmmmmm," Reggie Jackson said.

Even on the best of nights, the Yankees cannot entirely enjoy themselves.

Saturday, June 25

New York

The Red Sox home-run streak is dead and gone, thanks to Mike Torrez. Now it's the Yankees who are threatening to sweep the Red Sox.

Seven days after being strafed for thirteen hits and three homers in less than six innings, Torrez stopped the Red Sox, 5–1. It wasn't quite what his agent, Gary Walker, suggested before the game when he said, "If Mike pitches a no-hitter, Gabe is going to give him everything he wants," but who's counting.

So it wasn't a no-hitter, but the Red Sox, who had amassed 33 homers in their last ten games, never got the lead. Mickey Rivers led off the first inning with a home run against Luis

Tiant and Graig Nettles hit a three-run homer in the fourth. With the help of two extraordinary plays at third base by Nettles, Torrez got fifteen outs on ground balls.

Tomorrow Torrez' agent and Gabe Paul are to meet to discuss a long-term contract. And Martin has announced that Torrez now goes into a four-day rotation—which is what he's wanted since he came—while the rest of the staff is moved around him. There is less encouragement on the contract front. "I'd like to get it resolved," Torrez said. "If not, I'll be a free agent in two months. If they don't have the money, someone out there does."

Sunday, June 26

New York

There won't be any better weekends for the Yankees this season—unless there's a champagne party involved. They beat the Red Sox in dramatic style Friday night, almost routinely yesterday, and then again today in high drama: 5–4 with two out in the last of the ninth. The Yankees have swept the series and can search themselves for the reasons why.

"We changed our attitude a little bit," Thurman Munson said. "But I'm not gonna expand on that. That's horseshit over the dam."

They won the game because the Red Sox loaded the bases against Don Gullett with none out in the first inning and got only one run. That was a team that scored 30 runs, hit 16 homers in their three-game sweep in Boston last weekend. Now the Red Sox have been held without a homer for twenty-five innings and have lost three straight games for the first time since last July. The Yankees, who were on the verge of disintegration, have won four in a row and are within two games of first place.

They convinced a crowd of 55,039, largest regular-season crowd at the new Yankee Stadium, and reminded themselves of the joy it is beating the Red Sox. "I never knew this thing between the Yankees and Boston was so big until I got here," said Nettles, who came from the Indians five seasons ago. "When you play in Cleveland, you don't hear much about what goes on every place else. Last week, let's face it, we were embarrassed."

The winning run came on a single by Paul Blair with two out and the bases loaded in the last of the ninth. It was a suitable conclusion to the kind of game the Yankees played. Chris Chambliss made three fine plays at first base. They stole three bases, including a double steal. Gullett pitched until one out in the ninth. Dick Tidrow pitched to one batter for the second out and Sparky Lyle came on to get the final out.

"When you're doing things right, hit-and-run, stealing bases, doing everything you're able to do, well, that just makes baseball fun," Roy White said. "It was a pleasure to play in a game like that."

White had two hit-and-run singles, each resulting in a run. Rivers and Munson each had three hits. And they won, which can be the most fun of all. They had a 4–1 lead and the fans were beginning to beat the rush out of the ball park when the Red Sox scored three runs in the top of the ninth to tie the score. The game won, Nettles brushed off that threat. "All it did," he said, "was get all those people back out of the parking lots."

In the bottom of the ninth Campbell got the first out, but loaded the bases on a walk to White, a hit-and-run single by Munson, and an intentional walk to Chambliss.

That brought up Blair, who had replaced Jackson in right field in the top of the inning. With the infield drawn in, the count went to two and two, and Blair chopped a single over third base. "I was trying to hit a grand slam," Blair said, "but I would have been satisfied with a fly ball."

It was such a terrific weekend for the Yankees that the pitchers who had been shell-shocked last week in Boston could joke about it.

Hunter could tell about the phone call he received from his father, Abbott, after giving up four home runs in six batters. "Boy, what ails you?" the father asked.

"Nothing," the son said. He says he could hear laughter at his father's end of the line.

"You got to throw one at their head and, next, one at their feet," the father said. "And then they won't be hanging in there."

Hunter said he even dreamed about that game afterward. He dreamed his home was being dive-bombed by airplanes.

Tidrow pitched twice in Boston for an ignominious total of six home runs in five innings. "No," he said, "pitchers do not get whiplash from experiences like that. Most guys turn slowly and say, 'Stay?' " There was a question mark at the end of the plea.

As a result, he was given himself a new nickname. He's been known as "Dirt" for some time. Take three Yankees, nude and fresh out of the shower, ask which one is called Dirt and you automatically pick out Tidrow. He even had Dirt written on his undershirts for identification. Now he has crossed that out and relettered, "The Long Ranger."

It was the end of the series, but hardly the end of what goes on among the Yankees. "When all this is over," Martin said, "I think I'll open a nursery." In his day, ball players were ball players.

Monday, June 27

Toronto

Jimmy Wynn had wanted to show New York that the Toy Cannon was not just a tall tale in miniature from Texas. It's going to be hard for Wynn now. Staying with the Yankees—staying in the big leagues—may be a problem. Those saddest of thoughts filled Wynn's mind as he dressed.

Wynn had two hits in his last fifty at bats going into the ninth inning. Now the figure is two hits in fifty-one and the expansion Blue Jays beat the Yankees, 7–6. Wynn was called out on strikes while the Yankees were making their last menacing gestures. Billy Martin and Dick Howser said they thought the pitch was outside and that the umpire hurt them with a lot of other calls, too. It was Martin's first complaint—however modest—about umpires since the shock of nearly losing his job last week.

But then Wynn thought the first pitch he saw as a pinch hitter with the bases full was a pitch to drive, a fastball high and inside, right where the Toy Cannon wanted it. "I knew exactly what he was going to throw and I couldn't pull the trigger," Wynn lamented. "I haven't played in so long I can't judge velocity."

Wynn said he had experienced tougher situations in his fifteen seasons, but not many and not much tougher. With one out and trailing, 7–4, the Yankees filled the bases. With Lou Piniella serving the first day of his delayed three-day suspension, Wynn was sent up to bat for Chicken Stanley knowing just how important the opportunity was for him.

"I had to put a lot of emphasis on that one at bat; I may not get up again for two weeks," Wynn said. "I thought, 'Hit one good and they'll think of me sooner next time.' The walk back to the dugout was three miles long."

With two out, Mickey Rivers singled home two runs and Roy White walked, filling the bases for Thurman Munson. Munson struck out, ending the game, and Martin turned back to the umpiring. "What happens if Wynn walks?" Martin insisted. "We tie the score."

Wynn had his own thoughts. He is thirty-five years old, and with this season approaching the halfway point, he has only 76 at bats and a .145 average. He can see little opportunity ahead. That makes matters worse; he never has been able to adjust his long stroke to part-time action. "With Piniella playing now, unless somebody gets hurt, I can't see any action ahead in the next three months," Wynn said. He is a superior base runner and not a bad outfielder. "I feel good, my legs are good. Give me a chance and I'll prove I'm still alive." It was a plea, but it looks like all the chances are gone now."

Tuesday, June 28

Toronto

After sweeping three games from the Red Sox, the Yankees are not supposed to find the Toronto Blue Jays so difficult. Actually, it's the Yankees who are so difficult for themselves. The way they played against the Red Sox.

"We needed to continue playing the Red Sox ten more days," Dick Tidrow said. "Crush them out of the race, and then squabble among ourselves. This is a completely different team two days later."

Maybe the letdown was natural. The Red Sox have lost two more since leaving New York.

It took everything the Yankees had and less to salvage a

doubleheader split with Toronto, and it was difficult at times to determine which was the expansion team. "If we keep playing like this," Lou Piniella said, "it won't matter how many games the Red Sox lose, we'll lose more."

The Blue Jays made it two in a row by winning the first game, 8–5, with the benefit of four runs in an inning right out of the case histories of the 1962 Mets. Then it took eleven innings before the Yankees could win the second game, 5–1. The embarrassment of that seemed to escape some of the Yankees. "Why don't you write about the good things that happened?" Reggie Jackson advised.

Well, basically because there weren't too many. A nice job by Ken Clay was squandered in the first game and an even better job by Ken Holtzman was nearly frittered away in the second game. The rest was a lot of negatives. But as sophisticated as Jackson may be, he often thinks the reporters covering the team should be rooters, that they should be writing for the good of the team.

Before the first game Martin joined Jackson in the newest round of insult and overreaction. Until that time it was just Jackson who was upset because Martin had replaced him on defense in the third game with Boston. Jackson concedes that he has not been playing well in the outfield, but refuses to concede that he should come out even for Paul Blair, among the most gifted fielders ever. Word of Jackson's upset was carried back by the coaches, and now Martin is upset that Jackson is upset.

"It's nothing personal against Reggie," Martin said. "It's not a matter of likes and dislikes. I do what's best for the team."

The change is a valid tactic, but the way Martin goes about making it turns it into another insult. Martin was going out to the field before the game tonight to speak with Pedro Garcia, a second baseman who is looking for a job after being released by Toronto. "I wonder if he can play right field," Martin said. It was kidding, but it was kidding on the square.

And that was before Jackson dropped the fly ball that let the Yankees down in the seventh inning of the first game. With the score 2–2, Rivers, an excellent center fielder last season, misjudged Ernie Whitt's fly ball into two bases. Whitt was sacrificed and was coming home on a squeeze sign when Hector Torres mistakenly lifted a fly to right center. Whitt hurried back toward third as Jackson overtook the ball and reached up to catch it. And missed it. Whitt scored, breaking the tie. Errors by Chris Chambliss and Thurman Munson followed, and the Blue Jays had five runs. All the while a biplane circled above, pulling a sign: "I love you, Ella."

And when everything was over, it was the fried fish in the clubhouse that displeased the Yankees. "These guys feed us like I play right field," Jackson said. It wasn't clear whether that was supposed to be a laugh line.

* * *

Holtzman illustrated his own argument in the second game, pitching one out into the ninth inning in his best performance of the season. The Yankee pitching needs Holtzman—or somebody—and if he can give another reminder of what he did at Oakland, it will be hard for Martin not to be impressed. Holtzman says he needs just two things to win—a fastball and regular work. Not even a sign from the catcher.

When he pitched in Oakland, the textbook on pitching was revised by something close to a prohibition on a curveball for Holtzman, Hunter, and Vida Blue. Holtzman made it work so well that last season he pitched a game in which Munson never gave a sign. The fastball was understood, and the variation and the location were up to Holtzman. "The philosophy at Oakland was, no matter what your repertory is, no pitcher who ever lived could have as good control as with a fastball," Holtzman said. "It's not the pitch, it's the location."

Holtzman lived on the outside corner at the knees and fielded a lot of easy grounders back to the mound. He had seven assists tonight. That kind of control is a function of regular work, which is what Holtzman has been saying since last June. "I've been telling that to Billy," Munson said.

Thursday, June 30

Toronto

This has the makings of an awfully good stop on the road when it isn't raining. The Yorkville section is like a combination of Greenwich Village and Fifth Avenue, with outdoor sidewalk cafés in the afternoons and lots of fine shops.

There's also an atmosphere of security about the city. The stadium is right in the middle of the site of the Canadian National Exposition, which is open one month a year. Between times the rides are closed and left unguarded. The crowds walk past the exposition equipment on the way to and from the ball park and nobody bothers anything. There isn't even graffiti. How many other cities could say that?

The Yankees can be fun, but on their own terms. All it takes is three home runs by Cliff Johnson, two of them in one inning, and an eight-run inning. Simple.

Call him "Heathcliff"—not after the character in *Wuthering Heights,* but after a television bird. The classics are not exactly Thurman Munson's strength. "Remember Gertrude and Heathcliff on the Red Skelton show?" Munson said, flapping his wings gleefully. "Oopdee doop doop doop doop."

"Heh, heh, heh." Johnson laughed deeply. "Our fat little catcher came up with that nickname."

Johnson is six feet four and 220 pounds, long and broad and lean. He's a condor, a roc, a pterodactyl. He may even be the right-handed designated hitter the Yankees have looked for since the rule was invented in 1973.

He can hit a ball like Dave Kingman and few others can, sometimes long enough and high enough to carry over Death Valley in Yankee Stadium. That would make Heathcliff one of the rarest of birds. He can hit home runs in a place like Exhibition Stadium here by accident. Three home runs in a game is the most Babe Ruth ever hit. Two in an inning is the most anybody ever hit. And when Johnson was hit on the rump by a pitch, he laughed at it. When he was knocked down on his second turn at bat in the eighth inning, he got up and hit his third homer.

Including the ones at Houston, Johnson has 14 homers, and his presence might discourage other teams from throwing so many lefties at the Yankees. Martin says he will even use Johnson against selected righties in place of Carlos May, who is in exile. The owner is offended about equally by May's overweight and by his .160 batting average with runners on base, according to Steinbrenner's private figures.

* * *

Catfish Hunter pitched efficiently until stiffening in the long eighth inning and then uncharacteristically refused even to explain why he wouldn't talk about it. Apparently he is angry about the suggestions by a player on another team that he has a torn rotator cuff in his shoulder. There is no known cure.

* * *

The word out of Lorain, Ohio, is that according to court documents, the Department of Justice is investigating alleged fraudulent billing practices on government contracts by American Ship Building Co., George M. Steinbrenner, chairman of the board.

Friday, July 1

New York

Minutes after the 5–1 loss to the Tigers, Martin was summoned to meet with Steinbrenner and Gabe Paul. The issue was Jimmy Wynn's .145 batting average and his late arrival at the park. Martin gave a "flexible" arrival time after the late-night return home, but Wynn was later than "flexible."

* * *

Poor Fred Stanley. A newspaper reporter isn't supposed to root for the team, but it's impossible not to want some guys to do well. So hurray for Fred Stanley. He hit the home run in the eighth inning to beat the Tigers, 6–4.

"Of course you fantasize those things," Stanley said, "but still . . ."

Martin has told Stanley that it was George Steinbrenner's maneuvering that brought in Bucky Dent and took away Stanley's job. Steinbrenner insists that Martin had virtually demanded Dent. Whoever was responsible, Stanley was at bat for only the fourteenth time this season, with the winning run on second. He had been preparing himself to play 150 games this season, until the deal was made on the last day of spring training.

"So I go out there and do the routine stuff," Stanley said. "I go out early and catch my hundred grounders and make my hundred throws and then I'm like the batting practice pitcher. They give me my twenty bucks and say, 'Take a hike.'"

But for the moment, Stanley put disappointment aside. "All I wanted to do was get around the bases and get home without laughing or grinning," he said. He couldn't make it. As he turned third he saw Cliff Johnson, Carlos May, and Elston Howard fainted dead away in the dugout. Stanley welcomed being the butt of the jokes. "I guess that cheapens every home run hit this season," Graig Nettles said. It was Stanley's home run that put the Yankees back in first place, a half game over the Red Sox. Stanley loved that, too.

* * *

Sunday, July 3

New York

Just what if Ron Guidry had been judged on his spring training debacle and dispatched to Syracuse or Kansas City or someplace? What would the Yankees have done without him?

On a staff that includes Catfish Hunter, Ken Holtzman, Ed Figueroa, Mike Torrez, and an overworked bullpen, Guidry is the best.

Guidry struck out nine and beat the Tigers, 2–0, in the first game of the doubleheader. Holtzman lasted one batter into the third inning of the second game before coming out with a sore arm. Dick Tidrow was permitted to absorb a four-run ninth inning while the Yankees were losing the second game, 10–6. There was nobody else.

Hunter has had recurrent arm trouble and his sudden reluctance to discuss it seems to indicate he is discouraged. Figueroa has a tender shoulder, hasn't pitched in two weeks, and has lost his last three games. Gullett has often been unavailable but has pitched well lately; Torrez has been available but has not pitched well lately.

And that leaves Guidry. Roy White doubled home two runs in the eighth inning and that was enough.

* * *

Mickey Rivers, who feels he should be running on his own, was caught stealing in the first game for the eleventh time in twenty-seven attempts. He was caught only seven times in fifty attempts last season.

And in Boston, where the Red Sox have lost nine in a row, Don Zimmer's contract was extended through next season at a raise in pay. Martin is sure to notice that tomorrow.

Monday, July 4

New York

Jimmy Wynn never will get to show New York any more Toy Cannon than he showed opening day. Gabe Paul asked him to go to the minor leagues and Wynn refused. Cliff Johnson and Lou Piniella have left no job for Wynn here. "Paul just said, 'Go down for two weeks and try to get your stroke back,'" Wynn said. "No player-coach or anything. I said no to that."

That Paul would have handled a sixteen-year veteran in that manner was considered a measurement of Yankee corporate sensitivity. "For a guy that's been in the big leagues as long as he has and as good a man as he is, and plays so hard as he does—he plays hurt and never says anything—you gotta feel compassion," Munson said. "Asking a guy like that to go to Syracuse is downright belittling."

The Yankees have ten days to place Wynn or release him. Dell Alston was recalled. And Martin said he was surprised. Asked whether Wynn's late arrival Friday night had anything to do with the move, Martin said, "I don't want to get into any controversy, if you don't mind."

* * *

Ed Figueroa put up with a tight shoulder and an ache in the back to pitch into the eighth inning of a 7–5 victory over the Indians. "I told him before the game," Martin said, "that if I ever needed eight innings from him, I needed it tonight." Guidry can't pitch every game.

Tuesday, July 5

New York

It was the Yankees' eighty-first game—exactly halfway through the season. It was Sparky Lyle's thirty-fifth appearance—and there he drew the line. Rubber arm or no rubber arm, he needs some rest before he can pitch his thirty-sixth.

Lyle is a short-man, but when Martin needs a longman, sometimes that's Lyle, too. Theoretically, that's more to Martin's advantage than it is to Lyle's, so Lyle watches out for himself. There is no such thing as pacing himself for a pitcher with Lyle's job. The danger of a manager's going with a hot relief pitcher until he is burned out is always there. That's why many relief pitchers are one-season flashes or are effective only in alternate years.

Lyle has been remarkably consistent since he emerged as a bullpen star with the Red Sox in 1969. He knows how to take care of himself, is strong enough to mean no when he says so, and sophisticated enough to know that he'd better watch out for himself.

"Once I can't get 'em out, nobody's gonna give a shit about me," he said. "Once that happens, there's no place left to go. A starter can always become a long reliever. A long reliever can always become a short reliever. But where's a short reliever gonna go? I'm gonna go according to what I think is best for me."

Wisely, Martin permits Lyle to make his own schedule. Monday he told Martin he could pitch to a batter or two, but wasn't needed. So last night he told Martin he could pitch a couple of innings, and Martin took him up on it. Martin may have overdone it a bit, at that, to bring Lyle into the game in the fifth inning, but certainly it didn't hurt on the scoreboard.

Mike Torrez was disappointing for the second time in a row on his preferred three days' rest and came out in the third inning. The Yankees have had only twenty-four complete games. Dick Tidrow, himself overworked, replaced Torrez and ran into trouble in the fifth. The game can get out of hand in the fifth as well as the ninth, so Martin called for Lyle.

Lyle has pitched seventy-five innings in half the season. He's never pitched more than 114 in a season and doesn't like the idea of doubling his first-half total. Even if he got hitters out tonight, he didn't strike any out. "They hit like I was throwing," Lyle said. "Softly." That's a good indication that he could use a vacation.

"My arm doesn't hurt, but I've only got so much left in it. That [burning out] will never happen to me. I'm not going to let them blow me out, and they're not going to try."

Certainly Lyle won't make believe the fifth game of the playoff is beckoning him when it's the sixth of July. That would be beyond the call of duty. "Some guys would think, 'Go, go, give that hundred and ten percent,' " he said. "It's that extra ten percent that gets you your release."

* * *

Thurman Munson stopped a foul with his bare hand and needed seven stitches in the little finger. He'll get a bit of a vacation, too.

* * *

The question of Jackson in right field is less clear-cut. He may not be the greatest outfielder, but he hasn't been as good as he was at Oakland. "I've had outfield problems before, but not for this long," he said.

It might be a good idea to make him the DH for a while to take some pressure off him. Several players have suggested it. But that gets into the area of Jackson's psyche, and Martin is showing some awareness. "You don't like suddenly to make someone a DH," Martin said.

Jackson says he wouldn't mind, but his words lately have not jibed with his thinking. Underneath everything on this team is the question of what people are thinking. "I think we're in pretty good shape emotion wise," Munson said, "but you can never tell when something will be said or something written that will set something off."

The chemistry of the people on the ball club is still the same. They still irritate each other in too many places. The eye of media scrutiny is still to be suspected. "People are not going to allow it to be calm," Jackson said. This is a man who courted media exposure as recently as spring training.

It seems inevitable that the Jackson-Martin situation will flare again. Then there is Martin vs. Steinbrenner, and the players aren't sure who they'd root for—or against. "This team would confuse a psychiatrist," Tidrow said. "Anybody can say there are going to be clashes, but to say why, or how to avoid them, that's something else."

The most obvious evidence is the game on the field. Statistically Jackson is hitting well. He's hitting .283, has 13 homers and 42 runs batted in. He has seven steals in nine tries. He had three hits tonight and leads the league with 26 doubles. His double in the seventh inning drove in the winning run. He leads the team in game-winning hits with eight. Multiply that by two, and it makes a pretty good season. But he still hasn't shown the bursts of fence-busting that can carry a team for a month. He's hit only one homer in a month. Many of his hits have gone to left field. His head is still as muddled as the prospects for peace in his time.

"If he had Sparky Lyle's makeup," Tidrow said, "he'd have forty home runs by now and this team would be a paradise."

But not yet. "My stroke has been raggedy, my head's been fucked up. I've been out of the game in my mind," Jackson said. "I'm thinking about things I shouldn't be and I've let them affect me.

"Right now I can't hit the ball out of the ball park. It's taken me this long to adjust. I'm not a pull hitter, I'm an alley hitter. The right field seats being so close doesn't affect me. It affects the people that influence me. Therefore I try to hit the ball that way and foul myself up."

Lately he has been avoiding questions that draw any kind of introspection. He used to enjoy displaying his insight. "I don't want any interviews," he said. "I'm entitled to not getting my ass ripped all the time."

He feels too many of those interviews have been intended to find flaws, and that has made the season a nightmare in his estimation.

"Most successful major leaguers learn to block out that aspect," Ken Holtzman said. "One of the most difficult adjustments for an athlete to make is the switch from relative obscurity to total recognition.

"If this team were playing in Oakland with one full-time reporter on the team, you wouldn't hear nearly what you do here. The interaction would be the same among the players, but it wouldn't be magnified as it has. That tends to strain the emotions of certain players."

To an extent what Holtzman says is true. Issues that might

open and close in one edition in a city with one newspaper keep getting replayed in New York. If one newspaper has a strong story, the others are required to catch up with another aspect of the story or a response from the other side. If there is a story in the papers, then all the radio stations send people around with tape recorders. Then the television cameras come. If there's a big story around the Yankees, then at each stop on the road each newspaper will assign its own man to probe the same areas.

At each city players are strafed with references to Jackson's salary, his accumulated wealth, and his IQ. Some of the references come from the local media and some of them come from Jackson. Jackson means no offense when he counts his roll of pocket money on the bus, but the constant emphasis creates offense. "He never fails," a teammate said.

The money is still an issue. Ball players bitch the way soldiers bitch. Several players here feel they are getting less than they deserve, or experienced more difficulty getting what they wanted. Their vague complaining has stung Jackson. Their normal clubhouse ragging, another manner of probing a man's character, has been taken hard by Jackson.

"Reggie took it personally when it really may have been directed at the owner," Munson said.

From the beginning Jackson has taken things personally, beginning with what he perceived as coldness when he was broadcasting the Yankee competition for ABC's Superteams in Hawaii. They did not warmly welcome him to the club, and when spring training opened Jackson was already on guard.

He has been caught in the tug-of-war between Martin and Steinbrenner. Jackson still feels he is being deliberately held out of cleanup by Martin's need to show up the owner. Jackson gets a bad jump on nearly every ball in the outfield, as if he were startled. A man who was a decent outfielder and often made a spectacular play has been confused by routine fly balls. Yet he feels demeaned when Martin replaces him with Paul Blair's gifted glove. When he is hurt, he is offended that Martin does not directly ask him if he is well enough to play.

He is disturbed to the extent that he has dreaded going to the ball park. He has driven home from Yankee Stadium in tears. He is so overwhelmed by New York that he has felt near a nervous breakdown.

His unhappiness and his teammates' impatience with his

manner may have been inevitable wherever he chose to play. "I refuse to believe it was inevitable," Jackson said. But Martin's handling has made the conflict worse. He did not try to guide Munson and Jackson out of their dispute. That remained for Healy and for Steinbrenner's final appeal. Where others recognized Jackson's needs, Martin has not until this consideration of the DH.

"If asking Reggie directly whether he can play meets a need, why not? Time is cheap," a player said. "Why not substitute two defensive outfielders [for Roy White in left field as well as Blair for Jackson] on occasion and preserve the man's self-image?" another suggested.

Not every player is as solicitous of Jackson's self-image. Others feel that image is really the problem. "We had a better pitching staff than hitting team, so Gullett should be resented more than Reggie," a player said. "But Don is so unassuming you don't know he's making as much as he is. If you come on like your sweat don't stink, nobody is receptive. If you're a good old country boy like Catfish Hunter, the guys accept you.

"Reggie needed to be shown up like he was in Boston. He can be awesome when he's trying, but he's been just cruising, just playing hard enough not to look bad. Maybe that's what it takes to get him ripping."

Jackson feels the conflict and the attitude toward him have kept him from being all of himself, the man who could hit a towering home run onto the roof of Tiger Stadium in the 1971 All-Star Game or carry a team for a month. Others feel the conflict around him has kept the whole team from playing nearly its best—even Munson. "Let's say it's stalled us," Munson said.

Despite his extraordinary concentration, Munson finds himself distracted. "I can't give one other reason I've struck out thirty-five times," he said. He struck out only thirty-seven times all last season. "I know my concentration is not what it should be. Sometimes there's just a lack of it."

Emotionally, many of them feel as if they've played a whole season and it's just the halfway point. Things are quiet, but you can hear creatures in the night.

Thursday, July 7

New York

Graig Nettles won the home run championship last season and is ahead of his own pace in his own silent manner.

Graig Nettles is the most overlooked home run champion in recent years, but the talent that nobody misses any more is the wonder he works at third base. It once was that Nettles was an uncertain fielder. When the Yankees played at Shea Stadium, Nettles hated the condition of the field. He anticipated bad bounces and when he got good bounces he couldn't handle them. He sulked himself into two bad years with the glove.

Now that Brooks Robinson is sitting out the last year of his marvelous career, Nettles is the best glove at third base in the league. He earned a standing ovation for the play he made in the 8–2 victory over the Indians tonight. He brought the crowd to its feet in the top of the eighth inning by diving full-length behind the base to stab a line drive by Frank Duffy. It saved a run and enabled Catfish Hunter to pitch the complete game. Nettles got another ovation for the same play when he came to the plate in the bottom of the inning. Nettles responded with a sharp single that brought Reggie Jackson home from second with the final Yankee run.

"I've made better plays," Nettles said, "but I've never gotten a hand like that. The fans are really happy now that we're winning. Maybe that was their way of showing appreciation for the whole ball club."

Yankee attendance passed a million tonight and they've won eleven of fifteen. The fans even chose not to boo Jackson. He made an interesting play that produced the first Yankee run. With two out in the second inning, he singled and broke for second as the Cleveland pitcher made a pickoff move to first base. Jackson beat the relay from the first baseman, and then Nettles drove the run in with his first single.

In the last home game before the All-Star Game, Steinbrenner was delighted. The best team money could buy is in first place, going well, and now he gets to show off his ball park as host of the All-Star game. "There's unification now; there's leadership," Steinbrenner crowed.

Leadership apparently comes from Jackson's five hits in his last eight at bats, and from Thurman Munson's refusal to concede that he's hurt.

After taking seven stitches in the gash on his little finger, Munson rested on last night's rainout and then volunteered to play tonight. The trainer told Martin that Munson would benefit from another night off and Martin had Fran Healy in the original lineup. But Munson took infield practice and threw well. So Martin went to Munson and Munson said, "Whatever you want to do." Martin wrote him into the lineup.

In the third inning Munson ripped a long double that broke the 1–1 tie. "You'd have to hit that son of a bitch with a truck to keep him out," Steinbrenner said.

Munson said all those things earlier about refusing to play without rest, and now that he had a chance to sit, he wanted to play. "I feel guilty when I don't play," Munson said. That's more like Munson. It used to be when Rick Dempsey was with the Yankees and impatient with his place on the bench, Munson saw any praise of Dempsey as a threat to the job. Now that Healy is not a threat, Munson still can't sit down.

Friday, July 8

Baltimore

Whenever he gets the chance, Munson mentions "security," as in "I've got security" or "I'm secure." He likes to drop it into conversation with a smile because security is just what Jackson said Munson didn't have in that magazine piece. Munson says it was his sense of security that enabled him to make peace with Jackson when the war was at its hottest three weeks ago.

Security, Munson says, will enable him and Jackson to maintain their peaceful coexistence. Munson's security, that is.

Munson's security comes from the knowledge of what his awkward-looking body can do on a baseball field. "I like to play," he said. "I might not enjoy some of the things that go on or some of the people I'm connected with, but I enjoy winning." That enables him to close out thoughts that he has been cheated by the owner or insulted by a teammate, and concentrate on the little white ball.

He can put his last failure out of his mind when the next opportunity comes. As in the two-run homer and the two-run single he hit tonight after hitting into a double play his first time up. "I really do have the ability to concentrate on 'right now,'" he said. "When I strike out or hit into a double play, the next time I put it out of my mind. That's security, not just as a ball player but beyond baseball."

He drove in four runs and made a good hard tag on Lou Piniella's throw to the plate in the 7–5 victory over the Orioles. The Orioles had won seven in a row themselves and are proving stubborn contenders. Munson's home run went to left field. The single went to right. "You've got to know yourself," Munson said. "If I don't feel good, I may try to go to right field four times. If I feel good, I try to do what I can."

What Munson can do is remarkable. He has a .317 batting average and his 64 runs batted in are second in the league. What makes that remarkable is that Munson is a catcher. Sometimes it's painful for a catcher merely to hold a bat. Munson has the scar from the staph infection behind the first finger of his right hand and will have another where the seven fresh stitches form railroad tracks on the little finger. When he pulled on his shirt before the game, he winced when the stitches snagged on the fabric. "You think it hurts?" Munson said. "It feels good. I'm ready for another staph infection; that intravenous treatment was fun.

"The doctor told me if I didn't have it treated when I did, I might have lost the use of the finger." He laughed and said it really wasn't an important finger, just a signal for a fastball, half a peace sign, and the main finger in throwing or holding the bat.

If Munson finishes this season over .300 it will be his fourth in the last five and fifth in his nine as a big-league regular. He's headed for his third straight season of 100 RBIs. Now consider that Yogi Berra hit .300 three times in his seventeen full seasons and he's in the Hall of Fame. Carlton Fisk has never hit .300 or batted in 100 runs. Johnny Bench has topped 100 RBIs five times, but has never hit .300. "What the hell catcher does hit .300?" Baltimore manager Earl Weaver said. "Four times in five years is fantastic." He regards Munson as one of the two or three toughest outs in the league.

Munson, in fact, can be the first player both to drive in 100 runs and bat .300 for three consecutive years since Al Rosen did the trick for Cleveland in 1954.

Munson reminds listeners that he also has sizable real estate holdings and considerable independent wealth even if he doesn't have Jackson's 160 IQ. "I'm not exactly a dummy," Munson says. The hint of his own insecurity is his offering those aspects of his life as if he were in a competition with Jackson's comments.

In a sense, that insecurity is a wonderful thing for Munson. It pushes him to his physical limits, even to playing when it might be wiser to take the night off. It's important to him for his efforts to be acknowledged.

He feels he has been denied that recognition by Steinbrenner. There was that unwritten promise that convinced Munson to sign in the spring of 1976 for progressive salaries of $120,000, $155,000, $165,000, and $195,000. The promise was that Munson would remain the highest-salaried Yankee other than Catfish Hunter. To Munson the promise acknowledged his contribution no matter what was paid to any free agent. When Jackson was brought in at an annual salary of $332,000, Steinbrenner first contended that there was no such agreement with Munson. Then Steinbrenner argued that Jackson's salary was the $200,000 he is to be paid right now, and that the $132,000 annual deferred payments didn't count—and neither did the Rolls-Royce and the interest-free loan.

In January Munson signed an extension of his contract with salaries of $260,000 for 1980 and $275,000 for 1981. But Munson was still convinced Steinbrenner was reneging. Finally a package was worked that Munson says will pay him $1.7 million over five years. What he resents is that he had to scratch and claw to get what he feels was due him without arguing.

What pleases him is the thought of how far he has come since he worked with his father on the farm in Randolph, Ohio. They were tenant farmers and the work had to be finished before the ball playing began. "But I never minded hard work," he said. "When I was finished, I'd play ball, mostly. I loved to play. I'd come home at night and my collie—Fritz was his name—would be waiting for me. Jeez, that was a long time ago."

When he was eight, Munson's family moved to Canton and his father worked as a long-distance trucker, coast to coast out of Canton. "He didn't make much money, maybe four or five thousand, but there was always food on the table," Munson said.

"I remember he came to watch me play in a Class A game once. I went something like five for five, with two homers. After the game, he said, 'You really looked horseshit behind the plate tonight.' To my face he'd tear me down, but to others, he'd praise me to the sky."

Munson enjoyed the brief moment of nostalgia. "It's funny how I'm forgetting all the hard times, all the work," he said. "Ever notice how people's visions of things only include the good moments? Like I remember playing ball, but I forgot about picking potatoes."

Maybe someday Munson will look back on this season and remember the good moments, like tonight. He is afraid that the bitterness is indelible.

He would like to be known as a good guy underneath his gruff exterior, but doesn't know how to go about showing it. "I like to kid around a lot, but I do it in a kind of grouchy way," he said a year ago. "If you don't know me, you think I'm serious. It's just the way I am. And I like to be complimented as much as anyone else, although sometimes I don't seem to like it. Compliments are things which supplement your ego, something all of us need."

A year ago Munson was on his way to being voted Most Valuable Player and winning the recognition he craved. I don't think he would admit that same need today. The rivalry with Jackson is too great for that, although Munson would never admit that, either.

The rivalry he does acknowledge is with Fisk, the tall and handsome Boston catcher. Munson does have to live with his own image as characterized in nicknames that range from "Squatty Body" to "Turtle" to "Stump."

"I go out and stumble and a guy will yell, 'Lose some weight.' I can be in better shape than a lot of guys, but it doesn't seem to matter," Munson said.

He enjoys the speculation that he might even win the MVP award for a second year in a row. "Would a scientist like to win a second Nobel Prize?" he asked. "Would a writer want to win a second Pulitzer Prize? Does a President want to get reelected?"

But it bothers Munson that Fisk is a rival as the All-Star catcher—or that anybody might be considered serious competition. He says he's only kidding when he says that if Fisk is voted the All-Star then the American League will have a hell of a backup catcher. But it hardly seems like kidding.

He says often that he would like to retire and spend his time with his family in Canton and not have to travel. He says he doesn't need the money.

But then it takes ten years in the big leagues to qualify for the Hall of Fame, and this is only Munson's ninth season. The Hall of Fame—now, that is recognition. A bronze plaque is security.

* * *

Graig Nettles' homer in the ninth inning was his seventeenth. He didn't hit his seventeenth last year until August 13. And Paul Blair made a beautifully graceful over-the-shoulder catch steps short of the fence in center field, where he played fourteen seasons as an Oriole. It is reported that Blair is the owner of the territory and rents it to the Orioles.

Saturday, July 9

Baltimore

The issue on the surface in the Yankee clubhouse was the umpire's call on Dell Alston's slide home on a double steal in the seventh inning. "It's tough when you work a perfect double steal and come out on the short end," Martin said.

"I don't care for the umpire, either," Alston said. "I couldn't believe the call. I thought I was in there; I turned around and saw them going to the dugout and I couldn't believe it."

Alston's single had just given the Yankees a lead of 4–3. A two-run lead is always better than a one-run lead, especially looking back after losing the game, 6–5. But that call wasn't the undoing. The Yankees did give three unearned runs to the Orioles in the bottom of the eighth in as ragged an inning as you can imagine. It included an error by Willie Randolph, an error by Roy White, a wild pitch, and a throw home by Graig Nettles that hit the runner.

But the puzzler was the removal of Ron Guidry with a 4–3 lead before the Orioles came to bat in the seventh. That put Guidry in an awkward situation. Martin explained that Guidry's ankle was bothering him—an old high-school injury—and he was limping around the mound.

When Guidry was asked, he said it was the heat that got to him, and presented the case of a small man trying to throw a big fastball in the heat and humidity. When he was told Martin's explanation, Guidry flushed. "Well, if he said that," Guidry stammered, "I guess one of us is not telling the truth."

As it turned out, Martin had pulled the switch by telling the truth. Guidry's ankle was sore, but the trainer—anticipating Martin's thinking—had told Guidry not to mention it "because the reporters will make a big thing out of it."

So Guidry was victimized by Yankee custom.

Sunday, July 10

Baltimore

It's been a frustrating weekend for the Yankees. To begin with, they are staying at the Hilton Inn in Pikesville, a $12 cab ride from the ball park or downtown. There's nowhere to walk and it's too hot to walk, anyhow. The hotel closes down its food service at intervals that coincide with the ball players' mealtimes.

The newfangled combination locks on the doors are irritating. They're a nice idea: Specify any four numbers when you check in, and you don't have to carry a key. Except that more often than not the combination system is fouled up and you have to make a return trip to the desk in the middle of the night to get the door opened.

Then tonight Ross Grimsley shut them out, 6–0, and dropped the Yankees into second place. He made them look bad. He allowed five hits—all singles—struck out one, and got sixteen outs on ground balls. And the Yankees accused him of cheating. At least Martin thought that was important.

"Grimsley was throwing a greaseball, or whatever he gets

off his eyebrows and his hair," the manager said in another installment of what is now anticipated commentary on any defeat. If it isn't the umpires, then it's something else. Players thought they should have jumped on Grimsley's slow stuff.

Their insults didn't bother Grimsley. "They had nine innings to do something and didn't," he said. "I won and it's over; why should anything they say tick me off?"

Ken Holtzman was a teammate of Grimsley's last summer and remembers that pitch. But Holtzman is a pitcher and thought that anyone who demeaned what Grimsley had done was demeaning himself. "If the hitters say he had no business beating them, who does it reflect on?" Holtzman said. "The hitters, of course."

Lou Piniella wouldn't knock anything Grimsley did; he was too impressed by the way Grimsley kept his pitches at the knees. Piniella, though, is a stand-up guy. Also a sit-down guy. He was willing to express admiration for the pitcher and, contrary to Yankee custom, discuss the two balls he did not catch while playing right field in place of sore-legged Reggie Jackson. On one, Piniella found himself playing too shallow and too wide and leaped too soon for a drive that hit the base of the wall for three bases and two runs. The next inning he broke in and stumbled on his way back, and a fly ball dropped for two bases and the Orioles' fourth run. Piniella denied that Jackson had left right field unplayable for any mortal outfielder.

Jackson pulled his groin slightly last night but said he would be able to play tomorrow night. When he heard the manager's accusations of the greaseball today, Jackson shook his head and laughed.

Monday, July 11

Baltimore

You don't have to go looking to stir up controversy on the Yankees, it comes looking for you. At least, it's waiting.

Murray Chass and I were walking back through the lobby from the tennis courts that soften a sentence at the Pikesville Hilton, and there was this "prominent unidentified" Yankee who just had to make his complaint heard. He charged that

Steinbrenner had grown so impatient with the Yankees' failure to tear the race apart that he had taken to dictating the lineup to Martin. "George tells him who to play," the player said as if this were the final indignity.

"George doesn't want competition, he wants a slaughter," the player said. "To win, you need nine good players, plus some capable utility players and a pitching staff. George wants twenty-five superstars. George doesn't care about anybody's feelings. To him, we're not professionals, we're all employees. He treats everybody like that. Everybody on the club has experienced it. He's done something to everybody. He's destroyed Billy. He's made him nothing.

"Not a single guy on the club is happy except Willie."

That would be Willie Randolph, who has played his second base whenever he's been physically able and, in his second season, hasn't yet felt the crush of negotiations as others have.

Both Steinbrenner—at his office in Tampa—and Martin insist that the lineup comes from the manager. "Do you believe that?" the player said.

Whether the charge is totally correct or not, there is another crisis building. The mistrust is genuine even if the charge isn't. Martin immediately demanded to know who the player was. Steinbrenner immediately assumed it was Carlos May because he isn't playing. Steinbrenner can't stand May because he is overweight, and he constantly brings up May's batting statistic with runners on base. Each time Steinbrenner mentions it, it drops a few points.

First a note about journalistic procedure—at least Chass's and mine. The player remained unidentified because he asked to be. Before either of us would write what he charged, the player had to be someone who was important on the team and was playing, so his charge couldn't be strictly personal. Otherwise it would have been a dishonest story, used for purely sensational purposes. It could not have been used if it had come from Carlos May. And the story had to have the ring of some truth.

"It's a lie," Steinbrenner said. He said the only influence he's had is in urging more use of Lou Piniella as DH, not in ordering it. The prominent unidentified player says Steinbrenner's influence is more pervasive than that—like the use of Cliff Johnson as cleanup on one occasion and the periodic benching of Roy White and Mickey Rivers.

"How do you bat Johnson cleanup on the team that won
the pennant last year?" the player said. "What's he ever
done?"

Johnson did hit three home runs in one game in an impressive display of power. "George is ignorantly impressed
with Johnson," the player said.

Steinbrenner said he had not been that impressed with
Johnson.

The player also said that White and Rivers couldn't be
happy with the way they've been used. "They should be batting one-two like last year and let them go," he said. "They're
the only ones on the team who can run. If you want to play
Blair, put him in right field and DH Jackson. But Rivers
sitting down? How can he do that? And White is much more
productive than Johnson."

The player also questioned Jackson's sitting down with his
groin pull while Munson is playing with seven stitches in his
finger.

Martin called a clubhouse meeting before the game to discuss and deny the charges. "George sends a lot of notes on
statistics but I don't pay attention to them," Martin said.
"The players know George isn't making the lineups—but I
think our whole club is changed since we got Reggie, as far
as the lineup."

Later he asked again who the player was.

After that the Orioles beat them for the third time in a row,
4–3. The Orioles won it in the last of the ninth after tying the
score with two runs in the seventh. It was the second time in
the series that the Yankees had lost a two-run lead late in the
game. And the decisive run was driven in by Eddie Murray,
who has battered the Yankees for 12 runs batted in in their
twelve meetings. He has delivered the decisive blow in four
of the Orioles' six wins. Steinbrenner is angry that the brain
trust still hasn't figured out how to get him out.

Before too long the players had generally decided among
themselves that the unnamed player was Thurman Munson.
But Steinbrenner was more concerned by what was not happening on the ball club than by who was speaking out. Indeed,
he does not like the competition of the race.

He said he had taken the lineups of the Yankees, Red Sox,
and Orioles and written them side by side. "If I had to pick
them player by player, you know how many Yankees I'd
pick," he said. He put together the best team money could

buy and it still isn't in first place. "I said by the All-Star Game we should be three games ahead," Steinbrenner said. "We're not going to be." He said he had lain awake fretting over that.

He admires the way the Orioles have hung in the race under Earl Weaver's hand. "He must be a magician," Steinbrenner said. "If he can keep that team hanging in there, he should be Manager of the Year." And if Weaver is Manager of the Year, then Billy Martin cannot be. That's Steinbrenner's point.

"We got Billy everything he asked for," Steinbrenner said. "I shelled out a hell of a lot of dough. If we don't win, then I'm stupid for spending all that money, Gabe Paul for picking the players, and Billy for handling them."

Steinbrenner is most critical of the pitching and the pitches being called. Tonight he assembled assistant Gene Michael, player development director Jack Butterfield, and coach Elston Howard in the press box with binoculars to see if the Yankees were giving away their pitches or whether they were being stolen. If they saw anything, they weren't saying.

"We should have the five best starters," Steinbrenner said. "If this is the way they're pitching, the question is if they're being handled right."

* * *

The Yankees had led since the second inning on the first of Nettles' two home runs and Mike Torrez was pitching well until the seventh, when the Orioles tied it at 3–3.

In the ninth Al Bumbry led off with a looper into short left. White lunged, the ball skipped past him, and Bumbry reached third. Sparky Lyle took over the pitching, and Torrez kicked a row of batting helmets as he descended into the dugout.

Lyle deflected a line drive off his bare hand to Randolph for the first out, but had to leave the game. Dick Tidrow, who has accumulated a 9.60 earned run average over his last ten appearances, came on and intentionally walked Pat Kelly to set up the double play. Tidrow threw once to first base and on his first pitch to the plate, Kelly stole second. So Ken Singleton was intentionally walked. With the bases full, the infield halfway in and the outfield shallow, Tidrow threw three unintentional balls to Murray, one strike, and Murray hit the next too deep for anybody to bother chasing down.

"I'm not going to penalize Billy during the season," Steinbrenner said. "If we don't win, then he's got to stand up and take the blame." Poor Billy Martin. He's been returning phone calls and keeping himself available and everything.

" 'Don't tell me how many storms you encountered,' the ship owner said to the captain. 'Just tell me if you brought the ship home safely.' " That was Martin in his most melodramatic tones. The seas are rough again.

Tuesday, July 12

Milwaukee

This time Martin's clubhouse meeting was with the writers. He had read the story about Steinbrenner picking the lineup and Steinbrenner's dissatisfied comments, too. Martin wasn't as angry as he sometimes gets, but was irritated about having to endure another round.

"Number one," he said, "managing this team is tough enough without picking up the papers and seeing the manager against the owners, the owner against the players." And more.

"I listen to the owners. I listen to the general manager. I still do my own managing. The day I let an owner or general manager tell me how to manage, I will quit. And that has not happened."

Martin did not list any "number two." He did express his editorial judgment that if such stories continued, he would be forced to take some sort of action. "I'll keep the press off the buses and planes and out of the clubhouse," he said. He can keep the press off the buses and planes, which would be an inconvenience. He did not mention how he would prevent players who had opinions from expressing them.

But they did win a game and Steinbrenner is due in town tomorrow. Dick Tidrow—he of the inflated earned run average—came on when Don Gullett ran out of gas in the seventh inning and issued one walk and no hits in 2⅓ innings. So they beat the Brewers, 5–2. Tidrow had not saved a game since May 3. "I'm part of the reason we've been losing," he said.

If Tidrow can find himself again, he could make a lot of difference to the pitching staff. Especially if there is anything to the ominous signs about Gullett. He had no velocity in his last inning, and he refused to answer when asked how his arm felt.

Wednesday, July 13

Milwaukee

Steinbrenner met with Martin and the coaches in the morning and had the word passed to the players: "Stop complaining and go out and play ball." Then Steinbrenner watched Catfish Hunter driven out after five innings as the Yankees lost, 9–8.

* * *

Late at night there was a meeting in Steinbrenner's suite that became the best-kept secret of the season. What went on did not come out until October. Even then all sides did not agree on just what went on. There are two sides to everything on this team.

In attendance at the meeting were Steinbrenner, Munson, and Lou Piniella—and, an hour or so later, Martin. Piniella said he was involved because he was with Munson when he was summoned by Steinbrenner. Steinbrenner said it was the players who called the meeting. "They banged on my door at twelve thirty in the morning," he said.

Part of the discussion was over the players' suggestion that Jackson be moved into cleanup because that might get him to producing to his capability.

But the bulk of the talk was over Martin and the restrictive clauses in his contract that put him in continuous jeopardy. Piniella said, "If we have a lame-duck manager worrying about his future, we're going to have a manager who can't do his job." Piniella was not entirely on Martin's side at the time. "Straighten out his contract and remove the clauses," he said. "If not, fire him."

The issue, according to Steinbrenner's version, was that Munson and Piniella "admonished" him for not being more involved in the team. He said they told him, "You run your businesses, why not your team?" He said the question of

Martin's restrictions did not come up until Martin joined the meeting—uninvited—an hour later.

It was one thirty when Martin was going to his room and heard the voices of Munson and Piniella in Steinbrenner's suite. So Martin knocked. Steinbrenner answered. "I said, 'What's going on?' " Martin said.

"George answered, 'Nothing, I'm going to sleep.'

"So I pushed the door open and I saw there, in the lavatory, Piniella and Thurman. George said, 'Calm down, Billy.' "

So Martin was accepted into the conversation and, according to Martin, the dialogue went like this:

Steinbrenner— "Come on, Billy, what's wrong with the club?"

Martin— "You really want to know? You; you're what's wrong with this club. You're meddling with the club."

Thursday, July 14

Milwaukee

Life in the squirrel cage has gotten to Catfish Hunter, too. Milwaukee broadcaster Merle Harmon put a microphone around Hunter's neck and Hunter tore into his teammates for their selfishness, and into his manager for his handling of the pitching staff. And Hunter is the most unlikely man to make his complaints public.

"The Yankees could repeat if they put their minds to playing ball instead of what the other guy is making," Hunter said into the Wisconsin air. " 'He's making more than me.' That's all they ever think about over here."

The troubles on the Yankees have often been compared with conditions on the Oakland club when Hunter was there, but Hunter no longer thinks of the A's as the paragon of troubled ball clubs. "In Oakland, if one guy didn't hustle, the guys jumped on him and made him hustle," he said. "Over here, if you jump on a guy, he'll quit on you."

Hunter's complaint about no established pitching rotation is less clear. At one time or another five of the starters have been hurt, and he has been unavailable most of all. Two days ago Martin said he wanted to go with a four-man rotation— Torrez, Figueroa, Guidry, and Hunter, with Gullett spot starting. Hunter refused. By his own admission, he is a once-a-week pitcher. "I don't understand it," Martin said. "I never expected this from him."

Hunter refused to clarify his comments. "I don't want to stir up any more shit," he said, "because the more you stir it, the more it stinks."

Friday, July 15

Kansas City

No more passing the word through coaches to the players. George Steinbrenner, the former college assistant football coach, gave his own address to the troops for the third time this season. He is embarrassed.

Leo Durocher is fond of saying the first thing he'd like to do is bar owners from the clubhouse, but it's Steinbrenner's team and his chagrin. He has his own concept of motivation.

Not all of the players take George's concepts seriously. Sparky Lyle slept through the meeting and Ed Figueroa came in late. Dick Tidrow was not staying with the team because he has family in town. And Roy White had to pick up his wife at the airport; he said he would rather take his chances with Steinbrenner's wrath than hers.

Essentially, what Steinbrenner did was again remind them that the problem is on the field, not in the clubhouse. And he called for the "Yankee pride" that used to be parts of movie scripts.

Then he threatened them with something like the mummy's curse. "Either this team is going to make a great comeback, or it will be known forever as 'the team that choked,' " he said. And, you know, he's right. If the Yankees don't win at least the pennant they will go down in history as one of the greatest flops ever.

When the lecture was over, Steinbrenner displayed another part of his motivational concept: More has been accomplished by strong words and a check than by strong words alone.

He said: "Here's $300. Go out and have a nice time during the All-Star break." Then he had checks handed out. He was urging the players to spend it on something frivolous—a vacation to escape the tension of the club.

"I thought it was a nice gesture, a super gesture," Reggie Jackson said. "I mean, how nice can you be?"

It was something Steinbrenner didn't have to do and few owners consider. But it makes my head spin to think of ball players making $75,000 and $150,000 needing to be stimulated by gifts of $300.

Actually, it wasn't $300 for everybody. Lyle and Figueroa were each docked $100 for missing the meeting.

Mike Torrez, who feels he's being taken advantage of in the Yankees' unyielding negotiations, said he thought it was a "first-class" gesture. So did Mickey Rivers. "I need more than $300," he said, "but I like anything I get free."

And as the others were opening their gifts, Catfish Hunter went to Martin's office, closed the door, and apologized.

* * *

The Yankees responded to the lecture and the cash by roaring out the door and getting beat, 7–4, by the Royals. Ron Guidry struck out the side in the first inning without so much as a foul tip, and was driven out by the Royals' five-run fifth.

Saturday, July 16

Kansas City

Now they've fallen three games behind. The Royals beat them, 5–1, and the Yankees have lost six of nine games on the trip. Two in a row since Steinbrenner's motivational session. They placed lousy.

"The fact that I made an error and let in a run tonight didn't cost us the game," Jackson said. "The fact that Willie Randolph made an error didn't cost us the game. The fact that I didn't get a hit didn't cost us the game. We just got beat. It's that simple. We're gettin' outplayed.

"It's no one player, even though some of the guys would like to think so."

The meaning was clear: Jackson feels that the others feel he is the reason. Some of them do.

Sunday, July 17

We have more harsh words concerning Jackson. Today it was learned that Lyle indeed blamed Jackson for last night's loss. Jackson bobbled Hal McRae's triple into four bases and when Jackson returned to the dugout, Lyle said: "Get your head out of your ass." Several players heard the suggestion.

By game time today word of the incident had seeped out. "Lyle said somebody had said something to him about it," Jackson said quietly. "I told him it didn't come from me."

After today's game, an 8–4 loss that concluded a trip of three won and seven lost, Martin ordered the clubhouse guards to clear out the writers. "Get them the fuck out," Martin hollered. "And stand by the door. We've got some eavesdropping suckers."

There were two controversies that Martin hoped to keep from the public: Steinbrenner's gift, which is now being questioned by the commissioner's office, and the Lyle-Jackson thing. Both are out.

On the bus to the airport, Jackson overheard two reporters discussing his incident and asked, "You're not going to quote me, are you?" The reporters said yes. Suddenly Jackson became aware that Martin, in the front of the bus, was listening to the discussion as were several others. So Jackson announced loudly: "I want everybody to know that I didn't volunteer anything. I was approached. And I answered the question." Jackson wanted it understood that he didn't squeal to the press.

But his disclaimer made no difference. The identity of the leak was more important than the incident, as it was when the charge was made that Steinbrenner was running the team, as it was when Steinbrenner's gifts were revealed.

When Munson was asked about the gifts, he barked loudly: "What about it? Why is that shit going to be in the papers? Who the hell told everybody about that?"

"Who do you think?" said Graig Nettles.

Who, they knew, had to be Jackson. Of course, Jackson.

Again Jackson is the outcast, his failures to be broadcast

and the failures of others overlooked. Today Willie Randolph lost a pop fly in the sun because he had neglected to wear his sunglasses. Two runs scored because of the blunder and finished the Yankee chances, but nobody made anything of that in the clubhouse.

And that's how the Yankees go to the All-Star break. Martin hopes the time off will cool their tensions.

"I don't see how it can continue like this," Nettles said. But then when they get together again on Thursday, there's every chance that there will be some new issue. "That's the way it's been all year," Nettles said. "I think it'll be with us all the rest of the year. It's still the same personalities."

Tuesday, July 19

New York

For Jackson there is no escaping even for the benign All-Star game. He was leaving Yankee Stadium for his car, lingering to sign a few autographs, when he was involved in an incident with a thirteen-year-old boy. Jackson ended his signing because he had an appointment to meet the people from Standard Brands. "Hey, I've got to go home," he said.

Some boys said abusive things and one made the comment that Jackson was going to keep a date with his mother. Jackson started to chase the boy across the parking lot. Jackson said he wanted to catch him and tell him he should have his mouth washed with soap. But the boy fell, and later filed charges that Jackson had knocked him down and kicked him.

Another, bigger youth, who was running alongside Jackson, said that Jackson had not touched the boy. A police official at the precinct where the complaint was made said it did not warrant an assault charge.

But Jackson has again been wounded, he feels, by New York. "I don't want to be here," he moaned.

Thursday, July 21

New York

Just when the Yankees were blithely sliding down the banister of a double shutout of the Brewers, it turned into a razor blade. A split, and of the worst kind.

Catfish Hunter pitched a five-hitter in the 7–0 first game and Ed Figueroa took a 4–0 lead into the ninth inning of the second game. And they lost it, 5–4, in the tenth. It was shocking.

Cecil Cooper hit a home run, a bloop dropped off Fred Stanley's glove. Figueroa got an out, gave up a single, and Sparky Lyle relieved. Lyle pitched three straight ground balls. One oozed past Graig Nettles. Stanley tossed past Willie Randolph. And one went off Chris Chambliss' glove. Paul Blair tried to cut off the tying run at the plate, but his throw from right field was wide and the winning run went to third.

Dick Tidrow got the third out, but the Brewers scored in the tenth and the Yankees were left to survey the wreckage. The vacation hadn't changed much.

Friday, July 22

New York

A 6–3 defeat by the Brewers, and Martin decided to shake up his lineup. Paul Blair will be in center field tomorrow in place of Mickey Rivers. "Just for one game," Martin said. Roy White will be in left field and Lou Piniella will be in right. And Jackson will be the designated hitter.

As if by coincidence, Rivers had played a catchable line drive over his head into a two-run double. Martin said he wanted to rest Rivers, who just had three days off, against a left-handed pitcher. "It don't bother me," Rivers said. "I don't care if I don't play. I just don't. I don't see nobody doing so much greater than anyone else. What we need is a whole new everything."

Saturday, July 23

New York

Martin is in crisis again. He has more crises than Richard
Nixon. The rumor is that Martin is gone, that Steinbrenner
had decided to fire Martin after the second game of the doubleheader was blown Thursday night. There is no official
denial.

"The thing is all over the park," Martin said, his voice
trembling, tears hidden by sunglasses.

The Yankees won the game, 3–1, but the talk was thick all
day that it was Martin's last game—or maybe tomorrow
would be his last game.

Players asked newsmen what they knew. "Where did the
rumors start? I don't know," Martin said. "Probably the
people that are trying to fire me. Where are they? I don't
know."

Gabe Paul was at his Manhattan apartment, declining to
give even a rudimentary denial of the rumors. "I have nothing to say about it," Paul said. Steinbrenner could not be
reached at his home in Tampa. He will have the last word.

Martin called the players together for what might be considered a last few words. Martin plays on the histrionics of
the moment. He has a touch of theatrics in common with
Leo Durocher.

There was the time in 1962 when Durocher was a coach
for Walter Alston with the Dodgers. Durocher thought the
job should be his, and he and Alston shared no love. But one
night at the Polo Grounds Durocher suffered a violent reaction to penicillin before game time. Before a doctor could
come out of the stands to reach Durocher, the team had to
take the field. And Durocher looked up at Alston and said,
"If this is it, Skip, go get 'em." Leo recovered.

Martin told his players to "have pride in yourselves because
this is a proud organization."

Martin continues to think of the Yankees as the organization he played for twenty years ago. Nothing is the same except the name and the address. The old flannel pinstripes are

double-knits now and the ball park is rebuilt, but his emotional tie is unbroken.

When reporters asked him about his status, Martin identified them as "pallbearers." Then he slipped into a lament.

"I never thought I'd get to manage this team. It was like a dream for me when it happened." Then he stopped talking, a tear on his cheek, and sought the privacy of his bathroom.

He thinks he's fired. There is no denial. Players look at the situation and they see flaws that may have been Martin's undoing. Anybody who watches the team every day sees them. "You keep seeing certain things," Piniella said. "They happen and other people see them and it spreads. It's disgusting. That's what's happening now. Guys come to the ball park wondering why they should bust their butt when some things are going on."

Dick Howser, the third-base coach for nine years, is considered the top candidate. He is not denying anything. "We've heard the rumors before," he said. "What else can I say?"

The loudest defender of Martin is Jackson again, as he was in Detroit in June. He has accepted his turn as designated hitter. "The manager, he's a fine man," Jackson said politely. "We don't have to like the guy. You don't have to be his friend or wash his car, but we should stand by him for nine innings a day."

In his office, Martin sat alone, weeping softly.

Sunday, July 24

New York

What Martin is going through is brutal. You don't have to like him or even respect him to feel that much for him. This is torture.

He spent the night without sleep and then went to the stadium feeling he was driving to his own execution. And then he got a stay. For all we know that's what it is—no more than a delay—and the end may come tonight or tomorrow or who knows when.

Before the game he played the death scene from *Cyrano*, sitting barefoot at his desk, alternating sips of coffee and puffs of cigar, and delaying changing into his uniform. "I feel

like those guys on death row," Martin said, forcing a faint
smile. "But if they were going to make a change today, I
think I would have heard before this. You usually get a
phone call in the morning so you don't come to the ball
park."

The outgoing manager is spared the trial of a news conference at the ball park—or deprived of a forum to speak his
piece.

The rumors were riper after a day of waiting. But he wasn't
going to phone Gabe Paul. "I heard the same rumors when I
was managing the Rangers," Martin said. "Only that time I
made the mistake of picking up the phone and calling Brad
Corbett [the owner] and asking him about it.

" 'It's true,' Corbett told me. 'You're fired.' " Martin
smiled. If it was drama, then there would be comic relief,
too.

Then the phone rang and all those in Martin's office
reacted with a start. "I'll be up," Martin said into the phone.

"That was Gabe. I better keep my street clothes on."

He leaned down and pulled on his socks and shoes. He
lighted a fresh cigar and took some more coffee. "I'm not
rushing up there," he said.

"The first time you get fired, you think nothing can be that
bad again. But each time it gets worse. It was bad when I got
fired in Minnesota, but it was worse in Detroit and even
worse in Texas. And each time I cry. I guess that shows how
weak I am."

And this time, losing this job, will hurt most of all. Martin
wasn't crying, but if he could have been alone for a moment,
he would have. Instead he lapsed into a stream of consciousness, taking leads from questions and taking the answers
where his mind led them. He was asked if perhaps Steinbrenner and Paul were having difficulty finding a replacement. He
agreed. "The man they want is at Montreal, isn't he?"

Dick Williams is at Montreal. He's the man Steinbrenner
first sought in 1974, before Bill Virdon and before Martin.
Montreal executives say that they were not contacted about
Williams and would not make him available, but Martin
thinks he knows Steinbrenner's thinking.

"Williams is firm," Martin said, "and George likes that. He
wants things run just so. He doesn't give a darn if we win, as
long as it's firm." Martin laughed sarcastically.

"You wait and see," he said. "When I'm gone, some of

these players will be at each other's throats. I've been keeping them apart."

Dick Howser apparently has turned down the job in a round-about fashion. "I'm sure they asked Howser," Martin said. Howser, like all the other coaches, is not a Martin selection. He came with the job. He wants to manage. He was interviewed in Texas a couple of years ago, but he's forty and can wait a little longer. "I was never offered this job, though I was considered for it," Howser conceded. "If I was offered the manager's job, I would have to think about it." Howser's difficulty here is that this may be an impossible task if Martin is fired. Howser has never managed any place and has no record to stand up for him. If the Yankees were to come apart under him, he might never get another offer.

"I don't think I would want to be the manager stepping into this job," Martin said.

Martin has thought of ending the torture by himself, by walking away from it, but he says he can't afford to. He said it as if needing $200,000 were something to be ashamed of. "I would have quit yesterday if I could afford it," he said.

He traced the cause of this moment's crisis to the Milwaukee game, and the 4–0 lead blown. "George must have been pretty upset after that," Martin said. "I think I was fired right then."

Martin was still talking as if only the elevator ride to Paul's office separated him from his firing. A functionary knocked at Martin's doorpost and asked permission to have some players sign autographs on the field. Martin agreed. "My last act of authority," he said. The pain was on his face.

He drew another line tracing the course of his difficulties with Steinbrenner back to the spring. Martin had his audience and he had their sympathy. He might not ever have a chance to tell his side of the story in New York again.

He told of the night in St. Petersburg when Steinbrenner and Paul followed the loss to the Mets with a charge through the clubhouse. It was the night Jackson felt Martin deliberately held him out of the game because it was televised back to New York.

"George came into the clubhouse and showed me up in front of ten players, calling me a liar. Said I was supposed to be on the bus. 'Why wasn't I on the bus?'" Martin said. "I told him I was talking to him on the phone when the bus was supposed to leave, that's why. Well, he's shouting at me in front of my players, so now I'm shouting back at him.

" 'Don't ever call me a liar,' I said. 'Never call me a liar.' Well, I slammed my fist down and it hit an ice bucket and the ice went all over him and Gabe, who was standing in the middle. Then I told him he could fire me, but to get out of the clubhouse."

The next morning Martin and Steinbrenner had breakfast together. Steinbrenner, Martin said, apologized. "Ever since then," Martin said, "I knew I was gone."

A half hour after Paul's call, Martin stubbed out his cigar and walked his last fifty yards to the elevator.

Out in the clubhouse, players watched the procession of the reporters in and out of the office. "Look at this scene," Reggie Jackson said. "It's cruder and cruder than anything I ever saw in Oakland. These guys, they just sit around and wait for the big story. It's like throwing a piece of meat to the lions. Nobody gives a damn."

He failed to suggest an alternative procedure for covering an execution on the best-known sports corporation in the country.

"Do you feel sorry for Martin?" Paul Zimmerman of the *Post* asked Jackson.

"Do you really think I'd say that?" Jackson said. "But look, I did go in and talk to him yesterday. Just one human being to another. The man's got a heart, you know. The man is human."

Another half hour later Martin returned smiling. "Everything's all right," he said. "Nothing's changed."

But what about the rumors? "He told me, 'Don't pay any attention to them.' "

Now Martin said he didn't really think he was going to be fired when he stepped out of the elevator. "I think they would have done it another way," he said. "Gabe's a classy guy."

He didn't sound very convincing.

But it was still his job, if only for a matter of hours. When he took the lineup card out to home plate, he was cheered loudly by the big crowd. When he returned to the dugout he was cheered again. Twice, while the Yankees were beating Kansas City, 3–1, Martin ran out to argue calls at first base and each time he was cheered.

"The fans are great," Martin said. "Now if I can only get George to be a fan."

After the game Paul treated the issue of rumors as if they were merely rumors. "There will always be rumors," he said. "Rumors are what brought forty-one thousand people to the ball park this afternoon."

The company can profit even from the torment of one of its employees.

Steinbrenner was still out of contact with the press. He's at the University of North Carolina, where his daughter recently won a scholarship. And Paul was discussing the day as if it were business as usual. "Billy is in no more precarious position than he was last week or the week before. Managing is a precarious job."

Now the Yankees have won two in a row and both on strong pitching. Pitching, among other things, has put Martin in his jeopardy.

By the end of the day, Martin was exhausted.

"What all this is doing," he said, "is making a martyr out of me."

He did not exactly object to the role.

Monday, July 25

New York

Steinbrenner doesn't like the role Martin is playing; it makes Steinbrenner look like the bad guy. On a night with only the slightest excuse to call a rainout, Steinbrenner and Paul assembled the press, not to fire Martin but to lay out the standards by which he would be judged.

I never heard of a team in any sport where the owner and the field leader constantly felt they had to refute the other guy. Maybe this kind of internal squabbling goes on all the time and we just don't know about it and the people here are merely more open. But I can't believe that. This must be a one-of-a-kind relationship.

Steinbrenner poured drinks in his office on the club level of the stadium and said Martin was still the manager, but that not everything Martin said should be taken at face value. "He's saying, 'They're making a martyr out of me,' " Steinbrenner said. "The same thing was said in Texas and in Min-

neapolis and Detroit before that. I don't want any part in
making a martyr of Billy Martin.

"When is somebody going to have enough intelligence to
see through this? Maybe this guy is in the wrong profession."

Steinbrenner was calling Martin a liar.

"He's been creating an opinion that people have been on
him all the time," Steinbrenner said, "and that is not the case.
I'm not out to get Billy Martin. That's a cop-out. That's a lot
of crap. It's a cop-out, but it's not new.

"Any time George Steinbrenner or Gabe Paul, who are
footing the bills, can't make suggestions, something's wrong.
He's not being dictated to and if anybody says he is, they're
not telling it like it is."

On his desk, Steinbrenner had a scrawled list of seven
qualifications for the manager. "They're short of the Ten
Commandments," Paul said. The original were cut in stone;
they may as well be for Martin.

The Seven Commandments, in order, are:
*Won-lost record.
*Does he work hard enough?
*Is he emotionally equipped to lead the men under him?
*Is he organized?
*Is he prepared?
*Does he understand human nature?
*Is he honorable?

By the view of Steinbrenner and Paul, Martin falls short
on six counts. The one that has to save him is the won-lost
record. He won last season; he isn't winning now. This is not
how a dynasty is begun.

After the rainout and before the session, Martin expressed
his feelings about the whole chain of command up to Steinbrenner. "Loyalty to him is a one-way street," Martin said.

It's something other than a matter of loyalty. It's more like
Earl Weaver's reference to understanding that the manager
works for the owner. On more grandiose terms, there's a quo-
tation from Aristotle: "He who has never learned to obey
cannot be a good commander."

The players are caught in the middle. They know they
have to win some games or the whirlpool will be even more
violent. Performance seems to be a product of atmosphere
and it becomes more unsettled every day. "Every day is criti-

cal for Billy," one regular said. "You know how impulsive George is. He's continued to make a mockery of this. I don't have the same respect for Billy I had last season, but George has less than he ever had before. The whole league is laughing at us. Every time we start to come together, something happens."

The responsibility is Martin's. It's not an excuse for him to say of his players, "I can't play for them," as he said.

Steinbrenner likes what he sees and hears of Sparky Anderson, the Reds' manager. They were talking at the All-Star dinner and Anderson claimed the blame for the Reds' standing, despite their offensive might. Steinbrenner said it wasn't Anderson's fault that he didn't have the pitching, and Anderson replied, "Yes it is, unless I find the answer."

Steinbrenner banged his fist on the table as he told the story. "God damn, that's what I like," he said. "I don't like a guy—and I'm not saying it's Billy [but, of course it is]—who will look for other reasons and other people to lay something off on."

* * *

Steinbrenner thinks Jackson has done well, that his mistakes have been made headlines and his successes relegated to the box scores. He sees no excuses. "This team is a great team," Steinbrenner said. "Martin won when nobody was looking for him. The mark of a true champion is to win when everybody is looking for you." That's how Steinbrenner's dynasty begins.

It really isn't a great team. It's not the Yankees or the Dodgers of the 1950s. It's not the A's or the Reds of its own time. The great teams were great defensively; the Reds had no flaws. This team is mediocre at best in the outfield. The infield is sound but not great. In fact, if the Red Sox had pitching you could argue that they were as good as the Yankees.

But these are Steinbrenner's gems and they are certainly better than they've played. And Steinbrenner takes that back to Martin, whose history should have been a warning. "I thought because it was the Yankees, his love of the Yankees, and that it was his fourth time might make a difference," Steinbrenner said.

But like so many managers with the idea that their handling can turn a troublesome player into a winner, Steinbrenner thought his handling could reshape Martin. He should have known better.

Steinbrenner also knows that in every city where Martin has been fired, there has been a backlash at the gate. Martin gets great ovations when he is in trouble here. Management becomes the ogre. A boss I once had put it in simple blue-collar terms: "Bosses is Bastids."

"Billy is the little man and the people can identify with him," Steinbrenner said. "But . . .

"There's no more sword hanging over Billy's head than there is over yours. If you want to say 'sword,' there's a sword hanging over every man's head working in the world."

And until there's a union for managers, the sword drops when the owner says so. This is a very important week for Martin. Again.

Tuesday, July 26

New York

Cliff Johnson's pinch-hit two-run home run in the last of the ninth inning tied the score at 4–4 and Jackson led off the tenth inning with a homer to beat Baltimore, 5–4.

* * *

In the meantime, Jackson has been dropped as host of his syndicated television series *Greatest Sports Legends*. He will be replaced by Tom Seaver. "Jackson was arrogant, egotistical, and extremely hard to work with," said the show's executive producer, Berl Rotfield. Jackson says he anticipates being very busy over the winter when the show is being taped, and gave the producers a convenient way to end his contract.

Wednesday, July 27

New York

The Orioles bombed Catfish Hunter, scored five times in the eighth inning to even the series, 6–4. The big hits were back-to-back home runs by Eddie Murray and Lee May. They still can't get Murray out.

Thursday, July 28

New York

The tumult still pays dividends. There were 40,918 fans out for an afternoon game to see two contenders, and they saw the kind of show Steinbrenner talks about. The Yankees collected fifteen hits; Munson, White, and Nettles hit home runs. Mike Torrez pitched a four-hitter. And they beat the Orioles, 14–2. It was the Yankees' highest run output of the season.

The negative note is that Munson has a sore knee.

But the Yankees have won four of five and now go to the West Coast, where they have every chance to get rich against the A's, the Angels, and the Mariners.

West of Eden

Winning really is a simple equation: Pitch Ron Guidry against triple-A hitters and there's every chance that he'll pitch a shutout. He might not finish the game, but that's a story for another year.

On nights like this, it's even pleasant to be around the Yankees. Guidry isn't yet caught up in the web of suspicions.

The way he remembers it, the International League wasn't ready for him last year. "Many times I thought I was too good for the hitters; they can't hit me," he said. "A lot of times I would come in with the bases full and nobody out and strike out three guys."

(A Southerner drawls. What is it that a Cajun does?)

He would strike out guys like the five A's who have spent time in triple-A this season, one as recently as yesterday. These are Charlie Finley's new A's, the ones he's trying to unload in a big franchise sale. So the Yankees beat the new A's, 4–0. Guidry didn't need help until the A's filled the bases with two out in the last of the ninth.

Then Sparky Lyle came on for his sixteenth save and chased the ghost of the four-run lead the Yankees blew last week, the game that pushed Martin to the brink.

At Syracuse last year Guidry pitched forty innings, struck out fifty batters, allowed only fifteen hits, and had a microscopic ERA of 0.68. Only "nothing" is better than that. "He don't be change nothing," said Oakland center fielder Tony Armas, who hit against Guidry the last two seasons in the International League.

220

Guidry pitched all of 134 innings the last two seasons and has 120 innings this season. He is not one of those who complain about extended rest. The question is whether he can last.

Munson took a half day off as DH, and Jackson, who bruised his elbow yesterday, did not play. He did find an opportunity to tell a familiar Bay Area reporter about his trials with the New York press. "Playing in New York has been a different experience," he told Glenn Schwartz. "It's calloused me; I haven't said much lately.

"There's no comparison between the media here [San Francisco/Oakland] and media there and the way you're treated. The press has written a lot of controversial things that I've had to deal with. I still have fun on the field, but there's no more show biz side to me."

Since when is he having fun on the field?

Saturday, July 30

Oakland

Underneath the droning of the clubhouse radio piping in the postgame interview, Chris Chambliss asked the questions of Roy White, in the adjoining locker. "How many ribbies you get today?" Chambliss asked.

White shrugged at the innocence of the question. "Four," he said.

"Is that all?"

"What do you mean? Is that a bad day's work?"

"It just seemed like there was more."

White had a home run and three singles, scored two runs and batted in four as they beat the A's 9–3. A lot of what White has done since 1966 has been more than it seemed.

From the speaker came the commentary from Reggie Jackson, who homered for the first run of the game, to the A's official broadcaster. "Ninety percent of what the New York press has written about this team has not been true," Jackson said. He blamed the press for having "used human beings" for their own purposes, and so on, attributing some of the Yankees' shortfall to the pressures inflicted by the press. He doesn't miss a chance.

White doesn't look to place blame. He's hitting .287, has scored 41 runs and batted in 40, which is about his normal pace. He doesn't complain about being moved up or down in the batting order. He does know last season was more fun. "It has been a more unpleasant year," he said. "It hasn't been much fun to come to the ball park."

It was their sixth victory in their last seven games. They have begun the trip by winning the first two. They are still 24–27 on the road, which makes even the soft underbelly of the league dangerous. Plus, White finds the media out of New York trying. "When we win, nothing is said," he said. "When we lose, were 'millionaires.' I can't stand the stereotype; we're not all making a million."

What White doesn't understand is that the old Yankees who won every year were hated more deeply by the rest of America.

What Jackson said he didn't understand when he made his diatribe was that it was being piped into the Yankee clubhouse—as it was the night before and the night before that, and back to the day the speaker was installed. "I wouldn't have said those things if I knew the New York press was listening," he said. He was "embarrassed" when he was later told he had taken "a cheap shot."

There was little doubt of the outcome of the game until Don Gullett came out after six innings. "Are you going to write about the game or about Gullett coming out?" Jackson demanded. The game comes and goes in a day; the condition of Gullett's arm has a more profound effect. Billy Martin said Gullett "just never got loose." That's been Gullett's problem for two seasons. He will not pitch on four days' rest as planned.

After the last time Gullett pitched, he said he would make a statement but would answer no questions. He pitched 8⅔ innings then and pronounced that he was happy the team won and his arm felt good. He said he would answer no questions because he had "made an ass" of himself answering questions the time before that.

Today, with a three-hour differential ticking off New York deadlines, Gullett never came out of the trainer's room to say whether he was happy the team had won or how his arm felt. Sometime I feel there's a better way to make a living.

Sunday, July 31

Oakland

Even when they sweep a series from the A's, the Yankees leave an aftertaste of laughter with the players who know the difference between good and bad. The A's are bad enough to laugh at themselves, but it wasn't supposed to be this difficult for the Yankees.

"I laugh in an ironic way," Bill North said. He was the center fielder next to Jackson in the A's noisy championship years. He is a confidant of Jackson, Hunter, and Holtzman. "That's why I laugh," he said. "You see all the talent they have and they're caught up in all that bullshit. It's human nature to do what they're doing, but a man should be above that. They shouldn't be tied up in kids' games. They're like a bunch of hens getting together."

They beat the A's, 9–2, and are a game out of first place, but still in third, and that's what makes people who thought they knew better roll their eyes. "That team, I said even if they didn't get along, they should win by ten games," North said. "I was mistaken. They've lost the objective."

Also watching the Yankees from across the field is George Medich, the pitcher-to-be doctor who was a Yankee from 1973 to 1975. He knows a number of the people quite well. "They're not enjoying playing as much as they used to," he said. "They don't seem to be getting along. Maybe they're taking the game and their problems too seriously.

"I always felt fun made the game a lot easier. If there's fun in the clubhouse and guys get along with each other, you're not afraid to make mistakes because your teammates will criticize you."

North and Medich blame the Yankees' own unwillingness to cope with the scrutiny. "For that money, they conscripted to every bit of that scrutiny," North said.

"With the Pirates last year," Medich said, "guys teased each other about things that were written. Here—the Yankees—they get mad at what's written and when they get teased they get even madder."

The convenient excuse among the Yankees is the introduction of Jackson. North, having been Jackson's teammate and having had a fistfight and a long period of silence with him, doesn't buy it. "A player can't upset the whole thing," North said. "You're dealing with Billy Martin and he has to eat it. His job is to win; his ego is getting in the way of getting players to win and he's defeating his own purpose. The manager cannot compete with his players for recognition. The owner should not be in competition, either.

"The owner is supposed to get the players. The manager is supposed to get the most out of them and do whatever needs to be done to get it. You don't ride Reggie Jackson; you'll get him so tight he can't do anything."

North is a student of Jackson, dating back to 1964 at Arizona State. He sees Jackson as still not a big-city person, still finding New York strange. "He puts so much pressure on himself," North said. "He wants to live up to the reputation he has as a superstar. He suffers more than people understand. He was sensitive at college, too, but at Arizona State he did what he was told. Little things he does here, he does out of sheer impulse.

"He likes a close friend who's near him. If you're close to Reggie, he'll confide and lay his heart out to you. Everybody who's as intense as he is needs to do that."

With the A's, Jackson had a family situation, growing up with the same people. Back in Fort Lauderdale, Jackson already mourned the separation from Joe Rudi. In the most difficult times with the A's, Jackson was able to have dinner with Rudi and pour his heart out. He was able to weep—actually shed tears—with Dick Williams, too. Jackson has not found anything like that relationship on the Yankees—not with the team as a whole, not with any individual, and certainly not with Martin.

* * *

A more academic opinion comes from Dr. Thomas Tutko, professor of psychology at San Jose State and co-director of the Institute of Athletic Motivation. He has a similar view. "Martin is so feisty and blind in terms of winning that he doesn't take how people feel into consideration," Tutko said. "And Jackson is so sensitive.

"Martin made it as a player by working his ass off, and in people like that there's a basic dislike and a jealousy for people with raw, natural talent. The moment a gifted player doesn't show a second effort or doesn't do what Martin would have done, that becomes a reason to get heavy on him."

Tutko sees Martin as feeling he's still playing—in competition, as North put it. "He wants to be playing," Tutko said. "The really good managers have removed their personal winning and losing and doing well from the game. They're really mediums through which the players on the field can become better. Martin is still on the field, not in the dugout.

"He is out of tune with the modern players. As sensitive as Jackson is, he's also intelligent. He says, 'Why should I run into the wall when we're losing, 9–0? It's not going to win the game, it's only going to get me hurt! And Martin didn't know any other way to play the game. The minute he sees anything other than what he would have done, he takes it as a personal affront."

North and Tutko also have an identical forecast. "What happens is the function of a very talented team with a lot of guys with big egos who all want to be superstars," Tutko said.

The feeling is that somewhere along the line the Yankees will realize that they're at the brink of ultimately embarrassing themselves. "The team that choked," Steinbrenner warned them. Then they will be shocked into remembering what their business is all about.

Then other teams and people will stop laughing at them. "Right now," Jackson said, "they all think of us as a zoo."

* * *

The Yankees didn't announce it until after the word came through the Oakland side of the grapevine, but Gullett and Hunter are to be examined by Dr. Frank Jobe, the savior of arms, in Los Angeles on Tuesday or Wednesday while the team is in Anaheim.

Hunter said he still feels something uncomfortable in his shoulder. Gullett said, "No comment."

Why should anybody refuse to admit that he's going to see a doctor? Does denying a condition make it go away? Is a sore arm a social disease?

Monday, August 1

Anaheim

Recall George Steinbrenner's list of commandments. There are several involved every day.

After a one-game rest for his ailing elbow, Reggie Jackson played Saturday and hit a home run. Yesterday he sat while left-handed Vida Blue pitched for Oakland. Martin said that Jackson wanted to play but "his elbow still wasn't one hundred percent." He said Jackson would play tonight "whoever is pitching.'

When tonight's lineup came through, Jackson wasn't in it. "They told me I was hurt," Jackson said, deliberately cryptic.

Lou Piniella played against left-handed Ken Brett, the classic by-the-book managerial maneuver. Left-handed or not, Jackson remembered hitting a home run this season while Brett was pitching for the White Sox, and a grand-slam and a three-run homer off Brett last season. Brett wasn't quite certain about the three-run homer but the others were clear enough in his mind.

One of the commandments was that Martin do sufficient preparation.

Brett pitched nine innings and the Angels beat the Yankees, 4–1. He allowed six hits, and eighteen of the Yankees' twenty-seven outs were on grounders. Roy White called all those ground balls "the mystery of the year."

With the Yankees—hardly.

Catfish Hunter also pitched a complete game and the Angels' four runs were the product of an infield hit, an infield error, a bunt single, two sacrifice flies, and a suicide squeeze. He said he still had not decided whether he would see Dr. Jobe. But it was learned later tonight that Hunter and Gullett have appointments for tomorrow. No announcement. The Yankees always have to stir in some intrigue.

That's really nothing new to Brett, who began last season with the Yankees, pitching two innings in five weeks. "Gabe Paul lied to me," Brett said.

First there were the contract negotiations that left Brett unsigned. "Gave told me the Pirates were going to cut my salary before they traded me to the Yankees," Brett said. "So I called Joe Brown with the Pirates and he said no way he would cut me with my statistics."

Then there was the trade that sent equally unused lefty Larry Gura to Kansas City for Fran Healy two days before Brett was traded to Chicago. Brett wanted to go to Kansas City, where his brother George was playing third base. "I was told the Yankees offered a list of six players," Brett said. "Gabe told me I was offered and not taken. George told me he learned the Royals would have taken me if I had been on the list.

"That's what I remember about the Yankees."

Tuesday, August 2

Anaheim

If this is Anaheim, Disneyland can't be far away, and who else belongs there by the Yankees? At the base of the simulated Matterhorn Thurman Munson's simulated bobsled came out into the light and lurched to a halt, with Munson seated behind two dating teenagers. Fran Healy, an earlier arrival, greeted them. "Pardon me," he said to the couple, "is that your son in the back seat?"

The couple turned and looked, and Healy and Munson broke up. "It was so funny," Healy said, "those kids and then big Thurman scrunched in there with his mustache and beard."

Mustache and beard? Yes, by the hair of his chinny-chin-chin, Munson has a five-day beard to go with his traditional walrus mustache. He's had a beard before, in 1975 when he hit .318 and had 102 RBIs. "I looked good in it," he said when bearded in his locker. It was also the year Steinbrenner, the rules maker, was not around the team. "George was expelled for a while," Munson explained.

It was a precious rare moment of lightness. They battered the Angels, 9–3, with 19 hits, and they haven't had that many hits since before July 12, 1975. That was as far back as the Yankees could trace the information. Hunter and Gullett had come back with hopeful medical reports, according to the team.

What Munson is doing is subject to speculation. Either his beard is a gesture of his feeling of well-being with the team on a comfortable pace, or a gesture of defiance. Steinbrenner does not like beards; he tolerates mustaches.

"I like beards," Munson said, puffing a cigar. "I didn't ask George about it. Billy Martin doesn't mind. If he doesn't mind, it probably means—" Munson laughed. He slid his hands across each other in front of him."—George is the other way." He laughed again.

Munson's knee is well again. He accounted for five of the first six runs. Jackson and Mickey Rivers each had three hits, Mike Torrez pitched a complete game, and the Yankees have won nine of twelve. And Munson was twitting the boss. They have not been closer than a shaky armistice. Martin is identifying Munson as the man who charged that Steinbrenner is running the team, and now the beard. Can Munson force a trade for himself by embarrassing Steinbrenner?

Munson isn't saying. "Somewhere," he said, "is that against the Constitution—to say I can't grow a beard—or an employment contract? I'm worried about my health, not my beard."

And what if Steinbrenner objects? "Then," Munson said, "I'll blame it on the writers. Writers have beards."

Gullett was advised to rest briefly for the tightness in his shoulder and said he was relieved to be told as much. Hunter who is to pitch in turn, was not so comforted. "The doctor told me a pitcher ain't supposed to pitch," Hunter said. "He said your arm is not made to come up here." He made an overhand motion, which is just the way he pitches. He was advised to build up the muscles by exercise.

Jackson was to see Dr. Jobe, also, but was in a car on a freeway when he was struck from the rear. Nobody was hurt, but Jackson didn't have his elbow examined.

And, to introduce another issue, Kentucky State Police found a cultivated growth of marijuana among the corn of Gullett's farm in Lynn, Kentucky. The police said they had no suspicion of Gullett, and Steinbrenner proclaimed his pitcher the "modern-day Jack Armstrong," the all-American boy.

"I told the doctor," Hunter said, "I'm going to go home to my farm and do what Gullett's done."

Wednesday, August 3

Anaheim

The pretty road trip doesn't look so pretty anymore. The Angels beat them, 5–3, with a mediocre Nolan Ryan, and the Yankees lost two of three here. "After we won three in Oakland, I was hoping we'd win two out of three here and go in and smoke Seattle," Munson said.

Instead the Yankees gave away runs and missed chances to make the kind of good plays winners make. Now they are four games behind Boston in the loss column. It's too early to cry about it, but then they didn't laugh much on the way to the airplane. They would win all three games in Seattle and still go home having lost ground. The Red Sox, on an identical trip, haven't lost.

The Angels exploited some Yankee difficulties. "If you're playing guys who can throw, your basic thinking when the game starts is to stop," said Angels third-base coach Del Crandall. "You're going to run on anything you can against the Yankees."

With bases full and one out in the second inning, Rivers caught a fly in medium center. A good thrower would have had a chance on the runner coming home from third, but Rivers is a weak thrower. Rivers, who will not acknowledge that, threw for the plate instead of preventing the runner on first from advancing. So when the next batter singled, two more runs scored instead of one. And the Yankees lost by two.

The Angels are suffering in the light of their big spending in the free-agent draft. Joe Rudi and Bobby Grich have been injured for most of the season. Don Baylor is having a bad year. The Angels are not contenders as expected and Larry Sherry has been fired as manager. That's the kind of evidence the owners like to display to show how players' freedom has hurt the game. They do not mention that players like Mike Schmidt and Mike Luzinski of the Phillies got equivalent contracts to keep them from moving, are having fine seasons, and have the Phillies in first place. The same thing with many of the Dodgers, who are running away in their division.

A reporter asked Martin what he thought of the results of

the open market. He said, "Some players have good statistics but haven't contributed to the team." The clear inference is that he was talking about his own man, Jackson. Martin also often mentions that Munson does not love Jackson.

Friday, August 5

Seattle

Times are explosive again. Martin has requested that Munson shave, but has too much regard for Munson to be more demanding. The story that Jackson has the power to break his contract—and will do so—is around again and Jackson isn't denying it. The Yankees are playing lousy and Martin is at the brink again. The Mariners beat them, 5–3, and the Red Sox beat Oakland, 1–0. If the Red Sox get some pitching . . .

"I'm an optimistic-type guy," Martin said. "I got a little more patience in me than a lot of guys. I feel this club is going to win. I've been in races like this as a player."

But if they do come on, will he be around to smell the roses? Never mind smell the roses; how much longer will he be around to smell the sweat?

It seems appropriate to mention that the original Skid Row was in Seattle. When it was a big logging town, the tall trees used to be gravity-fed downhill through the town into Puget Sound. It was, of course, lined with cheap hotels and bars, but there is a rebirth of the old part of the city, perhaps prompted by the presence of the crowds at the Kingdome. The city even has a fine restaurant, El Gaucho, that serves until 4 AM, which is a delight after a night game. Now it's the Yankees who are on the skids. Appetites are for quick-service hamburgers, not leisurely dining.

Saturday, August 6

Seattle

More and more the Yankee script looks like anything but what Steinbrenner had in mind. It looks like something by

Gilbert and Sullivan as adapted by the Marx Brothers. There's the cast: the ruler of the queen's navy, the very model of the modern major general, the captain of the *Pinafore*, the pirates, and the recurring refrain: "Things are seldom what they seem. Skim milk masquerades as cream." You'd expect Groucho to show up as Captain Jeffrey Spaulding, the African explorer.

Beards and trades and tirades, and telephone calls from the home office to deny everything. Munson is directly defying Steinbrenner but insists he isn't trying to force a trade. "That doesn't even have anything to do with it," he said.

This morning Gabe Paul phoned the team hotel to issue a statement denying, among other things, that there is any kind of "escape provision" in Jackson's five-year contract. Paul said there is nothing to Jackson's contract that is not on file with the league. According to the rules, there couldn't be such a covenant, but that doesn't mean there couldn't be a letter in a safe somewhere or a verbal agreement. Paul has been party to such things in the past.

Jackson, who earlier indicated he had his way out, now nods and shakes his head but clarifies nothing. His attorney, Steve Kaye, will not clarify anything either. "Actually, I don't remember what all the agreements were," he said. Does a lawyer in this business not remember if there is an agreement of that magnitude? Come on.

When Jackson has been in his deepest depression, people such as Kaye, agent Gary Walker, and business agent Matt Merola have advised him to postpone any kind of decision until the cool of the off-season. Then, if the Yankees have won and Jackson has had a good season—he does have pretty good figures now—continuing in New York might not look so forbidding. And there's every chance in the world that Martin will be gone.

When it was suggested to Jackson that Frank Robinson might be the next manager, he said: "Just say, 'Jackson smiled for the first time all season.' "

Jackson missed the appointment to have his elbow examined when the team was in Anaheim and couldn't go on the off-day Thursday because he was buying a homesite in Monterey. He planned to go for the examination next Monday while the Yankees are playing an exhibition game in Syracuse. Imagine the reaction of the other players if they had to play that game while Jackson went to see a doctor he should have seen before! So the ball club decided to cancel that appointment, and Jackson will go to Syracuse.

And by Monday night Munson's beard—eleven days old by then—will be seen by Paul and Steinbrenner. In the meantime, the Yankees are struggling with teams they should be beating easily. They will not be in first place when the boss sees them. "One thing I do know," Paul's statement said, "is that we are leading the league in loose talking."

Tonight the Mariners beat them, 9–2. Sparky Lyle gave up the first indoor inside-the-park home run in American League history to Ruppert Jones. Mickey Rivers hit three doubles, but ran the bases and played center field as if in a trance. And Lou Piniella scorched the silence of defeat in the clubhouse by demanding that the dissidents speak up at that time. Nobody spoke up.

Nobody had to. It's already insanity here. So legally, Jackson had no termination clause. And the Marx Brothers have already explained that there is no sanity clause.

Sunday, August 7

Seattle

The Yankees are coming home by way of Syracuse—figuratively and literally. They have two months to come from five games behind the Red Sox and have the talent with which to do it. But there are doubts building within the Yankees that they can pull themselves together enough to do it. They are picking at themselves and each other.

They beat the Mariners, 7–1, with Mike Torrez' third straight complete game, which might be considered a good sign, but there's no intensity in their play. There are subtle signs of their disease. There was the blaring of Mickey Rivers' tape player in the clubhouse after the game, boring into the thoughts of those players who can't brush off the games won and lost.

Rivers jiggled in rhythm to the music while he toweled himself. Reggie Jackson walked across the room to lower the volume. When Jackson resumed dressing, Rivers restored the sound.

Rivers didn't play because he is involved in his personal financial problems again, and Martin thinks that's what causes

Rivers to forget what he's doing on the field. In his place, Paul Blair hit a two-run homer that was the big hit in the six-run inning.

Martin says the time may come soon to bat Jackson cleanup, but there isn't all that much waiting time to make the move. Jackson is wound up in several other issues now. He feels deliberately put down because he doesn't get permission to hit on a 3-and-0 count while others do. Yesterday he was denied permission to skip the exhibition game for the doctor's appointment in Los Angeles. Today he was refused permission to stay behind because of a death in his girl friend's family in Oakland.

And the clubhouse is still ringing with the aftermath of Piniella's denouncement last night. Some players accept Piniella's sincerity. Some others think he made a grandstand play. Piniella said he'd like to speak to each of the doubters individually.

"I didn't say 'you,' I said 'we,'" Piniella said this afternoon. His face was flushed. "If I was not to care and just kept my mouth shut, I could just collect my money, play out my option, and drive home to Tampa at the end of the season. I've got this one-year contract. I've got more to lose by speaking out here than any of the guys who have five-year contracts. I'm about twentieth on this club in salary." Piniella cares.

Martin cares like anything. He shows it in his eyes and the quavering tone of his voice more than in anything he says or does. He shows it when he reminds everyone that he played six seasons with the Yankees and they won each season.

Martin shows it when he tries to relate how he does things to the way Casey Stengel did them. Stengel used to push hard when the team was winning and ease up when it lost. "We won seventeen in a row in 1953 and every day he was worse," Martin said. "Then we turned around and lost seven in a row and he didn't say a thing."

So before today's game Martin had a soft-toned meeting with the players to suggest that if they were professionals they could forget their squabbling and rally themselves.

The distinction is that Stengel's Yankees didn't have this kind of bickering, and Stengel never let things get so out of hand.

Martin did make one more specific request that Munson shave. "I can ask," Martin said. "He's too hard of a player, too good of a player, to force him. If it's a reflection on me, it's a reflection on me."

In Steinbrenner's eyes, it may be the last reflection necessary to show that Martin can't control the team. Piniella has suggested as much to Munson. "If the owner is looking for an alibi to fire the man, that's bullshit," Munson said. "He doesn't have to look to me as an excuse."

Munson still insists he isn't trying to force a trade with his whiskers. He says he has too much leverage to need that. But he won't explain why he has added one more issue to a team drowning in issues. He said he had not decided what he would do if Steinbrenner himself requested that he shave when the team returns to New York.

"I've been here seven years before this," Munson said. "Doesn't anybody remember? I get blamed for whatever was between Reggie and me, and George and Billy, and Reggie and Billy."

But now Munson, probably the player most loyal to Martin, is violating the rule the manager is hired to enforce. "What's a rule?" Munson said.

That's just the point, said Piniella, both a critic and a supporter of Martin. "There are no rules on this club," he said. "People are making a lot of money. They're told to get to the ball park at a specific time; they come whenever they feel like it. We're told no loud music; we have loud music in the clubhouse, in the shower, in the shithouse, in the bus. Maybe it all gets back to the manager. A lot of the problems may come from the manager."

And Steinbrenner, back home in Tampa, said he knew of no plans to change managers at this point. While the Yankees were struggling to win five of nine on the trip, the Red Sox were sweeping all nine against the same weak opposition. The Yankees are six games behind in the loss column. And Steinbrenner is embarrassed. "I apologize," he said, "to the City of New York."

* * *

Just to keep in practice, on the plane to Syracuse—after it was too late to make the New York morning papers—the Yankees announced that Don Gullett and Ed Figueroa had stayed beyind to see Dr. Jobe.

Hair Today, Gone Tomorrow

Monday, August 8

Syracuse

A crisis was averted in front of the mirror in room 302 of the Sheraton Motor Inn. A Syracuse restaurant owner and friend of Thurman Munson's brought a razor and shaving cream and took it to Munson's room. Munson shaved. The eleven-day-old growth of trouble went down the drain before Gabe Paul could see it. If you can believe it, George Steinbrenner, in Tampa, said he never even heard about the beard.

When the team got to MacArthur Stadium, Martin said Munson had done it "all himself." Munson wouldn't say anything. "I ain't talking to any writer the rest of the year," he said.

To add insult to insult, the Syracuse farmhands beat the big brothers, 14–5. Ken Holtzman pitched the last two innings and didn't give up an earned run.

When the game was delayed by rain, Munson was excused to catch a plane home to Canton. Rivers told Martin if Munson didn't have to play, then he didn't have to play. Munson left. Rivers returned to the locker room without playing and was fined.

Wednesday, August 10

New York

A flourish of trumpets, or something like that. Reggie Jackson batted fourth tonight.

235

The Yankees knocked out Vida Blue in the first inning and beat the A's, 6–3. Cause and effect? Who knows?

But it was an important concession for Martin to make. It was only the eleventh time in 110 games that Jackson has batted cleanup and the first time since July 16.

A lot of people think Martin was being deliberately contrary. The owner did want Jackson batting fourth. Jackson did want to bat fourth. Martin insists he was merely waiting for the right time.

At this time there was no denying either the need of the team or the evidence. Since July 4, Jackson had batted in twenty runs in twenty-three games, while Chris Chambliss, Martin's monument to last season's wisdom, had driven in nine runs in twenty-nine games.

Ten days ago in Oakland, Jackson didn't even play against Blue. Martin then offered that Jackson's elbow was still sore even though he had hit a home run the game before. It took a long time for Martin to read the evidence—or for Steinbrenner to read it to him.

Now Martin says, "If he keeps swinging the bat good, he'll stay there."

Graig Nettles and Munson walked and Jackson singled the first Yankee run home. Nettles and then Munson? It was an odd lineup for Martin. Roy White and Mickey Rivers also sat out. And when it looked for a while as if the game might be rained out, Martin delayed announcing the lineup. "What's the point?" he said. "If we get rained out, then the players who aren't in the lineup won't know and they won't get mad."

Martin made one other strong concession. He said that the newspaper stories relating many of the team's problems—other than his own psychological warfare—had often been correct and newsworthy. "If you worked for me and didn't write that stuff, I'd fire you," he said.

* * *

The pitching remains problematical. Don Gullett had pain throwing before the game and may have to go on the disabled list. Ed Figueroa is available to pitch.

For Saturday, Martin plans to start Holtzman, who last started on July 3, and either Dick Tidrow or Ken Clay on Sunday.

Thursday, August 11

New York

The last time Mike Torrez talked about it, he was still uncertain about the good faith with which the Yankees were negotiating, and he was upset. Now he has formed a conclusion and it's easier for him to handle the darkest thoughts than the uncertainty.

He pitched a 3–0 two-hitter over the Oakland A's and pronounced himself "a hired hand." He is unsigned, and as time wears on, it has become clear that the Yankees aren't all that interested in signing him. "What they offered me makes me feel like I'm not wanted," he said. "They offered me what a utility player is making."

For all of the games Torrez has won over the last three years—an average of seventeen a season—Paul and Steinbrenner are not impressed enough to regard Torrez as a player they are afraid of losing. What they have done is rent him for the season, beginning April 27 when it was clear that Catfish Hunter was going to have problems.

"I just feel that George Steinbrenner has not been honest with me, the way negotiations have gone," Torrez said. "I felt in my heart they wanted me because they traded three players for me. Steinbrenner said they would negotiate, and then they didn't for two months.

"I feel like they're using me. They got me for a year and that's all. I'm just fed up with making changes. Now I know I'll have to make another one."

Having reached that conclusion, Torrez has settled into his best pattern. He has pitched four straight complete-game victories and allowed five earned runs over that span. He has maintained that he pitches best on a four-day rotation and this was his first time around on the fourth day. "I'm convinced," Martin said. Historically, Torrez has pitched best in the second half of the season. He has 10–3 last season in the second half and has a career record of 24–8.

He even counted a game over a team being nicknamed the Oakland Triple A's. It was the A's thirteenth straight loss, matching the team record set when their first name was Kansas City.

Again Jackson produced in the cleanup slot, singling home the first run in the first inning. And Chambliss followed with a double for the second run.

Graig Nettles left the game after injuring his knee. That was officially diagnosed as "a twisted knee" by team physician Dr. Maurice Cowen. In his first season, Dr. Cowen fits right in with the Yankees: Ask him a question and he runs into the trainer's room.

If Nettles has a worse injury, the Yankees will recall Mickey Klutts, who is playing well at Syracuse. He has recovered from what the Yankees still are calling a "jammed sprain."

And Don Gullett has been put on the disabled list, so Gil Patterson was recalled.

Friday, August 12

New York

Less than a week since their last crisis, it looks as if they are ready to go on a tear. Jackson is already on one. He hit a double and a triple in the first game and knocked in three runs. He hit two mighty home runs in successive at bats in the second game. He also threw out a runner at the plate. The Yankees beat the Angels, 10–1 and 9–3, and now they've won five in a row. They haven't had a streak like this since early May.

"I think this is the way it is planned by the master architect, the man upstairs," Lou Piniella said. On this team, the man upstairs is Steinbrenner.

Catfish Hunter and Ed Figueroa pitched complete games and the team has scored 35 runs in its last five games. That is what the man upstairs had in mind. It has taken just a little longer than he had in mind.

"Asking this team to win seventy-five percent of the time is asking too much," Jackson said. "I looked at this team when we began and thought we could win sixty-five percent or sixty percent." Either of those percentages usually means a championship.

Finding his own level for Jackson means applause and cheers, which usually means more inspiration and confidence for him. Twice he turned and doffed his cap to the crowd. "That's what it's all about," he said. "It should be fun for me and for the fans."

Chris Chambliss hit two home runs in the first game and Paul Blair played center field in both games. It is not always fun for Mickey Rivers. He has been out of the lineup for five straight games. Martin thinks Rivers is still "distracted" by his personal problems. Sometimes sitting Rivers down gets him over his distraction. Sometimes he is more distracted when he gets back in the game. Immediately after he replaced Blair in the second game, there was a fly ball to center that Rivers barely chased and Jackson had to come over from right field to make the catch.

Hunter, who gave up three home runs his last game, pointed out that he gave up only one tonight. That one was the 338th allowed in Hunter's career, the American League record.

The third baseman in both games was Mickey Klutts. Nettles, with his sprain, was not present in the clubhouse. "I was in Syracuse, came home after the game, and heard Nettles had broken his ankle," Klutts said. "You know how rumors start." Klutts doubled in the first game for his first major-league hit. To make room for him, Dell Alston was sent down, wondering how someone batting .379 could be demoted.

And Art Fowler was taken on as the second pitching coach. Fowler, a portly, rheumy-looking man with a permanently red face, was Martin's pitching coach and drinking buddy with the Twins, Tigers, and Rangers. Every manager likes to have one coach he feels is completely loyal, to listen to gripes and pick up the vibrations in the clubhouse. Hiring him is either a gesture of support for Martin, or the front office is telling him no more excuses. Cloyd Boyer, the management man, operates in the bullpen and Fowler is at Martin's side in the dugout. He has also been given the listening post next to Jackson's locker in the clubhouse.

Saturday, August 13

New York

The reports of Nettles' broken leg were exaggerated. Klutts again played third base, all right, but Nettles pinch hit in the twelfth inning. And there's nothing wrong with Reggie Jackson's arm. He threw out no less a runner than Bobby Bonds at the plate, trying to score the potential winning run in the top of the ninth. That's two runners at the plate in two days for Jackson.

With the tie preserved, the Yankees left the game in the hands of Sparky Lyle, and in his sixth inning he gave up the winning run. The Angels won, 6–5, in twelve.

You have to figure, two outs and two strikes and Lyle is not going to give up the winning hit to Mario Guerrero, but Lyle can't do it all the time. He had allowed only two earned runs in twenty-five innings. And the Yankees had won five in a row, which isn't bad but not enough to keep them from running to the off-limits rooms.

Ken Holtzman, making his first major-league appearance since July 15, was given a 3–0 lead in the first inning and was out of the game losing, 4–3, in the third. That meant Ken Clay had to pitch four innings. By process of elimination, Dick Tidrow becomes tomorrow's starter. Lyly is available for one batter. The situation demands some heroics from Tidrow.

* * *

It was Old Timers Day at Yankee Stadium. They created the event in 1939 to announce Lou Gehrig's retirement. Most teams have copied the successful promotion, but nobody does it as well as the Yankees. After all, they do have the most noted oldtimers. This time they brought back Jack Martin, the oldest living alumnus, a Yankee in 1912 when they were called the Highlanders. He was born in 1887.

Martin told of being spiked and the trainer coating the wound with shellac, and of watching Ty Cobb assault a fan who'd been heckling. He told his tale to Reggie Jackson, standing bare-chested and listening intently. "I know about that heckling," Jackson said. "Let it roll off your back," Martin advised.

They posed together for a photographer. Jackson requested that Martin autograph a picture. Martin signed. "Put my name on it," Jackson insisted.

"Who are you?" Martin asked.

"Reggie Jackson."

"Reggie Jackson?" Martin said. "You look like him. I didn't know who you were. Listen, you keep on doing what the hell you're doing now and we'll win it."

The old man was thrilled. It was Jackson at his most charming. He wanted to make an old ball player happy. It was a simple gesture, but I can think of only a tiny handful of professional athletes who would have had such consideration for a stranger.

Sunday, August 14

New York

In almost three years as a relief pitcher, Tidrow has never stopped thinking of himself as a starting pitcher and wishing he were one. When he went to the mound to start today, he was clean-shaven around his thick, drooping mustache. That isn't Tidrow's custom as the Yankees' other relief pitcher. He hadn't started since last July, but he remembered what his pattern was back in 1974, when he was still a starter. He shaved before he pitched "out of superstition."

Life is different for a starter. "I realized the game wasn't on the line on every pitch; I could make a mistake," Tidrow said. He could, perhaps, but he didn't. He allowed only two singles in six innings and would have stayed longer if the Yankees didn't have an eleven-run lead. They won, 15–3, and they saved three innings of work by Tidrow at a time when every inning counts. Martin thinks he is better off starting Tidrow rather than Gil Patterson, who pitched the last three innings, or Ken Clay. Martin thinks Lyle can carry the bullpen without Tidrow for two weeks, until the rotation straightens out. It's a calculated risk. They do have to get the pitching in order if they are going to catch the Red Sox.

So they got a big bonus when five staggering innings from Tidrow would have been acceptable. They also got the return

of Graig Nettles to the lineup with a three-run home run.
And among the fifteen hits were four by Mickey Rivers,
whose enthusiasm is sometimes questioned by the manager
and doubted by teammates.

Rivers said there have been "little problems" with Billy
Martin. "Everybody says to leave your problems at home and
go out and play," Rivers said. "Anybody can say that, but it's
not easy to do, you know." He said he likes to play every
day, but other players say Rivers takes himself out of the
lineup more than any player they've ever seen. What he
would like is to be able to play every day when he wants to.
The evidence others cite is the fact that he has been thrown
out stealing thirteen times in thirty-three attempts, after being
caught only seven times in fifty tries last season. "The manager, he doesn't like to run," Rivers said.

Rivers doesn't like to concede that Martin is punishing him
for his inattention. "Yeah," Rivers explained, "he gives me a
little rest."

But when Rivers does his job, he is a wonder at leading the
offense. He began everything by leading off the first inning
with a home run. For a little guy, he can hit a ball a long
way. "You do something like that, it gives the team a lift," he
said, in his best good humor. He pointed to elongated Cliff
Johnson, who caught while Thurman Munson rested on his
slump. "Like this big guy over here," Rivers continued. "He
was trying to catch up to me all afternoon and he couldn't
make it."

Monday, August 15

New York

Intensity is the difference between a player thinking he has
been playing as hard as he can and realizing there is something more involved. The best of teams in third place in the
middle of August can make the discovery.

Intensity is twenty Yankees after their own game is over,
groaning and cursing in front of the lounge television as the
Red Sox survive a ninth-inning threat. "Usually they would
have been out of here a long time ago," said Mike Torrez,
who spent the last four months observing much and saying
little.

Intensity is a suicide squeeze play with a 1–0 lead in the second inning. Or maybe intensity is in the eye of the beholder, as Dick Howser said. Torrez sees it, or rather feels it.

Torrez pitched his fifth consecutive winning complete game as they beat the White Sox, 6–2. After a thoroughly disappointing first half, he has emerged as the Catfish Hunter of the pitching staff. He has also emerged from his zone of silence.

"Everybody is more enthusiastic," he said. "You can feel it. It's a time of the season when we feel we have to pull together. It's a gut feeling. That wasn't happening before."

Torrez sees the Yankees with the semidetachment of a relative outsider. He sees them in the way of a number of other players in the league who said they were waiting for the Yankees to feel they were embarrassing themselves enough to kick themselves in the ass. "They were the New York Yankees and they won last year and they bettered themselves so much," Torrez said. "I think they were taking it for granted."

Through the turbulence of his four months here Torrez kept his observations to himself. "People have learned by now that if I dislike them or they dislike me, they know I'm going to go out and do a job," he said. "I've been sitting back and looking—and hearing a lot of things. Now they got to do it now—or don't do it."

Other than a fist double in the second inning, Torrez didn't allow a base runner until the Yankees had a 6–0 lead. His last two times out he didn't allow a hit until the fifth inning. The big plus for him was the squeeze play. With one out in the second, Martin had Chris Chambliss breaking from third on the pitch and Dent put down a perfect bunt. "It broke the game open," Dent said.

There's a whole world of difference between pitching with a one-run lead and with a two-run lead. There's also a psychological boost. "I don't know anything about psychological," Martin said. "I just wanted to get the run."

Squeezing in the second inning when the hitter has the advantage of hitting with the infield drawn in is unorthodox. But Dent leads the team in sacrifices and the man on deck was Fred Stanley, subbing for sore-legged Willie Randolph. And who knocks success?

It was the third time this season Dent has been given the squeeze sign. Once he missed the sign. Once he missed the pitch. "That started all the trouble," Dent said. Oops. He caught himself, smiled, and quickly added, "I'm just teasing." He had hit the hammer right on the thumb.

It was June 17 in Boston when Martin had Dent squeezing and got an out at the plate. The next day Martin asked Reggie Jackson in front of Dent if Jackson thought it was a good play. Jackson said no. And later that afternoon the television world saw the Martin-Jackson battle of the dugout.

The squeeze is Martin's favorite play. Some managers use it hardly at all. Ralph Houk, who used to manage here, for one. "Which managers don't use it?" Martin responded. "Ones who aren't here anymore."

It was the Yankees' seventh victory in their last eight games.

A word about preparation: Before the game, Martin did not know whether the White Sox had won yesterday or not.

A word about employee relations in baseball: George Zeber, the first choice as second-string second baseman, is to be examined for possible hernia surgery. "They want me to wait four or five days because of Randolph," Zeber said, "but it hurts too much to play well. If the doctor says I need the operation, I'm going to have it right away." Zeber is a twenty-seven-year-old rookie. He will not be pushed around.

Tuesday, August 16

New York

It was a natural high as Chris Chambliss sat in front of his locker with the biggest of smiles. He didn't know the name of the White Sox pitcher he faced. In fact, he thought it was somebody else. He was not sure how many games the Yankees had left with the Red Sox. There was even the suspicion that he did not know the score of the astounding game he had just won.

He hit a two-run home run with one out in the last of the ninth to snatch an 11–10 victory from what would have been an agonizing defeat. Losing a 9–4 lead in the top of the ninth can do dreadful things to the mind of a team with problems enough.

"I'm just happy," Chambliss declared. It was as much emotion as he has shown before or since his triumphal thrust of his fists when his sudden-death home run won the deciding game of the play-offs last year. He grinned constantly for his teammates and even for the assembled cameras and notebooks. Then he resumed his composed posture.

"That first-in-the-air thing was more than I've ever seen from Chris," Roy White said. "He doesn't display any more than a big smile. Inside, he's got to be feeling something."

Chambliss had played the consummate professional. "Of course I get butterflies all the time," he said. "Tonight I was worried we were going to lose the game."

The fear was established in the top of the ninth. "It would have been awful to lose," said Lou Piniella, who took over when Jackson bruised his knee in the last of the eighth. Boston won and the Yankees can't afford to fall another game back. And the Yankees did have the game won. "I played only one inning," Piniella said, "and it seemed like I was out there a damn hour."

Ron Guidry couldn't get any of the first three White Sox out in the ninth, and Sparky Lyle gave up three hits and got two outs, one of them when Piniella caught Richie Zisk's bid for a three-run homer above the top of the fence. The inning ground down with Chicago manager Bob Lemon maneuvering Martin into just the spot Lemon wanted. Rightly Ken Clay, a mid-season rookie, replaced Lyle and walked a batter, filling the bases. Then lefty Oscar Gamble pinch-hit a two-run single to put the Sox ahead, 10–9. Martin did have Ken Holtzman, left-handed and experienced, in the bullpen.

The Red Sox' victory must have been posted by then. "Well, yeah," Chambliss said. "I felt bad about Gamble getting that hit there."

It was quiet in the Yankee dugout as the bottom of the ninth began. Randy Wiles, a lefty, walked Thurman Munson. Martin had righty Piniella sacrifice rather than risk a double play. That brought up lefty hitting Chambliss. Wiles had pitched all of an inning and a third in the big leagues before tonight. "I faced him last year and before this year," Chambliss said. No; Wiles had never pitched against the Yankees. "Who was it then?" Chambliss said. "Hamilton, wasn't it?" No, Hamilton was knocked out in the eighth. "Oh, I'm sorry," Chambliss said, chagrined at displaying an imperfection. "I face all left-handers the same way, anyhow."

Left-handed pitchers don't intimidate Chambliss. As many

as the Yankees see, he is forced to cope. He is a professional hitter. He hit the second strike high and forty feet beyond the 340 sign in right field.

It was their eighth victory in their last nine and they have some momentum. But the Red Sox have won sixteen of seventeen. "It is kind of frustrating," Chambliss said.

* * *

George Zeber got a second opinion on the six-month pain in his side and no hernia was found this time. No explanation was found, either, and he said he would play if he had to.

* * *

Elvis Presley died this afternoon, and that offered another insight into the mentality of the ball player.

Fred Stanley, who would give anything to be a superstar and busts his butt to remain a utility player, thought of how Presley didn't take care of himself. "For a superstar I heard he had a very poor diet," Stanley said. "How can a guy of that status not care for himself?"

Jackson remembered Presley's comment about race. "I remember two things," Jackson said. "One time he said, 'All black people can do for me is shine my shoes and buy my records.' And once an old woman was admiring his car in Lake Tahoe and he just gave it to her."

Presley's life and career was much like that of a ball player. He had that enormous talent, he had so much money, he had humble origins, he had that great adulation, and he had the drain of the travel and of having to do his thing again and again.

"He had all kinds of money and he still had problems," Dick Tidrow said. "It sounds like some ball players, doesn't it?"

Some Yankees, indeed.

Wednesday, August 17

Detroit

For people who loved last night's game there was no reason not to like tonight's, too. You just have to love near heart attacks, that's all.

Like last night, there was a ninth inning to be survived. What had been a comfortable 7–2 lead over the Tigers was 7–4 and there were Detroit runners on second and third and one out. Jason Thompson, the Tigers' best RBI man, was waiting to hit. Sparky Lyle was coming in to take over from Ed Figueroa and Graig Nettles waited at the mound with Thurman Munson. "Maybe they ought to change the rules and let us play only eight innings," Nettles said.

Willie Randolph waited at second base and his mind took him back to the last time the Yankees played the ninth inning, and the White Sox scored six runs. "You would have to be a cigar store Indian not to think about it," Randolph said.

Lyle makes his life on the razor's edge and has learned to put yesterday's failure from his mind as well as any man can. But nobody's perfect. He does, however, maintain his sense of humor.

He made one pitch and Thompson grounded out, the fifth Detroit run scoring. Now Ben Oglivie was the tying run at the plate. Lyle's first pitches were high. Lyle throws a slider. A high slider is known as a "hanging slider." It is the pitch hitters hit out of the ball park. Oglivie is a home-run hitter. Nettles called time and took words of advice to Lyle. "Try and mix in a low one," Nettles said.

"I'm trying," Lyle said.

On the scoreboard was the news that the Red Sox were losing to Milwaukee. It was a rare opportunity to gain on them. Lyle got his next slider down where it belonged, Oglivie struck out, and the Yankees had their eighth win in nine games.

And Lyle was able to go into the clubhouse and tell Figueroa, "You've got a lot of guts, getting me in there after last night."

In the process, they made another fifteen hits. The game began with Mickey Rivers hitting the first pitch by Fernando Arroyo for a home run. Roy White hit Arroyo's second pitch for a triple and Thurman Munson hit the third for a double. The crowd applauded when Reggie Jackson took Arroyo's fourth pitch for a ball. Chris Chambliss hit the first of two triples and Willie Randolph singled to make it a four-run first. With that kind of lead, even a ninth-inning scare isn't too hard to take.

Chambliss, who was struggling, has come alive with Jackson's move to cleanup. In his last fourteen games Chambliss has raised his average from .290 to .304 and has batted in 20 runs.

* * *

Thursday, August 18

Detroit

The report of the Red Sox' victory was already in the clubhouse by the time the Yankees got to the ball park, but what the Red Sox do doesn't seem so terribly important now. The feeling is strong among the Yankees that they have found their pace and the Red Sox can't hold them off. "Boston can't keep winning," Lou Piniella said. "They don't have to lose too many. Just enough. A few should be enough."

The Yankees beat the Tigers, 5–4, and showed the effect of the depth in their batting order. Munson, Chambliss, and the Jackson/Cliff Johnson combination were a collective O for 13. But Mickey Rivers had three hits and three runs batted in, Graig Nettles had two hits and scored two runs, and Willie Randolph had three hits and scored two runs.

Rivers, who was so distracted not long ago, is on a streak of .386 over his last nineteen games. If he can stay hot, it's an awfully destructive lineup.

And Lyle came on when Catfish Hunter got into trouble and pitched two scoreless innings for his eighteenth save.

Friday, August 19

Arlington

It's fascinating to watch the attitudes change around this team. It doesn't mean that people love each other any more in August than they did in May, but they have learned respect for each other. "Our professionalism is starting to show" is how Jackson describes it.

They beat the Rangers, 8–1, for their twelfth in thirteen games and they see cracks in the Red Sox. The Red Sox have won seventeen of twenty, but the Yankees are quick to point out that the Red Sox have lost two out of three.

More important is the way the Yankees look at themselves. "At one point, we were down, there were lots of little problems," said Mickey Rivers, normally not the most analytical of men. "Whatever was happening on the field, people didn't really care a lot of times. There was too much worrying about too many other things, who didn't like who, how much money was this guy making."

Jackson's turn of mind is indicative. When life was stormiest, he was at the eye of the storm. Now he has seen what the others can do. He listed Mike Torrez as their best pitcher, "him and Sparky." Torrez has been a friend and ally of Jackson's all along; just a few weeks ago Lyle put down Jackson's hustle in front of the others in the dugout.

Jackson still feels no warmth toward Graig Nettles, but admires what Nettles does every day at third base and how he has driven in big runs. Munson, whom Jackson cut so deeply, is acknowledged as "a bear-down competitor even when he isn't hitting."

There is a determination that wasn't around earlier; call it intensity, if you wish. "It's business time, professional time," Jackson said. "You notice changes. Sparky knows we rely on him so much. His routine has changed. He wants to be sure to be ready."

After one day as a pinch hitter because of a sore knee, Jackson pushed himself back into the lineup; he feels that in May or June he would have saved himself. His third hit was his twenty-second home run. Everybody knew he could hit home runs. His second hit was more indicative of what the other players have just come to respect. The Yankees had a 4–0 lead in the fourth inning, runners were on second and third with one out, and the Rangers were playing the infield in. Rather than swing for the long ball, Jackson deftly bounced a single through the middle and the lead became 6–0.

"The Red Sox are aware of the Yankees now," Jackson said. "They can't shake us and they can't ignore us because what we're doing demands notice. We're blessed with so much, it's coming out of us now."

They are also getting pretty good pitching almost every day. It's a tough combination.

Saturday, August 20

Arlington

Sparky Lyle relieved Dick Tidrow in the eighth inning and threw a double-play ball. Lyle threw another double-play ball in the ninth and they beat the Rangers, 6–2. It was Lyle's nineteenth save. It was hardly dramatic enough to count.

What he would really like would be to be on the mound in the ultimate confrontation with the Red Sox, two out in the last of the ninth, runners on second and third, Jim Rice at bat. If Rice gets a hit, the Red Sox win the pennant. If Lyle gets him out, the Yankees win the pennant.

Lyle pondered the implications of that suggestion for just a moment. He took a soulful drag on his cigarette. His eyes narrowed and glistened. His red mustache bristled. He straightened his shoulders as he sat on his stool and grinned. "I'd love to be in that situation," he said. "I'd love to do it, winner-take-all. The guys might not want to have all their money riding on one man, but I'd like it. Hell, yeah."

Lyle is the classic go-to-hell guy. When the game boils down to its most primitive contest, when he can feel the ball in his hand, the breath in his chest, and his juices flowing, he loves it most.

"I feel that way," he said. "I've always felt that way. I get excited like a tightrope walker, like the guy who walked over New York between the towers of the World Trade Center. Except to me, it's like his stick fell out of his hand and there he was: you're in trouble. Especially when I got a guy on third base and none out; even if I give up a fly ball or a slow grounder, that sucker is going to score.

"You got to pitch in a way that you feel: 'Here it comes; try to hit it.' That's the way you got to approach it when you go three and two with the bases loaded and the guy knows I'm going to throw a slider ninety-nine times out of a hundred. I love it. It's hard for me to explain. People ask me what type of feeling I have. I tell them, 'It's me alone.' They ask, 'What do you mean?' I can't explain it. All I can say is that I love it."

And what if he fails? That's something Lyle does not consider. "Some guys are hurt by being afraid to fail," Thurman Munson said. "Sparky is not afraid to fail."

The way Lyle looks at it, there is no failure. He's already succeeded. He's thirty-three years old. He's making classic money after growing up in Reynoldsville, Pennsylvania, in the mountains northeast of Pittsburgh, where the temperature in the mold room of the pottery factory where he used to work ran to 180 degrees. If he weren't a ball player, Lyle figures he'd be working on a garbage truck or on the Alaska pipeline, or would have gone through both. Maybe he'd still be in Reynoldsville working for Jackson China, which would be worse.

"Who the hell ever thought Sparky Lyle would be in the big leagues, let alone eleven years?" he said. Every year Lyle goes back to Reynoldsville for a drink with the old friends and for a look at the old town. It renews his perspective. "I like to buy a round of drinks for the guys. Friends who are still there, we do the same things we used to do together. Sometimes they come to see me play. We have a good time; we go drinking. I'm sure a lot of people think I've changed.

"Life never changes for them. I guess they're happy there. There's not much to do there. Guys at home, they leave or they go to work. They say they'll save a couple of years and then get out. They get married and they save and the wife wants a house and there they are, still right there."

Lyle got out with that one pitch, that hard slider that comes in at a left-handed hitter's rib cage and 85 miles an hour and then swerves low and away. The hitters know it's coming. Sometimes Lyle will begin his stretch before he gets a sign from Munson. Sometimes Lyle will wait for a sign and Munson will just wave his hand, like what're you waiting for?

The pitch was self-taught during four clearly mediocre years in the minor leagues. Ted Williams told him what the pitch was supposed to do, so Lyle tinkered. One night in Pittsfield, the story goes, he was lying in bed beside his wife—now his ex-wife—with a baseball in his hand. "It was three AM and suddenly it came to me," Lyle said. "I went outside and threw against the wall of the tavern next door by the streetlights. It never broke then like it does now, but I had it."

He swears it's a true story. That it was a tavern wall gives it a ring of truth.

He said he signed because he wanted to find out if he was

as good as he thought, striking out all those sandlot hitters.
He once struck out thirty-one in a seventeen-inning game; he
would have struck out more but he played three innings at
first base. He wanted to show those people who said anybody
could do what Lyle was doing against that competition.

And he wanted to get out. Even at nineteen the Reynoldsville life-style wasn't enough. The work was too much.
His job was taking racks of soft pottery out of the bake room
and getting them to the skilled molders. At first Lyle broke
more than he delivered. By 3:30, quitting time, he was exhausted. "Everybody has worked at some horseshit job to
make a living," Lyle said. "I was happy to have that; guys
don't make all that much money at home. I took home $116
every two weeks for working in that heat. I watched one guy
cut his fingers off.

"When I signed, I went back to my supervisor and asked if
I could have my job back if I didn't make it. He said I could,
but I knew at least I was going to get a chance."

Lyle may not be the best relief pitcher in baseball. Bill
Campbell has a few more saves for the Red Sox. Rollie Fingers can make a good argument, too. But nobody has more
fun at his work than Lyle. He gets to the ball park at three
o'clock for an eight o'clock game. He would get there earlier
if he thought anybody else would. He says that marriage to
his first wife gave him the stability to reach the big leagues,
but no longer was suitable. "I've always been outgoing," he
said. "She's quiet." Sometimes when Lyle was outgoing, he
went alone.

"I don't like to stay home," he said. "I enjoy being out doing something." When he goes home, he watches old movies
on television until the station goes off, and he sleeps until
mid-afternoon.

A number of Yankees think that when Lyle is watching
those old movies, he's really scheming new pranks. The Best
of Sparky Lyle is really a catalog of things Lyle insists are
done on impulse.

There was the time Lyle discovered that Fred Stanley just
happened to have a coffin in his van in the parking lot. So
Lyle lugged the coffin into the clubhouse, smeared glare
grease under his eyes, powdered his face, pulled an im-
provised hood over his head and slowly rose up in the coffin
while Bill Virdon was holding a clubhouse meeting. Lyle
sawed through the legs of Virdon's rocking chair and Bobby

Murcer's chair, too. He placed Murcer's back together so it would appear intact until it came apart in Mercer's hands.

He is given credit for planting a grasshopper in Gene Michael's jock, but Lyle says that's a bad rap. It wasn't a grasshopper, it was a white mouse.

One day he rigged a rubber snake to drop on Michael from the ceiling, scaring the daylights out of Michael. But the butts of Lyle's jokes generally love him for them. They say he's a kind, generous, and considerate person. "I could have put a harmless live snake up there, but some people are afraid, and they can get hurt trying to get away," Lyle said. "I don't think I've ever done anything that hurt anybody. I never messed with somebody's clothes; I don't care for that. I've jumped in a pool with my clothes on, but I can't remember pushing somebody else in—unless he wanted to be pushed in."

In spring training of 1975, he made one of his rare on-time arrivals, but showed up the first day with his left arm and left leg in plaster casts, complaining about Florida drivers. He would have had a full body cast, but it would have taken too long to dry.

One year when the team assembled in formal rows for the annual ritual team picture, it was not discovered until the prints were made that Lyle was there with his fly open and his equipment waving in the breeze. Mike Burke, who ran the team then, has a treasured copy.

Lyle's most popular trick is the old sit-on-the-birthday-cake caper. Ball players are always getting cakes from fan clubs and the like. Lyle discovered how much former pitching coach Jim Turner loved cake. "He loved it so much I made a deal with him," Lyle said. "I promised I would never sit in a cake that had a slice out of it." So whenever somebody got a cake, Turner would say, "Hurry up and cut it before Sparky sits on it."

That's been somewhat subdued this season in the general pall that hangs over the clubhouse, but it's just that Lyle has been more selective, more internal, perhaps. "It's as much fun playing ball as my first day in the big leagues," he said. "Some players can't wait until they retire. I hope I play until I'm forty."

He is fully capable of coping with the jolts of his job. They don't interfere with his life or his approach to the game. Once during a run the Yankees were making at the Orioles,

Lyle was on the mound with two out, a 2–1 lead in the ninth inning, and Earl Williams, a genuine home-run threat, at the plate. Lyle called Munson to the mound, then crossed his ankles and draped his arm over the catcher's shoulder. "Do you want me to throw my super fantastic change?" Lyle asked.

"Sparky," Munson replied in near shock, "I'll tell you something. We have a one-run lead. If he doubles off that change, it'll be my neck, not yours."

"That's the fun," Lyle said. "That's where it's at. I don't ever want to be a starter. I really enjoy this . . . the money just goes along with it."

The money, he concedes, has been considerable. If there is more to come, Lyle promises to spend it as he has the rest. "I've done just about everything with it but save it," he said. "I could walk out of baseball, whenever that is, and have nothing.

"People tell me all the time I got to do this and that with some of it. My dad is on me all the time, and I agree with him. But that's not my evaluation of the kind of life you live in baseball. A man with all the money in the world could not have any more fun than I have, even if he can fly to Paris for lunch. The only thing a millionaire has on me is money. If he has any more fun, I'd like to know what he's doing. I know he's not having any more laughs."

One of the things Lyle enjoys is photography. When he thinks about it, he says he'd like to open a camera store some day, but he doesn't often plan on saving for it. "My dad asks me what I'm going to do when it's over," Lyle said. "The only way I can answer is: 'Dad, you worked all your life. If you had a chance to work half your life and have a good time the other half, what would you do?' So I'll have to work the rest of my life. If I live to be sixty—who knows?—I haven't worked the first part of my life. I'm willing to work the second part. There's no way I'd do anything any different."

"If something happened," said White Sox manager Bob Lemon, Lyle's pitching coach last year, "Sparky would be the same person. He wouldn't groan and moan. He would have a lot of wonderful memories. He'd go out and live on them. He wouldn't second-guess himself. He's smelled the flowers."

When the end comes, nobody doubts that Lyle will shrug

and say, it was good while it lasted. And it has lasted longer than he expected. It sure beats Reynoldsville.

Sunday, August 21

Arlington

Now the Yankees are close. It's getting to look like the manifest destiny of the dynasty years. When they make a lot of runs, they win. When they don't make a lot of runs, they win anyhow. When they need a good defensive play, they make that, too.

They beat the Rangers tonight, 2–1. They have won thirteen out of fourteen, climbed past the Orioles into second place, and are a half game behind the Red Sox.

Lyle got his fourth save in the five games of the trip. Graig Nettles drove in one run with a home run, one with a double, and when the Rangers were threatening to reverse the flow of the game, Nettles made a terrific play at third base. Just like Jackson said.

Nettles often argues about the validity of using batting average as measurement. He kids about his own career .248. He says he's the strongest hitter in the league "because I hold up almost all the other guys in the Sunday papers." He says the run-production figures are the real standard for a hitter. In one respect, he's right. But then a .200 hitter makes an awful lot of outs, and there's production in the single that sends a runner from first to third so he can score on a fly ball.

Nevertheless, the Yankees' second run, driven in by Nettles' double, was Nettles' eightieth RBI of the season. He is tied with Munson for the team lead.

When the Rangers got runners to first and second with none out in the sixth, Texas manager Billy Hunter had them running. Munson's quick throw was into the runner and Nettles had to reverse his direction to grab the ball and dove to tag Bert Campaneris.

Lyle got the last six outs for his twentieth save.

Nettles feels the thrill of the race. "I went through the years in Cleveland where you were out of it in April and you played out the schedule," he said. "That the races are close doesn't bother me. I look in the paper and there are three or four big games instead of one and it's great to be involved in it."

Nettles came to the Yankees in the last big trade before the reign of Steinbrenner and Gabe Paul. In fact it was Paul at Cleveland who traded Nettles away. And when Paul first got to the Yankees, he said he never would have made that deal from the Yankee angle. Last winter, when Steinbrenner was desperately shopping for a shortstop and wanted Toby Harrah of the Rangers, he offered Nettles. That, Nettles said, is why he enjoys beating the Rangers. "They didn't want me." Nettles said, "Steinbrenner told me he offered me to the Rangers straight up for Harrah and they turned him down. That's according to Steinbrenner, if you can believe what he says."

Of course, Steinbrenner told that to Nettles at the time they were going over their springtime contract hassle. Bits of confidential information like that come out at times like that.

Monday, August 22

Chicago

First place will have to wait a little longer. The Twins beat the Red Sox, but the White Sox beat the Yankees, 5–3. Or rather, the Yankees beat themselves, giving away two un-earned runs in a two-run decision. And they blamed them-selves—or rather they blamed each other. Then they hid in the trainer's room. They forgot that they had just won eight in a row.

"I think they're going to win their division, but they have to recognize that they can't win them all," said Oscar Gamble, who was a Yankee until the last day of the spring and remembers the personalities well. "They have a game like this and, from all I hear, they overreacted. What they have to do is have some feeling for each other and not think you guys [the press] are trying to put them down all the time. I think they think everybody is trying to blame stuff on them because they're supposed to win."

They did have a 3–0 lead going into the bottom of the sev-enth when Reggie Jackson, playing on a sore knee, was slow running down a drive into right field and it fell for a two-run double. Some of the Yankees were sure that it would have been the third out even if Jackson did have a bad leg.

The 3–2 lead disappeared in the eighth. Thurman Munson's throw turned an attempted steal into the first out. But Alan Bannister singled and Richie Zisk's single rolled under Mickey Rivers' glove in center field. Bannister turned third for the plate and Rivers relayed to Willie Randolph to Munson, who was blocking the plate. Randolph's throw was in the dirt and Munson had trouble handling it. He thought he had the tag on Bannister in time, but the umpire ruled safe and Munson was charged with an error.

Munson was furious. At the umpire and the official scorer. It's amazing in the heat of a race like this that players get so involved in who is charged with the error. That decision has nothing to do with winning or losing, and by the end of the season those twists of judgment tend to even out. But not to the players. "I throw the ball to the second base in the dirt and it's my error," Munson argued.

Lyle replaced Ed Figueroa and Gamble singled again to center. Rivers had another chance at the plate. This time his weak throw one-hopped to the plate at the same time Zisk arrived. The ball skipped away and Gamble reached third. This time the error was charged to Rivers. The Yankees were behind. They got another run behind when Chris Chambliss hesitated starting a double play, made a bad throw home, and Gamble scored.

* * *

All of the Yankees' discomfort was a delight to White Sox owner Bill Veeck, who has his own problems on the field. The Sox, who led the Western Division, have lost sixteen of twenty-two, a dreadful slump. But then Veeck beat the Yankees and he did love twitting George Steinbrenner's football tactics.

The Yankees have been stationing Steinbrenner's left-hand man, Gene Michael, in the press box with a scouting report and a walkie-talkie. Elston Howard has the other end of the communications system on the bench and moves the defense according to Michael's direction. They won two out of three in Detroit and all three in Texas using the system.

But Veeck put his foot down—he would have said he put his stump down. He had Michael moved out of the vacant radio booth on the press level into a seat in the upper deck behind the plate. And he provided Michael with a telephone so the Sox could monitor Michael's directives—just so the Sox could be sure Michael wasn't illegally stealing signs.

Sox broadcaster Harry Caray listened in and relayed what Michael was saying to the fans, some of whom always listen to the game in the ball park. A person in a clown suit found Michael and entertained him. So did an usher—or several ushers. Michael finally abandoned his mission. "I was afraid the fans were going to throw me out of the upper deck," he said.

Steinbrenner was irritated that his efforts at progress had been thwarted. "This is just another example that Bill Veeck thinks he can run the league," Steinbrenner said. "He believes in doing things his own way. He never comes to league meetings. We have permission from the league to use the walkie-talkie."

Indeed the Yankees do have permission. And Veeck does believe in doing things his own way. But for George Steinbrenner to accuse Veeck of trying to run the league—well, who's accusing whom of what?

Gabe Paul accused Veeck of harassment. "What else would you call it when an usher comes to Michael ten times to check his ticket?" Paul said.

"How does he know it wasn't ten different ushers?" Veeck said. "We have very efficient ushers. Any team would be proud to have such efficiency."

As Veeck was saying, Weiss and Topping and Webb are gone, but the Yankees do have Steinbrenner, and Veeck loves just as much to make him uncomfortable.

Tuesday, August 23

Chicago

Reaching first place calls for some kind of acknowledgment—maybe a glass of domestic wine, or just a good substantial yell. But baseball players are very much into the image of cool. To make a big thing out of getting where they should have been all along would be gauche. Worse than that, suppose they fell out of first place after making a grand display?

So the Yankees beat the White Sox, 8–3, while the Red Sox were getting beaten, and the Yankees are on top for the first time since July 9. "A lot of guys are saying, 'Welcome to first place,'" Reggie Jackson said, but he's an emotional sort, and he said it quietly, anyhow.

Mostly they applauded themselves for bouncing back after blowing last night's game. They now consider that they don't absolutely need those five remaining games with the Red Sox to make up the difference. Nettles, being especially conservative, said that he didn't really consider it first place yet because they were still behind the loss column. "You're never in first place until you have fewer losses, no matter how the paper reads," he said.

But there still are other issues beneath the surface. Mickey Rivers is still touchy about the onus of last night's error, but he did get five hits in five times at bat tonight. No Yankee had five hits in a game this season. His single broke the 3–3 tie in the seventh.

Nettles, despite a gimpy leg, hit his thirtieth home run to tie for the league lead.

And Mike Torrez managed to survive his own mediocre stuff to complete another game. Torrez is still not signed. "There's been only one offer," he said. "That was about two months ago." He likes New York and he gets along with the crowd on the team, but it is getting late in the season. If he hasn't settled by the middle of September, there would be no reason for him not to go into the free-agent market.

"I hope he signs with us," Sparky Lyle said. The only games Lyle did not pitch in on the seven-game trip were Torrez' two complete games.

Wednesday, August 24

New York

Explanations are not always relevant from Mickey Rivers, or always desirable. There are those times when things are going so right for him that even things he does wrong turn out right. So don't ask why—or any of the other four *W's*—who, what, where, or Wyoming. Like when he calls someone "gozzlehead." There's no need to ask just what it means. Just accept it.

He had a double, single, and home run tonight while they were beating the Twins, 11–1. When he struck out in his last time at bat, it ended a streak of eight successive hits interrupted by only a bad bunt that turned out good. His average has streaked up to .330, fourth in the league, and it's hardly coincidence that the Yankees have won fifteen of seventeen to take over first place by two games. The Red Sox lost two tonight and their streak is now seven in a row in the other direction.

But if you give credit to Rivers, you make him uncomfortable. His thinking is like that of the fabled Billy Loes, the Brooklyn pitcher who once lost a World Series ground ball in the sun. Loes said a pitcher should never win twenty because once he does, he'll be expected to do it again.

"They look for me to do a little bit more," Rivers said. "People say, 'You make the team click.' I see a lot of other guys who make the team click. I like to make the team click. Some days you're not going to have that click.

"The guys on the club know what I'm doing every day. The manager looks for me to do things. He gives me that little prod." The problem is whether Rivers needs a pat on the back or a kick in the pants. Last season Oscar Gamble, Dock Ellis, and Sandy Alomar had a feeling for Rivers' turn of mind, but they're all gone. Willie Randolph tries, but he's young. And Martin is not the manager to cajole Rivers.

Rivers concedes he lost his chance at the Most Valuable Player award last season when he sat out much of September with a shoulder injury. Martin says Rivers took himself out of the running by lingering too long on the bench. "I tried to play, I just couldn't do it," Rivers said. That man has a different concept of the ball player's work ethic.

Part of the problem in Rivers' mind is his great speed. "When you run 3.4 seconds to first base, you got to run it consistently," he said. "It doesn't work that way."

Rivers doubled leading off the first inning, singled in the second, and homered in the sixth inning, when they were breaking the game open. But in the fourth inning, when it was still a 3–1 game, runners on first and second and one out, Rivers bunted toward first base. Back in the early days of spring training Rivers railed at advice that he try to drag bunt for a hit more often. Too many demands were being made of him, he said. This time he was bunting on his own, "because in the other inning we got three men on and didn't get them in." He was out, but the runners advanced and both scored on Graig Nettles' single.

Rivers was 22 hits in his last 50 at bats. Actually, his streak is 43 for 103, a .417 pace, but right in the middle of that streak was an interlude of five games when he was benched. It was in Seattle at the end of the dreadful trip that threatened to rip the last bonds of unity. Martin said he thought Rivers was distracted by his personal problems and would be better off on the bench.

"He came to me and said I look a little worried, like I got problems," Rivers said. "I said I still want to play. Different problems bother you. You can't say you don't want to play . . . I get tired all of a sudden of doing little things. Everybody has problems sometimes."

Some of the problems, Rivers concedes, involve personal finance. He is on a closely budgeted allowance from the team. He has had advance after advance on his salary. The front office says that Rivers' wife is a terrible drain on his income. Recently, she had an accident in the ball players' parking lot and it turned out that Rivers hadn't taken care of his car insurance. The ball club had to get him out of that.

"Money ain't all of it," Rivers said. "Money ain't causing all the problems. Personal problems are always there. You try and cope. You worry 'cause you're like anybody else. I'm not saying it all gets too much for me, but it's there."

Martin feels if he tries to drive Rivers, he will quit entirely. But Martin does prod. And Steinbrenner prods. And Rivers resents. Like when Steinbrenner gave the pep talk before the play-offs last year. Rivers responded with a fine play-off series. When Steinbrenner gave another pep talk in the World Series, Rivers was insulted and wound up hitting .167 in the four games.

Rivers feels he is being denied his greatest asset. His only goal, he said, is stealing bases. He once stole 70 bases for the Angels, and 43 in 50 attempts last season. Under this year's tight rein, he has stolen only 20 in 34 attempts. "I'm not running consistently," Rivers said. "If I run consistently, I'll make it more often. Now it seems like I'm running every other week. So I do other things. That's why I'm hitting now. It gives me something to do."

Martin says he hasn't had Rivers running as much because the team has been behind too often. Rivers doesn't buy it.

"We never talked about it," he said. "I just go along with the program."

He goes along in his own way. That was how Rivers got along in California when stern Dick Williams was the manager and easygoing Whitey Herzog was the third-base coach. Williams turned Rivers over to Herzog and the two called each other "Chance," as in Chancellor. "Whitey let me do things the way I like them," Rivers recalled. "He didn't mind if I did something different."

One weekend Herzog left the Angels for his daughter's wedding; when he got back he learned that Rivers hadn't run out a ground ball "and everybody on the team was mad at him," Herzog said. "Williams told me, 'Hey, you better buy your friend an ice cream cone and have a long talk with him. He doesn't like to play if you're not here.' "

Herzog told Rivers, "Look, I'm not always going to be around." Rivers, Herzog recalled, said, "I know. I know."

But what did Rivers know? He knows he doesn't like to be singled out. Today he concedes he was insulted when he was dropped out of leadoff at times early in the season. He agrees that he hasn't been the outstanding center fielder he was last season. "We got a lot of guys out there," he said. "I don't have to cover as much ground."

"He didn't point out how they could use more than three men in the outfield at any time. But then you shouldn't look for too many explanations from Mickey.

Thursday, August 25

New York

While Jackson has been beating the daylights out of the ball since he was moved to cleanup, other things have been happening. Chris Chambliss, who was not producing, came alive. Over sixteen games, he's batted in 17 runs. And Dick Tidrow has pitched like hell.

While a group of players clustered around the table in the middle of the clubhouse eating the peppered crabs Martin had had flown in, while Jackson tried to explain how the minds got put in order out of sheer embarrassment, Tidrow tried to explain how he felt about his role. Sparky Lyle gave up the tying run, which took Tidrow out of the decision, and when Jackson singled the winning run home in the eighth, Lyle got credit for the victory. They beat the Twins, 6–4, making it sixteen of their last eighteen. Tidrow merely got credit.

He pitched seven strong innings again. After two years almost exclusively in the bullpen, Tidrow has started three times and pitched well each time. In all that time pitching relief, Tidrow still liked to think of himself as a starter. "I always thought I could start," he said. "I told everybody that. With this team, if you go out and give all you got for six or seven innings, you've got a pretty good chance of coming out on top. I wish I had started out as a starter with a team like this."

Chambliss is hot. Jackson is hot. Rivers got three more hits. And Munson is showing signs of coming out of his arctic slump even if he isn't talking to the press.

Jackson says it's fun coming to the ball park these days. He knows he's going to be hitting in the spot he feels belongs to him. Martin, at his most tactful, says a polite "no comment" when he's asked what Steinbrenner's urging had to do with the batting order.

But the problems that Martin says remain have been put aside while the business at hand is taken care of.

Chambliss, a UCLA man, sees how the change of lineups affected the team. "Something did happen when he changed the lineup. Reggie did get hot." What the cause-and-effect relationship is remains a mystery to him. The problem, Chambliss said, "was all created and made real. The controversies were being created by the press."

But they didn't bother him, of course. "I don't read most of the papers, anyway," he said.

Friday, August 26

New York

The first reaction comes from the fans, who are like gin rummy players working on three games at once. The numbers flash on the scoreboard behind the backs of the players, who have their own game to play on the field. The players hear the sounds, the shrieks or the groans, and then they react.

"We all hear them," said Willie Randolph, who plays second base with the scoreboard over his right shoulder. "Then we look around to see what's happening. Maybe the fans have spotted some celebrity in the stands." He said it with a straight face.

The Yankees made another impressive comeback to a 6–5 decision over the Rangers. On the night Randolph collected a walk, triple, single, and double to spark the comeback, he said he was most proud of his defense. If his chest holds out, he can be a pretty good infielder.

"Any more like that and I don't know if it will hold out," he said. "I got to be crazy to take those shots. But when you're winning, you got to do that—take it for the team." Besides, it wasn't his chest that hurt, it was his wrist, and despite three innings of ice packs he had the swelling to prove it. In the second inning a hard shot exploded in the dirt to the right of second base, skipped off Randolph's wrist and then his chest. He recovered and flipped to Bucky Dent to start the double play. "It's instinct," Randolph said. "First you get rid of the ball and then you feel the pain." He said the ball he blocked with his chest for the third out of the eighth wasn't hit nearly so hard.

"Defense," he said. "It's more gratifying than the hits—defense plus scoring runs. When I make a defensive play to save a rally, it gives me a bigger kick than hitting."

Of course, the runs Randolph scored did tie the game as the Yankees overcame the Rangers' 5–1 lead the way they overcome everything these days. Rivers started the two-run seventh with a single and Lou Piniella's sacrifice fly cut the deficit to 5–4. Piniella had already delivered a home run, double, and a single. When a team is going as good as the Yankees, it doesn't matter that Munson, on third base, missed the sign for a double steal when Jackson broke for second. Munson didn't try to score, but Jackson was safe and Piniella hit his fly ball, scoring Munson.

The next inning Randolph doubled and Rivers singled to tie the score. It was Rivers' thirteenth hit in 17 at bats. The statistics are numbing. Rivers has what Randolph calls "a seeing-eye stroke" right now. And when he's going like this, he isn't plain Mickey, they call him "Hardy," as in "Hard Mickey."

That's the name Randolph uses to keep Rivers pumped up. "Sometimes he needs it," Randolph said. The ghetto expression was the same in Brooklyn, where Randolph grew up, as in Miami, where Rivers was raised. "It can mean 'cruel' sometimes, but it doesn't here," Randolph offered. "It's hard to define. 'Relentless' is not quite it. Here, it's an affectionate thing."

Rivers said he liked it. He couldn't define it either, but he tried. "We used it for 'hard,' " Rivers explained "Just 'hard.' " I guess that's definition enough.

No sooner had Rivers driven Randolph home than Graig Nettles crashed a triple into deepest Death Valley in left center and they had the lead. Lyle made it stand up, with a little bit of help from the Rangers.

Juan Beniquez led off the top of the ninth for the Rangers with a walk, and Lyle relieved Ken Clay. On Lyle's first pitch Beniquez was out stealing second and Texas manager Billy Hunter threw down his cap in the dugout. The batter, Kurt Bevacqua, never offered at the pitch.

"Oh, shit," Hunter said. He laughed. "Well, I told him." Bevacqua didn't just miss the hit-and-run sign. Hunter had also told him the play was on before he went to the plate.

That's what happens for a team playing as well as the Yankees are. The breaks come to everybody, but the good teams capitalize on them. Munson could have thrown the ball into center field.

With that play, the fans playing the scoreboard reached the crest of their high. The Red Sox had lost. The Orioles had lost. And the Yankees had won for the seventeenth time in nineteen games. The Yankees and their fans are on one continuous high now. Most of the Yankees, that is.

Their two runs in the eighth—the tying and winning runs—came on a break, too, when Nettles' hard grounder went under the glove of the second baseman. It could have been a double play. Martin said he made that play when he was playing second base. When Nettles returned to the dugout after seeing the error light on the scoreboard, he put his hand to the crook of his elbow in the time-honored gesture of contempt for the official scorer. "I don't want to talk to no fucking writers about no fucking thing, including that hit," Nettles snarled. Of course, he was upset; an error instead of a hit may cost him a possible .250 average.

The games on the scoreboard affected the Rangers and the

Yankees from opposite directions. While Boston and Baltimore were losing, Kansas City and Minnesota were winning. It was only a week ago that the Rangers were first in the Western Division. But they've lost six of nine and Kansas City has won ten in a row to lead by three games. "It's just numbers up there," said Texas third baseman Toby Harrah. "I'm too involved in my own game."

"At this time of the year," said Billy Hunter, who was in a lot of races in the last fourteen years as a coach at Baltimore, "anybody who says he doesn't watch the scoreboard is full of shit."

Saturday, August 27

New York

The game was hardly over when Billy Martin had his attention fixed on the small portable television in his office. Gullett threw well on the sidelines; Piniella bruised his back against the wall, Martin said with an eye and a half still on the golf being played on the screen. "Hale Irwin, he's nineteen under," Martin explained as if he were more concerned with that than the 8–2 loss to the Rangers. Even though the Red Sox won, the Yankees are going so well even Martin can take a minor setback in stride. It's the first time they've lost ground to Boston since August 13.

It broke the four-game winning streak for the Yankees and ended Mike Torrez' streak at seven victories and seven complete games in a row. The loss was such a rarity that Martin kidded about the novelty of the two consecutive inside-the-park home runs the Rangers hit in the seventh inning. According to the august statisticians at Elias Sports Bureau, Marv Rickert and Eddie Waitkus of the Cubs did it in the Polo Grounds in 1946 and nobody else.

The Rangers had a 4–1 lead when they broke the game open in the seventh. Lou Piniella leaped and hit the padded wall and crumpled to the grass as Toby Harrah circled the bases. Then Mickey Rivers turned the wrong way on Bump Wills' drive to center field, and Wills also scored standing up. After that it was time for Ken Holtzman to pitch the ninth inning in his second league appearance since July 15.

After the Storm

New York

There was a bottle of champagne on the stool in Ron Guidry's locker when he came in off the mound, and bottles in the lockers of Lou Piniella and Mike Torrez. They were tokens of management's esteem honoring their birthdays. Each bottle was four-fifths of a gallon, a jeroboam. George Steinbrenner does not buy, give, or think small.

Billy Martin walked past Guidry with a can of beer in his hand and asked, "How do you get one of those?" One way would be to pitch a 1–0 two-hitter against the Rangers on your birthday. Another might be to be in the good graces of Steinbrenner. Martin's forty-ninth birthday came two days after he was fined $2,500 for insubordination. He had to drink his own California red.

Tonight, Martin had the gift of Guidry and a two-game hold on first place. In the two months Guidry has been a starter, he has been the most reliable starter on a staff that was supposed to be full of reliable starters. His 3.13 earned run average is the best. It was his eleventh victory and his third complete shutout, high for the team. Of the nine shutouts pitched by the Yankees, Guidry has had a hand in five.

On the day he turned twenty-seven, Guidry pitched his best game as a professional, man-to-man against a fine game by Dock Ellis, the pitcher Martin didn't want to give up in April. When Guidry didn't have any runs on his side, he didn't give up any; and when he had only one run on his side, he still didn't give up any. He struck out eight, didn't walk anybody, and pitched to one batter over the minimum. This was the pitcher who took such a dreadful battering all

267

spring while being tested as an immediate replacement for Sparky Lyle. If Guidry had had a good spring, there was every chance that Lyle, who was being almost as stubborn as Ellis about signing, would also have been traded. Then the Yankees would have lost both Guidry's brilliance as a starter and Lyle's in relief. Where would they be without either? Luck, you say? Branch Rickey used to say, "Luck is the residue of design."

Ah, yes. "There were some people who wanted to get rid of Guidry in the spring," Martin said. "I wasn't one of them. Gabe Paul wasn't. Maybe it was the trainer." Now that he is on top, Martin seldom misses a chance to throw a dart at Steinbrenner.

"That's a lie," Steinbrenner said. Steinbrenner said that he and Martin had wanted to move Guidry out, and only Paul's judgment kept him. Steinbrenner argues that Martin was reluctant to use young players at three previous jobs and Steinbrenner didn't want that stagnation to come about here.

But then contradiction has been commonplace all season.

The one Yankee run was both a gift and an indication of the way some other thinking has been changed. With one out in the sixth, Nettles hit a long drive to right center. Right fielder Tom Grieve angled toward it, slowed, touched the wall, and poised to make the catch. Just then center fielder Juan Beniquez dashed across, leaped, and deflected the ball away. "It was going over the fence," Beniquez said. Nobody else thought so.

Nettles wound up on third base. Ellis got Munson to foul out and fell behind 3 and 0 to Reggie Jackson. Rather than submit with two bases open, Ellis said he sensed Jackson might be swinging and made a tough pitch. If Ellis had been around the Yankees all season, he might have sensed the opposite. Jackson was more surprised that he was permitted to swing.

"Reggie's been swinging good," Martin said. He said he would have given the same green light to Munson, Chambliss, or Nettles.

"First time all year for me," Jackson said. What, never before? Well, hardly ever, Jackson conceded. The infrequency has been one of the most irksome slights to Jackson.

Anyhow, he fought off the pitch on the hands and dropped a single into short center. It was Jackson's sixteenth game-winning RBI, high on the team.

Guidry blew past the last six outs. Guidry's fastball baffles logic, coming from his 153-pound program weight. It's so good that Martin has reprimanded Guidry for shaking off his catcher and permitting himself to get beat on his slider. The last time Guidry pitched, the White Sox overcame his 9–4 lead in the ninth inning and Martin said that if Guidry didn't learn to go with his best pitch in critical situations he might not be permitted to pitch ninth innings.

"I want him to match their best with his best," Martin said. "He has a good slider, but he goes overboard with it." This time Martin said he liked what he saw.

In another Yankee era, Jim Bouton called his manager, Yogi Berra, "a second-guessing son of a bitch." Today Guidry thought his best pitch was the slider, but when Munson called for it, Guidry shook him off and threw fastballs. Until the last batter, right-handed John Ellis, who can take a bad pitch downtown. Guidry threw two left-handed fastballs and struck Ellis out on a slider to end the game.

"The thing is," Guidry said in his delicious Louisiana French accent, "if I use my head, he won't say anything. If I mess up, he'll say I messed up." It was as close as Guidry would come to calling Martin a second-guesser.

* * *

So what if the Red Sox won? "If we keep winning and the Red Sox keep winning, they don't stand a chance," Martin said. There was no contradiction in that.

Everything looks as smooth as glass. Dock Ellis was so inflammatory until April 27, he said he was glad to be going somewhere he was wanted and would be properly rewarded. He never did sign with Oakland. He said he is "signed and happy" with Texas. He said he isn't surprised that the Yankees pulled themselves together after a season of turmoil. "They were together when I left," he said. He wanted to find some kind of cause and effect there.

Monday, August 29

New York

The Yankees don't merely win games, they make people angry. "That organization is full of shit," Whitey Herzog said. "I don't mean the secretaries, so don't include them."

Herzog did not want to be in New York managing the Royals in the first place on what he felt should have been a day off. And getting beat, 5–3, didn't help his frame of mind.

Today they played the makeup of the game that was postponed on July 25 because of "wet grounds and a bad weather forecast." The Royals remember leaving LaGuardia Airport that day in bright sunshine at just about the time the game would have started. On that date the Yankee pitching was in a bind on the eve of a series with the Orioles, then in first place. The Yankees were in the midst of one of their periodic managerical crises. And that night Steinbrenner revealed the Seven Commandments for Martin.

Herzog, in first place and awaiting a series with the Rangers in Kansas City, responded tonight with a lineup intended to ridicule everybody concerned with his discomfort. While he was tied up in New York, the Rangers were lounging on a golf course in Kansas City. "I know they are," Herzog said. "I'm the one who called the place for them and set it up."

So Herzog submitted a lineup that listed one pitcher at DH, another pitcher in right field, a third at first base, and a fourth on the mound in his turn. His point was so clear that Bob Sheppard, a St. John's University speech professor who has been public address voice for the Yankees since the years of dignity, refused to announce the Kansas City lineup. Instead, Sheppard promised to write a poem. Having made his point, Herzog sent the regular hitters to the plate as pinch hitters in the first inning. When regular right fielder Al Cowens was sent to the plate, pitcher Jim Colborn tossed his helmet and bat away in simulated anger. "That," Herzog said," was part of the act."

*   *   *

What was not part of the act was the way the game was won. Chris Chambliss, the man who broke up the last game of the play-off last fall with a sudden-death home run, had been resting an 0 for 10 slump until he was called to pinch-hit with two on and two out in the last of the eighth. He hit a home run. Some people even thought it looked like the home run he hit last year. "You think so?" Chambliss said.

He did not. In fact, he is offended by his automatic identification with that home run. "People may tend to look at that home run as the peak of my career and what I do after that is not as important," he said. "I don't listen to people who talk like that."

Chambliss was excited that night. He even showed it. But he never was approached for outside appearances and endorsements. Perhaps it was because the Yankees were swept in the World Series. Perhaps it was because of Chambliss' personality. "I think my reputation has a little to do with that," he said. "They might not think I have the personality to want to do anything."

What Chambliss is, is a quiet man who goes about his own business. He is the kind of player a manager loves: He doesn't say a thing.

He is the product of the best trade Gabe Paul made. Chambliss survived the unhappiness of being unwanted by his teammates that first year. They resented the departure of four pitchers who were old friends. Chambliss hit under his head, fielded with hands of stone, and was as much fun in the clubhouse as the concrete pillars. "That's an awful thing when you walk in the clubhouse, look around, and get those fish-eye looks," Gabe Paul said. "It just proves ball players aren't the best judge of ball players."

* * *

When the game was over, Steinbrenner phoned Martin's office and there were cackles of laughter. "George," Martin said, "is a good winner."

And before they all went home, Bob Sheppard submitted his ode to Whitey Herzog:

In bush managerial pique,
He submitted a lineup unique,
But the tactic confusing
Couldn't keep him from losing
Though the game was a bit of a squeak.

If only Chambliss would write doggerel just once.

Tuesday, August 30

New York

Rivers is absolutely amazing. Not only did he get three hits, which is predictable, but he led off the bottom of the eleventh inning with a home run. It beat the Mariners, 6–5, but Rivers has his own view of life. "It was a little bit of a thrill because it got us out of the hole and enabled us to go home," he said, "but if it were just an ordinary home run, well, I'd rather steal a base."

Rivers' image of himself is not that of a long-ball hitter. Any time he hits a homer, it's a treat. But what he saw in his mind when he went to bat was more like a single slapped through the left side, a stolen base, an infield out, and a sacrifice fly. That would be doing his business. He still feels cheated that he is not permitted to do his business.

The home run was his tenth, two more than he has ever hit in the big leagues. The base he stole in the ninth was his twenty-first; he hasn't stolen fewer than thirty in his three years in the big leagues. He'd rather have the green light to steal on his own than the green light to swing on 3 and 0 that Jackson wants. "I'm not a home-run hitter, not me," River said. "What I need is another twenty stolen bases."

Lyle got credit for his eleventh victory, but he also got the negative mark for letting two runs score when the Mariners tied it in the eighth. The Yankees have too much trouble beating the Mariners. It must be that these big stars can't take the expansion team seriously.

Wednesday, August 31

New York

These are the Yankees: A home run by Rivers in their last at bat won yesterday's game; a home run by Chambliss in their last at bat won the day before; the second homer of the game by Nettles in the bottom of the ninth beat the Mariners today, 5–4. And Nettles is still angry.

Nettles is having his best season. The better his season gets, the more bitter he becomes over his contract. He signed a three-year contract for $375,000 last season rather than take his chances on the free-agent market. He won the home-run championship last season and saw what the prices in the market were. He has 93 runs batted in, a .254 average, and is leading the league again with 34 homers. He feels he is contributing more to the Yankees than the Yankees are paying him.

"I think I'm a better player than ever," Nettles said, "but you can't convince the owner of that." Nettles is thirty-three years old, and Steinbrenner thinks it would be foolish to tie himself to Nettles at a big price beyond the age of thirty-five. "He thinks you break down when you hit thirty-four," Nettles said.

Basically, Steinbrenner thinks he has every right to hold Nettles to the contract. If Nettles sold himself short because he was unwilling to gamble, then it's still his deal. Nettles, it should be remembered, negotiated his own contracts and paid no agent's fee until this spring when he decided he needed help. Nettles says he has been offered an extension of one more year with what he called a token raise. But, he said, Steinbrenner indicates the "token" raise was 20 percent.

Marvin Miller, the astute director of the Players Association, thinks there is no harm in asking for a raise based on Nettles' production highs, and says that some clubs think there is a morale advantage gained by raising some salaries. But Miller would never advocate what Nettles did when he jumped the team in the spring.

Nettles' resentment still has the same foundation. Reggie Jackson got his big money, at least in part, because he has color. "I lack recognition because I'm quiet and I don't cause trouble," Nettles said. "I'm not controversial. Maybe that's what you need to be around here. I've always felt people will notice you on performance. I've always felt it isn't what you say but what you do."

Perhaps Nettles might feel more favorably disposed toward Jackson if Steinbrenner raised Nettles. Maybe team relations can be bought. I doubt it. Nettles would still have the same feelings toward Jackson's flamboyance.

All the while, Nettles is playing a remarkable third base and has batted at a .390 pace for the twenty-four games during which the Yankees have taken charge of the race. "I hope somebody is telling these things to Steinbrenner," Nettles said, "I just want to be paid what I'm worth."

* * *

Lou Piniella was found to have a minor concussion, but is expected to be available tomorrow in Minneapolis. Thurman Munson also has a sore head. After striking out and grounding out to a chorus of boos from behind the dugout, Munson flipped his batting helmet over the roof and was replaced by Fran Healy in the seventh. "Thurman is not feeling well," Martin explained.

Friday, September 2

Minneapolis

This is the city Yogi Berra immortalized when he was managing the Yankees. Charlie's is one of the best restaurants in the league and a favorite stop for the press with the Yankees. But, Berra pointed out in 1964, "Nobody goes there any more, it's too crowded."

Ron Guidry is making a strong impression around the league. He beat the Twins, 4–0, with his second straight shutout. He held Rod Carew hitless. His earned run average is down to 2.96, fifth-best in the league. His strikeout ratio of eight a game is second only to Nolan Ryan's and better than Frank Tanana's.

There's no impression greater than that Guidry has made on his own teammates. He is even a little surprised himself. "I'd be lying if I said no," he said.

It was also his second straight game without walking a batter. That saves pitches, and once Guidry established himself on the pitching staff, the reservation against him was that he couldn't pitch nine innings. In the heat of midsummer, that was a problem, but it's getting into the cool weather and Guidry is pitching better than ever.

*   *   *

Another man outdoing his advance notice is Cliff Johnson, who came to the Yankees with a scouting report that he hit and fielded with the same bat. As Thurman Munson rested, Johnson caught and made two of the strongest, straightest throws to second base the Yankees have seen all season. He threw out Carew in the first inning and Larry Hisle in the second.

The last time the Twins saw Johnson behind the plate was in an exhibition game that introduced baseball to the Superdome in New Orleans. Johnson was in the uniform of the

Houston Astros then and he was charged with five passed balls in the first inning. There has been no knock on his catching in nine games here. What's startling is that nobody tested his arm in this league.

Lou Piniella had a home run, scored two runs, and played right field even though he said he still felt light-headed. The word he used was "floozie."

* * *

On the off-day yesterday, Maury Allen of the *Post* quoted Reggie Jackson extensively as saying he was considering not playing next year. Today Jackson wouldn't touch the subject. "I'm not even going to entertain the question," he said. "The question has no merit."

* * *

Saturday, September 3

Minneapolis

Fifteen minutes after Lou Piniella's home run turned a 3–2 lead into a 5–2 lead, Gabe Paul phoned the press box at Metropolitan Stadium from New York to announce that Piniella had been signed to a two-year contract for 1978 and 1979. And at a nice price, Piniella added.

Piniella met with Paul and Steinbrenner on Thursday and immediately reached the unannounced agreement. The sixth inning seemed like a good time to make the announcement. With the kind of year Piniella is having as part-time outfielder and the main designated hitter, he might profitably become a free agent at the end of the season. But he said he never gave that any serious thought.

He received a raise from his present $80,000 to about $105,000 and $120,000 for the next two years. "The whole thing took about fifteen minutes," he said. "I went up and took their first offer."

That's Piniella. His values are his own, like his sense of humor. "I like this organization quite a bit," he said. "In the four years I've been here, I've had more fun playing than at any other time in my life. I wanted to stay here, but I also wanted to get paid something that was fair to both sides. Of course, to get a two-year contract, I had to convince the owner I'm a young thirty-four and not an old thirty-four."

Unlike several of the players, Piniella likes Steinbrenner. He likes to tease the owner about his racehorses. Steinbrenner also likes Piniella as a ball player and as a man in the clubhouse. The owner says the one aspect of the lineup he urged on Martin was increased use of Piniella. And Steinbrenner has been right. Piniella is hitting a healthy .343 and his nine home runs are two short of his career high.

"I don't think I'm a star," he said. "I think I'm a good ball player. I'm probably the only guy who could be a free agent without an agent. I never once considered what I was worth on the market. Their first offer was a fair raise and I took it. If they had asked me what I wanted, I don't know what I would have told them. I don't care what others are making."

With that, Piniella made his bright smile. He can have instant rages of temper on the field and calm himself as quickly. When he talks about his anger later, the smile is there to kid himself.

"When you play baseball, it's a two-way street," he said. "The owner has an investment in baseball and without his money we wouldn't be in the game. I'm not going to get rich playing baseball. When I get out of baseball, I'm going to have to work like hell anyway, so what's a few dollars mean?"

At a time when players and agents are bargaining for the last dollar and grumbling about the one they didn't get, Piniella is happy with what he thinks is fair. At a time when players are boasting about their statistics, Piniella downplays his. His .343 does not impress him. He says it's misleading. If he had 350 or 400 at bats, or 500 like Rod Carew, then that average would mean something. By the end of the season, he could have 350 at bats. "Then," he said, "let's see if I'm hitting .343." He flashed that smile.

One concrete reason for the smile is that the new contract is guaranteed; all he has to do to collect is to live. One reason Graig Nettles refused the offer of a two-year extension of his contract—besides the money—was that it wasn't guaranteed for 1980. "If I had a bad year in 1979, they'd release me," Nettles said. And, Nettles said, the Yankees wanted him to waive his right to veto a trade as a player with ten years in the majors and five with the team. That would be a violation of the basic agreement governing all players.

Still playing out the end of one-year contracts are Mike Torrez, Paul Blair, and Carlos May. The most likely to move—or be moved—is May, who has been on Steinbrenner's shit list for a fat body and a thin average. "I don't think I'll be here, that's for sure," May said. "I think the feeling is mutual."

The victory was the sixth straight for the Yankees— eighteen out of twenty and twenty-three out of twenty-six. The statistics go marching on.

Sunday, September 4

Minneapolis

One good statement deserves another. Today George Steinbrenner called to deny Nettles' claims that he had refused the Yankees' latest offer. Steinbrenner said Nettles had accepted. Nettles said he didn't want to get into a name-calling match with the boss, but . . .

Steinbrenner's statement said that Nettles and agent LaRue Harcourt had agreed to a two-year extension. Steinbrenner said Harcourt had signed and Nettles would have signed, too, except that he had to rush off to play a baseball game. Nettles said it wasn't a contract, anyhow, and it had some illegal provisions.

He said he had asked Gabe Paul the next day and was informed that the agreement was a letter of memorandum. Nettles also said he accepted a waiver of his trade rights for 1980, and when he looked it up, the memorandum had him waiving those rights for '78, '79, and '80.

The last time the Yankees got into one of these situations was in the spring of 1976 when they announced that they had signed Andy Messersmith, one of the two original free agents. What they had was the signature of Messersmith's agent, Herb Osmond, on a memorandum. But the next day Messersmith said he had never authorized Osmond to sign for him, and when the contract was examined it was not the same as the memorandum of the night before. A hearing in the commissioner's office upheld Messersmith's claim. Just whom do you believe around here?

* * *

Ah, the game Mike Torrez says he needs to pitch on three days' rest to be sharp; Ron Guidry needs four. Today, thirty-five days since he last pitched, Don Gullett shut out the Twins on three hits, 4–0. He walked one and threw just ninety pitches. "This team has had a lot of fun since the All-Star break and I'm glad to be back and having some of the fun," Gullett said. They have been winning, but fun apparently is in the eye of the beholder.

All the runs came on Cliff Johnson's grand slam in the first inning. He didn't even hit it good and it carried 393 feet into the seats. And the Yankees, who were reputed to be impotent against left-handers, have lost a game started by a lefty only once in the last twenty-one starts.

Monday, September 5

Cleveland

Alfred E. Neumann, the sage of *Mad,* doesn't worry, why should the Yankees? Even when they lost a doubleheader to the Indians, 4–3, and 5–4. "We were bound to lose a game or two some time," Thurman Munson said. "We just happened to lose them both the same night is all." Withering logic.

"Did Boston win both?" he asked.

"Yes.

"Doesn't matter," he said.

The lead over the Red Sox is down to two and a half games, but the Yankees feel secure. They won seven in a row and have been hot for five weeks, which does breed a sense of security. They were not even especially annoyed at the handkerchiefs the Cleveland fans waved on the last out of "I Hate the Yankees Night."

"Don't people here know that's unsanitary, waving all those germs around?" Martin asked. It seemed the first time all year the Yankees could lose a double header and not worry about it. Martin recalled his own glory years in the uniform. "One year," he said, "they brought a black cat and let it run on the field on a day that Eddie Lopat was pitching."

Did Lopat lose?"

"Yeah," Martin said. "But we won the pennant just the same. Like always."

* * *

In Toronto George Scott was taken out of the Red Sox lineup for the second game because he told the manager "I am not mentally prepared." Scott was listed seventh in Don Zimmer's batting order.

Tuesday, September 6

Cleveland

Don Gullett called it fun. That's what the Yankees have been having since the All-Star break, right? Some fun.

Ask Thurman Munson. Winning is supposed to heal all wounds. Win the pennant after that lousy start and the whole season looks rosy. Bull. The Yankees are winning now and it looks as if there's no stopping them from winning their division championship, but Munson says it isn't any fun. He remembers last season as a joy, so much joy that he saw the change in his own disposition.

One night at batting practice he was accused of being a closet nice guy. He spun around and slammed his bat against the pipe on which the accuser was leaning. "Nice guy, huh?" Munson said.

There has been none of that visible this season. It has been a grind. And Munson feels that when he looks back at this season in the years to come, he will still recall it as a grind, still poisoned by the hostility.

The slump that leads him to say "I've been struggling harder than anybody in the league the last two months," is only part of it. Even Munson would not flip his helmet at hecklers solely because he isn't hitting. The ball playing is the one thing he is secure about.

The unending tug-of-war with Steinbrenner has been a punishment. Munson now sees the legacy of the ball player—packing and unpacking, going from hotel to hotel, being away from his family—as endless. There is more of it tomorrow and next year, as far as the mind can see.

He did not make life simpler with his growth of beard last month. Some thought he was growing it to irritate Steinbrenner and force Steinbrenner to trade him to Cleveland out of embarrassment at being shown up. Munson has suggested that he was growing the beard to tease his wife, who hates beards, but that's hard to believe.

"How could people say I don't want to play in New York?" Munson said. "New York has given me everything I want." He said he nearly asked the Yankee television broadcasters to permit him to explain himself over the air.

In a time of rare introspection early in the year, Munson reflected on his personal growth in the exposure New York has given him. He said he had only stereotyped images of Jews in his mind when he came to the city, prejudices formed on never having met Jewish people. "I used to go downtown and hear people talking loud or doing business and I identified them as Jews," Munson said. He didn't like what he thought he saw. Those loud people weren't all Jews.

"Then, after a while, I realized that some of the people I'd become closest to off the field were Jewish," Munson said. "I had no objections to them. They were no different; it was me who was different toward them. I realized people were what they were because it was New York, the big city."

Now Munson says, "If I ever do leave New York, it won't be because I don't like New York or don't like the fans. I do. If I ever do leave New York, it'll be for family purposes."

Skeptics dismiss thoughts that Munson would retire from his salary at his age. They say, if he were traded, a $400,000 salary would not be too high to expect. "But that's a fictitious figure," he said. "And with the money I have now, I can't spend $400,000 anyway."

He has this dream house that took eight years to complete in Canton. He has his burgeoning real estate business—an empire, some people say. He has this feeling of being demeaned by Steinbrenner.

"This is no phase I'm going through," Munson said. "It's based on reality. I'm tired of the bus rides, plane rides, the travel, I'm tired of being called a son of a bitch.

"I'm just a kid from Canton, Ohio, that's all. I get happy

at little things. My kids. My home. My wife. I'd like to be home."

Maybe at the end of the year— "This isn't a phase," he interrupted. "I'll just have to wait and see how I feel at the end of the year."

* * *

Munson got one of the big hits, a single that broke the 2–2 tie and brought Jackson to the plate in time to hit a three-run homer. The combination of Dick Tidrow and Sparky Lyle beat the Indians, 8–3, and put a stop to the thoughts of negative momentum. After two losses last night, there might have been some thinking with another loss and another Boston victory.

"Teams get tired physically and mentally," Tidrow said. "So much of the game is mental. If you get started down now, it's hard to stop. We needed to jump right back up and get it going again."

Which they did.

* * *

In Toronto, George Scott was still not "mentally prepared." Batting seventh does not appeal to him. The Yankees are not the only team with allergic reactions to batting orders.

Wednesday, September 7

Cleveland

Wayne Garland, the pitcher-turned-free-agent who has gone from $19,000 a year to $215,000 a year, had a 3–0 lead on the Yankees for eight innings. The score of Boston's 3–2 loss at Toronto was announced and things began to happen here. Chris Chambliss got a bunt single and Garland made a wild throw. Roy White beat out a dribbler. Willie Randolph beat a single through the infield and Dell Alston got a single in the infield. Mickey Rivers guided a roller past the second baseman's dive and the score was tied.

In the tenth inning, Munson singled hard. Jackson fought off an inside pitch for a bloop hit into left center. As Munson headed into third the throw hit him on the back and rolled into the dugout; Munson scored the winning run.

Even to jaded Munson, it was a memorable comeback. "You're playing and losing and doing nothing," he said. "You lose the game and your lead could be down to one. And then Boston loses and you come back and win like that. You remember the game."

Not only did Ron Guidry pitch nine innings, he pitched all ten.

* * *

A revealing vignette: Jackson had business to attend to and got to the ball park after batting practice had begun. He arrived at the batting cage and inquired, "How many we hitting?" Graig Nettles, in the cage, replied: "If you got here the same time as everyone else, you'd know." Jackson felt Nettles had said what had been on his mind from the very beginning. "Come out here and say that," Jackson said, his body tense. "Forget it," Nettles said after a pregnant pause. "I guess I'm just in a bad mood."

Thursday, September 8

Cleveland

For the second time this season Mickey Rivers dragged a bunt. That's what they were urging him to do on the first day of training. That's what made him unhappy on the first day of training. This time it led off an inning that produced three runs as they beat the Indians, 4–3.

"I know how to play ball," Rivers said. He had dragged his bunt with him toward first base instead of pushing it toward third, which is his custom. "That's it right there," Rivers explained. "Situations, you got to think in situations. The pitcher, the third baseman, the first baseman, you got to know your players out there, you got to know how they move. No, I ain't giving any of my secrets away. Well, they didn't break. When I faked a bunt, they didn't move."

Oh, but why toward first this time instead of toward third?

"You gotta play," Rivers explained. Oh.

* * *

Nettles broke his 0 for 22 and tied the club record for most RBIs by a third baseman, 95, set by Billy Johnson in 1947. Ed Figueroa pitched his second straight complete game, which he hadn't done since May. Jackson foolishly ran into two outs on the bases. But they won six of eight on the trip and are going home three and a half games ahead of the Red Sox, which makes for pleasant traveling.

Meanwhile, back to George Scott with the Red Sox. Scott had a $29 phone conversation with Reggie Jackson, reversing the procedure of the last time of trouble. Don Zimmer went to Scott and explained the facts of life—like the presence of Carl Yastrzemski, Jim Rice, and Carlton Fisk in the lineup. The issue was resolved after two days. Instead of declaring a war of words on Scott, Zimmer held his tongue. Zimmer understood that it was important to get Scott out of his funk, not to win an argument. Zimmer is a gritty veteran of the same era as Martin, but Zimmer was willing to go to Scott and explain. Martin can't bring himself to make that much concession to communication.

Friday, September 9

New York

The next trick for the Yankees is to remember that they don't play the Red Sox until Tuesday and there is a series with Toronto in between. It's only human nature to think ahead to the big ones. Anybody who doesn't can't understand what it's all about.

But the discipline of winning a pennant demands concentration on the job at hand. "Let me put it to you this way," said Elrod Hendricks, the elder statesman returned from Syracuse. "You block it out of your mind not because you want to but because you have to."

* * *

Apparently the Yankees had enough concentration, because Mike Torrez pitched a three-hitter, 2–0, and Cliff Johnson hit his tenth home run as a Yankee. Graig Nettles made a fine play, heading off a rally by charging a roller on the first-base side of the mound and boldly throwing to second for a force.

Saturday, September 10

New York

Sometimes the unavoidable fascination with the scoreboard brings amazement. Don Zimmer was watching the board while the Red Sox were beating the Tigers. He watched and he watched. "It was kind of weird watching that board, almost unbelievable," Zimmer said.

What he watched was the progression of runs for Toronto as they beat the Yankees, 19–3, and the succession of Yankee pitchers—Catfish Hunter, Ken Clay, Stan Thomas, Larry McCall, and Ken Holtzman. Each was thoroughly scathed, Hunter for six runs in 3⅓ innings. They wound up with a lineup that included Dave Bergman, Mickey Klutts, Hendricks, George Zeber, Carlos May, and Fred Stanley.

Martin refused to look at it as a catastrophe. He even smiled as he sat under a wall poster that read, "Thought for today; a smile makes a lousy umbrella." Actually, the thought for today came from both Martin and Zimmer: Whatever the score it was only one game. But the Yankees' lead is two games over Boston. They meet for three games in Yankee Stadium. It may still be a race to the end.

Sunday, September 11

New York

The Yankees and Red Sox are going to come together with the Red Sox only a game and a half behind. They won today and the Yankees split the doubleheader with the Blue Jays. A week ago the Yankees' lead was four and a half games.

Most of the Yankees decided to be unruffled by the turn of events. Lou Piniella decided to be ruffled. "I don't like it," he said. "We had that lead and now look where it's at."

They won the first game, 4–3, with Dick Tidrow the winning pitcher and tomorrow he returns to the bullpen. Tidrow has built a 10–4 record and Martin's decision to start Tidrow and leave Sparky Lyle on his own in the bullpen has been the brainstorm of the season.

The Blue Jays won the second game, 6–4. The big series doesn't start until Tuesday, but Don Zimmer likes to make a point about his 1951 Brooklyn Dodgers. If they had won on opening day, they wouldn't have had the play-off with the Giants and Bobby Thomson never would have hit his home run.

Monday, September 12

Boston/New York

This was supposed to be a day off, but nobody has a day off at a time like this. That's what a pennant race is. Some players are more honest with themselves about it, or more intelligent.

With the season 144 games old, with today the only unscheduled day in weeks, Carl Yastrzemski was at Fenway Park in Boston at ten thirty this morning to take forty minutes of batting practice even though he had two hits each on Saturday and yesterday. No Yankee player hit at Yankee Stadium. "I've always been honest with myself," Yastrzemski said. "I didn't like the way I was swinging, whether I was getting hits or not."

Yastrzemski has been a special kind of superstar for some years. At thirty-eight, with touches of gray in his beard and at his temples, he has played nearly every game. He has a .300 batting average with 88 runs batted in and 87 runs scored. He has hit 23 home runs and struck out only 36 times. Amazing.

More than that, he feels the race. "I'll probably be as emotional as anybody, if not more so," he said. "Maybe it's going into Yankee Stadium, or being from Long Island. Or maybe it's the pennant race, the feeling of chasing the Yankees."

A pennant race means living the tension every day for as long as two months. Players—especially the best players—try to relax in front of television or at the movies, but they dis-

cover they have lost the flow of the plot because thoughts of
the race have boiled to the top of their consciousness. They
struggle to sleep. No other sport has anything like it.

"I try not to think about the game, but I can't do it," Yastrzemski said. "The last three or four days it seems I've
watched the scoreboard constantly to see what the Yankees
were doing. The last couple of days I've gone to sleep at
eleven o'clock and woke up at five. I never woke up at five
AM in my life. I just lie there wishing it were eleven and time
to go to the ball park so I don't have to wait another six
hours."

That's what a pennant race is. "I don't find myself tired,"
Yastrzemski said. "This is the situation you want to be in."

* * *

Ironically, neither of the big-name pitchers, Catfish Hunter
or Ferguson Jenkins, is scheduled to pitch in the big series. It
opens with Ron Guidry, having emerged from his understudy
role as the Yankee stopper, and Mike Paxton, who was at the
Red Sox' Pawtucket farm until May.

The Red Sox did lead the division as recently as August
22. They had five games over the Yankees on August 10, but
in the next twenty-three days lost nine and a half games in
the standing. They have won five in a row and eleven of thirteen since a seven-game losing streak dropped them out of
first place. The Yankees have cooled since their 24–3 surge
took them to the top.

Billy Martin has expressed some unhappiness with Reggie
Jackson's baserunning, his having been picked off first and
thrown out at third Friday, and running into a kindergarten
out trying to go from second to third on a grounder to short
last week. Martin kidded about it: "If I could only keep
Jackson on the bases," but it's kidding on the square. Jackson's chill toward Martin is deeper and increasingly evident.

But the Yankees have emerged from those spells again and
again. "I haven't been able to understand either team," Yastrzemski said. "When we were behind, we played like hell.
When we got in front we played lousy. We got behind and
are playing like hell again. It seems both teams have reacted
to falling behind. We'll see how long it lasts." For New York
there hasn't been a series like this since the Yankees came
from behind to pull out the pennant in 1964. And this is the
last of the great rivalries. The city welcomes it.

Tuesday, September 13

New York

Guidry was too much. He threw ten pitches in the first inning, all strikes, and struck out the side. He struck out the last two Red Sox in the ninth inning. All fastballs, coming in at the waist and leaping across the letters. "He is so skinny you don't expect him to have that velocity," Yastrzemski said. "But he's got good rhythm. Everything explodes at once." The Yankees won, 4–2.

The Red Sox provided their momentary scare when Yastrzemski hit a 400-foot triple in the second inning when the Red Sox took a 2–0 lead.

Lou Piniella singled home the first Yankee run in the fourth. Bucky Dent singled and Mickey Rivers hit his eleventh home run to make it 3–2 in the fifth. And Guidry said to himself in the dugout, "If you don't let them score again, you win this game." Then Jackson ran hard to score from first on Chris Chambliss' double and Guidry had a cushion on his lead.

The crowd was 55,269, the largest for the regular season since the ball park was rebuilt, and now the lead cannot escape the Yankees this series. The emphasis in the standings has changed entirely. "What I'm thinking," said Piniella, Sunday's pessimist, "is this thing can be over by the end of the weekend . . ."

The emphasis in the clubhouse has not changed. In the original lineup, Martin had Piniella in right field and Jackson DH. Shortly before the game, they were reversed. "I asked him if I could play," Jackson said. "My leg is still bothering me but this is no time to sit down. I wanted to be out there."

After the game Martin electioneered for Nettles or Rivers for the Most Valuable Player award. How long ago was it that Martin benched Rivers for not having his head or his heart in the game? Rivers is playing well and Martin has his ways to keep Rivers pumped up.

While Martin was talking, the phone in his office rang. "What?" Martin said into the phone. "A five-year contract?" The Yankees lead by two and a half games with seventeen to

play. The manager is still Billy Martin; he thinks there should
be some reward for him too.

Wednesday, September 14

New York

This was the moment that makes people feel it's worthwhile to be a baseball fan. This was the moment for George
Steinbrenner to feel his investment in Reggie Jackson was
worthwhile. This was the moment Jackson could feel that his
own investment in heartaches was worthwhile. The sound of
the crowd of 54,365 demanding that he come out of the
clubhouse to take one curtain call and then another, the
crowd of journalists around his locker, and the backpounding
surge of teammates around him at home plate said everything
Jackson wanted to hear.

A ball game full of the tension of 400-foot outs, diving
catches, and runners stranded ended on one last swing of
Jackson's bat. With none out and one on in the last of the
ninth of a scoreless game, Jackson swung and the crowd
gasped. Jackson danced at the plate for a moment and then
he ran out his home run. It was no time for his home-run
trot, there was an ovation waiting at the plate.

"When I hit it, it was like a fairy tale," he said. "It was an
exciting feeling. You can feel everybody loving you, you can
feel your friends feeling it, the people pulling for you. When
I hit it, I had the feeling I was sharing it with everybody."

Jackson thought he felt love. He had provided the jolt that
may have clinched the pennant. People who had scarcely spoken to him all season patted his back. He welcomed the display from people who had turned his stomach. If that was
love, then love must come from the mouth of a cannon.

But it was what Jackson wanted. He had showed them. He
had won the biggest game for them. He won it with his bat,
which they all knew he could do. And before that, he saved it
with his glove, which he felt had been so harshly criticized.
That made it his "most satisfying" game as a Yankee.

He made two remarkable catches. Once he leaped near the
fence to spear a double and save a run. Once he dove to the
grass after a long run to catch a dying quail and save another

run. "Tonight they got something back from me," Jackson said. "I'm supposed to hit. I'm not supposed to field. But sometimes you think with all the money I'm making and George Steinbrenner sticking his neck out, it's great to do well."

Only a cruel person would point out that Jackson could have gone back another step before jumping for the first catch, that he misjudged the second and forced himself to make the diving catch. Only Paul Blair is perfect, and not many outfielders would have caught either ball.

The sound of the fans calling Jackson back onto the field ten minutes after the end of the game reminds the skeptical world of why Steinbrenner made his investment. Jackson has his magic. Steinbrenner reminded Jackson of that last night at P.J. Clarke's, a fashionable oasis on Manhattan's fashionable East Side. Jackson had struck out three times in four hitless tries in the opener of the series and Steinbrenner told him, "Don't worry, tomorrow night you'll win the game for us." The owner does not spend his drinking time with many players. Not many players call for the premonitions Jackson does. Not everybody reads the signs the same.

With Thurman Munson on first base with a single, Billy Martin's first inclination was to have Jackson sacrifice. Dick Howser walked in from the third-base coach's box to give the sign orally. He wanted to make certain Jackson knew the bunt was on but was subject to change with each pitch. "I don't ever know the bunt sign," Jackson said. "I had to look at Howser's lips." Jackson thought it was the first time he had been asked to bunt all season. Perhaps at an earlier time—or with other results—Jackson would have been annoyed, but at this time he sees the Yankees playing "connoisseur's baseball" and this was the play for the time. He joked about his own unfamiliarity. "It was really kind of funny," Howser said. "I asked him where he bunted the ball best and he had to think about it."

When Reggie Cleveland threw a ball on the first pitch, Martin decided to give Jackson a chance to hit a fastball on the next, and Jackson fouled it back. With Jackson squared around to bunt the next, Cleveland's pitch was wide. Jackson took a call strike and Cleveland missed with the next. Full count. Then Jackson swung. "It was ball four, it was so low," Cleveland said. "If he hits it, you figure it's on the ground for a double play. He picked it up. He's so strong, you know."

The pitch was near his ankles and Jackson hit it 430 feet into the bleachers in right center. In all these years, Jackson thought he had never hit one there before. It was so dramatic it was a cliché.

"I've never played in a game that exciting in my life," Bucky Dent sighed.

The Red Sox thought about the cruel fates. "Reggie Jackson" said his friend George Scott, "I'm not saying he's not a good outfielder, but he made two plays tonight he ain't made in ten years. If he's been making them all year, then why does the man take him out for defense?"

Bill Lee, Boston's mystic pitcher, saw it was the result of a pact between Steinbrenner and the devil. How else could the Red Sox hit so many balls so hard and get nothing for it? "Steinbrenner sold his pancreas to the devil," Lee said. Was Steinbrenner selling the devil one organ a year? "Yeah," Lee said, "but last year he tricked him. He sold him a Wurlitzer."

Ed Figueroa pitched in and out of trouble and admired the game Cleveland pitched. "But I think I pitched better," he said. "I win."

He won on Jackson's twenty-sixth home run and ninety-second and -third runs batted in. Jackson made $3,000,000 look like a bargain.

Thursday, September 15

New York

The Red Sox were entitled to win one game. They are a good team. But until it was safe in the clubhouse, they refused to think about the unthinkable. When it was safe, they sat quietly, in no mood to rush and dress to get to Baltimore.

The unthinkable was the question of where they would have been if they had lost. They had to look at it, but they had to refuse to see it. "If you looked at reality all the time, you couldn't function," said Bill Campbell, the relief pitcher who recorded the last five outs for the Red Sox as they beat the Yankees, 7–3. Campbell is used to living on the razor's edge, where one mistake is terminal. "You condition your mind," he said. "You care, but you don't really care. It's the only way."

Of course, the Red Sox cared the hell out of it. Reality after the game was that they were still alive. The Yankee lead is two and a half games with fifteen to play; the Red Sox have sixteen remaining. "If we hadn't won," Carl Yastrzemski said, "I think we'd have been all done. We came in all keyed up. The first game was so important. Then all of a sudden this game took on more importance than the first game."

The fact of life was that the Red Sox have to win two of three in Baltimore and beat the Yankees twice in Boston Monday and Tuesday.

After the first two games of the series, which are memorable, tonight's was eminently forgettable. No stirring plays or thunderous hits. For two nights the size of the ball park was an enemy of the Red Sox. They won this one with one line-drive single, a succession of grounders and bloops that produced four more hits, and then a three-run triple inside first base by Denny Doyle, batting ninth because he is the smallest and lightest-hitting of the Red Sox. "It's a strange game," Yastrzemski said. "I still haven't figured it out. You see something different every game." What was different tonight was that the scoreboard showed the Orioles had lost at Toronto by forfeit. "Who could believe that?" Yasztremski said.

Then it was safe to joke about the conduct of the fans— 55,218 of them, bringing the three-game total to 164,852 for the biggest three-game series in the league since the Yankees played at Cleveland in 1950. The Red Sox surveyed the scene in the grandstand where there were a dozen fights worth watching.

Campbell said he was glad to get out of the bullpen where he was strafed by flattened beer cans, a beer bottle, and a whiskey bottle. "Empty, of course," said bullpen resident Jim Willoughby. Campbell was struck by a flying lime. Yastrzemski noticed that several souvenir Red Sox helmets had been flung into left field. "They must have been taken away from Red Sox fans," he concluded.

The fans lost some interest after the six-run Boston sixth. The Red Sox had their interest revived. "We got a hell of a chance," Don Zimmer said. "Things would have looked a little dull if we had lost. I knew it. All the players knew it."

* * *

The other item of interest of the night was the appearance of Dave Kingman in pinstripes. The Mets couldn't sign him, nor could the Padres or Angels—all this season. He has been holding out for $2,500,000 for five years. He has hit 21 home runs with a .219 average and 71 RBIs. You say, what do the Yankees want with him while they have Cliff Johnson and Lou Piniella as right-handed designated hitters and that's the only position Kingman can play safely?

What they have is one more fence buster to keep the left-handers away from the door. What they have is one more player with star quality, and Steinbrenner likes star quality. The Yankees were unable to get him before they got Johnson. For two weeks Kingman will cost $7,500 in salary. Maybe he can break up a game in Detroit or Boston. The Yankees are able and willing to pay that price. And if they can't sign him for next year, they can absorb the price that brought him here.

If the Yankees do sign Kingman, who is not regarded by his peers as one of the greats of his generation, there will be great gnashing of teeth among better players who won't be paid as much. Like Nettles. But Steinbrenner is prepared to cope with that, too, as long as the fans come to watch.

The Yankees are going to pass the two-million mark in attendance next week. That's the tyranny of the new baseball; the good teams are rewarded and those with good management can afford to invest to remain good. That's called the merit system.

Friday, September 16

Detroit

At thirty-three, the greatest quality in Paul Blair is that he knows who he is and where he is. He can cope with the sitting after years as a regular. When he is told he is playing, he is ready. When he was told Mickey Rivers' ankle was sore and he couldn't play, Blair played center field and hit a two-run tie-breaking home run in the eighth inning as they beat the Tigers, 5–4. The pressure of the race is just fine with him. When a man does not have a contract for next season, the spotlight is a place to shine.

"It's good to know you're going to be out there when it's

going down the stretch," he said. "I still feel as I used to feel, that I have the ability to be the difference."

Once he was a star. Once he hit 26 home runs in a season. But he had his cheek shattered by a pitch early in the next season and has never been the same hitter. The tendency to bail out on an inside pitch is all too natural. But it never hurt Blair's ability to catch a ball. Bill Virdon, as Yankee manager then, once analyzed Bobby Murcer's shortcomings as a center fielder by a comparison with Blair. "You hear the crack of the bat and you look up and you never see Blair take his first step; he's already on the run. You always see Murcer's first step."

Blair's job with the Yankees has been to catch a ball and make a throw in a barely adequate defensive outfield, and to provide a viable alternative when Rivers is in one of his moods. He is expected to make the catch that saves the game; he is not expected to break up many with home runs.

This one, matched with the Orioles' defeat of Boston, left the Yankees with a lead of two and a half games, now measured against Baltimore.

Saturday, September 17

Detroit

This is the kind of glitter Steinbrenner has in mind for Dave Kingman:

On his first turn in batting practice against Dick Howser, Kingman hit a ball into the upper deck, then plopped one on the roof in left field, just foul. Only twice in thirty-nine years since Tiger Stadium was rebuilt has anybody cleared the left field roof in a game.

On his second turn, Kingman saw three pitches and hit all three into the upper deck, just short of the roof.

In his third turn, Kingman hit one more into the upper deck. He popped his last pitch into the netting of the batting cage and left the cage smiling to an ovation from the early arrivals.

How many ball players ever could get an ovation in batting practice? "I hope they sign him," Jackson said.

In his first game as a Yankee, Kingman was Kingman. He

struck out three times, hit a two-run homer, and a double. Thurman Munson, Graig Nettles, and Reggie Jackson also hit two-run homers and Jackson added a regular one-run homer as they bombed the Tigers, 9–4.

Jackson's first homer gave him the team lead in RBIs with 96 to Nettles' 95. Soon after, Nettles hit his homer to take the lead back with 99. And then in the eighth, Jackson homered, giving him 99.

It is a competition.

* * *

Not to be ignored, Dick Tidrow returned as a starting pitcher and allowed four hits in seven innings. He has started six times and the Yankees have won all six, with Tidrow the winning pitcher in five.

Sunday, September 18

Detroit

Ron LeFlore, the Tigers' center fielder, chuckled as he described the looks on the faces in the Yankee dugout as he stood on third base with the tying run and two out in the last of the ninth. The Yankee lead that had been an overwhelming 6–0 after eight innings was just 90 feet away from disappearing completely. It turned out to be only a scare, but LeFlore loved it. Everybody loves it when the Yankees squirm.

"They were laughing at us earlier in the game," LeFlore said. "Everything was going their way and they thought they had it wrapped up. They can be awesome hitters. Then there's that skinny kid Guidry knocking the bats out of our hands. But when I got to third base in the ninth and looked in their dugout, there wasn't a smile left."

Guidry took a four-hit shutout into the ninth inning. Kingman and Jackson had homered. Then in the last of the ninth, Willie Randolph messed up a grounder and Bucky Dent made an error and young Dave Bergman missed a catch in right for Jackson and Cliff Johnson made an error at first base. Then Sparky Lyle had to get the last out in a hurry. It brought back memories, but they managed to win, 6–5. Graig

Nettles remembered the game blown to Milwaukee just before the All-Star Game, which resulted in one of Martin's near firings. "Maybe we're getting better," Nettles said, "but I wouldn't want to go through that again."

Lyle got his twenty-fourth save with two pitches, and a handshake from Guidry. "But it was in the shithouse," Guidry said. "And when Sparky grabbed my hand, it was like this." He gave a precise impersonation of nervous Don Knotts' quiver.

* * *

In nine at bats as a Yankee, Kingman has struck out five times, homered twice, and doubled. He is an enigma. "I don't know if he inspires me, but he can embarrass a legitimate slugger," Jackson said. "If you don't do your thing, he can make them forget you."

Billy Martin said he will not have Kingman in the lineup in Boston tomorrow night, but will return Chris Chambliss and Roy White after their rest. Kingman has impressed players here with his power and with his obvious inabilities. They wonder what future—or present—he has here. "If he will settle for batting sixth or seventh and being a DH," one player said, "he can be helpful. But that is asking a lot. He would have to lower his salary demands and no other club has made any headway there."

Monday, September 19

Boston

What Billy Martin didn't need was more controversy. Maybe he didn't need Kingman, either. He got both.

Martin put Kingman into the game as a pinch hitter for Bucky Dent in the eighth inning, and Kingman hit a home run high over that beckoning left-field wall. When the Red Sox' 6–3 decision was complete, the question immediately became why Martin didn't hit Kingman for Dent in the fourth inning with two on and the Red Sox leading, 4–1. Dent hit into an inning-ending double play and a home run then would have tied the score. A second guess is always right. And why hadn't Kingman been in the lineup as DH?

Maybe the real question is whether Steinbrenner has bestowed one more jewel on Martin than he can handle. At first Martin ducked all questions by retiring to the trainer's room while Kingman asked questions of his own. "I thought they had obtained me to play in Boston," Kingman said. "This is what Mr. Steinbrenner told me. But then Billy went with the nine that have carried him this far, and why shouldn't he?"

That was Martin's comment, too: "The other guys got us here, didn't they?" he said testily. But if he chose to hit for Dent, why not in a more promising situation? Martin doesn't like to break up his defense in the fifth inning. His idol, Casey Stengel, used to do it when he thought he had a chance to break open a game. "I'm not Casey," Martin said.

There is sense to what Martin says about going with his own. It's the same sense that made Jackson such an outsider at the start of the season. It's the same thinking that sends the replacements in a combat infantry platoon out on the most dangerous patrols.

"I know I would want to come out of the lineup," said Lou Piniella, who was the DH. "I'm a damn fine hitter. If we're going to win or lose some money, the players who have been here all year should be the ones to decide it."

Of course, a long time ago the Yankees were famous for picking up castoffs late in the year and having them make notable contributions (see Johnny Hoop, Johnny Sain, Johnny Mize, et al.).

Now Kingman has seen Fernway Park. He would like to be with the Yankees next season, but the Red Sox have also expressed some interest. "I would like to play eight games here next year," he said. "But if not eight, then eighty-one."

* * *

More questions? of course more questions. Mickey Rivers was not in the lineup because of his still bad ankle. Martin said he was going to use Rivers, "but he told someone he couldn't play." Rivers said, "He give me another day off because it was just feeling good. I think I needed it."

Thurman Munson, the captain, said he had spoken to Rivers. "He's a good kid," Munson said. "He'll play tomorrow."

Tuesday, September 20

Boston

A rainy-day story: Now it can be told. It was on a flight to Seattle last month when Sparky Lyle put on his human-fly mask and hairy gloves and crept up on Phil Rizzuto in his front-row seat next to Billy Martin. Rizzuto is jumpy about things like snakes and bugs, and human flies at 33,000 feet. Lyle had it arranged with the stewardesses so that the food was off Rizzuto's and Martin's trays, but the trays were still in place so Rizzuto could not escape. Rizzuto reacted as predicted with a scream and a brief struggle to escape. I think Rizzuto puts some of that on after all these years. Maybe not.

It was minor key compared to the best of Lyle's pranks. "Well, I'm getting older," Lyle reflected. "I also didn't do too much this year because there was a lot of controversy going on and everybody was concerned about it."

Mail-order applications for the play-offs are being accepted at Yankee Stadium.

Wednesday, September 21

Boston

It was not time to look back. The Red Sox had beat the Yankees again, 3–2, and maybe there is some life in the race, after all. "Two games ahead with ten to go isn't bad shape," Billy Martin said. "We are in a lot better shape than the Red Sox and Orioles are."

It was the night the Dodgers clinched the Western Division in the National League. The Yankees were supposed to be the first team to clinch. Now they'll have to work a little longer. "It didn't matter, really," Lou Piniella said. "This only prolongs things."

Piniella homered and singled for both Yankee runs and blamed himself for blowing the chance to win the game. With runners on second and third in the eighth inning, Bill

Campbell relieved and struck out Piniella when a fly ball would have tied the score.

Reggie Jackson still has his own ghosts in this outfield. He made an error that cost one run and later played a hit into a three-base hit. And Mickey Rivers returned to center field to take a carom off the wall with his face. But the Yankees have that lead and Piniella asks, "What's all the commotion about?"

Thursday, September 22

Toronto

Getting here for a day off was not half the fun. The Yankee charter was taxiing down the runway at Logan Airport in Boston when a private plane zoomed too close for Yankee comfort. Ball players are notorious bad fliers to begin with.

Elston Howard said the incoming plane had come within 25 feet. He was shaken. The FAA said planes often appear closer to passengers than they really are. Billy Martin said they were close. "I got a look at the pilot and copilot of the other plane up close and will testify that it was Weaver and Zimmer," Martin said.

Mickey Rivers' face is swollen and sore after having his nose bloodied by the ball off the wall last night. "He thought his nose was broken," Martin said. "I was worried about his cheekbone. You can play with a broken nose. I know; I've had mine broken five times."

X-rays showed no break and the doctor said Rivers can play.

Friday, September 23

Toronto

From the standings, you would have to say the Yankees were a lot better than the Blue Jays, but you could hardly tell on the field. The Yankees had to score twice in the top of the ninth inning to go ahead, seven games to six, in the season's series. They won it, 5–3, on Graig Nettles' two-run homer.

Don Gullett pitched his most impressive game as a Yankee, striking out twelve. After Otto Velez homered in the second inning, Gullett struck out the next six batters. He has completed three of his four starts since coming off the disabled list.

The Yankees' third run came after Rivers walked in the third inning. It was the seventeenth time Rivers has walked in 567 appearances at the plate. Rivers has the highest batting average on the team. Nettles, who has the lowest average among the regulars, has been on base more often. One of the things that made Rivers mad in March was being told he ought to look for a walk more often.

The Red Sox won but the Orioles lost, and the Yankees' lead is two and a half games.

Sunday, September 25

Toronto

Ron Guidry pitched a shutout, 15–0, and Ed Figueroa and Sparky Lyle combined to pitch another, 2–0, and suddenly the Yankees and Blue Jays assumed their proper juxtaposition.

Now there's a magic number for clinching: five.

Jackson hit his thirty-first homer and drove in the first three runs of the day. Cliff Johnson hit two homers; of his dozen for the Yankees, a half dozen have come against the Blue Jays. Dave Kingman hit his fourth home run and struck out twice. Piniella homered and Nettles made a marvelous diving stab to start an equally marvelous double play that got Figueroa out of trouble.

But the question of their socks—the blue ones they wear over the white hose—was more typical of their season. As they dressed for the doubleheader, Roy White, Willie Randolph, and Bucky Dent found new blue socks in their lockers. When they asked, they were told that the ball club thought their stirrups were cut too high and not enough blue was showing beneath their pants. "Who'd it come through?" Mar-

tin shouted when he was asked. He said he knew nothing of
the socks and was displeased that the directive hadn't come
through him. "I was worried about winning the ball games,
which I stupidly thought was more important," Martin said.
"We can't be worrying about socks in a pennant race. Maybe
they do that in football."

Ah, football. A reference to George Steinbrenner's background. Martin is a baseball man; he makes the distinction
clear now that he is the manager of the team counting down
on the magic number.

Randolph and Dent wore old socks. White wore the new
ones.

Monday, September 26

New York

So much for keepsakes, mementos, milestones, and posterity. Sparky Lyle threw away the ball with which he got his
201st save. For him, such things have the life expectancy of
the bubbles in a glass of champagne. What was of value was
the double magnum of champagne in Lyle's locker in George
Steinbrenner's manner of congratulating achievers.

Lyle didn't know it when he got his 200th save yesterday
and threw that ball away. "What's the sense of keeping two
hundred and one?" he said. "I didn't know when I got two
hundred, so what good is it?" Ten seasons afterward, Lyle
can't remember his first save or his first win in the big
leagues. "I don't remember stuff like that," he said.

What is important to him is right now, where he lives. He
pitched the last three innings for Mike Torrez, who never did
get his shoulder loose, and held the 4–2 victory over the Indians. Now the lead is three and a half games and the magic
number is down to four, with six to play. "I can pitch till
we're done," Lyle said. "Every day."

Of course, don't expect the champagne to wait that long.
"He likes life," Reggie Jackson observed. "Sparky is a fun
guy."

That observation is from a man who had to learn how
Lyle has everything up front. It was just two months ago that

Jackson misplayed a ball behind Lyle and Lyle told him in front of the bench, "Get your head out of your ass."

The two have not discussed the incident since. "It's just been forgotten," Jackson said. "Sparky says what's on his mind at that moment and that's it. That's the way he is."

Jackson stiffened when he was asked about his relationship with Lyle since that time. Obviously, it has not been forgotten; Jackson doesn't let go of insults that easily. What Jackson has learned to accept is Lyle's nature, and Jackson has apparently learned to put aside some of what he cannot forget.

What Lyle got was his twenty-sixth save of the season, second in the league to Bill Campbell's twenty-eight. Lyle has won twelve and lost five. His earned run average is 2.23, best in the league. He has pitched in sixty-nine games. His 201 career saves are the most since the statistic was invented in 1969. Now remember when Lyle wouldn't take the contract being offered him and Steinbrenner was threatening to trade him, if only Guidry could get somebody out? Lyle held on and got what he wanted, three years for close to $450,000. The convincer, it now develops, was that at a breakfast meeting with Steinbrenner, Munson advised: "Sign him. We can't win without him."

Now, after years of thinking that a relief pitcher couldn't merit being chosen for the All-Star Game, Lyle feels that relief pitchers don't get enough credit. Nobody wins without a bullpen these days. Now Lyle pauses to consider that he might be worth a vote or two for the Cy Young Award as the best pitcher in the league this season. Mike Marshall is the only relief pitcher to win the award and he had to pitch in 106 games to do it.

"A relief pitcher never thinks of that, it's too far out of his reach," Lyle said. "It would probably be the greatest honor I could have in my whole life." He might even keep the award as a memento.

* * *

Gabe Paul has proposed to the league office that Dave Kingman be squeezed though the loophole in the rule that says a player must be on the roster by September 1 to be eligible for the play-offs. Paul argues that there is a vacancy on the roster because Carlos May was sold on the fifteenth, the day after Kingman got here. Of course, the vacancy was created deliberately for Kingman. If Paul gets his way, he deserves the Chutzpah Award for the year.

Tuesday, September 27

New York

Getting closer. Dick Tidrow pitched 7⅓ innings, his longest appearance of the season, and they beat the Indians, 2–1. Sparky Lyle got the victory because things happen for pennant winners. With the score 1–1, Thurman Munson led off the ninth with a single and was wild-pitched to second. Reggie Jackson was intentionally walked, and after the bunt sign was dropped, Lou Piniella bunted anyhow. With the winning run on third base, another wild pitch got Munson home.

Wednesday, September 28

New York

The magic number is one—one more game won by the Yankees, or one loss each by the Red Sox and the Orioles, clinches the championship for the Yankees. They beat the Indians, 10–0, to clinch (*shh,* say it softly) a tie, and it was about right that Reggie Jackson hit a home run with the bases full in the first inning.

The last seven weeks as they sought their level at the top have been a grand slam for Jackson. Since he became the cleanup hitter forty-nine games ago, he has hit 13 home runs and batted in 48 runs. And the Yankees have won thirty-nine and lost only ten. That's a searing pace.

At this point, Jackson is even included in the ritual ragging that indicates a man has been accepted by the others on a ball club. A man is not teased to his face if he is still rejected; those things are said behind his back. Jackson still gets some of that, but the balance has shifted somewhat.

The other day in Toronto, Jackson, Munson and Piniella were chatting with Dodger scout Charlie Metro, who was explaining how pitcher Tommy John was made bionic by the transplant of a part from his right arm to replace a worn out part in his left.

"Gee," Munson said, "do you suppose we could take some of Paul Blair's tendons and put them in Reggie?"

"I don't know, Thurman," Piniella said. "I figure Reggie was worth eight games to us."

Jackson delighted at the suggestion, but Piniella was only setting up Jackson.

"You were with Baltimore last year, right, Reggie?" Piniella said. Jackson nodded.

"Well, last year at this time we were ten games ahead of Baltimore," Piniella said. "Now we're two ahead. So I figure you're worth eight games, Reggie."

A man enjoys being insulted with that kind of wit, especially when he know what he has accomplished. Jackson knows that he was put on trial when he was batted fourth after insisting that was where he belonged. "Hitting fourth almost makes me perform because there's pressure in that spot," Jackson said. "Many people like to say Reggie Jackson thrives on the limelight and turmoil. That's not me. I go to pieces in turmoil. I thrive on pressure."

Obviously, he's right—by his definitions. At bat, he thrives on pressure. In the field, he found the pressure too much. At Oakland he wasn't a bad fielder, but on that team there was nothing like the kind of pressure he feels in New York. He doesn't have the kind of confidence in his glove to fight it off. He has come to that understanding. "Defense was my weakest link," he concedes now. "Under the pressure, the weakest link broke."

That is a strong and painful concession for the man. What he does not concede when he refers to the "first ninety-four nights" as torture was his own role in his discomfort. He still regards each success as a vindication in a battle with the doubting press. He may be charming and trusting with reporters he sees often, but he still regards the press as a whole as the main source of his torture. "The New York press to me was like a cobra in the jungle, almost ready to attack," he said. "If there was a fight in Oakland, the papers would say there was a fight. Or Reggie Jackson said something about Charlie Finley and Charlie said something about Reggie Jackson . . . Here you got whipped with it. Here it was projected with a maliciousness."

Some of that is true. The sheer numbers of media in New York, and the depth and breadth of coverage compared to that in Oakland, probably exacerbated the conflict that was actually there. That was inevitable and unavoidable. But I haven't seen any malice, nor has Jackson presented any evidence of it.

To his credit, he has rarely hid from the questioners, but sounds too much like the tales Barry Goldwater, who felt he was doing fine in his presidential campaign until the press decided to write what he was saying.

Thursday, September 29

New York

The delay caused by a 4–1 loss to the Indians isn't any cause for concern. When Ed Figueroa came out of the third inning with a muscle pull in his side, that was a cause for concern. Don Gullett and Ron Guidry, in whichever order, are supposed to start the first two games of the play-off, followed by Mike Torrez, whose shoulder has been stiff, and then Figueroa. Without Figueroa, they would be down to seven healthy pitchers, including Ken Holtzman and Ken Clay.

So George Steinbrenner assigned Gene Monahan, the trainer, to spend the night and maybe more nights with Figueroa at his hotel. Monahan phoned his wife to tell her he wouldn't be home tonight, he'd be sitting up with a sick friend. He'll be at the Sheraton in Hasbrouck Heights, N.J.,—everybody knows where that is—keeping Figueroa's side wrapped with ice bags until he's ready to sleep, then will put him in a back brace.

* * *

The Yankees passed the two-million mark in home attendance, making them the first American League team and third in history to draw a million both at home and on the road. Figure an average of $5 spent per fan at home, and that makes the Yankees a profitable operation no matter what their payroll.

* * *

Another medical report: After being told by "five other" doctors, by Catfish Hunter's count, that the ache in his groin was a hernia, the new diagnosis of Hunter is "seminal vesiculitis." It's an uncommon condition and has drawn snickers from cynics. It is an inflamation of the organ that stores seminal fluid, caused by a failure of the body's natural cleansing action. He says he's been told it can come from either too much sex or not enough sex. "I know it isn't from too much sex," he said. On occasion it has been known to be the delayed result of drinking unpasteurized milk. Hunter is a farm boy.

He said he asked the doctor to explain the likely cause. "On this club," Hunter said, "the doctor doesn't tell you anything. He looked at me and said, 'Get out of the room, I want to call the Yankees.'" In any case, Hunter thinks the antibiotics are working because he isn't in as much pain.

Friday, September 30

New York

There is no tension over another delay. Reggie Jackson doesn't jump to conclusions about what's said in the dugout. The Yankees are calm. Oh, sure.

Well, it was the third inning and the Tigers had just taken a 2–0 lead, on the way to a 5–2 defeat of the Yankees. Lou Piniella came in from left field and shouted into the dugout, "Come on, let's get going."

Jackson, who had struck out with two runners on base in the first inning and dropped a fly ball in the second, took it personally. "I'm tired of hearing that shit," Jackson snapped. "I know you're talking to me."

Piniella had been one of the few Yankees close enough to Jackson early in the year to speak frankly with him. "I wasn't talking to anybody in particular," Piniella said when asked about the latest incident. "I was talking to all the guys, trying to get us going. I wasn't the only one yelling. Hell, I wouldn't say anything to him because I know it would start trouble." Munson and Piniella, remember, were the ones who went to Steinbrenner's suite in the middle of the night at Milwaukee and urged that Jackson be put at cleanup to boost his ego and production.

Each time Jackson was asked about this incident, he replied, "Go ask Lou. He has all the answers."

* * *

Guidry was hit hard for the first time in a long time. He had a 10–1 record since the All-Star Game.

The American League office denied the Yankees' request to include Dave Kingman or Dell Alston on their roster for the play-off. And Kingman disclosed that he would not sign with the Yankees. The team was willing to meet his price for five years, but not his demand for a no-trade clause.

And the league returned Piniella's new contract to be rewritten. It is ambiguous. Piniella understood that he had agreed to a contract that would be guaranteed for both years. When it came back, he was informed that only the first year was guaranteed. The Yankees have this history of contracts looking different on closer examination.

Just Desserts

The champagne ran out of Billy Martin's hair and stung his eyes, and it ran out of Gabe Paul's hair and stung his eyes too. The manager and the president of the team drank to each other with the kind of feeling few of us ever have in life. "*Salute*," Paul said in Italian, tipping his cup toward the manager. "*L'chaim*," Martin said in Hebrew, raising his bottle to Paul.

Champagne baths are ritual for championship clinchings in baseball. Often they mean little more than the expected display for the television cameras. This time it meant something extra. There was a moment of love of some kind in there, the love of having worked very hard together.

Paul's plaid sports jacket was already drenched from his baptism in the clubhouse. George Steinbrenner, who had bought the champagne and the players, and counted the rewards at the turnstiles, had already passed through the clubhouse and the manager's office untouched, parting the downpour of champagne like a dry blanket at the party. His blue jacket and carefully styled short hair remained dry as he murmured about going on to beat Kansas City, posed a smile for the cameras, and withdrew from the scene. Nobody blessed him with the ritual; it was a championship to be celebrated in the trenches, not in the penthouse boxes.

"Stick with us dagos and we'll make all of you Jews dagos," Martin said to Paul. Whether you like him or not, it has been a relentlessly trying season for Martin. "Anybody who says it isn't sweet is flat full of it," he said. "It's worth

307

all the troubles we had this year." Of course, those troubles
never could be forgotten from the first day until today. He
created many of them. He had been fired who knows how
many times—at least four, by his own count. "I felt like
Caryl Chessman," he said about facing his personal gallows
and being reprieved each time.

They lost to the Tigers, 10–7, today, their third loss in a
row after clinching the tie, but during the three-hour rain
delay in the third inning they watched television as the Red
Sox lost to the Orioles. Elliott Maddox, who hates Martin
from Texas and the Yankees, caught the final out and the last
formal bit of suspense was over.

Martin's feelings were very strong. He has now won four
division championships with three different teams and has repeated for the first time. "There never has been a year like
this, as far as I'm concerned," he said. His tug-of-war with
Steinbrenner had been consuming. "If he ever gets to working
with me, it could be a lot easier," Martin said.

Working with Martin, it has been said, means giving in to
Martin. But he is a winner again—because or in spite of himself. "It proved a point," he said. "No matter who you signed,
it takes a melting pot to win. The melting pot came to be and
that's what it took. They came together." What they did was
put aside spinsterish annoyances and became professionals for
two months.

Reggie Jackson brought his bottle of champagne into the
manager's office where the press had congregated. "Here,"
Jackson said to Martin. "Have some of my champagne."

"I'll drink, if you will," Martin said. Each took a deep
draw. "You had a hell of a year, big guy," Martin said. "I
love you."

Martin's eyes were full then. "That's what it's all about,"
he said. Martin doesn't love Jackson. Jackson doesn't love
Martin. But they had been forced to share something both
thought was good and there's something to that, even if it
lasts just an instant.

Jackson said he wanted to play at least five innings tomorrow to keep his edge even though the game is meaningless.
"You can manage," Martin said. "You been wanting to manage all year." It was intended as a laugh line. Jackson
laughed.

There is a bridge of some sort between Martin and Jackson
that doesn't refute the canyon that separates them. "Whatever

there is between us," Jackson said, "there is an empathy I feel for him."

For himself, Jackson felt relief. He had established the ground rules in spring training: If they did not win, he knew he would be blamed, even if he had played in five play-offs before. "I got to prove I'm a good player, can play under pressure, can play in New York. It's a relief. One fucking relief. It's my toughest one of all."

Grudgingly, he compared these Yankees with his Oakland A's. It was the Yankees' ninety-ninth victory. "In Oakland, we won a hundred only once," he said. "For me, sometimes I amaze myself. All the adjectives and superlatives apply to this. I subdued my personality and it strengthened my character."

He had his championship and Martin had his. In eight full seasons as a Yankee, player and manager, Martin has been on eight champions. When he has been fired as manager, he has come back to win somewhere else. "You can fire me," he said, "but I'll haunt your ass and beat you. I've got that something inside me that nobody can deny."

Sunday, October 2

New York

They won their 100th game, 8–7, over the Tigers on Billy Martin's favorite play, the squeeze bunt. George Steinbrenner issued a statement accusing league president Lee MacPhail of being "intimidated" by Kansas City in refusing permission for the Yankees to use either Dave Kingman or Dell Alston in the play-offs. Yankee players say Steinbrenner's irritation is merely a smokescreen to obscure the club's own foul-up while trying to sneak one by.

Billy Martin issued a statement that he will never celebrate with champagne again. He said he got a phone call from Dodger manager Tom Lasorda and a nice telegram of congratulations from Boston manager Don Zimmer. He did not get one from Baltimore manager Earl Weaver. "He forfeited his telegram," Martin said.

On the last home date the Yankees' home attendance reached 2,053,038, highest since 1949. Steinbrenner indicates that the Yankees made close to $4,000,000 last season with 32,000 fewer customers. Prices have been raised somewhat. So has the payroll—to a total of $3,470,000 (an average of $139,000 a man), second only to the Phillies' $3,498,000. The club figures to make an estimated $2,000,000 more from the play-off and World Series. Recently, Steinbrenner said he turned down an offer of $18,500,000 for the franchise. His group paid $10,000,000 for the team and could probably sell for $20,000,000, a capital gain of $10,000,000. "That's the bottom line that's important, not winning and losing," Martin sniped.

It's hard to reconcile the thought that Steinbrenner could accept losing either way—in the ledger or on the field. He has ego needs on the field. He needs to be recognized as a winning owner not just as an owner. As a businessman he has been brilliant. Some say "ruthless," as well. He was, by business standards, virtually broke after his first basketball venture, the Cleveland Pipers, folded in 1961. He was living at the YMCA in Cleveland.

His father owned Kinsman, Inc., a fleet of five ancient ships that carried iron ore on the Great Lakes from the mines to the mills in Pittsburgh and Gary, Indiana. The mills were developing their own shipping armada. Steinbrenner borrowed money and bought out his father's business. Under George's direction, Kinsman prospered and added grain to its cargo.

By 1967 he and some partners had bought up enough stock in American Ship Building Co. to win control. Steinbrenner mounted a congressional lobby that won the inclusion of Great Lakes shipbuilding on federal maritime tax exemptions. Revenues soared and Steinbrenner had his first successful encounter with politics.

His interest reached in all directions. He now owns Kinsman Stud Farms in Ocala, Florida, is general partner in Kinsman Stables, a 10 percent owner in the Chicago Bulls of the National Basketball Association, and part owner of a fleet of taxis in New York, a hotel in Tampa, and a Cleveland harness track.

From his association with theater owner Harry Nederlander, a minority partner in the Yankees, Steinbrenner learned about show business. He owned pieces of Broadway hits *Applause* and *Two for the Seesaw* and came away with an understanding of the entertainment business few in baseball comprehend. "Steinbrenner has been an absolutely brilliant businessman," says Arthur Kaminsky, agent for athletes in three sports and for several entertainers. "George saw an opportunity, took advantage of it, and executed just fabulously."

Don't say he spent $2,900,000 for Reggie Jackson or $3,-500,000 for Catfish Hunter or $1,990,000 for Don Gullett. First divide those propaganda figures by the length of the contracts. Then don't say "spent," but "invested." He invested in American Ship Building. "You establish what you're willing to pay for a player by looking at the business return on the dollar," Steinbrenner says. "If you're in a market where you can get a profitable return on the ball club, you can pay it. You measure the value of a ball player by how many fannies he puts in the seats."

So Steinbrenner was able to bid for Bucky Dent to fill a gap that had existed since 1964. He was willing to go to a million in an all-cash deal if the commissioner permitted. He was willing to bid and win Catfish Hunter at a time the team desperately needed a star for identity, and then invested and reinvested. Instead of taking income to be taxed at say 50 percent, he reinvested and made the club more profitable. "Anybody who looked at a company with growth like ours in the stock market would say we were a well-run company," he says.

"I look at free agency in a way few other owners have. When I get a free agent, I am not giving up talent to get him. If I can generate dollars with a team easier than I can generate great talent, that's what I have to invest." And if the team is eventually sold, the capital gains would be taxed at 25 percent.

Steinbrenner hopes that his reinvestment in young players will enable him to raise that great talent at home and permit him to pick only an occasional choice selection from the competitive market. That would mean greater profit. In the meantime, he has no objection to the combativeness on the team as long as the team still wins; the action will put fannies in the seats.

And Billy Martin—or whoever replaces him—will squirm in the hot seat. Steinbrenner is still strongly critical—sometimes contemptuous—of Martin.

"I think our relations have been good lately," Martin said.

"He's been sincere and frank with me. I haven't missed a meeting and all that tricky crap."

He feels he deserves to be rewarded for having repeated a championship despite what he and many of the players feel were front-office obstacles. He feels he is in demand again and feels free to speak his mind again. "I don't think I have to have a—what do you call it when you're looking for a job?—a résumé," he said. "There'll always be a job in baseball for me. I'm not being cocky; it's just about time I said something."

Undoubtedly this has been Martin's most satisfying season. "The toughest part was having to put up with Steinbrenner," Graig Nettles said. "The happiest time for Billy has been the two and a half hours when the game was on, when there's no bull from people who don't know what they're doing. Now that it's football season and Steinbrenner is thinking about Purdue, it's been easier for us."

Nettles says it would have been a mistake to fire Martin, but says he doesn't know if the manager had anything to do with the turnabout of the team. Steinbrenner agrees that it would have been a mistake to fire Martin, but because it would have put the onus on Jackson.

Certainly Martin could have handled the Jackson problem more gracefully. There were other ways. "Not for Billy; he couldn't have handled it any other way," says one Yankee who asked not to be identified. Steinbrenner fired Pete Ward as his triple-A manager because Syracuse dropped its working agreement with the Yankees, and Ward said the wrong things to the Syracuse papers. "George is a vindictive man," the Yankee said.

But Martin is bold again. He has swallowed what he had to, swallowed more than he ever would have before. "Or again," he said.

Monday, October 3

New York

Never a day of rest. Billy Martin is pumping for a new contract. He may be fired if he doesn't win the play-off and the World Series, but he is agitating for a raise. "If we win everything," he said. "I think it's a must for George to come up with a new contract. If he didn't, I'd have to think seriously about asking permission to talk to other clubs."

Martin loves the byplay with the press now. The attention is on him, on his terms. "The front office," he said, "they always get smarter the second year. It's amazing how brilliant they get."

He recalled the rivalry between his Yankee teams and the great Brooklyn Dodger teams; they met four times while Martin was a player. "You know those comparisons they put in the papers?" Martin said. "They used to piss me off. They would say Jackie Robinson gave the Dodgers a big edge at second base. They'd give second base completely to the Dodgers—like it wasn't even close."

You're not saying you were better than Jackie Robinson, are you, Billy? "In the World Series I was," Martin said. In twenty-eight World Series games, Martin batted .333 with five home runs. He was a big-game player.

Martin held up and admired a team picture for the World Series program. He looked for an inset of Mickey Rivers. Rivers didn't show up for the picture taking.

The phone rang and Martin got involved in a lengthy conversation. Was it Rivers? Martin laughed. "You know," Martin said, "I'm getting to understand him. That's what worries me."

Tuesday, October 4

New York

Last-day preparations and batting practice. "Larry," Reggie Jackson says to Larry McCall, the batting-practice pitcher just up from Syracuse, "would you hold the ball across the seams, please. Across the seams. Do you mind?" Jackson wants the ball rising to him.

The scrubs replace the regulars. "This is the trash lineup batting," Chicken Stanley announces. "Would you hold the ball across the seams, Larry?"

Jackson calls for Elston Howard to hit fly balls to right field. Howard runs for a clubhouse meeting. "Will you come back out and hit some, please," Jackson requests.

This would be no time for the weakest link to break.

Wednesday, October 4

New York

Confidence is vital in a play-off game, but confidence and a 6–0 lead is more useful. The Royals had both. The Yankees had no lead at all.

In the top of the eighth inning, Kansas City pitcher Paul Splittorff passed his comparisons with last year's opening play-off game along to third baseman George Brett on the bench. "I told George how much more settled we were than last year," Splittorff recounted when the scoreboard showed the conclusion of the Royals' 7–2 victory.

The Royals, who had the best record in baseball, didn't make any mistakes. The Yankees did. The Royals challenged them. "Today was very important," said Splittorff, the obligatory left-handed starter in Yankee Stadium. He kept the Yankees in hand for eight innings. "We know we can play here," he said. "Before, we hoped we could play under pressure. Last year we were shy and timid and hopeful."

Splittorff, who started the first game last year, recalled that he felt light-headed on the mound. Last year the Royals laid the first game in the Yankees' hands in the first inning with two throwing errors by Brett giving away two runs. "Last year," Brett said, "I was in awe of the play-off."

Of course, it always helps confidence when the first batter of the game walks and the second batter, Hal McRae, hits a home run. Don Gullett, the Yankees' left-handed starter, was finished after two innings, behind 4–0 and complaining about an ache in his shoulder.

Actually, what the Royals had planned was to pit their speed against the Yankees' arms. "In the past, some clubs have been leery, scared to run against Munson," Frank White, the Royals' swifty, said. "He may throw some of us out, but we know he's capable of throwing the ball into center field." That much the Royals recalled from 12 stolen bases in 13 tries against Munson during the season. They challenged him three times this afternoon. Munson made one bad throw, saved by a leap and a great tag by Bucky Dent, one awful throw into center field, and once Fred Patek got a hit when White was running.

On that play, Patek, a miniature at five feet four, pulled Gullett's limp fastball inside third base, against the facing of the grandstand. Lou Piniella read the umpire's hand signal that the ball was in play to mean that a fan had touched the ball and it was dead. White scored the second run of the inning, and Piniella argued that the umpire normally makes no sign except to call the ball dead.

The Royals feel they have made their point to themselves. Having gone through the pressure of one play-off can make a world of difference in the next. "Today we were aggressive," Splittorff said. "It's something we do when we play well; it was definite that we do it today."

It should not be forgotten that last year was the first play-off for the Yankees as well. "All I hear is how much experience they got," said Munson who homered for both Yankee runs. "Do you think they were the only ones who learned anything last year?"

* * *

The needs caused by having 300-odd reporters around at a play-off have evolved into a procedure by which players from the winning team and both managers are taken to a special interview room as soon as the game is over. Billy Martin resents being asked questions in his natural habitat, let alone being separated out like this. When he was asked if Piniella should have played out the hit down the line, Martin threw a blank gaze across the room. "Any more questions?" he asked.

One question later, a pause followed another sarcastic answer. "It's been a pleasure," he said and left.

He was willing to discuss the problem of Gullett's arm in the familiar confines of the manager's office. "Gullett's arm is hurt and it looks like he'll be lost to us for the rest of the play-offs and probably the World Series, if we get there," Martin announced.

As good a body as Gullett appears to have, he is remarkably fragile. This is the third year in a row he's been hurt in some way in the play-off or World Series. Martin referred specific questions about Gullett's recurring "muscular soreness" to Dr. Maurice Cowens. In his first play-off game, Dr. Cowens has learned the Yankee system well. When questioners approached him, he fled to the trainer's room and left Yankee Stadium soon after.

Thursday, October 5

New York

The World Series seldom creates hard feelings on the field. The play-offs are somewhat different. Maybe getting angry was what the Yankees needed. They were angry when they left for Kansas City tonight and may still have some of it left for tomorrow night's game. Mild Willie Randolph does not throw a ball at the Kansas City dugout without anger that ought to last longer than a plane ride. Thurman Munson does not slide deliberately late and hard without intending to leave a message.

"I'm beginning to think these two clubs do not like each other," Lou Piniella said. His smile conflicted with the hostility he was describing, but then Piniella smiles a lot. For a change, it's the other team the Yankees are angry at.

The Yankees evened the score in games by beating the Royals, 6–2, but many of the Yankees think they still have a score to settle with Hal McRae for the body block he threw on Randolph at second base. A cheap shot, the Yankees thought—or worse. "It could have turned into a war," said Mike Torrez, who is tomorrow night's Yankee starter. "When you're ahead, 6–2, you don't want that. Tomorrow is another day."

It sounded like a warning. The Yankees gave a lot of warnings.

The Yankees broke a 2–2 tie with three runs in the bottom of the sixth when it looked as if they were falling into some kind of lethargy and wasting Ron Guidry's fine pitching. "McRae did wake us up," Munson growled. "It had its effect. It turned the game around. I think we were a little more aggressive after that, don't you?"

Unquestionably. But not quite aggressive enough for Billy Martin. "Our second baseman is a gentleman," Martin said, enjoying the taste of the kind of baseball conflict he enjoys. "I did not always play like a gentleman," he said. He loves to remind everybody that he was a scrapper.

McRae was trying to get a run home in a tied game and that was justification enough for him. He spent his formative years with Cincinnati in the National League and is still an unreconstructed National Leaguer. There was one out, Fred Patek on second base and McRae on first when George Brett hit a half-hopper to third base. Graig Nettles struggled for a grip long enough to lose a chance for a double play. Randolph took the throw for the force and looked toward Patek turning third.

Then McRae struck, going directly over the base in a half crouch and sending Randolph cartwheeling. Randolph held the ball long enough for the out but when it rolled free, Patek scored the tying run. "Hard slides are part of the game; that's not part of the game," Randolph said. "If he comes in on me again and does that slide, next time I'm going to throw it right between his eyes."

Randolph and the Yankees argued to no avail that McRae should be charged with interference and the run he wiped out. Then, in frustration, Randolph heaved the ball into the Royals' dugout. Randolph later insisted that he was just trying to throw the ball into the dirt, but there are acres of dirt in Yankee Stadium and only one visitors' dugout.

Guidry pitched a nifty three-hitter, but all he had to show for his work until then was a tie. If the Yankees couldn't beat Andy Hassler, who could they beat? Whitey Herzog passed up three starters with better records in order to start Hassler because he is left-handed and Herzog's move was looking good.

Then with one out in the Yankee sixth, Munson singled. Lou Piniella singled and Munson went careening into third base, high and hard. "You don't think that was bad blood?" Brett, the third baseman, said. "That was foul play."

"I slid as late as I could, as hard as I could," Munson said. "If I had wanted to hurt him, I'd have rolled him like they rolled Willie. I wanted to let them know I was there. If Brett thought I was trying to hurt him, maybe it was a guilt complex. They knew McRae was wrong."

There were opportunities for further retaliation, but the Yankees didn't want to take any chances with their lead. McRae has the protective coverage of being DH; he doesn't play the vulnerable positions of shortstop or second base. When McRae went to bat in the ninth inning, Guidry was instructed to treat him like any other batter. "There's a time

and a place for everything," Martin said. "Not leading off the
ninth inning of a play-off game. In spring training, maybe, or
early in the season, that's the time. Sometimes a pitch slips."

The Yankees' anger was acceptable to McRae, who once
broke his leg on a slide like that. "If I get a chance to get a
run home by knocking down an infielder," he said, "they're
going to get a lot more angry."

It's an interesting thought. The game is supposed to be
played hard. One player shouldn't deliberately try to hurt another. But the combativeness is welcome. For years the
American League was known as "the brother-in-law league."
A man doesn't want to take away his brother-in-law's liveli-
hood, does he? The Orioles and the A's played National
League ball and they dominated the American League for
nearly ten seasons. Perhaps some other teams have learned
from it.

Cliff Johnson, who had homered for the first run, doubled
and the Yankees had their lead again. Chris Chambliss was
walked and Randolph's sharp grounder went between Brett's
legs for a two-base error and two more runs.

Munson admires Brett too much to hurt him. "If there's
any player I compare myself to, it's Brett," Munson said.
"We're both hard-nosed. If there was anybody I was going to
get, it was McRae."

Friday, October 7

Kansas City

Whatever aggressiveness the Yankees thought they had last
night was lost somewhere en route. They were as flat as last
week's champagne. Now the team that lived in crisis off the
field all season is in crisis on the field. This time it may be
their last crisis. Now they have to win two in a row and if
they don't, there's no predicting the explosion that could follow.

The Royals beat them, 6–2, tonight to take a lead of two
to one. The first team to win three games goes to the World
Series. If it isn't the Yankees, then they have to go home to
George Steinbrenner. It would be a crashing disappointment
in the countinghouse and in the evaluation of Steinbrenner,
who had his finger on the button all season.

The Royals beat the Yankees because Dennis Leonard pitched a masterful game, because a pivotal umpire's call went against the Yankees, and because the Royals were aggressive while the Yankees were not. Billy Martin predictably chose to blame the umpires first. Several of the Yankees preferred to question the quantity and quality of desire in their clubhouse.

And if the Yankees don't win two in a row, what happens to Martin? "You ask questions about baseball; just ask about the game," Martin instructed. His voice was hoarse from screaming at the umpires and perhaps somewhat choked over the issue at hand, as well.

Munson sat on his stool, tired as always, and wondered aloud about effort. "If you have more talent, you think you can do it if you want," he said. "Superstars don't have to be aggressive because they have so much talent. These guys, the Royals, they have guys who know what they have to do to win, instead of guys who can bust things open."

Munson refused to point an accusing finger at any Yankee and he backtracked to say he wasn't saying the Yankees were "deadass," which was exactly what it sounded like. But his open admiration of the Royals' approach made it clear that he identified with them; he was separating his own efforts from that of his teammates. "I can win," he said. "I think the team can win."

The lone bold venture by the Yankees turned out to be the play on which the game turned. It came before Leonard established his mastery over Reggie Jackson, Graig Nettles, and Chris Chambliss. With one out in the top of the first inning, Roy White hit a ball to the opposite field—not too hard but close to the left-field line—and set out to run it into a triple. "We wanted to get the momentum," White said later. "We were flat."

The throw and White arrived nearly together at the feet of George Brett, the third baseman, and umpire Bill Deegan called an out. The Yankees made a scene. "I didn't think it was particularly close," White said. "When your legs are extended and he tags you, you know it's a close play. My legs were already folded against the bag. I was shocked. I'm not one to argue about anything."

Martin is. He argued. That's why his voice was so hoarse. He challenged, among other things, the practice of assigning umpires to postseason games by rotation. Unionism, it seems, has reached the umpires too; play-off money is too good now to be restricted to a select few. "How Deegan is in the play-offs, I don't know," Martin rasped. "You don't see Seattle playing here."

Brett conceded there was room for question. But instead of a man on third and one out, there were two out and none on. Then Munson hit a sharp one-hopper that Brett grabbed as a reflex at his chest. If White had been on third, Brett would not have been playing so deep, and if the Yankees had taken the lead in the first inning . . .

That was the thought that kept Martin raving until his voice was worn to a whisper. "I would have been thrown out three times if they could have heard me," Martin said, finding a little humor at his own expense. "The plate umpire, he said, 'If I could have waited one more day, your voice would be entirely gone and I'd have loved to be behind the plate.'" The umpires still have not come to love Billy.

As it turned out, the Yankees did not hit another ball hard until the ninth inning and only three all night, one of them foul. The Royals nibbled away and forced Yankee infielders to hurry on every play. The Royals rushed themselves into their second run, which is always a big run. Hal McRae doubled to open the Royals' third and Brett beat out an infield hit. Chambliss juggled Al Cowens' hard grounder, took one step, and touched first base. He looked to second for a possible double play and then threw home too late for McRae. Munson called for the throw to the plate. Torrez called for the throw to the plate. "You'd think he'd know what to do with that ball," Torrez said.

"You got to keep them guys off the bases and keep them from getting the big inning," Chambliss said, shifting the responsibility. "That wasn't the run that beat us."

Well, what was it then? Was it the fatigue of arriving at the hotel at 4 AM? The Royals didn't get home until five thirty. "Guys twenty-four and twenty-five like them bounce back faster," said Munson, thirty.

Or was it something else? "I have a lot of admiration for those guys," Munson said. "I told Brett not long ago they have eight of the most hard-nosed guys who want to win. He said to me, 'You'd fit in real well.'"

Munson liked the thought. It meant that whichever side won, he was associated with a winner. The Yankees' condition was described quite adequately by the sign paraded

through the stands, referring to the Yankees' defeat of the
Royals last year—and to the thin ice under Martin. "Maybe
once, never twice," one side read. "Bye, Bye, Billy," the other
side read.

Martin is still playing his defiant role. Tomorrow's Kansas
City pitcher with the chance to put the Yankees away is
Larry Gura, an old acquaintance. The Royals accepted him
in exchange for Fran Healy when the Yankees would not
part with Ron Guidry. Gura, a gentle fellow with effective
but unimpressive stuff, is not Martin's type. Martin cut him
at Texas in 1975, traded him away last year and, Gura says,
was not truthful to him in between.

Martin guarantees the play-off will go to five games because they will beat Gura. Martin can demean with the best
of them. "If I had my way," Martin said, "I'd put a body-
guard around his house tonight and get him a chauffeur so he
didn't get in an accident on his way to the ball park."

In order to pitch the left-handed Gura, Whitey Herzog is
passing over Jim Colborn, who won eighteen games. The
Yankees have been tough on lefties for some time, but a notion is a notion.

To pitch the Yankees through the fourth game, Martin has
Ed Figueroa, with or without pain. "I got to go," Figueroa
said. "Right now we don't have no pitchers."

Martin refused to name a starter for the fifth game. Torrez
would love to have another chance. Figueroa has a candidate,
too. Turning to Ron Guidry, who overpowered the Royals
Thursday, Figueroa said, "Gid, you want to pitch Sunday?"

Guidry smiled faintly. "Why not?" he said. "I'm not doin'
anything."

"Okay," Figueroa decided. "You pitch Sunday."

Saturday, October 8

Kansas City

There will be a Sunday game, after all. Graig Nettles has a
patch of raw skin at the crest of a bump near his left temple
to show how they got there.

Billy Martin faced the possibility that he might be working
his last game as Yankee manager by barely containing his

emotions at a pregame meeting. He told the players to be aggressive. "I told them, 'If we're going to get beat, let's go out
like champions.' But it wasn't the meeting that did it."

Nettles' slide in the first inning had more to do with getting
the Yankees to take matters into their own hands. He still
couldn't see sharp edges of objects in the clubhouse after the
game as he talked about his role in beating the Royals, 6–4,
to tie the play-off after the Yankees were at the brink of ex-
tinction. "Maybe a slide like that, the guys on the bench and
the other team could see that we were not going to lay down
and let them beat us," he said. "You never know what goes
on in people's minds."

He blinked frequently describing the fuzziness of his vision
for the first half of the game and how it had frightened him.
He said he hadn't intended his slide as inspiration. Inspiration
was a day late. Nettles characteristically denies awareness of
psychology, but the Yankees did need something to give them
a kick in the pants.

They do get bound up in other issues. Mickey Rivers, who
picked the time after this game to tell everybody that he
again wanted to be traded, led off with a 385-foot double.
Nettles beat out a dribbler to shortstop. Thurman Munson
then grounded wide of third base and Ken Brett fed to Frank
White at second. Nettles, in a half-slide, hit White across the
midsection and forced a relay too wide for a double play.
Rivers would have scored on a double play anyhow, but the
point had been made that Hal McRae wasn't the only one
who could play that game.

In the process, Nettles caught White's knee on the head.
Nettles hung on to do the job, unsteadily, like the Yankees
held their lead. Fortunately for Nettles, the Yankees sent six
batters to the plate in the second inning, when they made the
score 3–0. Herzog figures Larry Gura hates Martin so much
that Gura will rise to the occasion. Instead, Gura tries too
hard.

Nettles needed the time to decide if he could continue. He
couldn't read the numbers on the pitcher's back from third
base. His first play in the field was a bouncer he played off
his protective cup and recovered for a throw to the shadow at
first base. But he reacted so slowly that McRae was able to
continue from first to third. Somehow Nettles was able to
field a gentle grounder for the third out. Behind the dugout
the doctor and the trainer tested how Nettles' eyes were track-

ing and asked him if he knew what was going on. "I could remember things; I couldn't see well," Nettles said. "It was very frightening."

The Royals cut the Yankees' 4–0 lead in half in the third inning when Reggie Jackson misplayed two balls in right field. But with two out in the Yankee fourth, Nettles managed to stroke a soft grounder through the right side to get home what turned out to be the winning run.

Sparky Lyle made it so. The fourth inning is too early to call Lyle, but Figueroa needed help, and Dick Tidrow was unsteady, too. With two runs in and a man on, somebody had to get George Brett out or the time of Lyle's entry into the game might be after the fact. Brett was the third out on a line drive, then Lyle got better and better. He faced only sixteen batters in getting the last fifteen outs. Then he promised to pitch five more innings in the fifth game if necessary. "I had good shit today," he said.

If Lyle hadn't, Martin conceded, he might as well have pitched any of the writers in the clubhouse for all the good it would have done. Lyle never considered not doing well. "I try to keep my mind on one thing," he said. "Pull down on the ball and keep my hand behind the ball. It sounds simple, but it's not easy to do. I'd walk back behind the mound and say to myself, 'Pull down. Pull down. Pull down.' "

He thought he could remember that until tomorrow's game, even if he had to work on that pitch in his hotel room overnight. "My wife is going to catch me," Lyle said. "Then I'm going to catch her." He put on a wide-brimmed beige cowboy hat with a tall red feather and beat the crowd out of the clubhouse.

He left behind the other customary boiling issues of the Yankees. Rivers got three singles and a double, scored two runs and drove in another, and considered that he had "set the pace for the other guys to carry on." Then he shrugged and announced, "I don't want to hurt the cause, but I want to leave."

Before the fifth game of the play-off? So maybe he has good reason to want to leave, but wouldn't it be clever to hold that declaration until after the play-off? But why should the play-offs be different from any other day? "I made up my mind," Rivers said. "I don't want to be back."

Rivers has his problems and is having increasing difficulties getting salary advances. Every time Rivers goes to Gabe

Paul's office lately, Rivers comes out annoyed. He insists it isn't bothering his play. He does have eight hits in 18 at bats. But he was on first base three times in steal situations and didn't even fake a move toward second base. Spite?

"I haven't been stealing the last three months," Rivers said. "Why should I take a chance on taking us out of that situation today? The next man [Nettles] might hit a home run."

Rivers has been piqued by the restraints on his running, but Martin said there were none on Rivers today. "He has the 'go' sign," Martin said. "I can't pull him to second. What is it they say? You can take a horse to water but you can't what?"

Martin rode easily over all issues after winning that gallows game. George Steinbrenner was off at Parents Day at the University of North Carolina, where his daughter is a freshman. Martin kidded about how the owner left suggestions but the manager decided whether to use the suggestions.

"What's the percentage?" he was asked.

Martin smiled slyly. "I want to keep this job," he said.

In the corner of the room sat Martin's son, Billy Joe, a fine-looking, quiet twelve-year-old, overcoated in a blue Yankee warm-up jacket and a red cap advertising a food company. He had walked up to his father in the tunnel behind the plate after the game. Martin put his arm around the boy's shoulders and proudly led him into the clubhouse. "Don't you have a Yankee hat?" the father asked. The first thing Martin did was find the clubhouse man and obtain a blue cap with the NY monogram.

"He's a polite boy," Martin said, introducing Billy Joe. "His mother's done a great job." Martin had someone to share his joy. "Winning isn't fun," he said. "It's beautiful." He laughed.

It may be a last taste of sweetness for Martin. The word in the clubhouse is that Martin's dismissal will come as soon as the last game is played. *Time* magazine was around last week developing a story on the Yankees to run during the World Series. What Steinbrenner said apparently has gotten back to some of the players. "It's not whether Billy won today or tomorrow," Jackson said. "He could win five more games [including the World Series] and he's gone. I've been told—one of the players told me—he's already gone, and I believe it." Jackson revealed no pleasure in saying it.

* * *

Late tonight Jackson was at his most charming, sitting over an enormous ice cream sundae in the lobby coffee shop of the Yankees' Crown Center Hotel. He was warm, unguarded and full of humor. He made himself the butt of the jokes about the two balls he mishandled in right field, finding an alter ego in Kansas City first baseman John Mayberry. Mayberry had a terrible day under the influence of a painkiller for a toothache. He struck out twice, butchered a double-play relay, and dropped a foul pop. Jackson got up from his table in great mirth, posed as if to catch a pop fly, and then looked down at his feet. "Even I could have caught that one," he said.

He's turned on about tomorrow's game. It is the last game of a postseason series. "This is the fifth time I've been in a do-or-die game," he said. "All the other four, we didn't lose."

Sunday, October 9

Kansas City

It's all hard to believe, but then it was the only way it could have been. Chris Chambliss stood in the middle of the clubhouse, closed his eyes, and said, "Ooooooh!" Thurman Munson and Reggie Jackson wept, and some others, too. Players who hadn't talked to each other beyond the foul lines all season hugged each other.

The emotions were deeper than the wild ones of the division clinching that the Yankees felt they had coming to them all along. This time, as much as they said they felt they were going to pull this game out, they had been behind from the first inning until the top of the ninth. That's as long as a team can be behind and still win.

And they had started one more game with one more jolt. Martin benched Jackson, the biggest star, for the fifth game of the play-off. Why should the consummate game of the play-offs be any different from the 166 that came before it? As great as the game was, the game is never the whole thing with this team.

The Yankees scored one run in the top of the eighth and three in the top of the ninth to beat the Royals, 5–3. They had come from a very low point to win two games in a row and win the play-off. The heroes of the eighth and ninth innings were Jackson as a pinch hitter; Paul Blair, who played right field in place of Jackson; and the reluctant Rivers. When it was over, the Yankees exploded out of the dugout onto the field. Jackson, the tormented man, bounded highest, bounded most often.

"I just feel grateful, all the stuff that went on," Jackson said. "We won, we're the champs. Nobody can say anything anymore. We're the best team money can buy. They can't say Reggie Jackson didn't play on a winner."

Now nobody could point a finger and say Reggie Jackson came to the Yankees and it was his fault they didn't win the pennant. He knew that's what the world would have done had they failed. He knew that's what the world had thought before the game. It was the big game and Jackson always thinks of himself as a big-game player, Getting the big hit, making the big throw, scoring the big run. It was his self-image, his guts. Then he got to Royals Stadium tonight and discovered he was not in the lineup.

In the final game of the 1972 play-offs for the A's, he tore a hamstring as he strained to reach home with the tying run. In 1973 he homered in the seventy-game World Series victory over the Mets. In 1974 he had the A's only hit in the deciding play-off victory over Baltimore. In the ensuing final game of the World Series, his throw from right field began the relay that cut down a run at third base in a one-run game with the Dodgers.

Then he came to the ball park tonight and found that history meant nothing. For an emotional man, the pain must have been sickening, but somehow crushed as he appeared, Jackson stood in the middle of a crowd of inquisitors and handled himself with immense dignity. For all those who felt Jackson was a crybaby and his emotions a sham, Jackson grew in stature.

He gave credit to the manager he had fought with and who had belittled him from the very beginning. "The easiest thing in the world for him was to leave me in the lineup and have me go oh for four," Jackson said. "That's if I would have gone oh for four. At the very least, he showed some guts."

Guts has always been Martin's trademark. However, Jackson got the bleakest of news not from Martin, but from Elston Howard. Later it was explained by Fran Healy, the Yankees' father-confessor. Later Martin said to the press,

"How do you tell a guy he's been butchering the outfield and not hitting worth a damn? How do you do that diplomatically?" So Martin did not even try. It was, he said, "probably the toughest decision I had to make in my life."

If he had lost the game, how would Steinbrenner have accepted the sight of his $2,930,000 star on the bench? Regardless of his reluctance to handle the matter himself, Martin had indeed shown nerve under pressure.

Jackson said he would have preferred to be told personally, but continued to grow as he spoke. "People do things in different ways," he said. "I can't expect them always to do things the way I would want. Right now it's as emotional time for me. It's hard to come out with a solid, well-thought-out statement in twenty minutes. I just hope the ball club wins tonight and we've got the best nine—make that ten—men out there."

Only yesterday he was still evading questions of whether he would come back to the Yankees next season. It still seemed to hinge on whether Martin would be back. If Martin lost, Jackson had been told, Martin was gone. Maybe he was gone even if they won.

Then in the eighth inning, Jackson pinch-hit a single and the 3–1 deficit was down to one run. Afterward Jackson was in the middle of the celebrants, delighting in each stream of champagne that ran over his head. "All season I had to hold it in here," he said, in the manner of Kirk Douglas, clutching the chest of his T-shirt as he sat in the clubhouse. "I had to eat it in here. Thank God. I can't explain it because I don't understand the magnitude of Reggie Jackson and the magnitude of the event. I am the situation."

* * *

By itself the game was memorable. The Yankees beat a very demanding team and survived the kind of fistfight in the first inning that you just don't see in a play-off or World Series. The two teams admire each other, but nobody says they have to like each other.

The fight came when McRae singled and Brett drove a triple over the baffled head of Rivers in center field, giving the Royals the lead. Brett slid hard into third base, as is his style, and Graig Nettles thought Brett had slid too far beyond the base. He shoved Brett and kicked him. Brett threw a big right hand and the Yankee dugout emptied. By the time the fight was broken up, Brett had spent a long time on the bottom of the pile. A ground ball scored him and it was 2–0.

Rivers stole a base and Munson singled him home in the Yankee third, but the Royals quickly got that run back. Ron Guidry gave way to Mike Torrez, who had wanted to start. Torrez immediately pitched well but seemed to be too late.

Lefty Paul Splittorff put the Yankees down until the eighth, when Willie Randolph led off with a single. Righty Doug Bird came on to strike out Munson, but Lou Piniella singled and that brought up Jackson. He hates to pinch-hit. He wanted to succeed right then, he said, "more than any time in my life." He singled, the Yankees were one run behind, and Jackson sighed.

Torrez, who grew up in Topeka, sixty miles down the road, held the Royals in the eighth. Seventy years ago Torrez' grandparents on both sides came from Mexico to work on the Atchinson, Topeka, and Santa Fe. People who had hunted with Torrez to put rabbit on the table were in the ball park on his tickets rooting against him.

Going into the ninth, Herzog had already spent two of his best relievers in conformance with the law of percentages in order to get out of the eighth. He brought in Dennis Leonard, who had overwhelmed the Yankees in the third game. Blair gave thanks that he wasn't going out for a hitter and gritted his teeth. With two strikes he fouled up two more strikes. "It was the hardest and toughest at bat in my whole life," Blair said. He has been in the big leagues since 1965, has been in six play-offs now and four World Series. As he spoke, his breath came in gasps. "Slow down, heart," he said.

Blair fought off his tendency to shy from pitches on the inside, the residue of a cheek-shattering beaning seven years ago. Leonard threw another pitch on the inside edge. "He did everything he was supposed to do, great pitches," Blair said. "God, I hated to see Leonard come in there. I was as nervous as I've ever been in my life." He fought off that pitch and singled gently to center. When he got to first base, coach Bobby Cox said, "You just won it for us."

"I'll never forget that feeling in my life," Blair said.

Roy White walked. Gura relieved because he is the Royals' best fielding pitcher and the Royals played for the bunt. But Rivers singled and Blair scored the tying run. Randolph's fly ball put them in front. Brett's wild throw made it 5–3. Against Sparky Lyle there was no more coming back.

The Royals had another crashing disappointment in a game they thought they had won. Herzog mused that Jim Colborn would have been his starter on Tuesday. And Brett thought of how he had taken a thrashing for a slide he felt was routine. "The only guy who didn't hit me was Thurman," Brett said. "At least it seemed that way. I was at the bottom of the pile and it seemed guys were lining up to hit me in the face. Not Thurman."

Munson, remember, was the guy who stirred emotions in the opposite direction when he slid hard into Brett in the second game, and later said he identified with Brett. Now Brett was saying thanks. "He put his hands on my face so I wouldn't get hit," Brett said. "It didn't do much good. But I really appreciate what he did for me. I went from respect for him as a ball player to respect for him as a man."

There was champagne only for the Yankees. Rivers poured it over Gabe Paul's head. Munson sat in the trainer's room and cried. ". . . Cheated out of money I deserved," he said. "I think I contributed some. I was pretty happy about that."

Blair hugged Munson and thanked the stocky catcher for helping him learn to stand in at the plate again. "Yeah," Munson said. "The beachball can't stir the fuckin' drink but he can teach you how to hit."

Even in joy, animosities lurk beneath the wine.

In the middle of the clubhouse was Steinbrenner, in a protective raincoat, this time thoroughly anointed by the celebration. As Steinbrenner tried to retain his dignity, combing his hair, there was Martin stalking his prey from behind, mischief in his eye and a bottle of champagne in his hand. Martin looked and poured.

"That's for trying to fire me," Martin yelled.

Steinbrenner spun around, then grinned. "What do you mean, 'try'?" Steinbrenner yelled back. "If I want to, I'll fire you." They embraced.

"See how smart you are for keeping me on," Martin crowed. Maybe the job situation has changed. "Let's not talk about it now," the owner said. "It's not important—tonight."

Good to the Last Spat

Billy Martin talks about the phone call he got from Tom Lasorda when the Yankees won the division championship. Martin says he was rooting for Lasorda to get to the World Series with the Dodgers. They have a feeling for each other that goes beyond the fact that this is the first World Series to be managed on both sides by Italians. Both men are quick to wave their ancestry like some red, white, and green flag.

Lasorda loves to tell about the time Steve Garvey had the lettering reworked on the manager's shirt to read "Lasagna." Martin calls himself "Dago" and calls other Italians "Daig."

And the Yankee-Dodger thing goes back a long way. Lasorda grew up in the Dodger farm system when the big team played in Brooklyn. He was never a good-enough pitcher to get there for more than two cups of coffee—demitasse, actually. His four major-league decisions—all losses—came from Kansas City. Martin played four of his five World Series against Brooklyn.

Martin says he wears Yankee pinstripes on his heart. Lasorda says he bleeds Dodger blue and refers to the "Big Dodger in the Sky." Both are full of baloney; I suspect, know that we know.

Both made reputations as scrappers. That's how they met. In 1956, after eleven seasons almost entirely in the Dodger farm system, Lasorda was pitching for the Kansas City Athletics and the Yankees were beating them out of habit. Lasorda recalls how that annoyed Lou Boudreau, the Kansas City manager. "Everybody is afraid of the Yankees," Lasorda quoted Boudreau. "Nobody will throw at them."

330

Lasorda, the Dodger, thought, "Now, wait a minute, the Dodgers are not afraid of anybody." So Lasorda threw first at Hank Bauer—he of the face like a clenched fist—and then at Martin.

"It didn't take long for Bauer to turn to me in the dugout and say, 'That son of a bitch is throwing at us,' " Martin recalled. "I agree and start yelling at Tom, and he motions me to come on out there."

Martin never needed to be asked twice. But as Martin ran for the mound, he was headed off by Hank Soar, the umpire who had been on football all-pro. Soar grabbed Martin around the throat. Then there came Bauer to the mound.

"I said, 'Hey, Bauer, this is between Martin and me. You stay out of it'," Lasorda said.

Martin and Lasorda became friends. Each counts Frank Sinatra as some sort of friend. "What makes Billy and I so very close is I feel like I'm talking to a Tom Lasorda and he feels like he's talking to himself," Lasorda said. "We were both the same kind of player. He was a much better player, but we both scrapped for what we got."

They went out and drank to each other tonight.

* * *

Tomorrow Don Gullett starts the opening game of the World Series for the Yankees. He had a shot of cortisone for the tightness in his shoulder after opening the play-off. Some Yankees, noting Gullett's history, question whether the tightness wasn't emotional. If Gullett is sound, he's the obvious choice.

The second game is Martin's gamble. He's leaning toward the emotional trump, Catfish Hunter. His nickname is Big Game Hunter. The Yankees are comfortable gambling with him.

After last night's arrival to a horror show at Newark Airport, where Steinbrenner wanted to treat a mob scene of fans to a glimpse of their heroes, the Yankees have settled down to some sort of reality.

"I'm looking forward to the season ending and I want to win," Jackson said. "Then when I'm out with my family or my friends, I won't have to hear Jackson is a disturbance. I want to win to make the winner peaceful. If we lose, it's because Reggie screwed up, Martin couldn't win the big one, or Steinbrenner interfered."

Tuesday, October 11

New York

Around the clubhouse jammed with the hundreds of news-paper reporters and broadcasters and photographers, the Yankees stood or sat back in their upright cubicles and looked at themselves with a detachment. They had played one game of this World Series and proved to themselves they would win a game.

And if they can win a game, who's to say they can't win four of them? "Not nobody going to sweep us no more, we proved it to ourselves," Mickey Rivers said. The language did not interfere with his message. Last year, the Yankees remember clearly, the Reds swept them in four straight and it was a long time before the embarrassment went away. Like until tonight.

It was the first game of the new World Series and the Yankees beat the Dodgers, 4–3, in twelve innings. It was the kind of hair's-breadth game when any mistake could have been fatal—and the Yankees didn't make it. "Last year, I think Cincinnati might not have known it was in a World Series," Paul Blair observed. "The Dodgers are going to know they were in a World Series."

Blair watched on television last year as a lame-duck member of the Baltimore Orioles. Sunday he got the hang-tough single to start the play-off's decisive rally. Tonight he got the single that drove in Willie Randolph with the winning run. The spotlight of the playoffs and the Series when everything is scrutinized so closely, can make unexpected heroes.

Rivers, who played a major role in last year's embarrass-ment, didn't get a hit tonight, but he made an aggressive charge in front of a reluctant Reggie Jackson in right center and threw out Steve Garvey at the plate when the Dodgers were trying to take advantage of the vulnerable Yankee out-field to build on a 2–1 lead.

Gullet pitched into the ninth inning after failing dreadfully in the first game of the play-off. Gullett came out of the fourth game of the Series against the Yankees last year with an ankle sprain. He was building an uncomfortable reputation and he knew it. "In a way I felt I had let them down," Gullett said. "I was dissatisfied with myself and I saw the dissatisfaction in Billy Martin's face." Without Gullett, the Yankees pitching is shaky at best. With him capable of pitching this well, they have enough pitching.

How much Gullett wanted to do well was his problem at first. He walked the leadoff batter, gave up a triple to the second. He walked the third, the fourth hit a long sacrifice fly, and the fifth walked. Right then the Dodgers had two runs. Gullett was on the brink of eliminating himself from the Series, and maybe eliminating the Yankees, too.

But when Martin hurried to the mound and got Dick Tidrow throwing in the bullpen, Gullett said he was throwing freely. Thurman Munson remembered that Gullett had the same thing last week. So when the manager left, Munson asked Gullett how he really felt. In the light of what he could see, Munson was satisfied with the answer, and Gullett gave up only three more hits into the ninth inning.

Rivers made the big play behind him in the sixth. Garvey, the Dodger with a sense of the old Brooklyn heritage, got a bunt single. It was a touch of the Jackie Robinson Dodgers by a man who led his team with 33 homers. On a one-out hit-and-run single, Garvey tried to score from first. Another Jackie Robinson touch.

In right field, Reggie Jackson, the only arm in the outfield, was ever mindful of his difficulties. Rivers, who still resents Jackson's salary, cut in front of him. "I looked at him and he looked at me," Rivers said. "Well, somebody better get that; we're playing to win." His relatively short throw bounced once, twice. Munson went out to get it, dove back to the plate, and Garvey was out.

Willie Randolph, who grew up a Met fan in Brooklyn after the Dodgers left, homered to tie the score in the last of the sixth. Munson doubled Randolph home to put the Yankees ahead in the eighth. But Lee Lacy, the first batter Sparky Lyle faced with one out in the top of the ninth, singled the tying run home.

Lyle retired the next eleven batters, but the Yankees still needed a run. Twice Jerry Grote converted Yankee bunts in front of the plate to forceouts, in the tenth and eleventh. Again they failed to sacrifice in the twelfth—and that was what won it for them.

Randolph led off with a double and Munson was intentionally walked. Blair, the defensive replacement for Jackson when the Yankees had the lead, was ordered to bunt. He fouled off the first pitch. As a Baltimore star, Blair had beaten Martin's 1969 Twins with a two-out, two-strike squeeze bunt in the twelfth inning in the play-offs. "I was the best bunter you could see then," Blair said. Martin remembered.

Blair fouled another and was so determined to make the two-strike bunt a good one that Dick Howser had to yell to make Blair notice the bunt was off. Blair pulled Rick Rhoden's pitch through shortstop and the Yankees won the game. Blair didn't realize he had missed the original hit sign until much later.

He said he wasn't nervous this time; there was no place for another fantasy. "When I was a kid I dreamed of game-winning hits," Blair said. "I thought I wouldn't even get into these games except on defense. I thought I might contribute with a catch or a throw, or maybe a bunt. I thought that would be contribution enough."

He was still displeased that he hadn't put his bunt down. "Don't look at me," Howser said. "I'm not the bunting coach; that's Phil Rizzuto."

The Yankees are "off the schneid" in the World Series. They can make jokes. "Last year," Randolph said, "I know for me, I was embarrassed."

*　　*　　*

Tomorrow is another night, and Martin has decided to take his shot with Hunter. If he can steal a game, the Yankees are in great shape. If Hunter can't do it, then the Yankees are no worse than tied. Martin is gambling with the Dodgers' money.

Emotionally the Yankees feel Hunter is a good gamble even though he hasn't pitched in a month.

Rationally, not everybody is sure of the wisdom of getting Hunter to this game. "They probably should have pitched him somewhere along the line, don't you think?" Jackson said.

Some people thought Hunter had at least been throwing. He hasn't been. "I wanted to pitch batting practice," Hunter said. "They said no."

He showed his best country-boy aw-shucks about his five diagnoses of hernia and the final one of seminal vesiculitis.

How did he contract it? he was asked. Hunter smiled. "Trick fuckin'," he said.

Wednesday, October 12

New York

The Dodgers beat the Yankees in the second game of the World Series. It would have been a big thing in a Dodger clubhouse of another era. Not that the Dodgers were the least surprised to be going home after splitting the first two games in Yankees Stadium, but back then any time the Dodgers beat the Yankees it was an event. It was even bigger than beating the Giants.

But the Dodgers are going home to Los Angeles, not to Brooklyn.

In the early 1960s, when I first began to fulfill a dream of covering baseball, in the back of my mind something was missing. After a year or so with the Yankees, I realized that I felt cheated because they weren't the Dodgers. I grew up when the world was just learning to count backward to zero, in the era of the great Brooklyn Dodger teams, excited by Jackie Robinson and charmed by Pee Wee Reese.

No fan was brought to the heights only to be let down as cruelly as a Dodger fan, nor was any fan more loyal. The Giants beat the Dodgers in the Bobby Thomson play-off in 1951. The Yankees beat the Dodgers in the World Series every year. If you grew up in New York, there were Giant fans and Yankee fans all around you. We argued about Reese and Rizzuto at shortstop, about DiMaggio—then Mantle—and Mays and Snider in center field. The Yankees and their fans were haughty and smug; I hated the Yankees.

In that first season covering baseball I met a number of men who had covered the Dodgers, and they told me how open and alive the Dodger clubhouses always were. That was at the time I was learning how cold and aloof the great Yankees were. I was told that Reese really was a delightful man. When I met him, I expected to be disappointed, but I wasn't.

When I was with the Mets at the first Oldtimers' Game played in Los Angeles, I felt, what right do these people have

to have an Oldtimers' Game? It was Los Angeles against
Brooklyn and Los Angeles had, for goodness' sake, Maury
Wills playing shortstop and he was still an active player. I
wanted Reese to show those Los Angeles people, who needed
Vince Scully on the radio at the ball park to explain the
game to them, that Wills did not invent shortstop. Reese, then
nearly fifty, did not disappoint me.

When I covered the 1963 World Series—Los Angeles and
the Yankees—there were still traces of the feeling among the
players. That feeling is almost all gone from the clubhouse
now, left to live in the minds of fans over thirty-five and in
the minds of aging, spreading reporters who choke up when
they hear Frank Sinatra sing, "There Used to Be a Ball Park
Right Here." The Dodgers—except for Steve Garvey, who
has his roots in Brooklyn by proxy—certainly don't feel it.

"We beat the Yankees, 6–1; it may as well have been Kansas City or the Red Sox," said Dodger pitcher Tommy John,
who grew up in Indiana. The Dodgers' biggest rivalry is with
the Reds. The Dodger-Giant rivalry that was the greatest of
all sports rivalries is gone now, too, concluded by three thousand miles and twenty years.

The Dodgers hit four home runs tonight, three off Catfish
Hunter in his gallant but futile effort. The Yankees never did
get into the game against Burt Hooton. In the one Yankee
threat, Garvey made a fine stop to turn Reggie Jackson's
hard shot into a double play as the Yankees' lone run scored.
It was a display more typical of the Brooklyn Dodger fence
busters than the pitch-and-scratch Dodgers of the West Coast.
These Dodgers accepted it as a matter of course. "We challenged Death Valley and this time we beat it," said Ron Cey,
who hit a two-run homer in the first inning. "It already took
two home runs away from me."

The Dodgers talked about losing home runs to Death Valley back then, too, but left center was 457 feet then, not the
430 of the "new" Yankee Stadium. Frank Howard, a Paul
Bunyan of a man, reached the 457 marker for the Dodgers in
the 1963 Series and Garvey remembers Junior Gilliam telling
about it in clubhouse sessions.

Garvey, who also homered, responds to the stories from
Gilliam, the first-base coach who was Jackie Robinson's replacement at second base in Brooklyn, because Garvey grew
up with that team. His father drove the Dodger bus in spring
training for Robinson, Gilliam, Reese, Duke Snider, Gil

Hodges, and the rest. He paid attention when Roy Campanella was wheeled into the Dodger clubhouse before the first two games. "I never went to Ebbets Field, but I have some key pictures," Garvey said. "I feel like I've been there from the talk of it." He's read books on the era—*Miracle of Coogan's Bluff*, he said. "That was a tearjerker; the Dodgers lost."

Cey grew up in Tacoma, when the Northwest didn't have big-league ball. He said he marvels at how Joe DiMaggio could have hit so many homes runs with that distant target in left center. He was ten when the Dodgers went West in 1958. He sees old Dodgers at Vero Beach in spring training. "But they really have no meaning to me," he said. "Dodgers-Yankees doesn't meant a thing to me at all."

At least Cey has a feeling for the measure of DiMaggio. Davey Lopes, the second baseman, says he has none. "History has no bearing on me," he said. "I'm doing what I'm doing now. They were Furillo and Robinson; we are Lopes and Cey. The connection means nothing to me."

That's what Gilliam observes without rancor, in his twenty-fifth season wearing Dodger blue. "I don't like to go back; that's past," he said. "These kids, they want to win as much, but it doesn't matter who they beat. They know and look at the records, but they don't relate to past players the way we did to DiMaggio. This is a different era. It's new to me; I don't know how to explain it. Maybe that's the way all young people look at older people today."

Bill Buhler, the Dodger trainer, remembers how it was back then when the Dodgers dominated the National League only to be dismissed by the Yankees in 1941, '47, '49, '52, and '53. Finally, the Dodgers beat the Yankees in 1955. "It was unbelievable in this clubhouse," Buhler said. "We were in this very same clubhouse. We were so elated. It had been building for so long. We didn't win, we didn't win. All of it built up. Then we won."

There was even a phonograph record about the winning pitcher in the seventh game: "Johnny Podres Wears a Halo Round His Head." It was popular for about ten days, mostly in Brooklyn. "When we beat them in Los Angeles in 1963, there was still some feeling left," Buhler said, "but not now."

Gilliam recalled the celebration that followed in 1955 in Brooklyn at the St. George Hotel, also long gone. "All those fans lining the streets," Gilliam said. "I came out of the party at one AM and the traffic light was red. They just stopped traffic and let me through.

"The Los Angeles fans, they aren't so sophisticated. Vince Scully has educated them, but they still sit back until something happens." The Los Angeles fans don't know to anticipate an inning with Gilliam, Snider, and Robinson.

Other things have changed, too. Yankee Stadium used to be the model of decorum, decked with the pennants of dynasties past. Tonight fans ran onto the field. One even threw a smokebomb onto the grass when it was clear that the Dodgers would win. "These fans are getting unruly, aren't they?" Gilliam said. "They're not like they used to be here."

It's too bad. A lot of people missed something by not being a part of what used to be when there were three baseball teams in New York. The Dodgers were in Brooklyn, which was a separate state of mind. If you were there, it's worth remembering. If you weren't there, then it's worth knowing.

*   *   *

Hunter chose not to make his a poignant moment. He preferred to find a laugh. "At least the people back home know I can still give up the home-run ball," he said. "As the saying goes, the sun doesn't shine up the same dog's ass every year. But it seems like when you have a bad year, it keeps goin' on."

Hunter would make two good pitches and then a bad pitch and the Dodgers would jump on it. A pitcher needs either good stuff or great precision. After his ailments and not having pitched for thirty-three days, Hunter had nothing but courage. "If he wants to use me again, I'll be out there again," he said.

He kidded when he said he would fulfill the two years left on his contract even if he just sat on the bench. "I can still do Holtzman's job," he said and laughed. "But Kenny can still pitch."

The bitching came from Jackson, who was with Hunter when he was winning twenty, five years in a row. "How could the son of a bitch pitch him?" Jackson said. "How could he be expected to do anything? Cat did his best, but he hasn't pitched in so long. Ah, the hell with it."

Thursday, October 13

Los Angeles

Maybe there's something to the psychology of all this. For the Yankees the World Series is no different from any other time.

Like, on the plane, Munson demanded better seats for the players' use. George Steinbrenner had three thousand box seats in New York and the players each had four. "I'll tell you this," Munson said, "unless we get more boxes, I'm not playing the rest of the Series."

Sparky Lyle, the voice of sanity, pointed out, "We have the best seats in the house—the dugout."

*   *   *

As soon as they got to Dodger Stadium for the workout, Martin was asked about Jackson's comments on the use of Hunter. That set off another round of Yankee madness. Jackson says the wrong thing, Martin can't hold his response, adds his own shot, and there they go again.

"Why do we have all this kind of talk now when we're trying to win the World Series?" Martin asked. He pulled the cap from his head and flung it onto his desk. It was a Yankee cap. "This is not the proper type of team spirit," he said. "It's not the Yankee kind of thing to do. A true Yankee wouldn't say that."

Martin never has regarded Jackson as "a true Yankee."

"He's got enough trouble playing right field without second-guessing the manager," Martin said.

This issue began to rise last night when Jackson was asked if he would be playing the third game against left-handed Tommy John after being benched for the fifth game of the play-offs because Paul Splittorff was pitching. Jackson said he wasn't sure. In appreciation of the way Jackson took that, Martin said Jackson would play every game of the Series. "Where's his memory? Where's his 160 IQ?" Martin said with great sarcasm. "I'm not going to take Reggie out. Splittorff's not pitching."

"I don't need to take that from nobody, especially from

him," Jackson said last night. "I know what I can do. If he did, we might be a lot better off."

They go around and around, each in reply to what the other said like a carillon (say it "carry on").

Today, Jackson was being more diplomatic. "In the emotion of wanting to win the World Series," he said quietly, "maybe I said something I shouldn't have said that was taken the wrong way. I have no desire to comment on anything Billy Martin does in handling the ball club because he has won the pennant two years in a row and I'm pleased to be a member of the club. I've had a good year because of the way he has handled me."

It must have hurt his teeth to say that. But he had another innocent way to make Martin angry. Jackson mentioned in a television interview that Graig Nettles' shoulder was sore. Martin was trying to hide that.

"Did you hear me criticize him the other night when Mickey Rivers had to come all the way over and make that play?" Martin said. "I didn't say a word then. If I'm going to back that ass, why doesn't he back me? What is this, a one-way street? He's got a lot of growing up to do."

Out in the clubhouse, Munson examined the lastest fuss. "It's just an overheated argument," he said. "Reggie's been struggling and would like to be doing better. Billy probably just doesn't realize Reggie is Mister October."

Then Munson recounted his own litany of slights. "I've got five more games at the most to put up with this crap . . . All year I've been trying to live down the image that I was jealous of somebody making more money. Somebody asked me, did you bury your pride? No, I postponed it."

He pointed out that Jackson was batting .136 in postseason games, and if it were Munson, he wouldn't be second-guessing the manager. "And I'm going to stop talking because the more I talk, the madder I get." Mister October, indeed.

At the batting cage Nettles was asked how he regarded Jackson. "Let me say that he is very interesting," Nettles said.

Does he bring laughter to the clubhouse? "No," Nettles said. "Laughter isn't what he brings."

In contrast, the Dodgers were calm and full of their image of brotherly love, preparing for the inevitable visits of Don Rickles or Frank Sinatra and considering their individual telegrams from Farrah Fawcett-Majors. Everybody loves a winner.

Few of the Dodgers know Jackson, Rick Monday does; they were teammates at Arizona State and then for four years at Oakland. "Reggie came after his time," Monday said. "They made a movie about him. Only he wasn't around so they gave the part to a woman. He could have played it if it was about a man. They called it *Three Faces of Eve*."

As the Yankees walked out toward their bus, Tom Lasorda teased some of them. "Let's just keep playing," Lasorda said. "What would you rather do than play baseball?"

"Our club?" Nettles responded. "Our whole club would jump the club."

Friday, October 14

Los Angeles

I can't help but see this whole thing as a morality play: peace and fellowship vs. turmoil and jealousy, soap opera vs. good clean baseball, Dodger Blue vs. Yankee Greenback, good vs. evil.

And evil is winning.

"So, the soap opera goes on," intoned Tommy John, the losing pitcher of the third game. "Will Billy Martin find success and happiness in a continuing shower of champagne?"

The Dodgers look at the Yankees and wonder, try to ignore them and wonder some more. Some of them say they couldn't care less, and some say they are amused by the kinds of things that make Lou Piniella say, "The circus is back in town." Some Dodgers regret that some good baseball performances they were taught to value are being obscured by the Yankee noise so foreign to the squeaky-clean Dodgers. Some of them object to being asked about it. And more of them resent the fact that it is the bad guys and not the good guys who are ahead.

"I'm sure it's got to pull them apart in certain areas; where and when remains to be seen," said Steve Garvey, the very model first baseman on the clean team. He said he was concerned that the Youth of America would perceive that the Yankees' new order was the way it ought to be, when the Dodgers knew their way was best. But he is willing to concede it is possible that the Yankees might win this thing.

The Yankees do just the sort of thing the Dodgers don't. They argued at the workout yesterday and had a news conference at the hotel this afternoon to quiet the noise and make more of it. Gabe Paul assembled the media after Martin invited Jackson for a bitter-suite hotel-room meeting about yesterday's rumpus. "Everything's resolved; everything's perfect," Martin declared. Jackson muttered an agreement. So what's perfect? Perfect is in the eye of the beholder.

Paul, smooth as ever, downplayed the effect all the noise had on the games. For his own state of mind, Paul said, "I was so excited about it that I woke up this morning and bought a new pair of shoes."

As for the tempest in the clubhouse, he said, "This is another chapter in the tumultuous life of the 1977 Yankees. Controversial ball players are many times better ball players because they are not afraid of the consequences . . . What I do mind is a miser who's going to worry about what's going to happen."

Then they went out and won. Mike Torrez, who is concluding that he won't sign here, pitched an efficient nine innings, allowing just two singles after the Dodgers tied the score at 3–3 in the third inning. Rather than play the infield in, the Dodgers conceded a run to the Yankees on Mickey Rivers' grounder in the fourth. It put the Yankees ahead, 4–3, and Torrez made it enough. Which, coupled with the sound and fury of the Yankees, pisses the Dodgers off.

"I get sick and tired of it," said Dave Lopes, who is hitless after three games and 13 at bats as leadoff. "It seems like everybody is having a tough time as to who's the top guy over there." That's not so on the Dodgers, of course.

Lopes does not laugh on nights like that. Don Sutton, who started the first game and pitches again in the fifth game, did give the matter a wry smile, especially the question of whether it might not be wiser for Sutton to have pitched in the fourth game so he could come back again in the seventh. "We are the All-American Boys," Sutton mocked. "We never squabble—publicly." Well, at least not since 1975 when they finished twenty games behind and revealed that not all thought Garvey was a saint.

Ron Cey, the third baseman who couldn't come up with the double-play grounder before the Yankees scored their fourth run, didn't see much to kid about. "Sure, we'll probably have problems here some day," he said. "Probably after Reggie and Thurman get along."

Cey will not answer questions suggesting that he had a bad second half of the season, batting .218. That he rejects as "negative questioning." Bill Russell snaps at references to his and Lopes's two for twenty-seven. But they snap quietly and only at people who don't wear Dodger Blue.

But still the Yankess won. "They make it a joke," grumbled Jerry Grote, who has left a three-thousand-mile trail of grumbling. "They really won tonight." Certainly Tommy John didn't have to be ashamed of his performance. But the Dodgers were reluctant to give Oakland credit in the 1974 Series either, even after the A's had beaten them in five games. The A's did also beat the so-clean Reds in another clash of good and evil in 1972.

"If the Yankees were a mediocre ball club, the conflict might hurt them," John said. He has read the Yankees very quickly. "I know Billy is headstrong. It's the irresistible force and the immovable object, but it seems they don't take it out on the field—except maybe Rivers. You can see it in the way he stands."

John sees the Dodgers as a team from another era, when age and authority were automatically respected. "We question sometimes," John said. "But when Tommy Lasorda tells you why he does something, that's it. Really, the Yankees are more typical of the new life-style.

"If they win, that won't be the reason. It won't prove that their way is superior; it will prove they played better ball. You can't say the end justifies the means. Who said that?"

"Karl Marx."

"Yes," John said, "Groucho, Harpo, Chico, and Karl."

Saturday, October 15

Los Angeles

A mere baseball game is a letdown. It's difficult to accept the Yankees on such quiet terms. Maybe it was the ease with which they won the game that calmed everything. Ron Guidry pitched a four-hitter, Lou Piniella made a fine catch above the left-field fence, Reggie Jackson got two big hits, and they won, 4–2. That gave them a lead of three games to one, and that's a big lead.

Plus, they think they have discovered the key to beating the Dodgers. "The key," Graig Nettles revealed, "is keeping them from hugging each other."

The Yankees put on a show of disciplined hitting in taking apart Doug Rau in the second inning. Jackson led off with an opposite-field double inside third base. Piniella went to right field with a single, scoring Jackson. Chris Chambliss, also going to the opposite field, doubled to left to finish Rau.

Again Lasorda played the infield back and Nettles' grounder scored Piniella. Behind, 2–0, Lasorda then reversed his strategy and Bucky Dent's grounder slipped through the drawn-in infield for a single, making it 3–0.

Jackson finally joined Willie Randolph on the Yankee home run list with a long shot to left center in the sixth.

Guidry told about how depressed he was last season when he was sent down to Syracuse and decided to drive south out of New York instead of north. He was going to quit and go home before his wife talked him into making a U-turn at a gas station.

Thurman Munson told of how exhausted he was, how sick he's felt, how his legs bother him, and how he concentrates almost exclusively on defense once the Yankees get a lead. Munson has been having trouble seeing the ball and has been striking out. But the Dodgers, who stole two of every three times they tried all season and all three of their tries in the play-off, have been caught four of six times by Munson.

Today the score was 4–2 in the sixth when Lopes ran. If he were in scoring position with none out, he had a good chance of making it 4–3 and the Dodgers would have had three more innings to catch up. Munson's throw was quick and strong and into Willie Randolph's glove knee high. "And you guys said I couldn't throw," Munson said, smiled, and padded off to the shower.

And Piniella told about his catch and about threading the mine field between Munson, Jackson, and Martin. "I've done my part," Piniella said with the black glare grease emphasizing the crinkle of his eyes.

Piniella can accept his reputation as a dangerous fielder as having once been earned. "Now I think I'm better than my reputation," he said. As he can stand that reputation, so he could play a mollifying role in the everlasting conflict. "Reggie is a strange dude at times," Piniella said. "He feels he's carrying the whole load of the ball club. When he doesn't go well, he broods. I tried to explain that he was only one of twenty-five, that he may be making the most money and getting his name in the paper most often, but all he had to do was his part.

"Thurman—I like both people. At times both parties are right.

"The owner pays me. I play for the manager. You can't tell strong-minded people what to do. I can only make suggestions."

The owner is fond of citing Piniella's use every day as the turning point of the season. The owner says he had advocated that move for some time before it was made.

Piniella shrugs and smiles at that thought. "I'm close to the owner, too," he said. He can also walk the line about the ambiguity of his rejected contract. "I don't think it was deliberately devious," he said. "I think it was just an accident. Heh-heh-heh-heh."

Lasorda had made his gamble on Rau when the Dodgers were behind and came out further behind. Lasorda went with the left-handed thinking about the Yankees. He said he had discussed the percentages with a lot of people before deciding. "I had no imput," said Don Sutton, their best pitcher. "No, I'll never know how I would have pitched today, will I? I could give you any one of several opinions on it, but we'll just never know, will we?" His lips were pressed together in as much of a second guess as the Dodgers allow themselves.

But the Dodgers had no hugging. So after the game, Martin and Jackson hugged for the cameras. And then Jackson said, "I plan on playing in New York in 1978. Hopefully, everything will be as smooth as it was today." What? Now, today, he decided?

Sunday, October 16

Los Angeles

Not even today could be as smooth as yesterday. Right up until the Yankees went out to play what could have been the game that won the World Series, they were caught up in charge and countercharge. There was Billy Martin giving his side of the story, and as we have seen all season, it wasn't the same as the other side. Apparently the argument is never over until the last man is out—or fired.

After the game there were other questions and other issues raised. Between, they played the game and the Dodgers won, 10–4. The World Series will go back to New York. The games have been played almost as afterthoughts all season, anyhow.

After the security people had cleared the press from the field before the game, Martin held an animated discussion in the corner of the dugout and held it until the lineups were introduced.

What Martin said was that he was not going to tell Steinbrenner to shove the job even if the Yankees won the Series. "I thought of it," Martin said. What he said he would do after the last game was ask for a raise. With the car and the apartment and other paid expenses, he will get close to $100,-000 this year on his base of $75,000. The third year base is not quite $90,000, Martin said. "I certainly think, if we win, I deserve a raise," he said.

This round of bickering was set off by advance publicity of the story that is to appear in *Time* magazine this week. It is to include the tale of the July 13 secret meeting in Milwaukee that supposedly rescued the season when it was burning up. That meeting was one of the few Yankee secret anythings that remained secret for any length of time. Martin contended that Steinbrenner leaked the story a couple of weeks ago for his own purposes, to ease the eventual firing of Martin.

During the game, seated in the stands, Steinbrenner maintained that he had to clarify for *Time* the version that had already come from Martin.

In either case—although the Yankees have won a division championship, a pennant, and need to win only one more game for the World Series—the owner and manager are still in conflict. However, indications now are that Martin will not be fired, although that was the plan a week ago. Evaluations change quickly on this team; perhaps they will again after Steinbrenner reads what Martin had to say today. Martin says Steinbrenner has been greasing the skids for him all along. Certainly, Steinbrenner has knocked Martin—on and off the record—often enough.

Now the stories of that midnight meeting in Milwaukee

again reveal the tenuous nature of the team. "The club teeters like we're talking now," Dick Tidrow said. "They're like world powers. They're not free and easy. Maybe what we're saying will make them explode. That's the makeup."

Today Piniella said he was with Munson that night in July when Thurman was summoned by Steinbrenner. Steinbrenner said, "They banged on my door at twelve thirty in the morning."

The question of whether the players sought Martin's firing brought a "no comment" from Steinbrenner. "I don't want to get them into something they might not want." It sounded as though that was just what Steinbrenner wanted inferred.

Piniella, who concedes that he was not entirely on Martin's side at that time, said that wasn't the point. Piniella said he and Munson said that the clauses in Martin's contract that said he could be fired without being paid the balance of his contract made Martin a "lame-duck" manager.

"We said," Piniella said, "straighten out his contract and remove the clauses. If not, fire him."

Remember, that was three days after Munson—eventually everybody knew it was he—accused Steinbrenner of dictating the lineup. And Steinbrenner's description of that Milwaukee meeting says that Munson and Piniella admonished him for not being more active in the team. "They said, 'You run your businesses, why not your team?' " Steinbrenner said.

Today Martin traced the conflict back to spring training and wondered why it all had to happen this way, why he had to manage by Steinbrenner's rules when Billy Martin had won before under his own rules. "It was like he was building a case against me," Martin said. "I don't say anything first, but I got to fight back."

The *Time* story also quotes Reggie Jackson, the best slugger Steinbrenner could buy, as saying he wouldn't return if Martin returned. Today Jackson denies having spoken to *Time*. He wondered if the source of his supposed quote had been "someone who's never betrayed me before." The inference there is that Steinbrenner himself planted the quote to further grease the skids under Martin when actually Jackson was leaning toward returning. Steinbrenner maintained again that there is no escape clause for Jackson.

And still Martin says he wants to return for more. Martin is a Yankee. "Believe me," Martin said, "I'd like him to like me and respect the job I do. If I fail, I fail; just let me go down the tubes my way . . . I don't want to be the hero, I just want to be the manager of the Yankees. I want it to be peaceful and quiet as it can be, for George to like me and respect me and I'll do a job for him as long as he wants me."

There will be a sixth game because the Dodgers knocked Don Gullett out in the fifth inning and because Don Sutton held the Yankees scoreless until Munson homered in the seventh. By that time the Dodgers had hit two homers and had a 10–0 lead. Jackson also hit a two-run homer in the eighth, too late to matter.

And somebody has to pitch Tuesday in New York. After the game Martin first announced his pitcher would be Ed Figueroa, who has been nursing a finger injury. Then, while they were dressing, Martin said he had switched to Mike Torrez. But nobody told Figueroa until Torrez dropped the word on the plane. Figueroa was devastated. When he recovered from the shock, he said he wanted to be traded. "I want to go some place where people have confidence in me," he said. Martin "has been lying to me for two years."

Monday, October 17

New York

Figueroa is normally among the most placid of men. Today he beat the workout crowd to the clubhouse, cleaned out his locker, and left his uniform hanging there as testimony to his anger.

"I was almost ready to leave for Puerto Rico today," he said. "But I decided to wait until after the last game. People are going to think I left the club and didn't want to be with the club. But now I want to get traded. I want to get out of here."

Martin said he'd inquired yesterday and was told Figueroa's finger was almost healed and decided, "This is not a game for 'almost.'"

If there is a seventh game, Figueroa might be all healed, but he says he isn't interested in pitching again. "If there's no way I can pitch Tuesday," Figueroa said, "there's no way I could pitch Wednesday."

Perhaps if Martin had gone directly to Figueroa in the first place, Figueroa would be ready if he were needed. But Martin didn't go to Figueroa.

* * *

So the assignment is Torrez', and he sat in his locker and contemplated the idea that, by his count, he is already the first Mexican to win a World Series game. The other day Munson was needling Piniella about how he got along with all of the many factions on the team. "He doesn't have any choice," Munson said, "he's Mexican." Piniella's ancestry is Spanish, not Mexican. And Munson's humor often runs to calling Cliff Johnson "Big Coon" or Henry Hecht, the man from the *Post*, "Hey, Jew." Munson does not intend to offend, but isn't very graceful, either. Torrez says he is withholding his judgment, "Thurman being German."

Torrez grew up in Topeka, which was East Topeka for him because that's where the Mexicans lived. He didn't feel there was any distinction until one night he went to pick up his date, "a nice-looking blonde from the rich section of town." Her father answered the door, looked at Torrez, and said, "Can I help you?"

Two days later the girl said to Torrez she wasn't permitted to date him anymore. "Damn, I liked that girl," Torrez said. "It still stays with me even now."

There is something in that kind of experience that toughens a competitor. He knows how far he's come and how far it is back down. "It's in you and you don't forget it," Torrez said. "And you know you have to bust your ass to stay on top."

It's also interesting to consider that it's probably the last game Torrez will pitch for the Yankees. They aren't terribly anxious to sign him. He is here because Charlie Finley, the Oakland Scrooge, goofed. He forgot Torrez was a six-year player and didn't have an option year. He sent Torrez a one-year contract at a slight raise, which still left him eligible to be free at the end of the season. He could have cut Torrez 20 percent.

"He's got so many things cooking at once that he forgets," Torrez said. "So I signed and he called me and said, 'If you're a man, you'll let me tear up your contract and cut you twenty percent.'

"I told him, 'Sorry, but I'm not that much of a man.' "

Torrez can count the days now like the rest of the Yankees. "I feel torn apart," Piniella said. "The thing the

players talk about now is not winning or losing, but how
many days we have left."

Tuesday, October 18

New York

It couldn't be merely the last game of the World Series,
not just the ordinary final game of a season. There had to be
a climax.

There couldn't have been more of a climax. Sports has no
greater superlatives. If saying Reggie Jackson with an excla-
mation point can be an expletive, then saying it with an ex-
clamation point can be a superlative. In the concluding game
of the World Series, Reggie Jackson hit three home runs,
magnificent home runs. He kept saying it in the swirling aftermath, "Damn, I hit three home runs tonight."

In the afternoon, a news conference was called downtown
to announce that Billy Martin had not been fired, but that he
had been given a bonus. He gets a cash bonus of about $35,-
000, a Golden Jubilee Mark V Lincoln Continental that re-
tails for about $22,000, and adjustments on the rental of his
$400-a-month apartment in New Jersey. Plus assurances that
the two remaining years on his contract will be paid. Considering the nature of the beasts involved, a cynic could say
that the new agreement represents an increase in severance
pay.

But the night belonged to Jackson, and so does posterity.

"It was like—it was like—" Bucky Dent stammered, "in a
fairy tale and like in a horror movie where Frankenstein
comes out talking, but in the end the wicked witch turned
good."

Jackson was the Frankenstein monster. Jackson was the
wicked witch. Jackson was the conquering hero, standing in
right field, tipping his batting helmet to the cheering crowd as
if to catch their adulation in it and then standing in the clubhouse in a cascade of champagne. Only Babe Ruth had ever
hit three home runs in a World Series game. Those were
Ruthian feats. Jackson hit his three on consecutive swings. He
had already hit one on his last swing in the fifth game. That
was four home runs on four swings. He hit five home runs in

the Series and nobody ever did that. Maybe nobody ever will again. They were Jacksonian feats.

On the last day—after 173 games that counted and one in Syracuse that counted only on the list of incidents—the figure of controversy all season hit three homes runs. And the Yankees won. "They won it, they're world champs," Martin said. "You can analyze how they got there. If you can." The man who managed the hell out of the play-off and the World Series breathed deeply. "Good luck," he said.

The whole season was not to be forgotten, most of all the last game. Jackson's accomplishment was the greatest ever in a play-off, an All-Star Game, or a World Series. The only reasonable feat that might surpass it would be to do the same thing in the seventh game. It will take someone with Jackson's flair for melodrama to do it—if not Jackson himself.

The only place Jackson fell short was in trying to explain what a man feels when the emotion inside is bigger than he is. "I felt jubilation, excitement, relief, gladness, joy," he said, counting out the words. "I felt all the adjectives you can think of." Maybe there really is no better way a man can relate it.

As in a work of fiction, Mike Torrez pitched the final nine innings after Ed Figueroa was withdrawn and said he wanted to be traded.

The Dodgers took a two-run lead in the first inning. Chris Chambliss tied the score in the second with a home run after Jackson walked on four pitches. Reggie Smith hit a home run to put the Dodgers ahead in the third.

Thurman Munson led off the Yankee fourth with a single, and when Jackson hit the next pitch from Burt Hooton on a line into the right-field stands, there was Munson waiting at the plate for him. The two men who had been antagonists all season—and probably always will be—clutched each other. The Yankees had the lead they never lost. Those two had admiration for each other, if not affection.

In the fifth inning, Jackson hit Elias Sosa's first pitch on a searing line into the right-field stands for another two-run homer. And in the eighth, against Charlie Hough, Jackson hit the third, higher and further than the others, 475 feet into the unoccupied blacked-out area in center field, a province reached only once before in the rebuilt Yankee Stadium.

"He's awesome," said Graig Nettles, one of the Yankees most distant from Jackson. "It was a very impressive per-

formance under pressure. As good as you can do. He even
caught everything that came out there."

Nettles made a little wry smile. It was one of those rare
Yankee days when it was perfectly safe to tease anybody.
"Twenty or thirty years ago you might have made a movie
like this," Nettles said. "Today people would never believe
it."

The movie twenty or forty years ago would have been
about Babe Ruth and the part would have been played by
himself. No one could have played Ruth but himself. And
nobody could play Jackson but Jackson.

Jackson is so melodramatic he is a cliché come true. If
wearing Jackie Robinson's number in New York would have
been too much grandstanding, Jackson could form his own
link with Robinson.

"I'm not Babe Ruth," Jackson said. "I never thought of
Babe Ruth because he's so far out there. I can't relate to
him." He could relate, he said, to Robinson. Jackson called
attention to the small medal pinned to the belt loop of his
pinstripes. Jackie Robinson's image was on the medal. "I've
been wearing his pin for the whole Series," Jackson said.

Jackson has such a gift for the emotional and the knack
for saying the right thing, you suspect he must be manipulat-
ing, that this has to be contrived. But then Jackson can be so
convincing.

All year he was convincing when he said he couldn't stand
the thought of another year in New York, and now he is
talking about his identification here. Joe DiMaggio, who was
a coach briefly for the A's when Jackson was young, threw
out the ceremonial first ball. "I can relate to Joe DiMaggio,"
Jackson said. "He's the living Yankee, the Yankee Clipper.
He symbolizes the Yankees for me. He came into the
clubhouse before the game and said hello. That meant a lot to
me."

Here was the man Billy Martin said could not be a real
Yankee because he didn't act like a real Yankee, being
turned on by a greeting from the Yankee Clipper.

Jackson came into the clubhouse after hitting the ball well
in batting practice and told Fran Healy, friend through thick
and thin, "I feel excellent." Eight innings later Jackson was in
right field amid the snow of bits of paper. The people had demanded him until he stepped from the dugout to take a bow.
The people waited impatiently for the game to be over, to

claim the Yankees' first championship in fifteen autumns. Jackson wanted them to settle down. "I wanted them not to cause too much commotion and not degrade themselves as New Yorkers," he said.

For the first time he publicly identified with them. The first time, he said, was when he hit the home run to beat the Red Sox in the ninth inning. Perhaps he felt that then, but he kept it to himself. This time he said it. "I feel like a New Yorker," he said. He deliberately pronounced "Noo Yawker," as if he were one.

Jackson was exhausted. They all were, drained by day after day of reading about themselves—reading what they did not want to see. "The field was like a refuge," Nettles said. "I like to read the papers. I'm a baseball fan. It made it tough to read this guy was unhappy and that guy. There were too many people fighting to be Number One on the club.

"It's tough to read that somebody is mad at you or you're mad at somebody else. I can't blame the papers. People like to read the spicy stuff. On this club, that's not hard to dig up."

They brought so much of their problems on themselves. But that didn't make their problems any less draining. "We've had the living hell beaten out of us psychologically," Jackson said. "Especially Thurman Munson. Especially Billy Martin. Especially George Steinbrenner. Especially Reggie Jackson. These guys have gone through living hell. They've been pushed to the line and over. I'm happy for the team, happy for New York, happy for George Steinbrenner. That man stuck his neck out. If I had been a bust, he would have looked like a fool."

Jackson and Steinbrenner, the man who had brought him, embraced. "You can't do anything to me now," Jackson said, all a laugh. "I've got a five-year contract."

"And," Steinbrenner said, "you're not going anywhere, either."

It wasn't the emotion of a baseball movie, it was the emotion of a war movie. In a sense, they all had been through their combat. Jackson spoke in forgiving tones. What forgiving Munson gave was mostly begrudging. He never did stop battling Steinbrenner and didn't stop believing in himself. "I never doubted I could win," he said. " 'We' is a tough word. I don't know what other people were thinking. There's a lot of 'I's' in 'We.' "

Somehow the "I's" came together. It would take a doctoral dissertation to explain why and how. Munson feels the turning point was the midnight meeting in Milwaukee in July. But people were maddest at each other when July turned into August, they had fifty-three games to play, were six behind Boston, and there was not the slightest sign that they would recover. But the egos were temporarily replaced by pride and the desire to win, which may be stronger than ego or may really be the heart of a ballplayer's ego.

At the end Munson felt he was able to goad Jackson to his greatest height. "I finally woke him up because I called him 'Mister October,'" Munson said. That was in Los Angeles when Jackson's bat was still quiet. "I told him," Munson said, "'I finally got you pissed off enough to get you off your ass.'"

They learned to live with themselves. They stopped being their worst enemies. "A lot of our problems arise when these people don't accept defeat," Healy, the father-confessor, said. "These people do not lose gracefully. It's a unique quality."

Eventually, when nothing short of winning would do, they won. "There was never a dull moment," Healy said. "And what an ending."

*   *   *

For the eternal record books, hidden in the fury of Jackson's slugging and the sound of the bickering, the Yankees beat the Dodgers, 8–4, to win the World Series, four games to two. "The last line in the history books will say, 'Semicolon, the Dodgers and the Yankees also played,'" said Steve Garvey of the Dodgers. He saw enough in one week in October to get an idea of the Yankee season that began in March—at least to understand a little bit of it. Nobody understands all of it even at the end.

The Last Bubble

In the great sodden aftermath of the Reggie Jackson Show there was a curious revelation of feelings for Jackson. Don't call it affection because that's not what Jackson stirs among teammates. Commiseration is more like it.

The feeling came from Ken Holtzman, a teammate from the last tie around, who had his own grief to bear. "He had the best year I've ever seen," Holtzman said. "He went through more than any player who ever played, except for Jackie Robinson." Probably Holtzman is right.

The feeling came from players who were most critical of Jackson for so much of the season, among them Munson, Nettles, and Dick Tidrow. They acknowledged that it had been a season of hell for Jackson—however much was self-imposed.

"Maybe he does stir the drink," Tidrow said. "Maybe any team Reggie is on has to be like Oakland."

The straw that stirs the drink. That's a line to be etched in bronze in Cooperstown some day.

That line prompted an awful lot of harsh feelings. There weren't any fistfights, but there were a lot of times when one more word would have set one off.

Tidrow was one of these who felt in the early days that Jackson was the wrong addition to a team that had won the year before. "I was a skeptic for half a year," he said. "What you see is what you believe. I didn't think he was going to do much for us. Then you see what he did, and we blew four teams out."

Nobody is about to give all the credit to Jackson. "Actually," Tidrow said, "we got two straws; we can't win minus Munson or minus Reggie."

Even before his final starburst, Jackson had begun to come through his feeling of isolation. Chris Chambliss still hadn't spoken to him, Jackson felt, and that hurt. And Nettles and Martin. But success was rebuilding Jackson's self-image and he began to think he could survive another year of New York. Not long before that, he was thinking it would be most convenient for him if Billy Martin were retained so he could provide the visible push that moved Jackson out. When he was at the brink of closing his mind to New York, his closest advisers were telling him to wait until the season was over and he had taken what it offered.

The way it came out, he had statistics comparable to those of 1973, when he was elected Most Valuable Player. If his fielding had been better, he would have been a strong candidate again. But, as he explained it in his most human terms, "The weakest link in my game was my fielding. It had always been good enough, but under the pressure the weakest link broke."

That was what Munson understood. At $1,700,000 for five years, he still felt cheated—"lied to about money"—but he understood the pressure. "I was happy for Reggie; he was jammed on, too," Munson said. The straw in the drink reference has not been forgiven. "I don't bury my pride very easily," he said. "But I think that one of the reasons I can talk to him is that I can understand how conspicuous he feels."

Munson spent his first eight seasons feeling he was denied due credit, then won the MVP award last season. "All of a sudden I was put on a perch," he said. "People's opinions change, they give you certain things they expect you to live up to. It's hard to say and do the right things in that position. For three million, you're supposed to do things you've never done before."

Certainly Jackson, who loved the momentary brushes with the New York media when he played for Oakland, had to adjust to the demands of New York. They are extrordinary demands. He did not adjust immediately. Whatever the education level of baseball players, given the normal distribution of intelligence, these are physical people. They are not in the big leagues because they have the gift for saying precisely what they want to say, or of reading precisely what was said or intended. There is inherent tension in what they do. Not everybody can ride the waves.

"I don't think this club could take another week of this," Lou Piniella, one of the most buoyant, said. "Not another season like this. If it's not going to be tranquil, this team is not going to win. This team can't stand this anymore. They can sign all the free agents they want and they won't win. It doesn't have to be a big happy family, but you have to have enough concentration to play the games.

"It surprises me that we were able to win. Whoever's function it is should learn from this year. If they think they can sell tickets with a fourth-place club, let them try."

What reason is there to think another season can be much different? I don't think that money was the root of all the animosity, although it was of some of it. Anytime you put Munson, Jackson, Nettles, Lyle, and the rest in one clubhouse, put Billy Martin in charge, and have them all accountable to George Steinbrenner, how can it be much different for very long?

Now they've had a season with Jackson. They have learned what Holtzman and Hunter knew about him from their Oakland years. "We knew you have to take things he says on face value," Holtzman said, "for what they are: bullshit. That's why he doesn't bullshit Cat and I."

And will they be prepared for whatever comes next? "I have all the confidence in the world Reggie will come up with something different," Holtzman said. "Rest assured you will be thoroughly entertained."

Don't doubt it for a moment.

Extra Inning

Billy Martin sent his Yankee shirt to Robert Violante, partially blinded in the last attack of the ".44-caliber killer," who marked New York the same summer.

Sparky Lyle won the Cy Young Award as the top pitcher in the American League.

Rich Gossage signed as a free agent for $2,748,000 over six years.

Lyle got a bonus.

Paul Blair got a three-year contract.

Dave Kingman signed with the Cubs for $1,375,000 over five years.

Mike Torrez signed with the Red Sox for $2,507,249 over seven years.

Mickey Rivers got a new agent and said he did not want to be traded, but wanted a new contract.

Andy Messersmith was obtained from the Braves. He said he was happy to be a Yankee. When his first negotiations with the Yankees broke down in 1976, he said George Steinbrenner and Gabe Paul represented all that was evil in America.

Rawly Eastwick signed as a free agent for $1,100,000 over five years.

Thurman Munson said he still wanted to be traded to Cleveland. Steinbrenner said Munson still wasn't going anywhere.

Gabe Paul moved to Cleveland as president of the Indians.

Lyle said that with Gossage and Eastwick in the bullpen, there wouldn't be enough work for him and he wanted to be traded.

Jim Spencer, a left-handed-hitting first baseman from the White Sox, signed as a free agent.

Ron Blomberg signed with the White Sox for $600,000 over four years.

Cedric Tallis, the architect of the Kansas City Royals, was elevated from vice president to vp-general manager, and Al Rosen, former MVP third baseman with Cleveland, was brought in as executive vice president.

During spring training Rosen was made president and chief operating officer and Tallis' duties were defined as player development. Steinbrenner said he was backing out of the Yankee picture to devote more time to his other businesses.

Torrez, speaking as a member of the Red Sox, predicted more thunder and strife on the Yankees. "Thurman Munson hates Reggie Jackson and Graig Nettles hates Jackson, too," Torrez said. When Torrez signed with Boston, Paul said the loss of a pitcher who was 17-13 and just two games over .500 with the Yankees (14-12) was "not catastrophic." Torrez said: "If it weren't for me, the Yankees wouldn't have reached the Series."

At a dinner in Boston, the enemy camp, Graig Nettles looked back at the notoriety of the season. "Billy would like you to think that the press made up all that stuff. But ninety percent of it was true."

When they returned to spring training, Jackson and Munson were still cool toward each other. Jackson's candy bar was ready for the market, but he still felt an outsider on the team.

Don Gullett's shoulder was too sore for him to throw.

And the Yankees played so poorly in exhibition games that Steinbrenner went to the dugout to deliver a lecture in the middle of an inning. "I threw him out," Martin said.

Believe it or don't.

About the Author

Steve Jacobson has been covering sports for *Newsday* since 1960, the year Mazeroski's home run beat the Yankees in the World Series. He has covered the Yankees from when they were five-time pennant winners, through the humbling years, to their present state of lordly champions. Jacobson graduated from Indiana University and can tell you what the editors ate for lunch on the 1956 New York *Daily Mirror*, where he was a copy boy. He lives with his wife, Anita, and their children, Mathew and Neila, on Long Island.